Private Company Valuation

Also by Gianluca Oricchio

BASEL III CREDIT RATING SYSTEMS: An Applied Guide to Quantitative and Qualitative Rating Models (*with L. Izzi and L. Vitale, 2012*)

CREDIT TREASURY: A Credit Pricing Guide in Liquid and Non-Liquid Markets (*2011*)

The Efficient-market Hypothesis (EMH) and Financial Crisis, in G. Zanda CORPORATE MANAGEMENT IN A KNOWLEDGE-BASED ECONOMY (*2011*)

MERCATI FINANZIARI E VALENZA INFORMATIVA DEL BILANCIO DI ESERCIZIO (*with F. Pistelli, S. Porro and A. Tresoldi, 2010*)

Active Credit Portfolio Management: l'approccio di Unicredit Group (*with F. Pistelli, S. Porro and A. Tresoldi*), in A. Resti (a cura di), IL SECONDO PILASTRO DI B ASILEA E LA SFIDA DEL CAPITALE ECONOMICO (*2008*)

Il modello di rating interno del segmento retail di Capitalia (*with L. Izzi and A. Ratini*) in G. De Laurentis, F. Saita, A. Sironi, RATING INTERNI E CONTROLLO DEL RISCHIODI CREDITO (*2004*)

GLI EFFETTI DELL'IRAP E DELLA DIT SULL'ECONOMIA DELLE SOCIETÀ DI CAPITALI (*with S. Lugaresi, E. Romanello and F. Cascone, 1998*)

DISCREZIONALITÀ DEGLI AMMINISTRATORI NELLA VALORIZZAZIONE DI TALUNE POSTE DEL BILANCIO DI ESERCIZIO ED ALEATORIETÀ DELLA STIMA DEL VALORE DEL CAPITALE ECONOMICO (*1996*)

LA VALUTAZIONE ECONOMICA DEI DIRITTI DI CONCESSIONE (*1996*)

LA GESTIONE DEL RISCHIO DI CREDITO NELLE AZIENDE DI SERVIZI: STRUMENTI E TECNICHE DI GESTIONE (*1995*)

LA STIMA DELL'ALEATORIETÀ NELLE VALUTAZIONI DEL CAPITALE ECONOMICO D'IMPRESA (*1994*)

LA VALUTAZIONE DEL CAPITALE UMANO DELL'IMPRESA (*with M. Lacchini and G. Zanda, 1993*)

Private Company Valuation

How Credit Risk Reshaped Equity Markets and Corporate Finance Valuation Tools

Gianluca Oricchio

palgrave
macmillan

First published 2012 by
PALGRAVE MACMILLAN

Palgrave Macmillan in the UK is an imprint of Macmillan Publishers Limited, registered in England, company number 785998, of Houndmills, Basingstoke, Hampshire RG21 6XS.

Palgrave Macmillan in the US is a division of St Martin's Press LLC, 175 Fifth Avenue, New York, NY 10010.

Palgrave Macmillan is the global academic imprint of the above companies and has companies and representatives throughout the world.

Palgrave® and Macmillan® are registered trademarks in the United States, the United Kingdom, Europe and other countries.

ISBN: 978–0–230–29144–7

This book is printed on paper suitable for recycling and made from fully managed and sustained forest sources. Logging, pulping and manufacturing processes are expected to conform to the environmental regulations of the country of origin.

A catalog record for this book is available from the British Library.

A catalog record for this book is available from the Library of Congress.

10 9 8 7 6 5 4 3 2 1
21 20 19 18 17 16 15 14 13 12

To Donatella, Alessandro and Allegra for their love and support

Contents

Tables

Figures

Foreword: How Credit Risk Reshaped Equity Markets and Corporate Finance Valuation Tools

The recent crisis in financial markets has seen a gradual erosion of the boundaries of asset classes previously regarded as risk-free. We have gone from a world largely free of default risk to one where credit risk is largely reflected in equity prices.

The cost of the capital of investment grade companies is mainly based on market risk. The cost of the capital of sub-investment grade companies, however, is primarily based on default risk.

The majority of risk in private companies is sub-investment grade, which means the task of establishing a private company's credit risk should always be a predominant concern when analysing equity risk.

If traditional valuation methods are to be integrated, this should be done in such a way as to take into adequate account a scenario in which expectations of growth are considerably reduced and credit risk is increased to levels unheard of before now.

This book sets out a new method for estimating private companies' cost of equity based on a Fixed Income Approach.

The equity of a sub-investment company is compared to the first loss piece of a securitization and the cost of equity calculated by applying pricing models traditionally used for the valuation of junior subordinated notes.

This new approach is also integrated into the Capital Asset Pricing Model. Business cases focusing on the valuation of private companies in the USA, Japan, China, Russia, India and Italy are presented and discussed in detail.

In addition to this book's undoubted theoretical insights, readers will also benefit from the practical experience the author has accumulated as risk manager within major banking groups.

Sergio Ermotti
Chief Executive Officer, UBS

Acknowledgements

I would like to extend my thanks and appreciation to Moody's Analytics Team for their valuable support and contribution (©Moody's Analytics, Inc, and/or its affiliates. Reprinted with permission. All Rights Reserved.). Credit is also due to Salvatore Marazita and Stefano Palladini for their input on business cases. Valuable input was provided by several referees at UBS, Goldman Sachs, JP Morgan and Barclays Capital and I am grateful to all of them for their help in improving aspects of the book.

1
Introduction

1.1 How the financial markets are changed: where is "risk free"?

The recent crisis in financial markets has seen a gradual erosion of the boundaries of asset classes previously regarded as riskfree. The classic divide between Developed Markets and Emerging Markets is largely meaningless.

The USA has lost its Standard & Poor's AAA credit rating, while the Peripheral Eurozone Nations have become the tail risk for financial markets. The differential between the government bonds of Portugal, Spain, Italy, Greece and Ireland, and that of the German Government – the Bund – has reached and exceeded a threshold spread that goes far beyond the usual "risk free" level.

In the years preceding the crisis, and against a prolonged background of low interest rates, the ongoing search for yield has been pursued via a continuous and progressive use of leverage. Widely differing methods for estimating equity fair value and the cost of equity, based to a large extent on market risk, have given little indication of the exponential increase in credit risk. The same ratings systems have shown themselves to be "unreliable" when it comes to credit risks relating to structured credit financial instruments (CDO (Collateralised Debt Obligation), CLO (Collateralised Loan Obligation), ABS (Asset Backed Securities), etc.), hedge fund credit risk and investment bank credit risk, although ratings in the corporate sector have proved more accurate.

Given the structural weakness of a system based on a high level of debt, a series of technical failures and defaults have suddenly followed one after another in all major asset classes.

Recent falls in values on share markets can primarily be attributed to an increase in the probability of insolvency (and in default rates) in both the financial and the corporate sectors. Credit risk, virtually

Table 1.1 Credit ratings and default probabilities

Moody's	S&P	Fitch	Risk level	Firm life
Aaa	AAA	AAA	Minimum	Going concern
Aa	AA	AA	Very low	Going concern
A	A	A	Low	Going concern
Baa	BBB	BBB	Medium	Going concern
Ba	BB	BB	Medium-high	Going concern
B	B	B	High	Going concern
Caa	CCC	CCC	Very high	Going concern
D	D	D	Default	Gone concern

Source: Author's estimate of the frequency of corporate default.

non-existent in the past, first appeared on the fixed income and equity markets in Western countries. From its beginnings in the financial system, the crisis has spread to sovereign risk level and to the real economy.

The credit risk component is generally much smaller for a company with an investment grade rating (AAA–BBB), tending to increase for companies with a sub-investment or speculative grade rating (BB–D) or with a high yield rating (see Table 1.1).

In the years leading up to the recent crisis in financial markets, the percentage of public (listed) companies rated by Moody's or by Standard & Poor's as being investment grade used to oscillate between 55% and 65% (and, conversely, the percentage of listed companies rated by Moody's or Standard & Poor's as sub-investment grade was contained within the 35–45% range).

Non-listed companies (and companies smaller than listed ones) of the kind that are the subject of the valuation exercises dealt with in this book do not usually have an external rating. Their probability of default, however, can be estimated on the basis of rating models compiled and fine-tuned for such business (Altman, 1968 and Altman *et al.*, 1998; Zijmieski, 1984; Dwyer *et al.*, 2004, 2006, 2009, 2010; Chan-Lau, 2006b; Zanda, 1996, 2012 and Zanda *et al.*, 2005, 2011, 2012; Oricchio *et al.*, 2012). Before the financial crisis struck, the percentage of non-listed companies assigned a rating similar to investment grade was around 35–45% of the total. At the same time, non-listed companies with a rating similar to sub-investment grade were within the order of 55–65%.

The level of credit risk has risen significantly over the past few years (see Table 1.2).

The percentage of listed companies externally rated as investment grade has fallen to 30–40%. At the same time, the percentage of listed

Table 1.2 Investment grade vs. high yield European corporates

	Public companies (%)		Private companies (%)	
	Before	After	Before	After
Investment grade	55–65	30–40	35–45	25–35
High yield	45–35	70–60	65–55	75–65

Source: Author's estimate of externally rated European corporate and internally rated European mid corporate.

companies externally rated as sub-investment grade has increased to within the 60–70% range. A similar phenomenon was observed with non-listed companies, with a significant increase noted in non-performing loans on the balance sheets of credit institutions. In particular, the percentage of non-listed companies rated as sub-investment grade rose to within the 65–75% range, while the percentage of non-listed companies with a credit rating analogous with the investment grade has dropped to around 25–35%.

The cost of credit risk has also suffered a serious re-pricing process: the i-Traxx IG 5-year index and the CDX IG 5-year index rose from 20–30 basis points to a peak of 170–80 basis points; indices used to express the cost of credit risk for companies rated as high yield (the i-Traxx Crossover 5-year index for Europe, and the CDX HY 5-year index for the USA) have reached levels of 700 basis points and even higher.

To sum up, *we have gone from a world largely free of credit risk in the financial markets to one where, for around "two thirds of businesses" the "subject of credit risk" has become the overriding factor in any risk and company valuation analysis.*

1.2 How equity valuation methods are changing: the growing role of credit risk

This substantial change has a number of very significant implications for the methods used to value a company's equity fair value. The techniques for estimating the probability of insolvency developed in the so-called fixed income world have now become a central element when estimating the value of companies and, therefore, in the "equity" market. This phenomenon is of even greater importance when switching from valuing the equity fair value of listed companies to valuing the equity fair value of non-listed companies (Zanda *et al.*, 2011; Banks, 2010).

Equity fair value is normally worked out using a method that takes account of the company's situation at the time of the valuation and of its future prospects. More precisely, in this context, and more or less implicitly, the *assumed value of the company's survival as an ongoing entity* (its going concern value) is calculated.

"Economic value" is in reality a weighted average between the company's economic value assuming its ongoing existence over time, and the company's value assuming its liquidation (see Damodaran, 2010). The formula (see Equation 1.1) is as follows:

$$\text{Firm Value} = \text{Going Concern Value (probability of survival)} + \text{Gone Concern Value (probability of default)}. \quad (1.1)$$

From the shareholders' point of view, in the event of the company being forced into liquidation following a default, the recovery value (and the gone concern value) is practically equal to zero (see Equation 1.2).

$$\text{Equity Value} = \text{Going Concern Equity Value (probability of survival)} + 0 \quad (1.2)$$

Credit-worthiness values expressed in the form of ratings are useful for determining a company's probability of survival over time. The following table shows the cumulative 10-year probability of default (as well as the cumulative 10-year probability of survival) depending on the particular rating category (see Table 1.3).

It is easy to see that equity value (when estimated on the assumption that the company is a going concern) tends to decrease in line with the

Table 1.3 Cumulative 10-year probability of default

Rating	Cumulative prob. of default (%)	10-year prob. of survival (%)	Equity value
AAA	0.07	99.93	Going concern
AA	0.50	99.5	Going concern
A	0.65	99.35	Going concern
BBB	7.5	92.5	Going concern
BB	20	80	Going concern
B	37	63	Going concern
CCC	60	40	Going concern
CC	67	33	Going concern
C	80	20	Going concern
D	100	0	Gone concern

Source: Author's estimate on cumulative corporate default rates.

increase in the probability of default, i.e. the credit risk (Zanda *et al.*, 2010).

Let us suppose that the estimated equity value of an A-rated going concern is 1 billion US dollars. The value that takes account of the risk of insolvency is equal to 0.9935 billion US dollars (1 × 99.35%), i.e. the error is immaterial. On the other hand, let us suppose that the estimated equity value of a B-rated going concern is 2 billion US dollars. The value that takes account of the risk of insolvency is equal to 1.26 billion US dollars (2 × 63%), i.e. the error is decisively material.

By this reasoning it can be argued that when estimating equity value on the assumption of a company being a going concern, account is already taken of the business risk when quantifying the risk premium within the scope of the discount rate of future cash flows. The observation is absolutely correct *providing coherence (consistency) is shown between business risk and discount rates.*

In order to identify a size of discount rate (understood as the cost of equity) that is consistent with the credit risk (understood as the cumulative probability of survival over a 10-year period), the familiar Gordon Model is used as shown in Equation 1.3. The results are illustrated in Table 1.4.

$$(\textit{survival prob.}) \times P/E = 1/(r + ERP - g) \qquad (1.3)$$

where:

survival prob. is the probability of survival for 10 years;
P/E is the price/earnings ratio;

Table 1.4 Ten-year probabilities of survival and economic risk premium consistency (assuming P/E equals 10x and growth rate equals zero)

Rating	10-year probability of survival (%)	ERP	Equity value
AAA	99.93	7	Going concern
AA	99.5	7.1	Going concern
A	99.35	7.1	Going concern
BBB	92.5	7.8	Going concern
BB	80	9.5	Going concern
B	63	12.9	Going concern
CCC	40	22	Going concern
CC	33	27.3	Going concern
C	20	47	Going concern
D	0	Na	Gone concern

r is the riskfree rate;
ERP is the equity risk premium;
g is the growth rate.

The economic risk premium (ERP) is measured in a manner consistent with the credit risk and is basically stable at the investment grade level. When high yield ratings are measured in a manner consistent with the credit risk, however, the ERP begins to increase significantly.

As will be seen, at very low annual probability of *default* values (investment grade companies), a failure to consider the credit risk has no significant impact on the estimate of the cost of equity. Conversely, however, failure to consider the credit risk when estimating a *speculative grade* company's cost of equity is the harbinger of a significant (material) error (Chan-Lau, 2006a; Rietz, 1988; Vassalou and Xing, 2004).

Traditional methods for estimating the economic value of companies must be integrated so as to take into adequate account a scenario in which expectations of growth are considerably reduced while credit risks are increased to levels unheard of before now.

Such considerations are more valuable if the intention is to estimate the equity fair value of non-listed companies which, generally speaking, are small to medium sized enterprises, have a greater business risk (and a greater credit risk) and less marketability of the share capital.

1.3 How this book is structured

Chapter 2 illustrates traditional methods for estimating the economic value of non-listed companies. Chapter 3 shows the model used to estimate the cost of equity known as the Integrated Pricing Model (IPM) in that it combines the Capital Asset Pricing Model (CAPM) with a second method based on a fixed income type logic known as the Fixed Income Approach (FIA).

The FIA is based on estimating the expected loss from the perspective of the shareholders, and on the subordinated junior notes pricing method. It requires the application of ratings models developed for estimating the probability of insolvency in small to medium sized enterprises.

The second part of the book looks at business cases of IPM equity valuations based on corporate rating models for private companies (RiskCalc type mid corporate rating models). The cases presented pertain to non-listed companies (with an equivalent of a sub-investment grade rating) and are divided as follows: Chapter 4 is devoted to the USA, Chapter 5 to Japan, Chapter 6 to China, Chapter 7 to Russia, Chapter 8 to India, and Chapter 9 to Italy.

About two-thirds of non-listed companies have a credit risk that is higher than investment grade level and, as we will show, traditional methods tend to overestimate the value of the equity fair value of companies with a medium to high credit risk.

2
Private Companies' Equity Valuation Methods

2.1 Equity value configurations

The equity value of private companies can be configured in different ways depending on the objective that the valuation process is intended to achieve (Coda, 1966; Zanda *et al.*, 1994; 1996; Damodaran, 1996; Burgstahler and Libby, 1997; Guatri and Bini, 2009; Annunziata, 2011).

However, to summarize, the following considerations should be borne in mind:

- *start-up equity value*, relating to the moment the company is first set up, (usually) represented in the form of the cash available and assets brought in;
- *gone concern equity value*, estimated at the end of the winding-up process, during which the assets and liabilities of the business are valued independently of each other (and not as a systemic whole) whereupon the net realizable value is estimated;
- *going concern equity value*, aimed at measuring the equity value of the businesses a set of elements that are co-ordinated and oriented towards the future operation of the company.

Depending on the perspective from which the valuation is calculated, the approach used to estimate the equity value can be divided into:

- *a buy-side equity valuation;*
- *a sell side equity valuation;*
- *the independent expert's equity valuation, or equity fair value.*

The equity fair value can be regarded as a particular configuration of the equity value that manifests itself once the subjective requirement of the position taken by the "independent expert" working for the valuation entity meets the objective requirement (the sale, in the broadest sense, of the business as a whole).

2.2 Reliability of equity fair valuation methods

The equity fair valuation process involves estimates, forecasting and conjecture; it is only natural, therefore, that such subjective elements should be examined in the light of the perspective of the evaluator and the way the valuation has been configured. There are three fundamental requirements that any reliable method for estimating equity fair value must fulfil (Guatri, 1998). These are:

- *rationality:* the method must be conceptually valid and the theory behind it must be consistent;
- *objectivity:* the method must be firmly applicable;
- *universality* or *fairness* or *neutrality:* the method must leave aside the specific nature and interests of the parties involved in the negotiations.

This last requirement shows how the evaluator must, when attempting to estimate the *stand alone* equity fair value of the business, put himself in the "position" of the independent expert. In other words, he must *completely disregard subjective conditions of the negotiation.*

The objective conditions should not reflect the various characteristics of the parties involved in the transaction or the potential probabilities for profits or losses that each specific subject (buyer or seller) might derive from the transfer of the business.

There is no methodology for estimating equity fair value that is fully capable of satisfying all of the requirements for rationality, objectivity and fairness; in other words, there is no valuation methodology that is "optimal" in every case. This therefore means it is necessary to carefully examine the purpose of the valuation, the situation of the business whose value is being estimated, and the data available or that can be acquired, and then, on the basis of these considerations, to identify the most satisfactory method or methods (Zanda *et al.*, 1996).

2.3 Relative valuation and fundamentals-based valuation approaches

The general criteria used to evaluate a private company are usually divided between a relative value approach and a fundamentals-based approach.

With a relative valuation approach, the equity fair value of the business is estimated on the basis of a sample of stock prices as these relate to public companies that can be "compared" with the private company to be evaluated. The "comparison selection" is a complex process and the companies selected to act as samples must be chosen with care.

In the fundamentals-based approach, meanwhile, three different criteria can be used:

1. net present value (NPV) of future benefits stream (flow-based methods);
2. net asset value (stock-based methods);
3. combined flow-stock methods.

Methods used to estimate the equity fair value on the basis of flow-based methods are in turn broken down into:

- cash flow-based methods;
- earnings-based methods;
- dividend-based methods.

Stock-based valuation methods rely on an appreciation of either the net asset value or the net asset value integrated with intangible asset values: the first equates the equity fair value with the sum of accounting assets valued at current prices less accounting liabilities valued at current prices; the second, on the other hand, adds the value of intangible assets (that have not been accounted for in the balance sheet) to the net asset value.

Valuation methods that are based on a combination of flow-based and stock-based methods try to "capture" both the strong points of the net asset value approach and the strong points of the flow-based method.

Table 2.1 summarizes the methods used for calculating equity fair value for private companies.

2.4 Relative valuation approaches

Relative valuation methods are estimation procedures that evaluate the equity fair value of a private company on the basis of the stock prices of "similar" public companies (this method is also called the comparison approach).

Two key points are essential if this methodology is to be used correctly and not abused:

Table 2.1 Equity valuation methods (private companies)

Methods for calculating equity value	*Relative valuation*	Comparison approach	
	Fundamentals-based methods	Flows -based	Cash flows-based Earnings-based Dividends-based
		Stock-based	Net Asset Value Net Asset Value integrated with intangible assets
		Flow-*stock*	Net Asset Value and Goodwill value Average value

1. sample public companies deemed to be "similar" to the private company to be evaluated must be carefully selected;
2. the multiples used to run the comparison (equity-side multiples or asset-side multiples) must be carefully selected.

The first point is usually the real weak point when the relative valuation approach is used for estimating the equity fair value of private companies.

The comparison between the value of listed companies and the value of private companies can be made on the basis of equity-side multiples (such as price/earnings, price/cash flows, price/sales, price/book value, price/tangible book value, etc.) or on the basis of asset-side multiples (such as enterprise value (EV)/EBITDA, EV/EBIT or EV/operating cash flows).

Generally speaking, asset-side multiples should be preferred to equity-side multiples because the leverage effect can be easily managed in the valuation process.

From an investment bank point of view it is useful to compare the EV/EBITDA multiple with the debt/EBITDA multiple in order to assess

Figure 2.1 Median values of EV/EBITDA and debt/EBITDA of 333 industrial and basic materials public companies that have been externally rated
Source: Our estimate based on 2007 Bloomberg data.

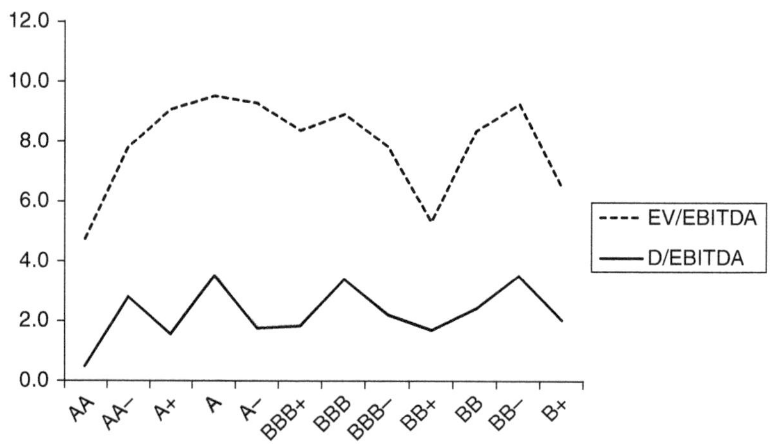

Figure 2.2 Median values of EV/EBITDA and debt/EBITDA of 135 public utilities companies that have been externally rated
Source: Our estimate based on 2007 Bloomberg data.

the feasibility of an M&A transaction and the best way of financing of the deal.

In the following figures the median value of EV/EBITDA and the median value of debt/EBITDA of public companies are illustrated from the point of view of industrial and basic materials, utilities, consumer cyclical and non-cyclical, and tech and communications companies (see Figure 2.1, Figure 2.2, Figure 2.3, Figure 2.4).

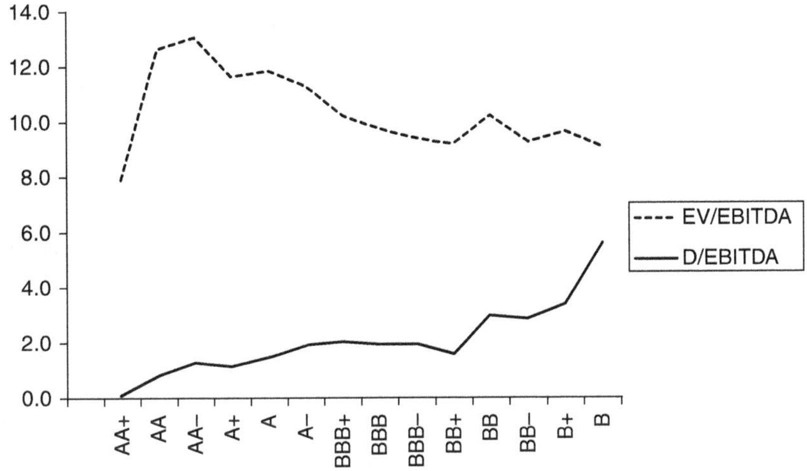

Figure 2.3 Median values of EV/EBITDA and debt/EBITDA of 405 consumer cyclical and non-cyclical public companies that have been externally rated
Source: Our estimate based on 2007 Bloomberg data.

Figure 2.4 Median values of EV/EBITDA and debt/EBITDA of 156 tech and communications public companies that have been externally rated
Source: Our estimate based on 2007 Bloomberg data.

As we can see, and if we exclude the highest and lowest rating categories, there does not appear to be a strong correlation between the EV/EBITDA multiple and the debt/EBITDA multiple in either utilities or industrial and basic materials; this situation is "ideal" for a leveraged deal. The key question, then, is whether market prices take the corporate credit risk into due consideration. The hypothesis underlying this book is that before the onset of the financial crisis, this relationship was so weak and the interest rate was so low that leveraged deals often had inflated stock prices.

2.5 Earnings-based methods

The equity fair value estimation is based on the NPV of expected and normalized earnings.

Figure 2.5 shows the relationship between operating and net earnings flows relating to a profit and loss account that has been reclassified and "normalized" so as to represent a standard administrative period (see Figure 2.5). The equity fair value is the present value of net future earnings; the enterprise value in the present value of operating future earnings; the debt value is the present value of future debt cash flows (Zanda *et al.*, 1996).

where

- *EBIT* is the operating income or earnings before interest and taxes;
- *t* is the rate of corporation tax;
- *IE* are the interest expenses;
- *E* is the value of the net income;
- *EV* is the economic value of the operating assets or enterprise value;
- *W* is the economic value of the net book capital or equity fair value
- *D* is the economic value of the financial debts.

From Figure 2.5 it is easy to deduce the formula for calculating equity fair value in the following two ways.

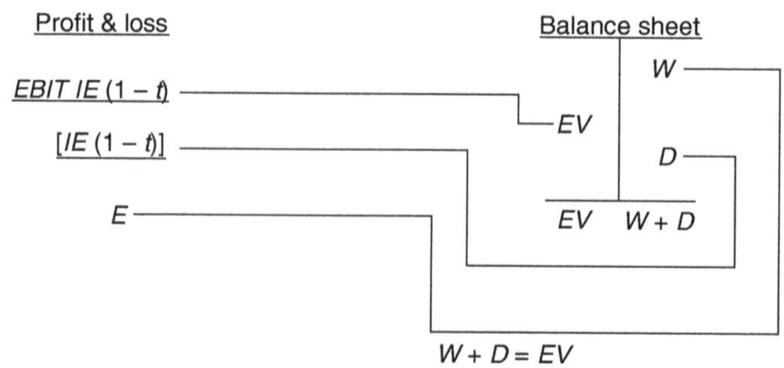

Figure 2.5 Stocks-income flows relationship (tax as a percentage)

In the first simplified case, the equity fair value is equal to the current value of the *standard* normal net income:

$$W = NPV\ (Earnings).$$

In other words, and assuming a constant and perpetual stream of earnings, the formula is the following:

$$W = E/ke$$

where

- W is the equity fair value;
- E is the expected and normal average of net income;
- ke is the cost of equity of the equity fair value.

In the second simplified case – the so-called "WACC (Weighted Average Cost of Capital) technique" – the economic value of the capital is equal to the difference between the economic value of the assets(EV)and the economic value of the financial debt (D). Rearranging

$$EV = W + D$$

gives

$$W = EV - D$$

where all symbols assume the meaning already noted.

As Figure 2.5 shows, the economic value of the financial debt is equal to the current value of the standard normal interest expenses net of tax:

$$D = NPV[(IE(1-t)].$$

In other words, of flows, the formula is as follows:

$$D = IE(1-t)/i_D(1-t)$$

where

- D is the economic value of the financial debt;
- IE is the expected normalized average value of interest expenses;
- i_D is the rate of remuneration from financial debt;
- t is the rate of tax.

The economic value of the operating asset is equal to the NPV of normalized and expected operating earnings, net of tax:

$$EV = NPV[EBIT(1-t)]$$

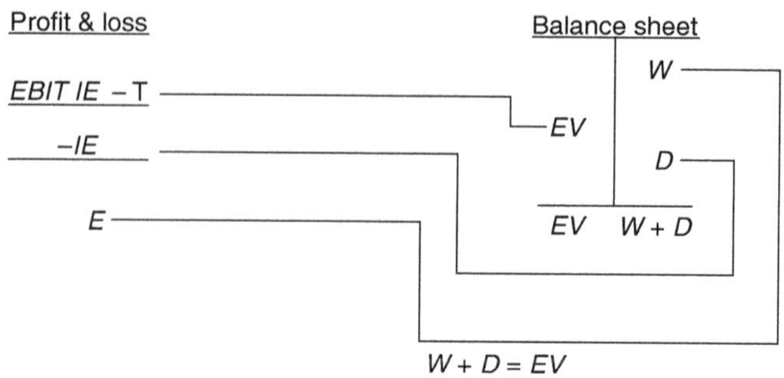

Figure 2.6 Stocks-income flows relationship (tax as absolute number)

or, assuming constant and perpetual flows:

$$EV = EBIT(1-t)/i_A$$

where

- EV is the economic value of the operating asset net of operating debts;
- $EBIT$ is the normalized and expected level of operating income;
- i_A is the asset's rate of remuneration, calculated as the weighted average between the rate of remuneration from the equity fair value and the rate of remuneration from financial debt (WACC):

$$i_A = ke\,W/(W+D) + i_D D/(W+D)$$

where all symbols assume the significance already noted.

It is interesting to observe how Figure 2.5 can be re-proposed as in Figure 2.6:

where to the symbols already noted are added:

T or the amount of tax.

Let us suppose that a company, Alpha AG, has an expected normal average operating income of 60,000 euro, that the expected normal average value of its interest expenses is 10,000 euro and that it is subject to 50% corporation tax. Here again we are assuming that the company has no assets, liabilities, income or losses of a non-operative nature.

Alpha AG's normalized and expected Profit & Loss accounts can therefore be alternatively represented as follows:

Profit and Loss Account (A.1)	Profit and Loss Account (A.2)
$EBIT\ (1-t) = 60,000$	$EBIT = 60,000$
$(1-0.50) = 30,000$	
$IE(1-t) = -10,000(1-0.50) = -5,000$	$IE = -10,000$
	$I = -25,000$
$E = 25,000$	$E = 25,000$

Assuming the *equity* rate of return is equal to 20%, in both cases we obtain:

$$W = 25,000/0.2;$$

$$W = 125,000 \text{ euro}.$$

If, on the other hand, we assume that the interest rate on financial debt is 10%, we have all the data we need to calculate the economic value of Alpha AG using the WACC technique.

Consistent with Figure 2.5 given we have:

$$D = IE(1-t)/i_D(1-t)$$

$$D = 10,000(1-0.5)/0.1(1-0.5)$$

$$D = 100,000 \text{ euro}$$

and

$$EV = EBIT(1-t)/i_A$$

$$i_A = ke\,W/(W+D) + i_D D/(W+D)$$

$$i_A = 0.2(125,000/(125,000+100,000)) + 0.1(100,000/(125,000+100,000))$$

$$i_A = 0.133$$

$$EV = 60,000(1-0.5)/0.133$$

$$EV = 225,000 \text{ euro}.$$

Thus:

$$W = 225,000 - 100,000 = 125,000 \text{ euro}.$$

It must be pointed out that every time the equity fair value of a company is estimated using the WACC technique there is a function of the type:

$$W = f(\ldots, W, \ldots).$$

Ultimately, the unknown equity fair value appears either on the first side of the equation and on the second side.

Every time the WACC technique is used there is a problem of circularity. To resolve this, one of the following alternatives can be used:

- iterate the function and determine the result of the convergence hypothesis – this focuses on an algebraically-correct solution;
- replace the value of W on the right hand side of the equation with the equity market value (if the company is public) or with the book value (if the company is private) – these give an approximated solution;
- replace the value of W on the right hand side of the equation with the equity fair value calculated using another method (e.g. an adjusted book value method). Such an alternative is applicable every time the equity fair value is calculated using different techniques – here again we arrive at an approximated solution.

One special case arises when the average expected EBIT flow is constant over time. On this assumption, no iteration is required because the valuation equation is reduced to a second degree polynomial. The algebraic relationship is shown below:

$$W = EBIT(1-t)(W+D)/(ke\,W + i_D D) - D$$

$$W + D = EBIT(1-t)(W+D)/(ke\,W + i_D D)$$

$$(W+D)(ke\,W + i_D D) = EBIT(1-t)(W+D)$$

$$ke\,W^2 + W(i_D D + ke D) + i_D D^2 = EBIT(1-t)W + EBIT(1-t)D$$

$$ke\,W^2 + W(i_D D + ke D - EBIT(1-t)) + i_D D^2 - EBIT(1-t)D = 0.$$

This polynomial can be re-written as follows:

$$aW^2 + bW + c = 0$$

where

W is the unknown;
$a = ke$;
$b = i_D D + ke D - EBIT(1-t)$;
$c = i_D D^2 - EBIT(1-t)D$.

The second degree equation requires that $a > 0$ and that $c < 0$; it follows that the parabola has its concave side facing upwards and the intercept with the y-axis is negative, as shown in Figure 2.7.

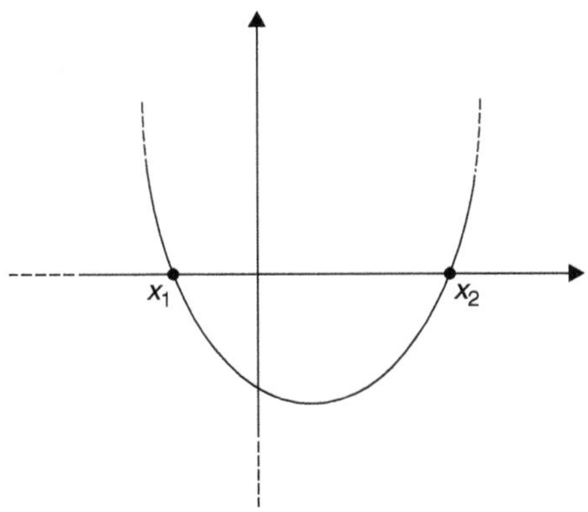

Figure 2.7 WACC double solution

The parabola expressing the equity fair value offers two possible solutions: the first root (x_1) is negative and is not therefore significant; the second root (x_2), on the other hand, is positive and constitutes the value sought (W).

Using an algebraic profile we arrive at the following solutions.

Root I : $x_1 = -b - (b^2 - 4ac)^{1/2}/2a$
(not acceptable).

Root II : $x_2 = -b + (b^2 - 4ac)^{1/2}/2a$
(acceptable).

By way of example, let us look at the following valuation.

WACC technique

Expected normal average of EBIT net of tax = 30,000 euro;
Financial debt = 120,000 euro;
Cost of equity = 8%;
Cost of borrowed funds = 10%.

Coefficient $a = 0.08$;
Coefficient $b = -8.4$;
Coefficient $c = -2,160$.

Discriminant $b^2 - 4ac = 761.76$.

Root I $= -120,000$ euro (not acceptable).
RootII $= 225,000$ euro (acceptable).

Classical technique

Expected average of EBIT net of tax = 30,000 euro;
Interest expenses (10% × 120,000) = 12,000 euro;
Expected normal net earnings (30,000 – 12,000) = 18,000 euro.

$W = E/ke$;
$W = 18{,}000/0.08$;
$W = 225{,}000$ euro

2.6 Cashflow-based methods

Cashflow-based methods determine the equity fair value on the NPV of a company's stream of expected cash flows.

On the simplified assumption that cash flows remain constant over time and are protracted indefinitely, the diagram most widely used in valuation practice to calculate equity fair value using cash flows is represented in Figure 2.8.
where

UCF	is the *unlevered* cash flow;
DCF	is the value of the flow generated by debt cash flows;
LCF	is the value of the *levered* flow;
EV	is the economic value of the asset (net of operating debts);
W	is the economic value of the net capital (equity fair value);
D	is the economic value of the net financial debt.

Figure 2.8 clearly shows that in the cash flows-based methods, as with the earnings-based methods, the equity fair value can be calculated in two ways.

In the first approach, the equity fair value is made equal to net present value of normalized and expected *levered* cash flows:

$$W = NPV(LCF).$$

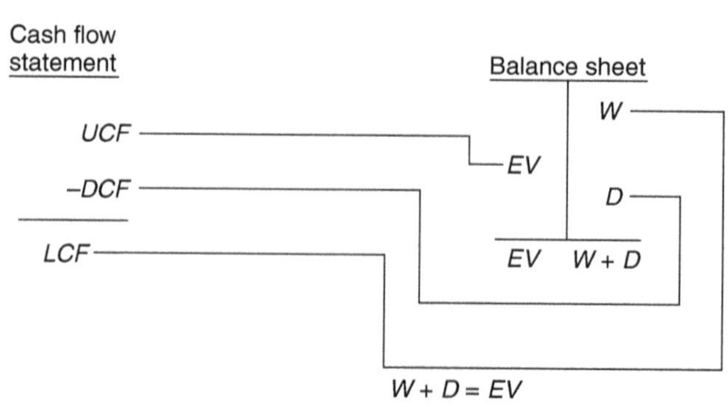

Figure 2.8 Stocks-cash flows relationship

Assuming a constant and a perpetuity of normalized *levered cash* flows, we will get:

$$W = LCF/ke$$

where

- W is the equity fair value;
- LCF is the value of the expected and normal average level of *levered* cash flows;
- ke is the rate of remuneration from the equity fair value.

If we move to WACC technique there are three different cash flows calculation criteria. As regards the principle of consistency that must be valid between the configuration of the cash flows to be discounted and the discount rate, we shall look at the following three hypotheses.

1. Unlevered cashflows (UCF) are worked out before tax; it follows that, in the relevant actualization rate (WACC), the cost of equity should be expressed before tax:

$$W = \frac{UCF}{\frac{Ke}{(1-t)}\frac{W}{W+D} + i_D\frac{D}{W+D}} - \frac{DCF}{i_D}.$$

2. The UCFs are computed net of tax; tax is calculated on the gross flow multiplied by $(1-t)$; the cost of capital(WACC) is determined in relation to the remuneration rate net of equity and the cost of financial debts net of tax:

$$W = \frac{UCF\,(1-t)}{Ke\frac{W}{W+D} + i_D\frac{D}{W+D}\,(1-t)} - \frac{DCF\,(1-t)}{i_D\,(1-t)}.$$

3. The UCFs are computed net of actual taxes (I); taxes are calculated on the operating income before tax net of interest expenses. It follows that the cost of the capital is estimated in relation to the net rate cost of equity and the cost of financial debts before tax:

$$W = \frac{UCF - I}{Ke\frac{W}{W+D} + i_D\frac{D}{W+D}} - \frac{DCF}{i_D}.$$

An example will clarify what has been said thus far (see Table 2.2). Let us suppose we are using the WACC technique to estimate the equity fair value of a company with the following data. Expected, constant, normal, average unlevered cashflow = 60,000 euro;

Table 2.2 Cash flow configurations

	Levered cash flow	Debt cash flow	Unlevered cash flow before tax	Unlevered cash flow net of virtual taxes	Unlevered cash flows net of tax calculated on operating income net of interest expenses
Operating result	60	–	60	60	60
Interest expenses	(20)	+ 20	–	–	–
Pre-tax result	40	–	–	–	–
Paid taxes	(20)	–	–	(30)	(20)
Net income	20	20	60	30	40

Expected, constant, normal, average debt cash flow(to keep things simple relating to interest expenses only) = 20,000 euro;
Tax paid in the financial year = 20,000 euro;
Expected, constant, normal, average *levered* cash flow = 20,000 euro;

$$ke = 12\%;$$

$$i_D = 10\%.$$

Let us also suppose that this data derives from the following situation (per 1,000 euro):

Suppose that the NPV of the interest expenses at the time of the estimate is 200,000 euro, that there is no liquidity, that the tax rate is 50%, and that the equity fair value is calculated in accordance with the three methods shown above.

First method

UCFs are calculated before tax:

$$UCF = 60,000 \text{ euro}.$$

It follows that the relative actualization rate must be calculated by considering the cost of equity before tax:

$$WACC = 0.12/(1 - 0.5)W/(W + D) + 0.1D/(W + D);$$

$$WACC = 16.3637\%;$$

$$W = EV - D;$$

$$W = 60,000/16.3637\% - 200,000;$$

$$W = 166,670 \text{ euro}.$$

Second method

UCFs are individualized net of tax; the taxes are calculated on the gross flow multiplied by $(1-t)$:

$$UCF = 60{,}000(1-0.5);$$

$$UCF = 30{,}000 \text{ euro.}$$

In this case the cost of equity is net of tax and the size of the interest expenses must be expressed net of fiscal impact:

$$WACC = 0.12W/(W+D) + 0.1(1-0.5)D/(W+D);$$

$$WACC = 8.18185\%;$$

$$W = EV - D;$$

$$W = 30{,}000/8.18185\% - 200{,}000;$$

$$W = 166{,}670 \text{ euro.}$$

Third method

UCFs are calculated net of taxes; the taxes are determined on the gross operating income net of interest expenses:

$$UCF = 60{,}000 - 20{,}000;$$

$$UCF = 40{,}000 \text{ euro.}$$

It follows that the average cost of capital is estimated using a net cost of equity and a cost of debt before tax:

$$WACC = 0.12W/(W+D) + 0.1D/(W+D);$$

$$WACC = 10.909\%;$$

$$W = EV - D;$$

$$W = 40{,}000/10.909\% - 200{,}000;$$

$$W = 166{,}670 \text{ euro.}$$

Although the three calculation methods set out above employ different WACC actualization rates and different gross flow methods, they lead to identical results.

At this point it should be stressed that the three methodologies above lead to the same final result if, and only if:

- the expected operating annual cash flows, as well as debt cash flows and levered cash flows, are normal and constant over time;
- the valuation time frame (the life time of the company) is unlimited.

On the other hand, if the sizes of the operating cash flows are different in the various financial years and/or the valuation time frame is restricted (e.g. 10, 15 years etc.), then the three methodologies are not rational and will not converge.

2.7 Stock-based methods

The stock-based valuation methods used to value equity fair value usually distinguish between "simple" net asset value(NAV)and "complex" NAV, i.e. NAV integrated with the valuation of intangible assets not accounted in the balance sheet.

The first method equates the company's equity value with its NAV at current market prices. The formula is:

$$W = K'$$

where

W is the company's equity fair value;
K' is the net asset value.

These methods basically assume that the company will generate a NPV of earnings equal to the NAV. In formula:

$$E \geq keK'\mathrm{E}$$

where

E is the company's expected normalized earnings;
ke is the discount rate / cost of equity;
K' is the company's net asset value.

As can be seen, however, even the simple net asset method is based on income-related considerations; it is assumed that the earnings of the company will be at least equal to the cost of equity multiplied by the NAV.

If this assumption is not correct, an income-generation capability adjustment (ICA) must be subtracted from the NAV. This adjustment is equal to the NPV of the difference between expected and normalized income (E)and the cost of equity multiplied by the NAV (*keK'*) for an infinite period, or by the number of years needed for the company to achieve a proper level of profitability. The formulae are respectively:

a) if the value of the ICA is actualized *ad infinitum,*

$$ICA = \frac{(E - keK')}{ke}.$$

b) on the assumption the company performs a good profitability within a limited period of time,

$$ICA = (E - keK')\, a_{n,i}.$$

This solution turns the simple NAV method into one of the flow-stock-based valuation methods that will be discussed below.

The process for estimating the adjusted NAV can be split into four phases:

1. identification of assets and liabilities of the company;
2. accounting and auditing review of the balance sheet;
3. estimation of any corrections needed to the accounting NAV;
4. the company's equity fair value calculation, as an algebraic total of its assets and liabilities at current market prices.

The following example shows how the simple asset value method can be applied.

Company *Beta AG* has a net capital of 1 million euro made up of fixed assets with a net accounting value of 4,000,000 euro, loans accounted for at 400,000 euro, a controlling shareholding (100% of the shares held) at 200,000 euro, and debts of 3.6 million euro.

The company's expected normalized earnings are considered to be 200,000 euro and the cost of equity (including the risk free rate and the risk premium) is equal to 8%.

It is also assumed that, once the assets and liabilities have been identified and the balance sheet has been reviewed, the expert will estimate the replacement value of the fixed assets at 5.5 million euro, the presumed value realized from loans is the same amount as shown on the balance sheet, the equity fair value of subsidiaries is 450,000 euro, and the value of debt is equal to the accounting value.

The adjustments (*Ap*), all positive, to the company's net capital can therefore be estimated at 1.75 million euro, as shown in the following equation:

$$Ap = (Vs_{FIXED\ ASSETS} - Vc_{FIXED\ ASSETS}) + (W_{SHAREHOLDING} - Vc_{SHAREHOLDING})$$

where

Ap is the value of the positive adjustment to the NAV;
$Vs_{FIXED\ ASSETS}$ and $Vc_{FIXED\ ASSETS}$ are the replacement value and the net accounting value respectively of the fixed assets;
$W_{SHAREHOLDING}$ and $Vc_{SHAREHOLDING}$ constitute the economic value and thc accounting value of the shares held.

By replacing the parameters of the formula with the numerical values we obtain (per 1,000 euro):

$$Ap = (5,500 - 4,000) + (450 - 200) = 1,750$$

On top of the capital gains, we need to calculate the tax charges, even if these are potential; in this case, it is considered appropriate to use a tax rate adjusted with the probability of the new values to be taxed. For instance, if we assume a tax rate on capital gains equal to 30% and a probability of being taxed of 50%, the rate of tax on potential fiscal charges is 15% (30% × 50%). Hence the potential fiscal charges weighing on the NAV can be estimated as 15% of 1.75 million euro, i.e. 262,500 euro.

The adjusted NAV will therefore be 2,487,500, calculated as follows:

Net accounting asset value (K) $= 1,000,000$ euro
Positive adjustments (Ap) $= 1,750,000$ euro
Negative adjustments (An) $= 0$
Potential fiscal charges = (262,500) euro
Adjusted NAV(K'K) = 2,487,500 euro.

The amount of equity fair value determined with the stock-based method of Beta AG is consistent ("minor of") with the present value of future earnings. The present value of net future earnings of Beta AG is 2.5 million euro (200,000 / 8%) and no ICA is necessary.

Stock-based "complex" valuation methods (NAV integrated with the value of intangible assets accounted in balance sheet) draw on the *going concern value* theory. Here the assumption is that, in order to create a business from scratch, certain costs will be incurred that do not arise for a company that is already trading. The equity fair value is estimated as the sum of the adjusted NAV and the value of intangible assets not accounted in the balance sheet, as shown in the formula:

$$W = K' + IA$$

where

W is the company's equity fair value;
K' is the adjusted NAV;
IA is the value of non-accounted intangible assets.

This formula implicitly supposes the company is in a position to reasonably remunerate the adjusted NAV inclusive of intangible assets, or, put another way:

$$E \geq ke(K' + IA)$$

where

E is the expected net earnings;
ke is the cost of equity;
K' is the adjusted NAV;
IA is the value of non-accounted intangible assets.

If this condition is not valid, the value obtained by adding the adjusted NAV to the intangible assets must be corrected using an ICA for the period of time which is necessary to reach an economic equilibrium or surplus ($E \geq ke(K' + IA)$).

Naturally, if expected earnings (E) is equal to break even margin ($ke(K' + IA)$) the ICA is zero and is not therefore shown when equity fair value is estimated using the complex asset value method.

The value of the intangible assets "explains" part of the goodwill, in the sense that it specifies the sources that help determine the value.

When it comes to estimating adjusted NAVs, the problems are clearly the same as those that arise when a company's equity fair value is estimated using the simple asset value method. Please therefore refer back to what has already been said on this subject.

The problem of assigning a value to *intangible assets* also needs to be looked at in more depth. There are three fundamental aspects that need particular attention if intangible assets are to be estimated appropriately. The first fundamental aspect concerns their identification;the second concerns the need to resolve problems of intersections and over-positioning between intangible assets; and the third is the choice of valuation criteria.

As regards the aspect, we must remember that an intangible asset is only worth being autonomously estimated if – and only if – it has the following three characteristics: it is the object of a significant flow of investment; it is capable of ensuring differential economic benefits to the company that owns it; and it can be transferred, at least sideways. This means, then, that in order to be able to rationally decide whether an autonomous estimate is appropriate, a case-by-case assessment must be carried out of whether the company's intangibles meet the requirements set out above.

As regards the second aspect, the thinking is that in order to eliminate or at least attenuate the problems of duplication and over-positioning of intangible assets, an adequately detailed list of the assets in question should be compiled and relevant relationships should be discussed and properly documented.

The third aspect is the criteria to be used for estimating the value of the intangible assets. Here the estimation methodologies tend to distinguish between empirical criteria and theoretic methods. Methodologies based on empirical criteria estimate the value of the intangible asset on the basis of the product of a market multiplier (based on progressive and codified experience in practice) and the magnitude of business that relates to the intangible to be valued (i.e. sales, operating income, excess earnings, cash flow and so on). Theoretical methodologies distinguish between methods based on costs (historic cost, re-valued historic cost, replacement cost, opportunity cost, cost of a loss, etc.), and income-generation or cashflow-based methods.

It might be helpful here to set out the main methodologies used for estimating the most important intangible assets.

2.8 Intangible assets valuation

In this section a number of intangible assets valuation methodologies for private companies are considered: human capital, commercial licences, order book, brand, customer portfolio and customer data base, mineral exploration and research concessions.

2.8.1 Human capital

There are many ways of estimating the value of *human capital* as an intangible asset. A distinction is often made between qualitative methods and quantitative methods. Qualitative methods are aimed at identifying those variables and relationships on which any increase or decrease in the value of human capital depends. Quantitative methods, meanwhile, are aimed at estimating the value of the intangible "staff organization" factor.

Quantitative criteria, largely derived from *human resource accounting,* especially distinguish between historic cost criteria, cost-opportunity and replacement cost methods, and earnings-based criteria.

However, since none of these are capable of fulfilling all of the requirements for rationality, objectivity and neutrality, we need to look for a method that, whilst it may not be "optimum" in the abstract sense, is nonetheless sufficiently satisfactory to meet the specified objectives of the value-attribution process.

In valuation practice, the methods most widely encountered and actually applied are without question based on replacement cost criteria. These equate the value of human capital with the total costs that would in theory have to be sustained in order to replace all of the staff available at the time of the estimate with other staff of equivalent quality under the same given environmental and market conditions.

The replacement cost criteria enable the requirements for conceptual validity, objectivity and fairness to be better met and, amongst other things, help to estimate not only the human capital value *per se,* but also its value to the company. Likert (1970), the principal author of this kind of valuation methodology, claimed that the cost of replacing human capital could be equated to three times the company's total annual salary costs. Empirical research (Zanda and Lacchini, 1989) has shown that recruitment, selection and training costs can oscillate between one sixth and half of the total annual labour cost, while hiring and induction costs can be between one sixth and twice the total annual labour cost. The staff cost multiplier to be applied to annual salaries must therefore be between one third and two and a half times the total annual labour cost.

The central question, of course, is the choice of multiplier and that largely depends on four factors: a) quality of in-house research; b) quality of the technology used; c) complexity of any financial, marketing, supply, staffing, and/or administrative problems; d) quality of the style of management.

The relationship between the business profile estimated according to these four qualitative variables and the quantitative value of the human capital multiplier can be reasonably established according to the data in Table 2.3:

A simple example will clarify how the methodology is applied.

Table 2.3 Human capital empirical multipliers

Multiplier	Company profile
between 0.33 and 0.50	Low
between 0.51 and 1	medium to low
between 1.1 and 1.5	medium
between 1.51 and 2	medium to high
between 2.1 and 2.5	high

Let us assume that *Company A* needs to conduct a valuation of its human capital. The balance sheet for the financial year shows wages and salaries, social security charges and the quota share of the final salary pensions scheme as 4 million euro. The company has 30 employees, most of them researchers and highly-specialized managers; the company operates in a *high tech* sector and its style of management tends towards the Participative Management by Objectives model. Let us also assume that following an examination of the company's staffing needs, no redundancies are planned of a kind that would require a staff restructuring.

Based on an examination of the four variables listed above, the company's profile is "high" so the multiplier to be applied to the labour cost in order to work out the value of the company's human capital can therefore be reasonably estimated at 2.1–2.5. The decision as to true value will be considered in more detail in the light of the independent expert's own experience and understanding of valuation techniques. In the case in question, if we assume a multiplier with a value equal to the average value within the high profile range, i.e. 2.3, the human capital can be estimated as 9.2 million euro. The formula is:

$$HO = ALC \times m = 4{,}000{,}000 \times 2.3 = 9{,}200{,}000 \text{ euro}$$

where

- HO is the value of the staff organization (Human Organization);
- ALC is the average annual labour cost;
- m is the multiplier.

2.8.2 Commercial licences

An administrative permit or "licence" constitutes the indispensable condition for the pursuit of many entrepreneurial activities (commercial ones in particular). It is characterized by having a "legal-administrative" need and its value is essentially linked to the fact that it makes it possible for the holder to operate in a certain location that offers pinpointed sales and income potential, irrespective of the characteristics of the entrepreneur and the capabilities of the employees. Given its intrinsic value, the economic value of a commercial licence becomes relevant when its granting is subject to stringent quantitative or quota restrictions.

Many methods have evolved in both theory and practice for estimating the value of commercial licences and these can be broken down into two basic types: fundamentals-based methods and replacement cost valuation criteria.

Fundamentals-based methods estimate the value of an administrative licence as the difference between the value of the company's equity fair value calculated using a flow-based method (earnings-based or cash flow-based) and its NAV, including the value of non-accounted intangible assets (except of course the commercial licence). The formula is:

$$L = W - (K' + IA)$$

where

- L is the value of the commercial licence;
- W is the equity fair value estimated using a flow-based method;
- K' is the NAV;
- IA is the value of non-accounted intangible assets (excluding the commercial licence).

On the other hand, replacement cost methods are for the most part empirical in nature. They equate the equity fair value of the commercial licence with the product after the application of a multiplier and a quantity linked to the volume of sales, i.e. to the income flows that can be achieved by reason of the location of the point of sale. In valuation practice the following are especially widely used:

a) The method that equalizes the value of the commercial licence with the product of average sales of the last 3 to 5 financial years and a multiplier of between 0.1 and 1.3. (in the foodstuffs sector, this range is limited to between 0.2 and 0.3, and in the clothing sector to between 0.3 and 0.5). The formula is:

$$L = S \times m$$

where

- L is the economic value of the commercial licence;
- S is the company's average sales;
- m is the empirical multiplier (between 0.1 and 1.3);

b) The method that equates the value of the commercial licence with the product of a value coefficient and the surface area of the commercial going concern. The formula is:

$$L = SA \times m$$

where

- L is the economic value of the commercial licence;
- SA is the surface area of the commercial going concern;
- m is the coefficient of the value assigned to the surface area of the commercial going concern.

c) The criterion that estimates the economic value of the licence as the product of the annual rental costs, real or virtual, relating to the commercial concern and a multiplier that in an average European valuation practice is usually 3. The formula is:

$$L = A \times 3$$

where

- L is the economic value of the commercial licence;
- A is the value of the annual rental costs, real or virtual, relating to the commercial concern;
- 3 is the empirical multiplier for valuing the administrative licence.

2.8.3 Order book

The order book represents all of those orders placed by the company's clients and awaiting completion. It is the typical intangible asset of a company that operates on the basis of orders; in other words, those businesses that only produce goods or services on the instructions of their clients.

The value of the order book derives from the fact that it is a resource capable of expressing the earnings potential of a company operating on the basis of commissioned work.

There are a lot of methodologies for estimating the equity fair value of the order book; these include, amongst others, the "basic method"; the method based on capitalization of costs already sustained and the actualization of future costs and revenues and their correction with the excess earnings value; the method based on calculating the presumed net realizable value, and the differentiated income method. Since no method fully meets the requirements for rationality, generality and objectivity, the choice of valuation criterion will depend, case by case, on the data that is available or that can be acquired, on the reliability of the data available, and on the characteristics of the order book that is the subject of the estimate.

The so-called basic method is fairly widespread in valuation practice. This methodology estimates the value of the order book through the following expression:

$$W_{pf} = W_{c1} + W_{c2} \ldots + W_{cn}$$

where:

W_{pf} is the value of the order book;
W_{c1} is the value of order 1;
W_{cn} is the value of the n-th order.

This can also be written as:

$$W_{pf} = \sum_{i=1}^{n} E_{ci} v^{ti} - \sum_{i=1}^{n} ke\,CI_{ci} v^{ti} = \sum_{1=1}^{n} (E_{ci} - keCI_{ci})\, v^{ti}$$

where

W_{pf} is the value of the order book;
E_{ci} is the value of the net profit deriving from the future completion of the i-th order;
CI_{ci} is the capital invested in the i-th order;
ke is the cost of equity and actualization;
v^{ti} is the actualization factor relating to the i-th order to be actualized by the time t_i.

As regards the net profits from the order book, this figure is given by the sum of the net profits the company will attain from completing the individual orders in the order book.

In the absence of any accurate and reliable analytical accounting, the first step towards arriving at the net profit on individual orders is to estimate the assumed value of the ratio between the company's total net profits and its total sales (hereafter *E/Sales*).

This indicator can be constructed using a range of methods:

- first and foremost, if the company has a financial plan that spans several years, it can refer to the revenues forecast in the budgets and the forecast results for the financial year;

- the trends of the two quantities of reference (total net profits and total sales) can be studied by extrapolating historical data from the previous year's balance sheet;
- it can refer to a simple average of the results for the current financial year and the revenues from the previous year;
- the quantity sought can be determined by referring exclusively to the previous financial year.

The *E/Sales* ratio determined using one of the four methodologies shown is successively applied to the expected volume of sales attached to each order. This enables an estimation of the profits that will probably accrue following completion of the orders in the order book.

We will then get:

$E_{c1} = \text{sales from order } 1 \times (E/Sales);$

$E_{c2} = \text{sales from order } 2 \times (E/Sales);$

$E_{cn} = \text{sales from sale} n \times (E/Sales).$

The inclusive value of the actualized net profits proceeding from the order book will therefore be:

$$E'_{c1v} + E'_{c2v} + \cdots + E'_{cnv}$$

In the absence of any accurate and reliable analytical accounting, the second step towards arriving at the net capital invested on individual orders is to estimate the assumed value of the ratio between the company's total net capital invested and its total sales (hereafter *CI/Sales*).

By setting k equal to the ratio:

$$\frac{Net\ Capital\ Invested}{Sales}$$

we obtain:

Net Capital Invested in the individual order $= k$ Sales from the individual order.

The net capital invested in the order book will therefore be equal to the net total capital invested in each of the orders, or:

$CI_{c1} = k \text{ sales from order } 1$

$CI_{c2} = k \text{ sales from order } 2$

$CI_{cn} = k \text{ sales from order } n$

for the n orders in the order book.

When defined in accordance with the criteria shown, the actual value of the net profits deriving from the order book, and the actual value of the cost of equity of the capital invested in same, the equity fair value of the order book will be able to be identified as the difference between these two quantities.

A simple example will clarify the application of the methodology just postulated.

The order book of the company Alpha AG has to be valued as at 31.12.201*x*. The sales forecast in the company's budget for the next three years (expressed in euros from 201*x*), are 1 million euro for FY201*x* + 1, 1.2 million euro for FY201*x*+2, and 1.4 million euro for FY201*x*+3, assuming expected net profits totalling 150,000 euro; 120,000 euro and 160,000 euro respectively, and share capital during the three financial years of 500,000 euro per year.

Lastly, the sales from the orders in the order book to be completed in the next three financial years are assumed to be 800,000 euro, 900,000 euro and 1,050,000 euro.

The actualization rate / cost of equity is established at 10%.

The first step towards calculating the value of the order book is to estimate the net profits on the orders. This involves calculating the ratio between average net profit and average sales – this quotient is 0.1194 as shown below (values shown per 1,000 euro):

$$\frac{E_{average}}{Sales_{average}} = \frac{150 + 120 + 160}{1,000 + 1,200 + 1,400} = \frac{430}{3,600} = 0.1194.$$

The expected profit on orders over the next three years can be estimated by multiplying this figure by the sales from orders from each individual year; Table 2.4 summarizes the expected net profits for the three sets of orders in question (values shown per 1,000 euro).

Once the expected net profit from orders from each individual year has been calculated, the amount of capital invested in each set of orders can be found. To do this, the ratio between average net capital and average sales must be calculated. In our example, this is as follows

Table 2.4 Net margin on sales

Year	Sales from orders	E/Sales	Profit on orders
201x + 1	800	0.1194	95.52
201x + 2	950	0.1194	113.43
201x + 3	1,050	0.1194	125.37

Table 2.5 Capital invested on sales

Year	Sales from orders	CI/SalesT	Capital Invested from orders
201x + 1	800	0.4166	333.28
201x + 2	950	0.4166	395.77
201x + 3	1,050	0.4166	437.43

Table 2.6 Excess return on capital invested

Year	Net profit	ke CI	E-ke CI	(E-ke CI)v[t*]
201x + 1	95.52	333.28	62.192	59.2977
201x + 2	113.43	395.77	73.853	64.0146
201x + 3	125.37	437.43	81.627	64.3209

(values shown per 1,000 euro):

$$\frac{CI_{average}}{Sales_{average}} = \frac{500+500+500}{1,000+1,200+1,400} = \frac{1500}{3,600} = 0.4166.$$

The capital invested in the individual orders over the next three financial years can be estimated by multiplying the sales from each set of orders by 0.4166 by the sales from individual orders; Table 2.5 summarizes the capital invested in the three sets of orders in question (values per 1,000 euro).

The cost of equity on individual orders will thus be obtained by multiplying the net capital invested in individual orders by the rate of actualization/cost of equity. The *ke CI* for each set of orders is 333,280 euro, 395,770 euro, and 437,430 euro respectively.

We now have all the information we need to calculate the value of the order book; the data required are shown in Table 2.6 (values per 1,000 euro):

Should it be assumed that the costs of and revenues from the individual orders have the same time distribution, the value of *t*will be 0.5, 1.5 and 2.5 respectively for the three periods of time in question.

Summing up the right hand column, the value of the order book is thus given as 187,633.2 euro.

2.8.4 Brand

Brand constitutes one of the intangible assets with major relevance when estimating the equity fair value of an industrial business.

The equity fair value of a brand can be estimated in many ways, although distinction is drawn between fundamentals-based and replacement cost methods. Fundamentals-based methods equate the economic value of the brand with the difference between the company's equity fair value calculated using a flow-based valuation methodology (earnings-based or financial) and the total value of the NAV of the company and of its non-accounted intangible assets (excluding the brand, of course). The formula is:

$$M = W - K' - IA \text{ (excluding brand).}$$

Replacement cost and empirical methods, on the other hand, estimate the value of the brand autonomously by leaving out of the company's equity fair value any value the said intangible asset might have. Distinction is made in particular between costs-based and earnings-based criteria. The use of empirical criteria has been especially widespread over the past few years so it is on these that we shall concentrate our attention.

So far as earnings-based methods are concerned, the one most widely used in the valuation of private companies is the actualization of royalties deriving from the brand over a period of time equal to the duration of the brand itself. The formula is:

$$M = (x \times S)a_{ni}$$

where

- x is the percentage of royalty on average business sales;
- S is the prospective average sales estimated on the basis of the results of the last three to five financial years and future sales over the same length of time;
- n is the duration of the brand;
- i is the actualization cost/cost of equity.

The empirical brand valuation method calculates the value of the brand as the product of a multiperiod quantity expressing the value of the brand. Depending on the European sector in question, and on the merchandising categories of brand-related assets, this can vary between 1.1% and 10% of sales.

2.8.5 Customer portfolio and customer database

The client portfolio is a typical intangible asset and it is susceptible to autonomous valuation.

The methodologies used for valuing the client portfolio are essentially empirical in origin: they equate the value of the client portfolio with the product of a multiplier and one of the economics capable of expressing the relationship that exists between the business and its clients. In practice, two valuation techniques are more frequently used than others when valuing private companies. The first estimates the value of the client portfolio as the product of the average annual sales and a variable percentage indicator of between 0.8–1% and 2%, the formula being:

$$CP = S \times m$$

where

CP is the economic value of the client portfolio;
S is the annual average value of the sales;
m is the percentage indicator (between 0.8–1% and 2%).

The second empirical method typically used to value the client portfolio bases the estimate of such intangible assets on the product of a multiplier (normally between 2 and 3–3.5), and the volume of annual profits. The formula is:

$$CP = PC \times m$$

where

CP is the economic value of the client portfolio;
PC is the volume of annual profits from the customer;
m is the multiplier - in Italian practice it is usually between 2 and 3–3.5.

Should the two methods result in notably different valuations preference is given to the second, i.e. to the criterion that equates the client portfolio value with the product of a multiplier of between 2 and 3–3.5, and the volume of annual profits from the customer.

2.8.6 Mineral exploration and research concessions

The task of valuing mineral exploration and research concessions poses special problems, any solution of which needs to include a consideration of both the specific geophysical features of the area being explored and the survey techniques employed. The valuations assigned to some of the parameters used to estimate the economic value of such permits must therefore be validated by an expert with the appropriate geo-engineering experience.

Typical examples of investigations and evidence-gathering techniques of relevance when identifying deposits with the potential for being economically exploited include core-sample analyses, log analyses, seismic studies, and reviews of local sedimentological and petrophysical features.

Any description, however approximate, of these or any other analysis technique is beyond the scope of this work. What is important, however, is that whatever method is chosen to compile the estimate should be the one that most validly applies in each specific case. Also, it is always advisable to employ the services and to follow the advice of someone particularly well-qualified in the fields of geology and engineering.

The two estimation methods primarily used are essentially the capitalization of historical costs sustained, which is designed to establish the technical and financial capacity needed for a research permit to be issued, and a technique based on the options theory, although this, as will become clear, is susceptible to multiple empirical parameters.

2.8.6.1 Capitalization of historical costs methods

This method involves the capitalization of the costs sustained in acquiring the technical know-how and financial capacity needed for a research permit to be issued. The task of estimating these costs is particularly difficult and complex and can cause significant confusion. On the one hand, the long-term utility costs that have helped consolidate the applicant company's image have to be evaluated – primarily its *know-how* and the investments it has made in classifiable *marketing*, such as intangible assets; on the other hand, the costs involved in obtaining a specific research licence need be taken into account. To be even minimally reliable, it must be possible to accurately analyse these valuations from an accounting point of view. The rate of capitalization and the duration of the reference period are both extremely subjective and will depend on the marketing and the technology used as well as on the valuation entity's own perception of the situation.

Similar confusion surrounds the valuation method based on calculating the replacement cost of the assets needed for an exploration and research concession to be granted.

2.8.6.2 The option theory

The main valuation variations of the model are:

- probability of success of a drilling operation;
- the number of attempts needed to discover an economically productive deposit;
- the research cost of every drilling operation;

- the approximate minimum value of the deposit that will presumably be identified.

The probability of success of a drilling operation depends on the specific geophysical and geological features of the area from which the extraction was made and on the results of preliminary tests carried out using specific surveying techniques. Defining this probability as p and supposing, for the sake of simplicity, that it remains constant even when the number of drilling operations varies, the probability of failure after n attempts is as shown in the following equation:

$$\text{probability of failure} = (1-p)^{n}$$

where

$(1-p)$ represents the probability of failure of the single extraction operation.

By defining a minimum probability of failure level that is acceptable across the entire research programme, we can identify the number of extractions reasonably believed to be sufficient to identify an economically-exploitable deposit. For example, assuming a 5% overall probability of failure, the number of drillings can be calculated as follows:

$$5\% = (1-p)^{n;}$$

$$\lg 5\% = n \lg(1-p)$$

$$n = \lg 5\% / \lg(1-p).$$

This clearly shows that when the probability of success of a single drilling operation p increases, n tends to decrease. Supposing p equals 25%, the number of extractions virtually sufficient to identify an economically-exploitable deposit is as follows:

$$n = \lg 5\% / \lg(1-25\%)$$

$$n = -1.301029996/-0.1249387366$$

$$n = 10.41$$

$$n \approx 10 \text{ trials.}$$

At this point, by estimating the unit drilling cost and the cost of the related preliminary tests,we can compile a reticular diagram (see Figure 2.9) for the options.

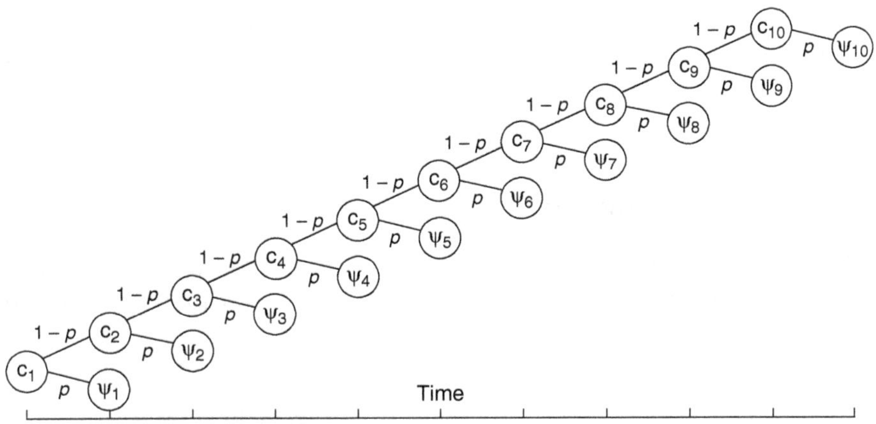

Figure 2.9 Option time-diagram

Drawing on past experience with similar specific geological and geophysical features, the minimum economic value of a profitable deposit can be identified. Variations are shown as Ψ, the cost of a prospective drilling operation is identified as C, and v is the periodic actualization factor relating to the duration of a drilling programme (monthly, bi-monthly, etc.).

By using the notions of probabilistic calculation, the following magnitudes can be determined.

Present value of profits from the *WG* deposit:

$$WG = p\Psi v + p(1-p)\Psi v^2 + \ldots + p(1-p)^{n-1}\Psi v^n.$$

Present value of exploration and research assets *VI:*

$$VI = C + (1-p)Cv + (1-p)^2 Cv^2 + \ldots + (1-p)^{n-1}Cv^{n-1}.$$

The economic value of the exploration and research concession can be quantified as:

Economic value of the exploration and research concession	=	present value of profits from drilling operations	$-ke \times$ present value of exploration and research assets

The options theory outlined above represents a particularly versatile and flexible valuation tool. It can be reliably applied thanks to the vast experience that mining companies have acquired in the fields of research and exploration and in the use of technology capable of improving geologists' forecasting efficiency.

The model illustrated means the problems associated with valuing an exploration or a research concession when it is already operational can be avoided. If this is the case, not only will the geophysical data be more reliable, the reticular structure will be less complex.

2.9 Flow-stock methods

These methods are a combination of earnings-based methods and stock-based methods. There most known flow-stock methods are the following two.

1. The Average Value methodology; that is, the simple average between the stock-based method and the earnings-based method. In formula, we have:

$$W = (K' + E/ke)/2$$

where

W is the equity fair value;
K' is the NAV;
E is the expected normalized earnings;
ke is the cost of capital.

2. The Goodwill Limited Life; that is, the sum between the NAV and the present value of the excess return. The excess return is the difference between the expected earnings and the cost of equity multiplied by the NAV. The time horizon of the discount process is limited to the range of 3–8 years. The reason behind this limited time horizon is that a competitive advantage, that is, the source of the excess return, cannot be maintained for a long period of time by a company. In formula, we have:

$$W = K' + (E - keK')a_{n,i}$$

where

W is the equity fair value;
K' is the NAV;
E is the expected normalized earnings;
ke is the cost of capital;
$E - keK'$ is the excess return;
$a_{n,i}$ a is the discount factor.

2.10 Majority control premium and minority discount

A company's equity fair value represents the theoretical exchange value that can be assigned to the company's entire share capital.

Particular problems arise whenever estimates have to be assigned to share parcels of differing sizes. In principal, the value of a certain number of shares should be the function of two considerations:

- the size of the share capital that makes up the parcel;
- the rights those shares confer upon the purchaser.

This second consideration is worth particular attention; as can be seen on closer inspection, the value of a parcel representing 3% of the share capital will be different depending on whether the purchaser already holds 48% or 80% of the share capital. In the first case, that 3% will allow the purchaser to gain effective control of the company, taking over the economic decision-making, whilst in the second the purchaser is only increasing and further consolidating his already controlling share.

It follows that the value of a parcel of shares is rarely exactly proportional to the economic value of the share capital represented. Therefore, any valuation problems need to look at whether there are any majority voting rights premiums (the first case in our example) or any minority voting rights discounts (the second case).

The objective of this section is to come up with a model that can be used to estimate the economic value assignable to parcels of shares in relation to their aptitude for allowing or disallowing corporate control. The tool we are using here is a box diagram (Figure 2.10) on which are

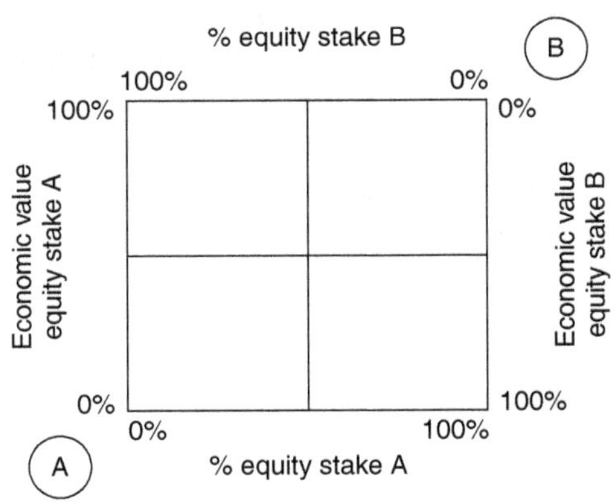

Figure 2.10 Equity value vs. equity stake

shown the positions of two co-partners (A and B) who between them own 100% of a company. As will be noted, this simplified assumption is easily removable if there are more co-partners (A, B and C, for example).

The diagram is constructed as follows:

- the parallel sides represent, respectively, the numerical percentage of the equity stakes held and the equity fair value, expressed as a percentage;
- the bottom left hand corner represents the starting point of the axis used to define the position of partner A;
- the upper right hand corner constitutes the starting point of the axis used to define the position of partner B.

The economic value of the parcels is only self-evident in three particular cases:

- a parcel representing 100% of the share capital is worth 100% of the company's equity fair value;
- a nil parcel has a value equal to zero;
- a parcel comprising 50% of the share capital is necessarily worth 50% of the overall equity fair value.

By marking these three points on the box diagram it is easy to see that the line that passes through them represents a bisector; if there are neither majority voting rights premiums nor minority voting rights discounts, the values of the parcels of shares would move along this line (see Figure 2.11).

In truth, the hypothesis of perfect proportionality between the percentage of shares that makes up a parcel and the percentage of the overall equity fair value that the parcel of shares represents has been shown to be somewhat inappropriate and scarcely representative of the underlying economic and legal reality.

We are therefore introducing a "leap" into the model, which involves the purchase of two shares by a co-partner who already holds 50% minus 1 share of the share capital. In listed companies, a majority voting right premium of between 25% and 35% of the equity fair value is normally recognized, but for the purposes of our model we shall assume an average rate of 30%.

This means that a holding of 50% minus 1 share of the share capital is worth 35% of the equity fair value, whilst a holding of 50% plus one share is worth 65% of the equity fair value. Thus if partner A, who

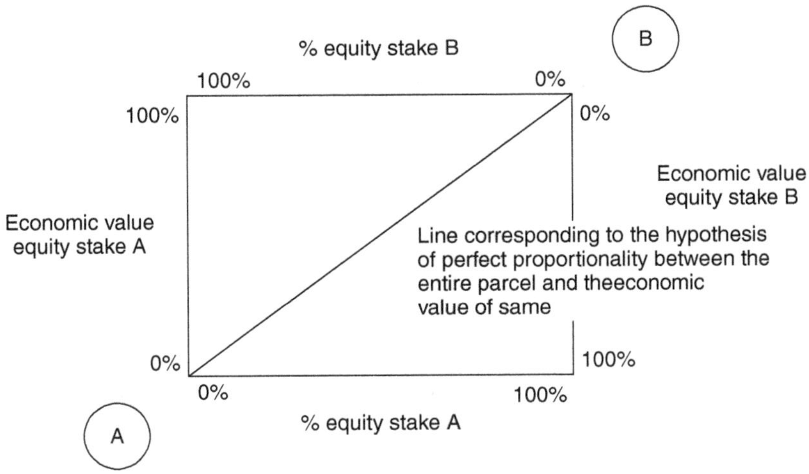

Figure 2.11 Equity value vs. equity stake, perfect proportionality

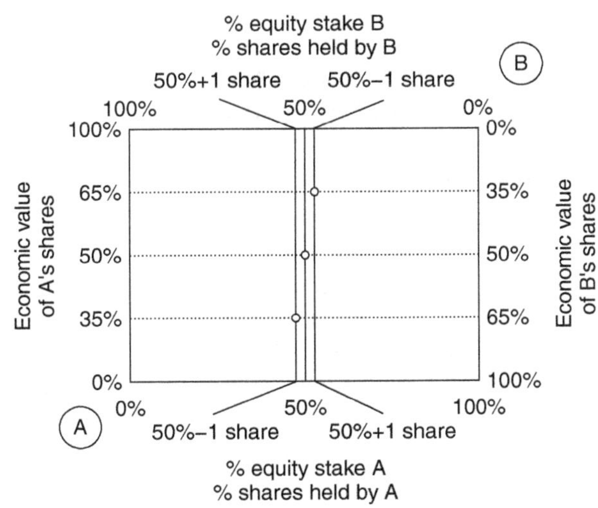

Figure 2.12 Equity value vs. equity stake, jump for control premium

holds the 50% minus 1 shareholding, is seeking to purchase two shares, he will need to pay out more than 30% of the company's equity fair value.

In view of this, we have a further two points that will almost certainly need to be added to the box diagram (see Figure 2.12).

First point:

no. shares held by A = 50% − 1 share no. shares held by B = 50% + 1 share

$Wa = 35\%W$ $Wa = 65\%W$.

Second point:

no. shares held by A = 50% + 1 share no. shares held by B = 50% − 1 share

$Wa = 65\%W$ $Wa = 35\%W$.

We now only need to carefully define the function that links the economic value of a parcel to the size of the equity stake that the parcel comprises. The simplest assumption that can be made, albeit one that, as will be seen, fully responds to the reality of the facts, involves supposing, in relation to the Cartesian axes that express the position of co-partner A, that there is a linear relationship between the starting point of the Cartesian axes that identify the position of B and the value of B's holding of 50% minus 1 share.

The function relating the economic value of the parcel to the whole of the parcel is represented in Figure 2.13.

This function can be easily determined via an analytical route for the purpose of arranging the equations needed to make the model operative.

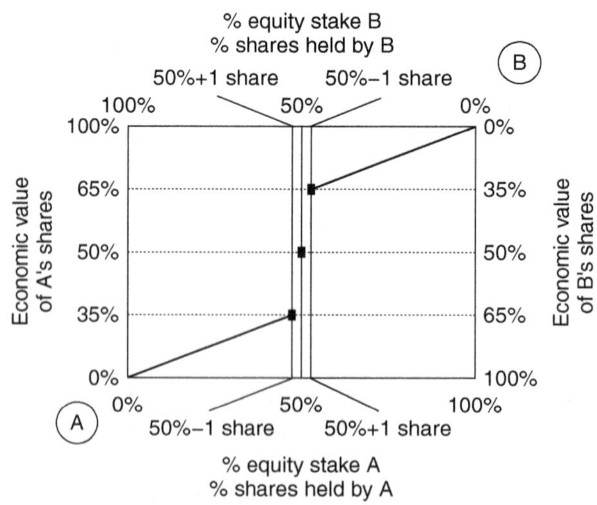

Figure 2.13 Equity value and equity stake, final relationship

The expression defined by the first part of the function, i.e. the one that in relation to the position of the co-partner joins the starting point with the point representing A's holding of 50% minus 1 share, is as follows:

$$y = \frac{35\%}{50\%}x$$

$$y = \frac{0.35}{0.7}x$$

$$y = 0.7x$$

The central point of the function, to coordinate 50% of the number of shares of A or the number of shares of B and 50% of the value of the parcel of A's or of B's shares, represents the second part of the function.

The equation that defines the third part of the function or, put another way, the line that, with reference to the Cartesian axes identifying the position of co-partner B, joins the point that expresses B's holding of 50% minus 1 share with the starting point of those same Cartesian axes, is as shown below. (Please note that this part of the function can also be identified with reference to the Cartesian axes that identify the position of co-partner A, joining the point that assumes the economic value of A's holding of 50% + 1 share with the point that expresses the value of A's 100% shareholding.)

$$\frac{y - y_1}{x - x_1} = \frac{y - y_2}{x - x_2}$$

$$\frac{y - 65\%}{x - 50\%} = \frac{100\% - 65\%}{100\% - 50\%}$$

$$y = 0.7x + 0.3.$$

However, using y to define the economic value of the generic parcel x in percentage terms, also expressed as a percentage of total share capital, in relation to the Cartesian axes used to identify the position of co-partner A, we have the following function:

$$y = \begin{cases} 0.7x & \textit{for } 0 \leq x < 0.5 \\ 0.5 & \textit{for } x = 0.5 \\ 0.7x + 0.3 & \textit{for } 0.5 < x \leq 1. \end{cases}$$

To verify that the results obtained using the above model adhere to the economic and legal logic underpinning the purchase of parcels of shares of varying sizes, we will use the following three examples (which are moreover based on a real valuation experience).

Supposing equity fair value of 25 million euro, we shall now work out:

- (*Case I*) how much should be paid by co-partner A who currently holds 30% of the shares and wishes to own 45% of the share capital;
- (*Case II*) how much should be paid by co-partner A who currently holds 30% of the shares, and who is trying to purchase a further 30%;
- (*Case III*) how much should be paid by co-partner A who currently holds 60% of the shares and who wishes to purchase a further 10%.

Case I: The economic value of the parcel to be acquired (equal to 15% of the share capital) can be obtained by calculating the difference between the economic value of 45% of the share capital and the economic value of 30% of that same share capital.

The economic value of a 30% parcel can thus be determined as $y = 0.7 \times 0.3 = 0.21$: i.e., 21% of the equity fair value of 25 million euro (5.25 million euro).

The economic value of a parcel representing 45% of the share capital can be calculated as $y = 0.7 \times 0.45 = 0.315$, i.e. 31.5% of the equity fair value, equal to 7.875 million euro.

On this hypothesis, co-partner A, upon acquiring a further 15% of the share capital, must pay 2.625 million euro, determined as follows:

$$\begin{aligned}&\text{Economic value of 45\% parcel} - \text{Economic value of 30\% parcel}\\&= 7.875 \text{ million euro} - 5.250 \text{ million euro}\\&= 2.625 \text{ million euro.}\end{aligned}$$

If direct proportionality between the economic value of a parcel and the parcel as a whole were deemed valid, 15% (45% – 30%) of the share capital would be valued at 3.750 million euro (0.15×25 million euro). The model thus asserts that a minority voting rights discount of 1.125 million euro should be recognized, i.e. the difference between the "theoretical" value (3.750 million euro) and the "real" value (2.625 million euro).

Case II: The economic value of a 30% parcel comes to 5.25 million euro (as calculated in case I); the economic value of 60% of the shares can thus be calculated as $y = 0.7 \times 0.6 + 0.3$:(on the basis of the third part of the model where $y = 0.7x + 0.3$).Thus, $y = 72\%$ of the equity fair value, or 18 million euro (0.72×25 million euro).

It follows that in order to move from owning his current 30% of the share capital to owning 60%, co-partner A must pay the following amount:

Economic value of 60% parcel – Economic value of 30% parcel

= 18 million euro – 5.250 million euro

= 12.750 million euro.

In this case the following majority voting rights premium (for the 30% parcel) will be acknowledged:

12.750 million euro – 0.3 × 25 million euro = 5.250 million euro.

Case III: The economic value of 60% of the shares is 18 million euro (as calculated in case II); the value of 70% of the shares, worked out using the third part of the model, can therefore be calculated as $y = 0.7 \times 0.7 + 0.3 = 0.79y$, i.e. 79% of the equity fair value corresponding to 19.750 million euro (0.79 × 25 million euro).

In order for co-partner A to move from owning 60% of the share capital to owning 70%, he must pay 1.750 million euro (the value of 70% of the shares minus the value of 60% of the shares = 19.750 million euro minus 18 million euro).

In this case, a discount of 0.750 million euro would be recognized (the proportional value of 10% of the shares less the actual value of those shares = 25 × 0.1 million euro – 1.750 million euro = 2.500 million euro – 1.750 million euro = 0.750 million euro).

Based on the above, we can conclude that:

- because the total value of the shares must correspond to the equity fair value at the moment the existence of a majority voting rights premium is confirmed, the subsistence of a minority voting rights discount must necessarily be acknowledged, and vice versa;
- when starting from one non-controlling position and moving to a new non-controlling position, the purchaser must acknowledge a minority voting rights discount; the same applies if a purchaser is starting from a controlling position and attempting to increase his quota;
- if a partner owning 50% minus 1 of the shares wishes to acquire the remaining 50% plus 1 of the shares, more than half of the premium must correspond to 50% of the equity fair value, in other words, 15% of the equity fair value (supposing, of course, that the majority voting rights premium is equal to 30%);

Table 2.7 Table showing the economic value of parcels of shares

% shares	Economic value (%)	% shares	Economic value (%)	% shares	Economic value (%)	% shares	Economic value (%)	% shares	Economic value (%)
1	0.70	21	14.70%	41%	28.70%	61%	72.70%	81%	86.70%
2	1.40	22	15.40%	42%	29.40%	62%	73.40%	82%	87.40%
3	2.10	23	16.10%	43%	30.10%	63%	74.10%	83%	88.10%
4	2.80	24	16.80	44	30.80	64	74.80	84	88.80
5	3.50	25	17.50	45	31.50	65	75.50	85	89.50
6	4.20	26	18.20	46	32.20	66	76.20	86	90.20
7	4.90	27	18.90	47	32.90	67	76.90	87	90.90
8	5.60	28	19.60	48	33.60	68	77.60	88	91.60
9	6.30	29	20.30	49	34.30	69	78.30	89	92.30
10	7.00	30	21.00	50	50.00	70	79.00	90	93.00
11	7.70	31	21.70	51	65.70	71	79.70	91	93.70
12	8.40	32	22.40	52	66.40	72	80.40	92	94.40
13	9.10	33	23.10	53	67.10	73	81.10	93	95.10
14	9.80	34	23.80	54	67.80	74	81.80	94	95.80
15	10.50	35	24.50	55	68.50	75	82.50	95	96.50
16	11.20	36	25.20	56	69.20	76	83.20	96	97.20
17	11.90	37	25.90	57	69.90	77	83.90	97	97.90
18	12.60	38	26.60	58	70.60	78	84.60	98	98.60
19	13.30	39	27.30	59	71.30	79	85.30	99	99.30
20	14.00	40	28.00	60	72.00	80	86.00	100	100.00

- if a partner owning 50% of the shares is attempting to purchase the other 50%, he must only pay a sum equal to 50% of the equity fair value.

In our opinion the above is a reasonable response to and is in line with the economic and legal reality that underlies the purchase of parcels of shares.

Table 2.7 has been compiled to make it easier and quicker to calculate the value of single parcels of shares. The table has been compiled on the assumption that the majority voting rights premium is equal to 30% of the equity fair value:

Looking at the table we can immediately see that 7% of the equity fair value corresponds to 10% of the shares; in reality, 40% of the share capital is only representative of 28% of the value of the company; 75% of the shares are worth 82.5% of the equity fair value and, naturally, 100% of the shares show a value equal to that of the equity fair value.

The purchase value of a parcel can therefore be estimated by subtracting the value of the initial number of shares from the value of the final number of shares and multiplying the percentage thus obtained by the total equity fair value.

Example: calculating the transfer value of a parcel equal to 15% of the share capital in the case where the co-partner acquiring the additional shares already has a 51% shareholding: economic value of 66% of the shares (76.20% *W*)-economic value of 51% of the shares (65.70%*W*) = percentage of equity fair value (10.5% *W*).

The whole of the majority voting rights premium and of the minority voting rights discount can be readily determined by subtracting from the transfer value of the parcel the value of same calculated proportionally at the economic value.

If

> *Economic value of the parcel* (VE_p) > *proportional value of the shares* (VP_p)
>
> $VE_p - VP_p$ = *majority voting rights premium.*

If

> *Economic value of the parcel* (VE_p) < *proportional value of the shares* (VP_p)
>
> $VE_p - VP_p$ = *minority voting rights discount.*

3
Cost of Equity for Private Companies: The Integrated Pricing Model

3.1 Introduction

In this chapter we shall be setting out a model for estimating the cost of equity that is based on valuation techniques similar to those developed in the Fixed Income sector for estimating expected losses and for the pricing of junior subordinated notes relating to cash or synthetic securitization (also known as the Fixed Income Approach, or FIA). More precisely, the following phases are mapped: firstly, fixed income techniques are used to estimate the expected losses for shareholders of non-listed companies (in other words the probability of default and the loss given default (LGD)); next the way in which spreads of junior and subordinated notes are calculated is outlined; and finally results from using the FIA model are integrated with those from the CAPM (see Figure 3.1), leading to the Integrated Pricing Model (IPM). The FIA is based on the assumed major valuation efficiency of credit market in respect to equity market (Blanco *et al.*, 2005; Chan-Lau and Kim, 2005; Hull *et al.*, 2004; Longstaff *et al.*, 2005; Oricchio, 2011).

3.2 Shareholder's expected loss

The integrated FIA–CAPM approach has proven particularly useful for valuing the equity fair value of the share capital of non-listed companies with sub-investment grade credit risk.

The first step when calculating the cost of equity using the FIA is to estimate the expected loss (probability of default and LGD) that would result should part or all of the capital invested in a non-listed company be lost. Hence there is a move away from estimating the expected loss caused by the company's debt to instead estimating the expected loss from the business equity point of view.

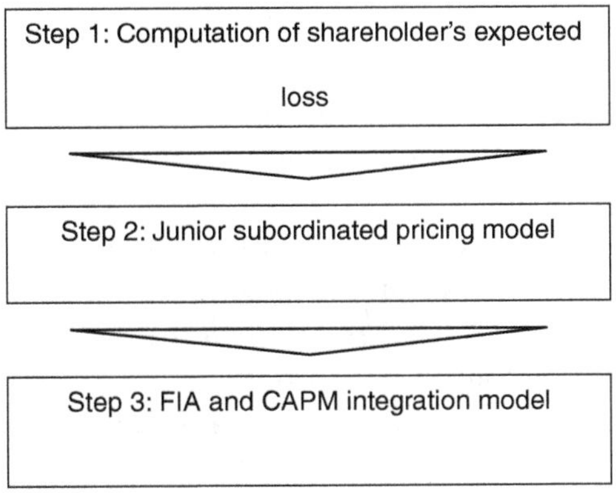

Figure 3.1 Cost of equity estimation process

To do this, (step 1 in Figure 3.1), the following procedure is adopted:

1) the case of the total loss of enterprise capital is studied (the so-called Floor Theorem);
2) the case of the loss of at least 1 euro on enterprise capital is studied (the so-called Cap Theorem);
3) the results of these two cases are systematized (the so-called Combined Rule).

3.2.1 The Floor Theorem

Ratings models for estimating the probability of default of a non-listed company are based on analyses of a sample pool of healthy (good) companies and companies in default (bad companies). The probability being estimated is the probability of insolvency within 12 months (or within a certain number of years). Within the sample of bad companies insolvency is defined as the loss of value of the bank credit facility, and for every bad company the recovery rate (or its complement, in other words the LGD) is estimated. For a bad company the recovery rate assumes a value of less than 100% (and the LGD is a value greater than zero). It follows that in the case of a bad company the bank suffers a loss on the credit it has advanced that is in a senior position with regard to the company's asset value. In other words, at this bad company the assets are reduced to such a value that its net capital is re-set to zero and a loss is generated on the bank credit facility. In such a case the net capital, which is in a subordinate position to the bank credit facility, is totally consumed and a 100% loss is generated for the shareholders.

It follows that when the bank credit facility has a recovery rate of less than 100% (if a company goes into liquidation, for example), this automatically generates a 100% loss for shareholders.

Based on the above, both of the following statements can be regarded as *simultaneously* valid:

a) internal rating models are normally developed on bad/good samples, in which the bad is a bank default with a recovery rate of less than 100% (and a LGD of more than zero);
b) internal rating models are normally developed using bad/good samples, in which the bad involves a 100% loss of shareholders' capital.

It follows that the probability of insolvency estimated for non-listed companies using internal rating models (or models available on the market such as Moody's RiskCalc) in fact estimate the probability that shareholders will lose 100% of their capital.

An initial simplified measurement of the equity risk premium can be formulated on the basis of the probability of default established using internal rating models, and from the relative LGD for shareholders in line with what usually happens to the credit risk premium in the following circumstances (see Equation 3.1):

$$\text{credit risk premium} \approx \text{probability of default} \times \text{debt loss given default}$$

$$\text{equity risk premium} \approx \text{probability of default} \times 100\% \qquad (3.1)$$

where the probability of default is identical in both cases.

The following will serve as a useful example. The company *Alpha* is attempting to launch an increase in its capital and to embark on new medium- to long-term financing arrangements that will enable it to prove that it has an average annual probability of default of 5% over 10 years. Alpha is asking the *Beta Bank* for a 10-year loan, which it is securing with a mortgage on its own property. In this case, the LGD for the bank is 20%.

Based on the above, the Beta Bank's credit risk premium for providing finance to Alpha is estimated at around 1% (see Equation 3.2):

$$\text{credit risk premium} \approx \text{probability of default} \times \text{debt loss given default} \qquad (3.2)$$

$$\text{credit risk premium} \approx 5\% \times 20\% = 1\%.$$

A new shareholder is trying to assess the level of equity risk premium to apply when calculating discounted cash flows over a 10-year period.

Throughout this period, every year the shareholder runs the risk of there being a 5% probability of his losing all of his capital. An initial estimate of the equity risk premium is 5% (see Equation 3.3):

$$\begin{aligned} &\text{equity risk premium} \approx \text{probability of default} \\ &\quad \times \text{equity loss given default} \\ &\text{equity risk premium} \approx 5\% \times 100\% = 5\%. \end{aligned} \tag{3.3}$$

This 5% equity risk premium is a "by default" estimate in that, above and beyond any considerations of the time frame, it measures the risk that shareholders face of incurring a 100% loss of their capital. Shareholders obviously also run the risk of losing just part of their capital, hence the need to integrate the first assessment with a second, as discussed in Section 3.2.2. Given that this first estimate is by default, the approach just outlined is referred to as the "Floor Theorem". In contrast, the following section illustrates the "Cap Theorem".

3.2.2 The Cap Theorem

The Cap Theorem is designed to estimate the probability of a shareholder suffering a partial loss of the capital he has invested. In order that the reasoning behind the valuation process uses the same calculation tools as in the previous section, i.e. internal rating models, we have introduced a concept of "mathematical limit". Internal rating models estimate the probability of insolvency with regard to the bank credit facility, in other words the probability of insolvency of the senior debt within the structure of the capital of the company being valued. As the level of bank debt rises, i.e. the relative value of the (senior) debt compared with the total sources of finance, so the company's probability of default significantly increases. If, in the end, the company is only being financed via bank debt plus a small amount of equity, the probability of default of the (senior) debt would be identical to the probability of default of the equity. In this extreme case, given the substantial lack of equity (subordinate and junior), the bank debt would lose its valency as the senior debt and the bank would in fact be the company's sole shareholder. Capital with a "full debt" structure of the kind just described is equivalent to a CDO (Collateralised Debt Obligation) in which there is only one type of note (untranched). As one gets closer to this "extreme case", the probability of losing at least 1 euro on the share capital get closer to the probability of losing at least 1 euro on the senior debt.

In analytical terms, the following equation applies (see Equation 3.4):

$$[1]\,PD\,equity = PD\,debt \;[2] \lim_{\frac{D}{(D+E)}\to 1} (PD\,debt) \Rightarrow PDEquity \quad (3.4)$$

where

D	is the senior debt;
E	is the junior subordinated debt;
$PD\,debt$	is the probability of default of senior debt;
$PD\,equity$	is probability of default of junior subordinated debt.

The probability of losing at least 1 euro on share capital can be estimated as the probability of losing at least 1 euro on the senior debt in the extreme hypothesis of the company being 100% financed through bank debt.

In the case of Alpha, the internal rating model simulates a nearly 100% leverage and we arrive at an estimate showing that there is an average annual probability of default of 20% over 10 years. It follows that over the course of 10 years the shareholder faces a 20% annual average probability of losing at least 1 euro on his investment. This estimation method is known as the Cap Theorem.

This means that two extremes have been identified: the probability that the shareholder will lose 100% of his investment (the floor estimate), and the probability that the shareholder will lose at least 1 euro on his capital (the cap estimate). The challenge now is to combine the two estimates so as to arrive at a single calculation of the equity risk premium.

3.2.3 The combined Rule for the expected loss for the shareholder

According to the above, a floor and a cap are defined when estimating the equity risk premium.

As regards the floor, we have managed to estimate the probability that the shareholder will lose 100% of his investment as a result of the probability of default of the senior debt, estimated using an internal rating model based on bank defaults (with a LGD higher than zero for the bank). When a company's liabilities are viewed from the logic of structured credit, the net capital can be compared with a junior subordinated tranche and the bank debt with a senior tranche. If a LGD is verified on the senior tranche following liquidation of the CDO, it is reasonable to suppose that the LGD for holders of junior subordinated notes is 100%.

So far as the cap is concerned, the probability that the shareholder will lose at least 1 euro on his own investment is estimated as the probability of default of a company that is totally indebted vis-á-vis its creditors. Notwithstanding the total sum involved from different sources of financing, as the weight of the senior debt increases (with the corresponding reduction in equity capital), so the risk position of creditors moves gradually nearer the risk position of the shareholders. In the final extreme, if the company is totally indebted, the creditors in fact become the shareholders. It follows that in this extreme case the company's probability of default with regard to equity corresponds to the probability of default for the creditors. This estimate is obtained by incorporating into the valuation model an amount of debt equal (or nearly equal) to the total obtained from the various sources of finance.

The following figure shows the probability associated with the LGD for the shareholder (see Figure 3.2).

The black area of Figure 3.3 identifies the floor probability; the grey area of Figure 3.4 identifies the cap probability. Without going into the statistics of the density function (where numerous technical solutions are possible), it was decided that the simplest and most robust approach

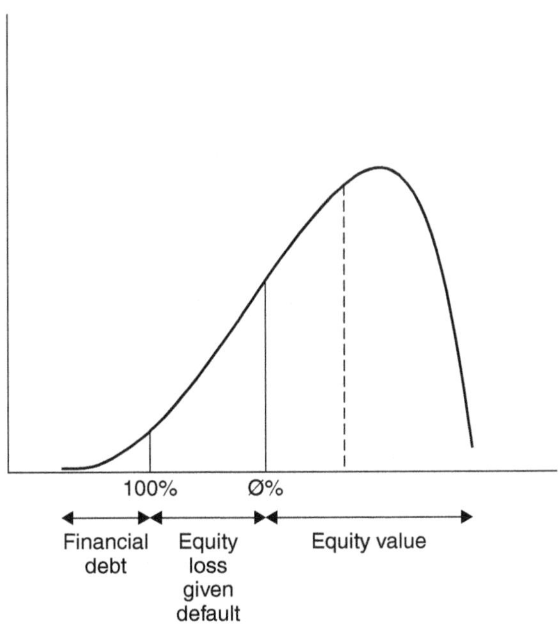

Figure 3.2 Equity loss/gain probability distribution

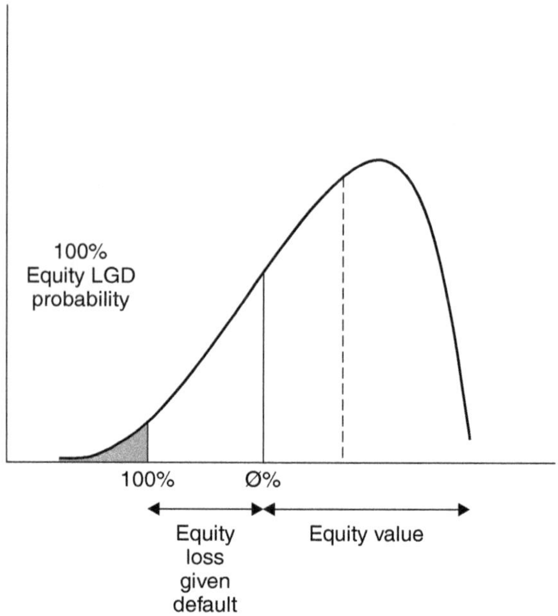

Figure 3.3 100% equity loss given default probability

would be to determine the equity risk premium as the amount between the black part and an average of the grey area net of the black area.

So let us more specifically suppose that an average LGD of 50% will be assumed within the 100–0% LGD range. By doing this, the hypothesis assumes that the area of overestimation of the LGD (relating to the 100–50% range) is similar to the area of underestimation of the LGD (relating to the 50–0% range)(see Figure 3.5).

The equity risk premium is determined thus (see Equation 3.5):

$$\text{probability of default floor} = \text{probability associated with a 100\% LGD}$$

$$\text{probability of default cap} = \text{probability of at least 1 euro equity loss}$$

$$\text{equity risk premium} \approx \text{probability of default cap} + 50\%(\text{probability of default cap} - \text{probability of default floor})$$

In the case of the company Alpha, Beta Bank will need to receive compensation for the credit risk equal to a loan credit spread of 1%; meanwhile the premium for the shareholder's equity risk premium is equal to 12.5%, as shown below (see Equation 3.6):

$$\text{equity risk premium} \approx 5\% + (20\% - 5\%) \times 50\% = 12.5\%$$

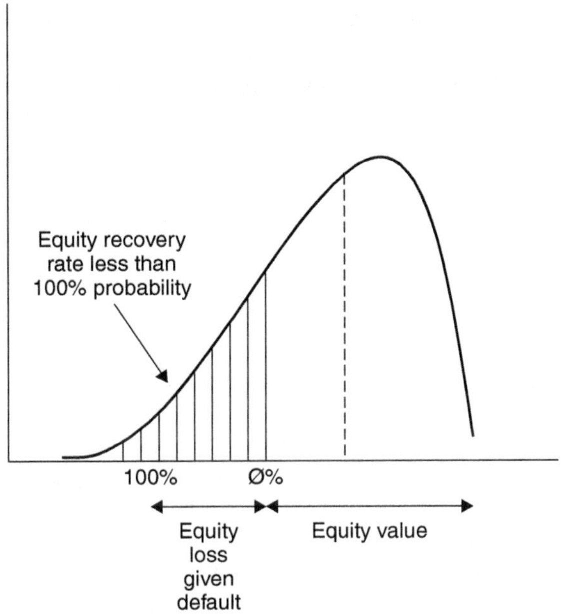

Figure 3.4 Equity recovery rate less than 100% probability

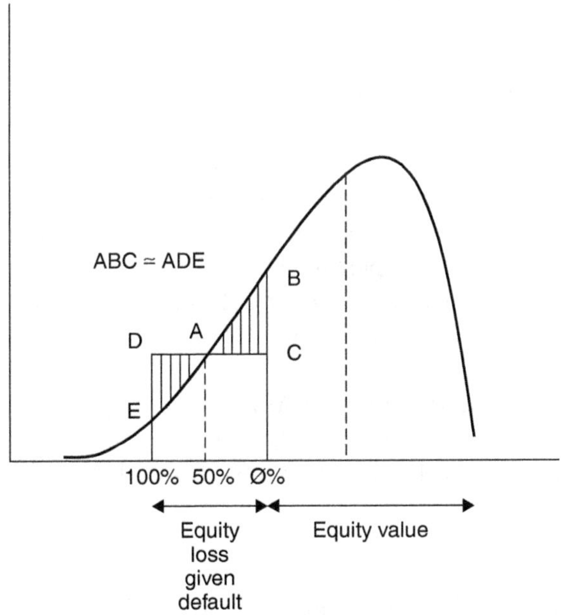

Figure 3.5 Over-estimation error and under-estimation error

To complete the example just given, if we assume a long-term risk free rate of 4%, the adjusted risk rate for the Beta Bank will be 5% (we are talking here about a simplified rate because no account is taken of the remuneration of own means, nor of the structural costs), whilst the cost of equity for the shareholder will be 16.5% (again this is a simplified rate in that it does not take into consideration the discount for the lack of liquidity of the investment, nor the duration of same).

3.3 Junior subordinated pricing model

On the basis of the above, we can now move on to the application of the pricing model for junior subordinated notes (step 2 in Figure 3.1) in order to work out the risk-adjusted spread that in our case corresponds to the equity risk premium (ERP). The advantage of switching from an approach based exclusively on expected loss to one based on a fixed income pricing model is that when considering how to define the ERP, it takes account of both the probability of loss and the relative amount, as well as the probability of "winning" and the relative amount. More precisely, the cost of the equity represents the win that makes the investment fair and reasonable from the shareholders' point of view (in other words, it represents a hurdle rate). The analytical development of a pricing model requires the introduction of ratings migration matrices over time as well as the term structure of the probability of default. In the appendix to this chapter we set out the arguments relating to the term structure of the probability of default and to state-dependent transition matrices (see Appendix 1).

In order to define the pricing model algebraically, the notions of Equity Risk-Adjusted Profit (ERAP), Cost of Capital, and Economic Profit need to be defined.

Equity Risk-Adjusted Profit (ERAP) is calculated over the lifetime of the facility (assumed to be perpetual) and is essentially the Net Present Value (NPV) of the facility's cash flows. It is defined as follows (Equation 3.7):

$$ERAP = \sum_{n=0}^{Maturity} \frac{1}{(1+r)^n} \cdot \left[(1 - PD_{cum,n}) \cdot (Earnings_n) \right.$$
$$\left. -(1 - PD_{cum,n-1}) \cdot (EL_n)\right]$$

where

$PD_{cum,n}$	is the cumulative probability of default for period n;
$Earnings_n$	is the earnings payment for period n;
EL_n	is the equity expected loss in period n;
r	is the monthly discount rate;
n	is the period of time in which the cash flow occurs.

The equity risk premium is present in both the discount rate and in the cost of capital. The cash flows included in the model consist of the expected losses and the target hurdle rate of return required on the shareholder's invested capital. The cost of capital in each period of time is calculated as the product of the shareholder's invested capital and the hurdle rate.

The Economic Profit of the Equity (junior subordinated) is calculated as follows (Equation 3.8):

$$Economic\,Profit = \sum_{n=1}^{Maturity} (ERAP_n - CostCap_n)$$

where

$ERAP_n$	is the equity risk-adjusted profit for period n;
$CostCap_n$	is the present value of the expected cost of capital for period n.

The formula for this calculation is shown in full below (Equation 3.9):

$$Economic\,Profit = \sum_{n=1}^{Maturity} [\frac{1}{(1+r)^n} \cdot \{[(1 - PD_{cum,n}) \cdot (Earnings_n) - (1 - PD_{cum,n-1}) \cdot (EL_n])] - (1 - PD_{cum,n-1}) \cdot CostCap_n\}$$

Under this framework, a junior subordinated note with zero economic profit would meet exactly the target hurdle rates of return, having paid for the expected losses. Thus, it is possible to calculate the "breakeven margin" (or the "value neutral margin"), the margin for which economic profit is zero, by solving the above equation for earnings having set the economic profit at zero. However, it is not possible to calculate the breakeven margin by using a simple analytical solution, thus iteration is required.

3.4 The relationship between the cost of equity and the credit rating: the Integrated Pricing Model (IPM)

The model just described estimates the cost of equity on the basis of the expected loss for shareholders within the scope of a pricing model for junior subordinated notes.

The application of the method in question, so far as a non-listed company is concerned, presupposes the use of an internal rating model.

As an example we will show how the cost of equity changes when the company's credit rating varies in the case of the private company Alpha Ltd. (see Figure 3.6).

As can be seen, the estimated cost of equity is particularly low in the investment grade share, primarily because of the low probability of default that characterizes higher ratings. More to the point, for investment grade companies not only is the expected loss in the event of default virtually nil, but in addition the probability of losing at least 1 euro's worth of equity capital rarely involves significant values. This last aspect is worth looking at in more depth.

The capacity for debt repayment is based on the ability to generate high and stable operating cash flows. In the best companies and in less risky sectors, there is a high ratio of operating cash flow to total assets. If such assets are being financed with little debt, it is clear that the ratio between operating cash flows and debt denotes a very low degree of

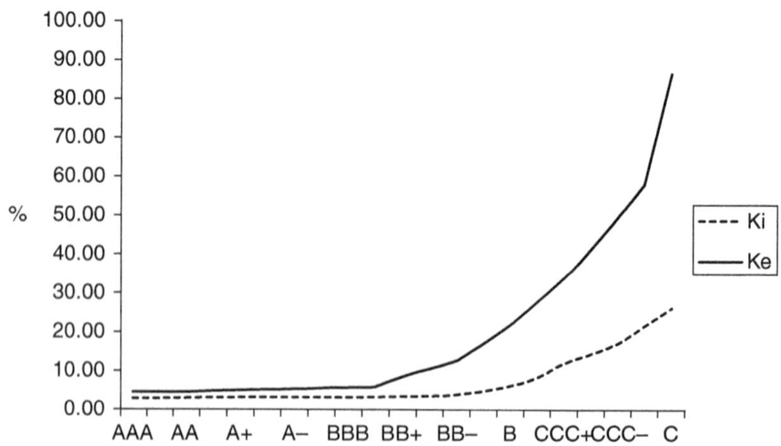

Figure 3.6 Relationship between credit rating and cost of equity for the company Alpha Ltd.
Source: Our estimate based on financial data held on Alpha Ltd.

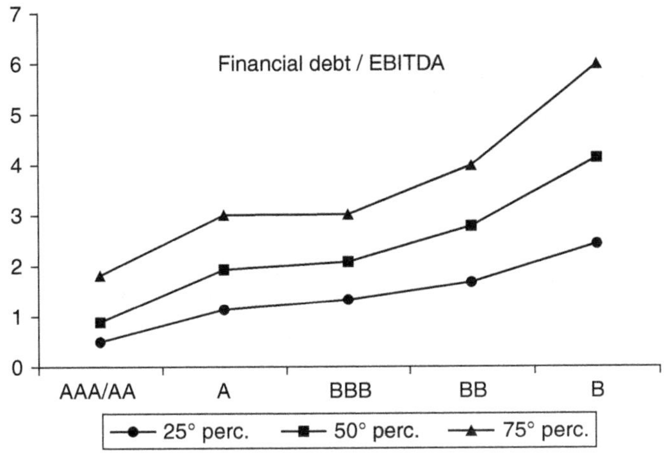

Figure 3.7 Relationship between D/EBITDA and credit rating
Source: Our elaboration on the Bloomberg database.

risk. On the other hand, if such assets are financed with a lot of debt (or even entirely through debt) the ability to service operating cash flows needs to be verified. Often, the size of operating cash flows is such as to service the elevated debt with a probability of default equivalent to a BB or BB– rating (as can happen in some utilities).

In order to give an immediate reading of the phenomenon described, let us suppose we are working in a simplified context where the internal rating model is based on a single variable represented by the debt/EBITDA ratio. The following figure (see Figure 3.7) represents the statistical relationship between the ratings and the values of the debt/EBITDA ratios of around 1,800 listed companies. The three lines in the debt/EBITDA ratio represent the median, the 25th percentile and the 75th percentile.

Alpha Ltd. shows an EBITDA/Total Assets ratio of 25%. Even if all of the assets were financed with debt, the ratio of EBITDA debt would still be 25% (or, if you like, the debt/EBITDA ratio would be equal to 4).

If we assume that the sector in which Alpha Ltd. operates reflects the line representing the 75th percentile, with a debt/EBITDA ratio of 4, Alpha's equivalent rating would be a BB–, corresponding to an annual probability of default in the order of 3%.

The model for estimating the cost of equity set out above is based exclusively on credit risk and, as a result:

a) it does not take the market risk into adequate consideration;

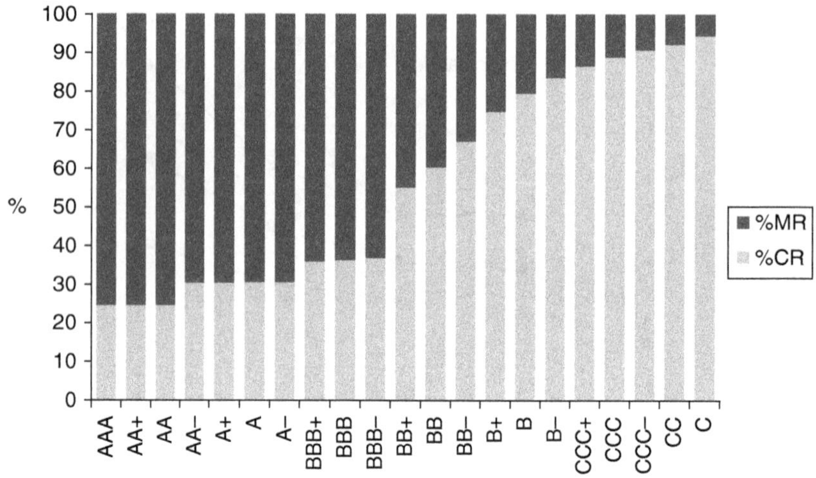

Figure 3.8 Relative weights of credit risk and market risk on the credit rating scale
Source: Our estimate of credit risk premium and equity risk premium by rating classification.

b) the ERP is very low in the investment grade share but rises rapidly in the sub-investment grade share (see Figure 3.6 and Fig. 3.8).

In order to arrive at a full and adequate estimate of the economic risk for non-listed companies, there is one final step. This represents the integration of the credit risk with the market risk (step 3 in Figure 3.1). To this end, we shall briefly examine the main method used to estimate the cost of capital for listed companies and formulate some valid conclusions for non-listed ones.

The model for estimating the equity risk premium most widely used in international practice is the CAPM (Damodaran, 2010) (see Equation 3.10).

$$\text{equity risk premium} = beta \times (Rm - rf)$$

where

$beta$ = is the non-diversifiable risk indicator;

Rm = is the expected return on the market index;

rf = is the risk free rate.

The "beta" factor, however, does not fully capture the credit risk, indeed it assumes a less susceptible value compared to the rating of the company being valued (Damodaran, 2011; Chan-Lau, 2006). Shown below is a representation of the median of the beta subdivided by the

Table 3.1 Sample of 355 public corporates with an external rating, beta factor and 5 years' CDS

External rating	Beta	Cost of equity (%)	5 yrs' CDS (%)
AA	0.92	10.45	0.43
AA−	0.92	10.76	0.51
A+	0.84	10.10	0.54
A	0.89	10.66	0.69
A−	0.90	10.66	0.78
BBB+	1.04	11.66	1.16
BBB	0.99	11.40	1.34
BBB−	1.12	12.31	2.08
BB+	1.05	12.48	2.47
BB	0.76	9.27	1.99
BB−	1.12	12.36	3.35
B+	1.25	14.17	8.71
B	1.36	14.58	9.76

Source: Our estimate based on Bloomberg data.

various classes of rating for listed companies (see Table 3.1). Table 3.1 also shows the scale of the cost of equity estimated using the CAPM and the average value of the CDS (Credit Default Swap) over 5 years.

If we examine data on listed companies that also have a credit rating it can be seen that the beta used when applying the CAPM is largely uncorrelated with the actual rating. To be more precise:

(i) the beta is highly volatile within the same sector and same credit rating;
(ii) the beta has no correlation with the credit rating;
(iii) the beta's range of variation is very modest (ranging on average between 0.8 and 1.2) and is not comparable with the range of variation in the probability of default underlying the credit rating.

It follows that the premium for the risk deriving from the application of the CAPM "moves" within a range that is significantly reduced compared with the breadth of values assumed for credit spreads, which are strongly correlated with credit ratings.

The sensitivity of the beta to credit risk appears to increase only for businesses that are near insolvency.

In order to correct this poor sensitivity to credit risk, various integrations into the CAPM model have been proposed. The main one (Hamada, 1969; Damodaran, 1997) consists of firstly determining an unlevered beta and then calculating a levered beta applying a multiplicative factor based on the leverage (see Equation 3.11).

$$levered\,beta = unlevered\,beta\left[1+\frac{D}{E}(1-t)\right]$$

The assumption underlying this correction is that the debt/equity ratio is a good indicator of the credit risk that shareholders are supporting. In other words,

i) the debt/equity ratio is used as a univariate rating;
ii) the multiplicative factor can be from one to infinity.

With regard to the first point, it will be observed that the credit risk can be measured using a multi-dimensional approach (see successive chapters) and the use of a univariate rating model can only work well in very simplified contexts. And yet if you really want to work with rating models to a single variable, in professional practice it is more common to use a rule-of-thumb based on the debt/EBITDA ratio rather than the debt/equity ratio. As we saw in the previous section, there may be cases of deeply indebted companies (including full debt) that still have a probability of default in the order of 3–4%.

The following graphs compare the valency of information on the debt/EBITDA ratio compared to the debt/equity ratio based on a sample of 1,800 listed companies (see Figure 3.9). As can be seen in the graph on the left, the relationship between rating and classic debt ratio appears less steep (weaker) compared with the relationship between debt/EBITDA seen in the graph on the right.

With regard to the second point, and for non-listed small to medium sized enterprises in particular, a correction of the beta factor based on the debt/capital ratio can be excessive. Non-listed small to medium sized enterprises obviously present a level of credit risk that is higher

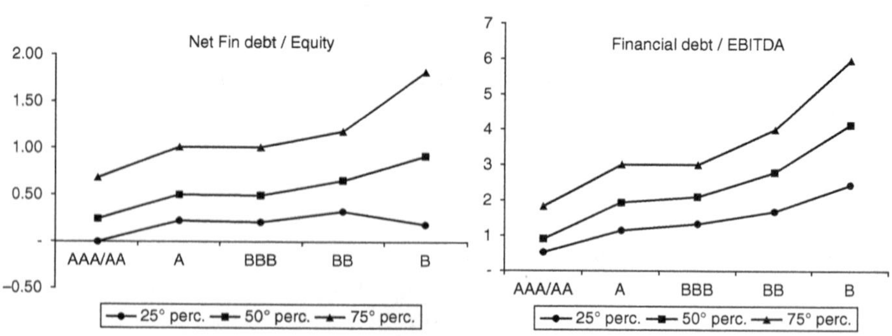

Figure 3.9 Financial index comparison
Source: Compiled by us on the basis of data from Bloomberg.

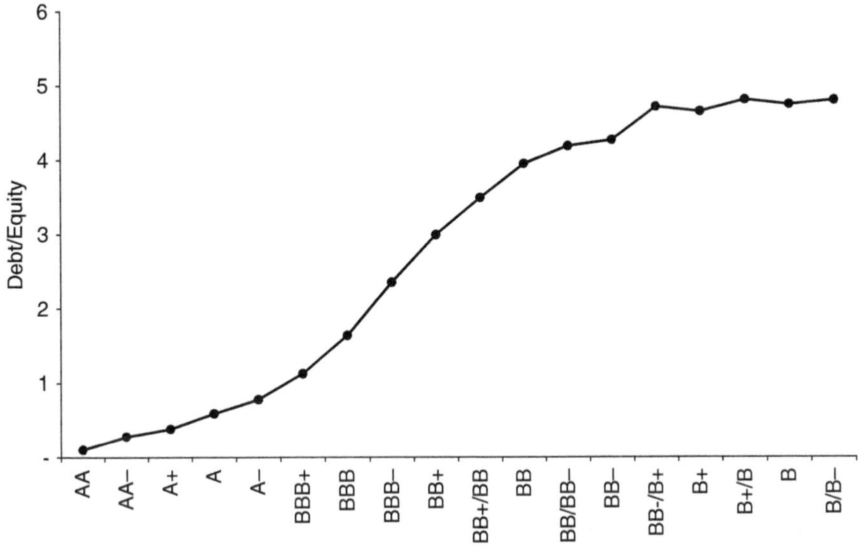

Figure 3.10 Relationship between leverage and classes of internal credit ratings
Source: Compiled by author from European financial databases.

than big listed companies that are only carrying a small amount of debt. However, the application of this factor would often prove misleading in that it is not suitable for reflecting the probability of default estimated using multi-dimensional rating models. See also Figure 3.10, in which for a sample of 60,000 European corporates, the classic indebtedness ratio (debt/capital) is related to the rating category deriving from the application of an internal rating model. Note how the debt/capital ratio in the sub-investment grade assumes values that are decisively higher than is the case for listed companies.

Both of the points illustrated above can lead to unrealistic results, especially when the subject of the valuation is a non-listed sub-investment grade company. If we examine the Fame-French three factor model (Fama and French, 1993, 1996), the two new explanatory factors (SMB or size factor and HML or "book-to-market" value) try to capture – in reality – the "default risk" (Chan-Lau, 2006a):

i) the default risk in small-firm portfolios is higher than in big-firm portfolios;
ii) the default risk in high book-to-market value firm portfolios is higher than in low book-to-market value firm portfolios.

Small companies with high book-to-market ratio usually are sub-investment grade companies.

In other terms, the excess return associated with small-firm and high book-to-market portfolios should not be a pure excess return, but it could be seen as the remuneration of the sub-investment default probability.

If we summarize the positive and negative points of the CAPM model when used to value the risk premium of the capital of non-listed companies from an operational point of view, we find:

3.4.1 CAPM for private companies:

Strong points: reliable estimate of market risk (most widely used method);

Weak points: (i) identification of listed companies comparable with the non-listed company being valued;

(ii) reduced capacity for capturing the credit risk; in other words, an underestimation of the economic risk for high yield companies.

Conversely, the method based on the application of rating models developed and "fine-tuned" for non-listed companies presents the following negative and positive points:

3.4.2 Fixed income approach for private companies

Strong points: (i) you do not need listed comparables for the company being valued;

(ii) the credit risk is correctly measured in terms of the probability of default and LGD;

Weak points: incapable of estimating the market risk; in other words, overestimation of the financial risk for investment grade companies.

A quick synopsis focusing on estimating the risk premium of non-listed companies shows a preference for the CAPM for companies with a low credit risk and a preference for the approach based on the pricing of junior subordinated notes (Fixed Income Approach, FIA) for companies with a higher credit risk (see Table 3.2).

One general model that is being proposed for estimating the value of the risk premium for non-listed companies involves valuing the cost of equity as the sum of the free risk rate and whichever is the greatest between the risk premium resulting from the application of the CAPM and the risk premium resulting from the application of the expected loss. The formula for this is shown in Equation 3.12:

$$\text{Cost of equity} = \text{risk free rate} + \text{equity risk premium}$$

$$\textit{Equity risk premium} = \max(CAPM,\ FIA)$$

Table 3.2 Benefits of the Integrated Pricing Model in valuing private companies

CAPM	FIA
Suggested for Investment Grade	Suggested for High Yield
Focus is on Market Risk, less on Credit Risk	Focus is on Credit Risk, less on Market Risk
Well known method, need for comparables	No need of comparables, new approach

In this way it is possible to build on the strong points of both approaches whilst at the same time mitigating the weak points. This is called the Integrated Pricing Model (IPM).

For companies with a low credit risk, the risk premium adequately reflects the market risk; while for companies with an elevated credit risk the risk premium correctly captures the whole of the loss expected for shareholders.

Returning to the example of the company Alpha Ltd., we are able to work out the risk premium by taking into consideration the general model that combines the CAPM with the FIA. Using the approach based on comparables, a beta coefficient of 0.8 is assigned to Alpha Ltd. (a non-listed company); the average market premium is 6% and the risk free rate is 3%.

The risk premium deriving from the application of the CAPM is 4.8% (0.8 × 6%). The cost of equity becomes 7.8% (3% + 4.8%). The risk premium in the CAPM is successively correct in line with the leverage of Alpha Ltd.

Figure 3.11 illustrates Alpha's cost of equity, calculated using both approaches.

As can be seen, the cost of capital is effectively steady for the whole investment grade and low investment grade share; with effect from the BB rating onwards, it begins to climb rapidly well beyond the estimate calculated using the CAPM.

Table 3.3 shows the process for estimating the cost of equity using the IPM.

To sum up, the general model proposed is designed to be "flexible" and to capture the benefits of both the CAPM approach and the FIA. For the world of non-listed companies it assumes special valency when it is remembered that two thirds of companies have a credit risk worse than investment grade level. More generally, the proposed addition could be useful in determining the value of investments in companies, sectors

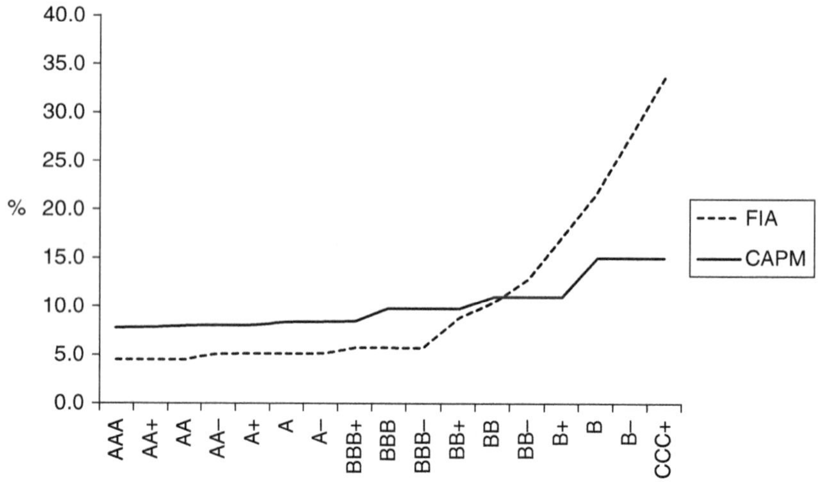

Figure 3.11 Relationship between credit rating and cost of equity at Alpha Ltd. using both CAPM and FIA
Source: Our estimate based on financial data held on Alpha Ltd.

Table 3.3 Process for estimating the cost of equity (Integrated Pricing Model)

Step 1: Computation of shareholder's expected loss: 1.1 Floor theorem 1.2 Cap theorem 1.3. Combined rule
Step 2: Junior Subordinated Pricing Model (FIA): 2.1 Equity Risk-Adjusted Profit 2.2. Economic profit 2.3 Risk-adjusted equity premium
Step 3. FIA and CAPM integration model: ERP = max (CAPM; FIA)

and economies with a high credit risk (primarily high yield private companies operating in developed markets and emerging markets).

It is for this reason that the second part of this work will illustrate the RiskCalc type of corporate rating models developed for six geographical areas and their relative application in the USA, Japan, China, Russia, India and Italy.

4
Integrated Pricing Model in USA

4.1 RiskCalc USA*

The Moody's KMV RiskCalc™v3.1 US model is built using the results of extensive Moody's KMV research, including:

- Moody's RiskCalc™v1.0 and the Moody's KMV Private Firm Model®;
- Moody's KMV Credit Research Database™(CRD, the world's largest and cleanest private company default database);
- Industry sector information, market information, and industry-specific default rates.

RiskCalc v3.1 incorporates the structural and market-based comparables approach (used in the MKMV Private Firm Model), and the localized financial statement-based approach (used in RiskCalc v1.0). This allows RiskCalc v3.1 to blend market-based (systematic) information with detailed firm-specific financial statement (idiosyncratic) information to enhance the model's predictive power.

RiskCalc modes

RiskCalc v3.1 allows a user to assess the risk of a private firm in two ways: Financial Statement Only (FSO) and Credit Cycle Adjusted (CCA).

The FSO mode delivers a firm's default risk based only on financial statements and sector information, adjusted to reflect differences in credit risk across industries. In this mode, the risk assessments produced by the model tend to be relatively stable over time.

The CCA mode adjusts the default risk by taking into account the current stage of the credit cycle. The CCA adjustment is a sector-specific factor derived directly from Moody's KMV Public Firm Model's distance-to-default. The CCA model reflects the market's current assessment of the credit cycle and is a forward-looking indicator of default.

The CCA adjustment is specific to the firm's sector and country and is updated monthly. The CCA mode also has the ability to stress test EDF (Expected Default Frequency™) credit measures under different credit cycle scenarios – a proposed requirement under Basel II.

RiskCalc v3.1 US versus RiskCalc v1.0 North America

Since the release of RiskCalc v1.0 North America, Moody's KMV has significantly increased the size of the North America database and substantially improved its data cleansing technologies. As a result of these improvements, MKMV has been able to separate the North American model into a US model and a Canadian model. The new model includes additional financial statement variables as well industry adjustments. Moreover, the EDF output can be adjusted for the credit cycle. We have also made substantial advances in our model development and testing techniques. As a result, the new model is more powerful and precise than its predecessor. Finally, the new model includes additional analytic tools that increase model usability and transparency.

4.1.1 Data description

The source of the data for RiskCalc v3.1 US is Moody's KMV CRD. The CRD collects data from participating institutions, working closely with them to understand the strengths and weakness of the data. As of May 2004, the CRD contained 6.5 million financial statements, over 1.5 million unique private firms, and more than 97,000 default events worldwide. Moody's KMV uses this data for model development and testing purposes.

4.1.1.1 Definition of default

Moody's KMV RiskCalc™ provides assistance to institutions and investors in determining the risk of default, missed payment, or other credit events. The proposals for the new Basel Capital Accord (BIS II) have stimulated debates about what constitutes an appropriate definition of default. RiskCalc applies the criteria used by most of the advanced economies in the world.

Default is defined as any of the following events:

- 90 days past due;
- bankruptcy;
- placement on internal non-accrual list;
- write-down.

4.1.1.2 Data exclusions

Excluded companies The goal of the RiskCalc model is to provide an EDF for private US companies in the middle market. The firms and industries covered in the model must have similar default characteristics. To create the most powerful model for US middle-market companies, those that did not reflect the typical company in this market were eliminated. The following types of companies are not included in the data.

- **Small companies** – For companies with assets of less than $100,000 (2001 US dollars), future success is often linked to the finances of the key individuals. For this reason, they are not reflective of typical middle-market companies and are excluded from the database.
- **Financial institutions** – The balance sheets of financial institutions (banks, insurance companies, and investment companies) exhibit higher leverage than the typical private firm. The regulation and capital requirements of these institutions make them dissimilar to the typical middle-market company. Therefore, they are excluded from the database.
- **Real estate development companies** – The annual accounts of real estate development and investment companies provide only a partial description of the dynamics of these firms and, therefore, their likelihood of default. This is because their financial health often hinges on a particular development.
- **Public sector and non-profit institutions** – Government-run companies' default risks are influenced by the states' or municipalities' unwillingness to allow them to fail. As a result their financial results are not comparable to other private firms. Non-profit financial ratios are very different from for-profit firms, particularly with regard to variables relating to net income.

There are many types of "project finance" firms whose success depends largely on the outcome of a particular project. We would recommend use of separate models for such firms. At the time of writing, this characteristic is explicitly recognized within the proposals for the new Basel Capital Accord.

Excluded financial statements The financial statements of smaller companies can be less accurate and of lower quality than those of larger companies. The financial statements in the CRI are cleaned to eliminate highly suspect financial statements. Plausibility checks of financial

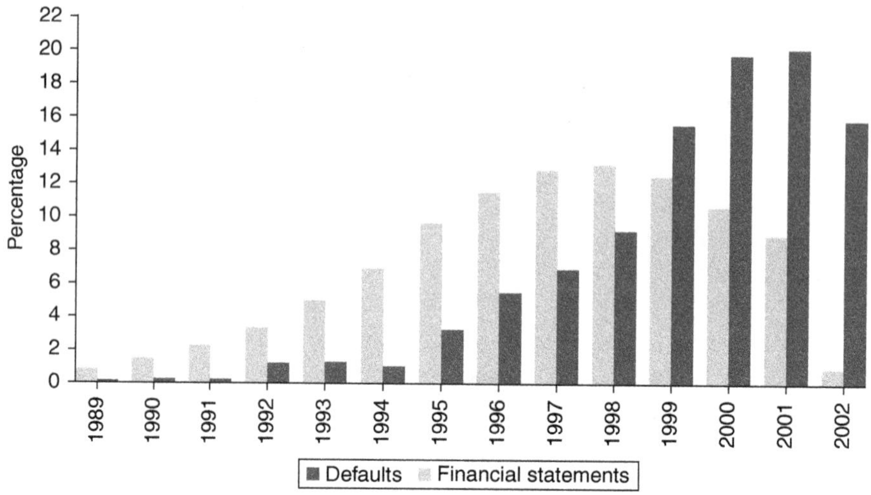

Figure 4.1 Date distribution of financial statements and default data

statements are conducted, such as assets not equal to liabilities plus net worth, and financial statements covering a period of less than 12 months. If errors are detected, those statements are excluded from the analysis.

4.1.1.3 Descriptive statistics of the data

Overview of the data The extensive data on both non-defaulting and defaulting companies contained in Moody's CRI has increased substantially since RiskCalc v1.0. In addition to the increase in time-series data, there has been an increase in the number of participants in the CRI.

Figure 4.1 presents the distribution of financial statements and defaults by year. The years 2000, 2001, and 2002 represent a period of intense default activity adding to the credit cycle information of the v1.0 model.

Table 4.1 summarizes the data used in the development, validation, and calibration of the RiskCalc v3.1 US model. The number of financial statements, firms, and defaults is considerably larger even though the original model was based on both US and Canadian firms.

Robustness of the data In building a model, potential database weaknesses need to be examined. Not only does the database need to cover a large number of firms and defaults, but the defaults also need to be distributed among industries and company types covered. For example, if the database has significant numbers of small firms, or firms in

Table 4.1 Information on private firm sample data

	U.S. and Canadian private firms	RiskCalc v1.0 North America	RiskCalc v1.0 Canada	Credit research database growth
Financial statements	115,000+	183,000+	44,000+	**T95%**
Unique number of firms	24,000+	40,000+	11,000+	**T112%**
Defaults	1,621	3,157	607	**T132%**
Time period	1989–1999	1989–2002	1989–2002	**T3 additional years**

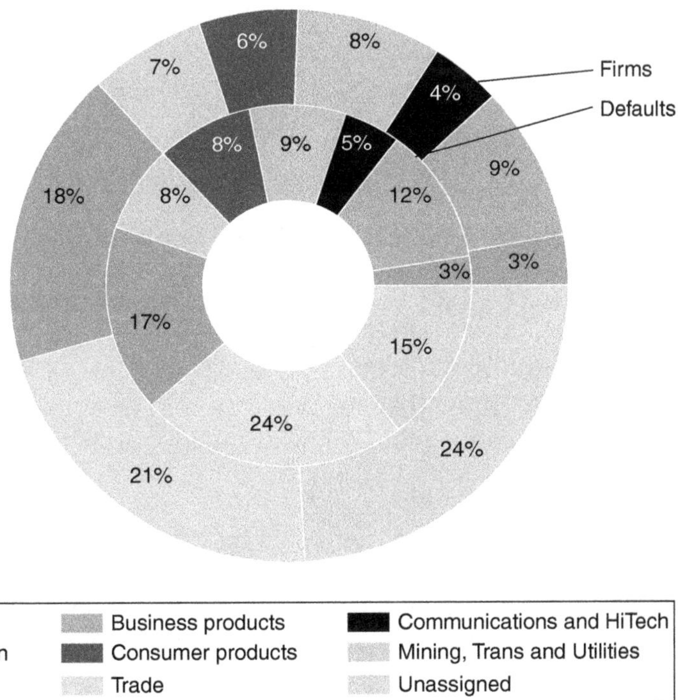

Figure 4.2 Distribution of defaults and firms by industry

one particular industry, and there are not sufficient defaults in those areas, the model may not be a good default predictor. The CRD used in developing the RiskCalc models has addressed both of these issues.

Figure 4.2 and Figure 4.3 present the distributions of defaults and firms by industry and size classification, respectively, as well as the

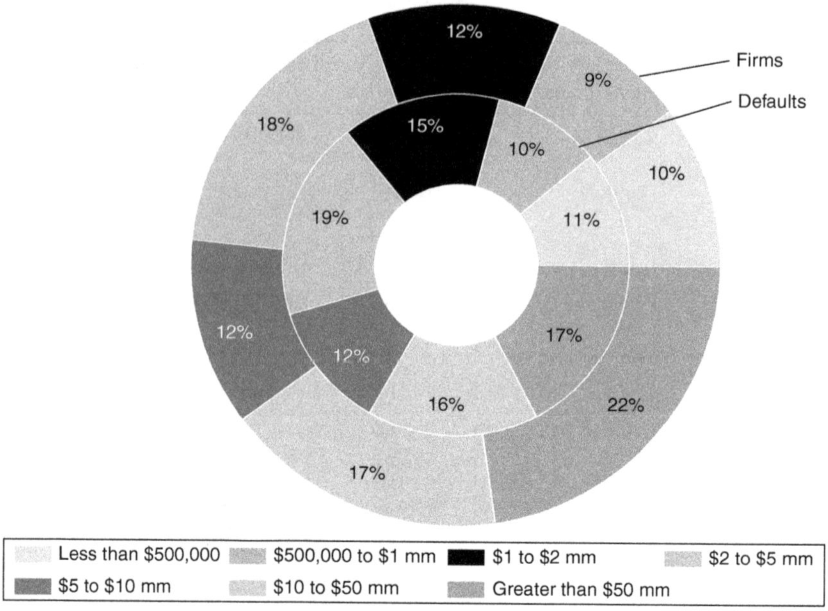

Figure 4.3 Size distribution of defaults and firms

proportion of defaults in one industry or size group. The largest industry groups are trade and services. Firm size as measured by assets range from $100,000 to $500,000 to over $50 million in assets. Figure 4.2 and Figure 4.3 show that the proportion of defaults in one size group or industry is comparable to the number of firms in these groupings.

4.1.1.4 Cleaning the data

In the development of a RiskCalc model, the first step is the collection of a large and appropriate database. In addition, data needs to be "cleaned" so that it is representative of the actual risk of the firms covered. MKMV has developed techniques for cleaning the database to improve the model results.

4.1.1.5 Central default tendency

Since most companies do not default, defaulting companies are relatively rare and thus more valuable in building default prediction models. Much of the lack of default data is due to the data storage issues within financial institutions, such as defaulting companies being purged from the system after troubles begin, not all defaults being captured, or other sample errors. Also, if the date of default is uncertain[1] the financial statement associated with the firm may be excluded from model development, depending on the severity of the problem. These issues can result in a sample that has lower defaults rates than occur in the general population. If the underlying sample is not representative, then it needs to be adjusted for the true central default tendency.[2]

In order to calculate the overall population default rate, the RiskCalc model uses a triangulation approach that integrates information from both private and public records. The central default tendency is typically triangulated using two different approaches:

- reference to reliable third-party data sources;
- analysis of bank charge-offs and provisions.

By triangulating the central default rate from a variety of sources, a more accurate central tendency estimate is achieved than that inferred directly from the development sample.

Reliable third-party data sources In order to determine the central tendency used in RiskCalc, we first examine reliable data sources representative of the underlying population and in which the default information is relatively complete. From these sources an average default rate is computed. In developing RiskCalc v1.0 NA, we had consulted a variety of sources and derived 1.7% as the central default tendency (Falkenstein, 2000).

Bank charge-offs and provisions An alternative approach one can implement to infer a central tendency is from provisioning or write-off data from banks. Banks make provisions for bad loans that are estimates of their expected write-offs. From the volume of losses and the volume of loans, an average default rate can be inferred given the LGD:

$$Volume\,of\,Losses = Volume\,of\,Loans \times Probability\,of\,Default \times LGD$$

Therefore:

$$Probability\,of\,Default = \frac{Volume\,of\,Losses}{(Volume\,of\,Loans \times LGD)}$$

The foundation approach to capital allocation as described in Basel II uses a LGD rate of 50%, so this assumption can be used to calculate the implied default rates. We applied this technique to US commercial banks as reported by the OECD (Organisation for Economic Co-operation and Development) (2002). For these institutions the average implied probability of default hovered around 1.7%. We also applied this technique to charge-off rates for Commercial and

Industrial Loans 1990–2003 as reported by the Federal Reserve Board. Using a LGD of 50%, the implied probability of default ranges from less than 1% during the trough of the credit cycle to over 4% at the peak of the credit cycle. The average over this time period turns out to be 1.7%, thus confirming the selected central default tendency for RiskCalc v1.0.

Calculating a 5-year central default tendency There is a lack of publicly available data for direct calculation of the central tendency rate of a cumulative 5-year default probability. Based on extensive MKMV research, a 5-year cumulative default tendency is derived from the 1-year estimate. This research, combined with the information provided by the CRD, shows that the 5-year cumulative default rate is, on average, 4 times the level of the 1-year default rate. Therefore, 6.8% is used as the central default tendency for the 5-year model.

Central default tendency in FSO and CCA modes In the FSO model, the central default tendency remains constant over time. In CCA mode, the central default tendency is equal to the central default tendency of the FSO mode when the effects of the credit cycle are neutral. When the forward-looking prediction of the credit cycle indicates increasing default risk, the central default tendency of the CCA mode will be larger, and when the effects of the credit cycle indicate reducing default risk, the central default tendency will be smaller.

4.1.2 Model components

The RiskCalc v3.1 model incorporates the various components to determine the EDF credit measure. The inputs to the model include selection of the financial ratios and transforms of those ratios, the inclusion of industry information, and the CCA.

The development of a RiskCalc model involves the following steps.

1. Choosing a limited number of financial statement variables for the model from a list of possible variables.[3]
2. Transforming the variables into interim probabilities of default using non-parametric techniques.
3. Estimating the weightings of the financial statement variables, using a probit model, combined with industry variables.
4. Creating a (non-parametric) final transform that converts the probit model score into an actual EDF credit measure.

In FSO mode, the models are based on the following functional form:

$$FSO\,EDF = F\left(\Phi\left(\sum_{i=1}^{N}\beta_i T_i(x_i) + \sum_{j=1}^{K}\gamma_j I_j\right)\right)$$

where

$x1, \ldots, xN$	are the input ratios;
$I1, \ldots, IK$	are indicator variables for each of the industry classifications;
$\gamma 1, \ldots, \gamma K$	are estimated coefficients;
D	is the cumulative normal distribution;
F *and* $T1, \ldots, TN$	are non-parametric transforms;[4]
$FSO\,EDF$	is the financial statement only EDF credit measure.

The *T*s are the transforms of each financial statement variable, which capture the non-linear impacts of financial ratios on the default likelihood. (This is shown in Figure 4.4 and discussed in detail later in the document.) *F* is the final transform (i.e. the final mapping). The final transform captures the empirical relationship between the probit model score and actual default probabilities. We describe the final transform as calibrating the model score to an actual EDF credit measure. The difference between the FSO EDF and the CCA EDF is that in CCA mode the final transform is adjusted to reflect our assessment of the current stage of the credit cycle, while in FSO mode it remains constant.

4.1.2.1 *Financial statement variables*

Selecting the variables Our variable selection process starts with a long list of possible financial statement variables. The working list of ratios is divided into groups that represent different underlying concepts regarding a firm's financial status (see Table 4.2). A model is then built with at least one variable per group. When it is possible to increase model performance while maintaining model robustness, several variables from each group will be used in the model. Criteria that must be met for variables to be included in the final model are:

- Is the variable readily available?
- Are the definitions of the inputs to the variable unambiguous?
- Is the meaning of the variable intuitive?
- Does the variable predict default activity?

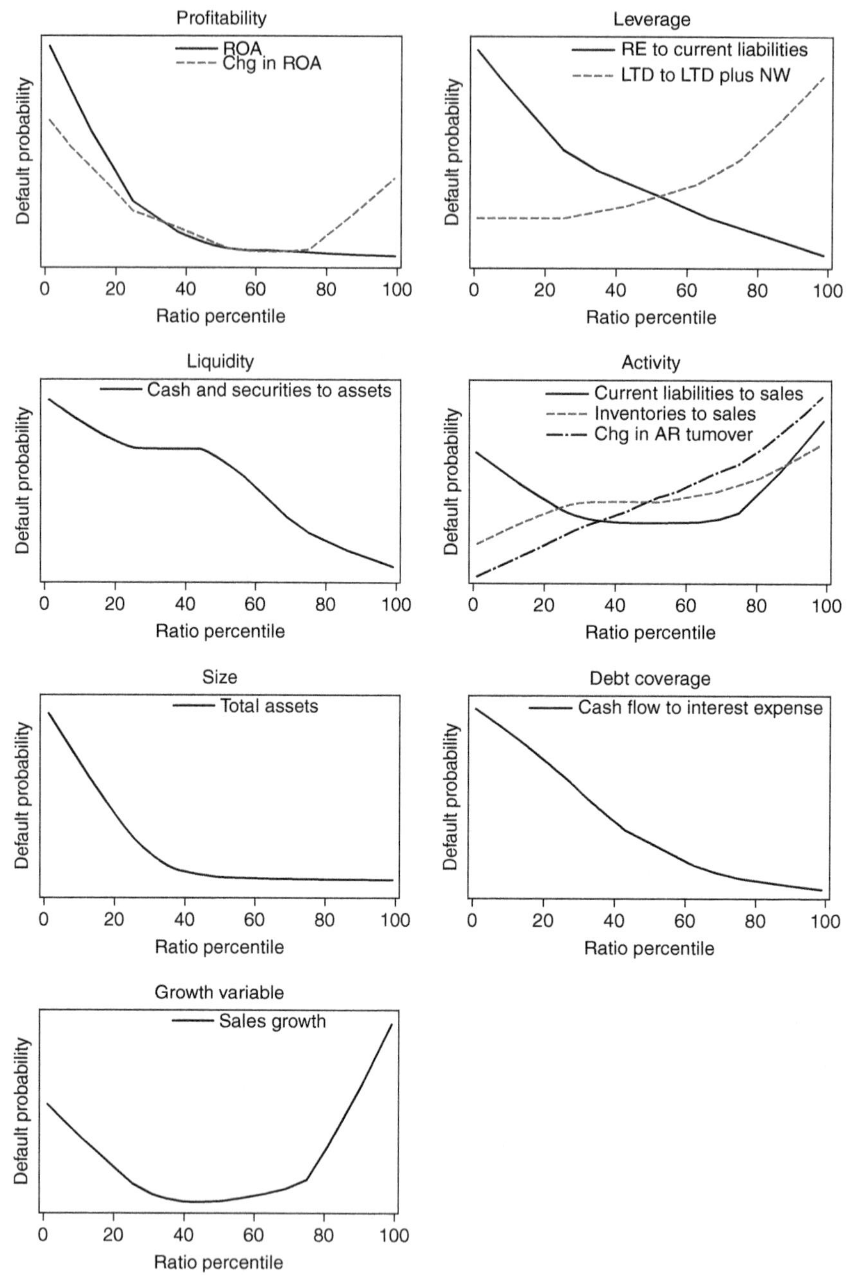

Figure 4.4 Transformations of financial statement variables used in the model

Table 4.2 Groupings of financial statement ratios

Examples of ratios in the **profitability** group include: net income, net income less extraordinary items, EBITDA, EBIT and operating profit in the numerator; and total assets, tangible assets, fixed assets and sales in the denominator. *High profitability reduces the probability of default.*

Examples of ratios in the **leverage** group include liabilities to assets and long-term debt to assets. *High leverage increases the probability of default.*

Debt coverage is the ratio of cash flow to interest payments or some other measure of liabilities. *High debt coverage reduces the probability of default.*

Growth variables are typically the change in ROA and sales growth. These variables measure the stability of a firm's performance. *Growth variables behave like a double-edged sword: both rapid growth and rapid decline (negative growth) will tend to increase a firm 's default probability.*

Liquidity variables include cash and marketable securities to assets, the current ratio and the quick ratio. These variables measure the extent to which the firm has liquid assets relative to the size of its liabilities. *High liquidity reduces the probability of default.*

Activity ratios include inventories to sales and accounts receivable to sales. These ratios may measure the extent to which a firm has a substantial portion of assets in accounts that may be of subjective value. For example, a firm with a lot of inventories may not be selling its products and may have to write off these inventories. *A large stock of inventories relative to sales increases the probability of default; other activity ratios have different relationships to default.*

Size variables include sales and total assets. These variables are converted into a common currency as necessary and then are deflated to a specific base year to ensure comparability (e.g. total assets are measured in 2001 U.S. dollars). *Large firms default less often.*

- Is the variable generally uncorrelated with other variables in the model?

RiskCalc v1.0 versus RiskCalc v3.1 variables Since RiskCalc v1.0 NA was completed, MKMV has been able to collect more and better (cleaner) data in the CRD. The impact of this is that the variables originally used in v1.0 can be improved. This is because more data and cleaner data provide a clearer picture of the predictive power of alternative ratios. Table 4.3 presents the variables used in RiskCalc US v3.1. They differ from the variables chosen for RiskCalc NA v1.0 in several important ways. The following are some of the major changes:

- Operating cash flow is used in the numerator of the debt coverage ratio instead of EBIT.[5] Cash flow is used because a company that has profits but no cash flow is at risk. Also, since cash flow is a more difficult number to manipulate, the impact of accounting

Table 4.3 Financial statement variables used in RiskCalc v3.1 US*

Category	Variable
Leverage	LTD to (LTD plus Net worth)
Profitability	Retained earnings to Current liabilities ROA
	Change in ROA
Debt coverage	Cash flow to Interest expense
Liquidity	Cash and Marketable securities to Total assets
Activity	Inventories to Sales
	Change in AR Turnover current liabilities to Sales
Growth	Sales growth
Size	Total assets

*LTD is long-term debt, ROA is Net Income to Total Assets and AR Turnover is the ratio of accounts receivable to sales.

irregularities is reduced. Using cash flow in the model penalizes a firm that has negative cash flow even if both its net income and EBIT are positive.

- LTD (Long-term debt) to the sum of LTD and NW (Net Worth) is used as the primary leverage variable instead of Total Liabilities to Total Assets. This change reduced the degree of multicollinearity in the model.[6] Including Total Liabilities to Total Assets would have increased multicollinearity due to the relatively high correlation between [Total Liabilities to Total Assets] and [Net Income to Total Assets].
- LTD used in this analysis is the non-current portion of LTD and typically includes capitalized leases. If capitalized leases are not explicitly included under LTD, users should include them.
- ROA (Return on Assets) is Net Income to Assets whereas in v1.0 ROA was Net Income less Extraordinary Items to Assets. Not allowing for the subtraction of extraordinary items makes the model more objective. The user no longer needs to decide whether an item is truly extraordinary or an accounting ploy.
- A new variable, the Change in Accounts Receivable Turnover (accounts receivable to sales) is included. This variable indicates potential collection problems within the firm. A dramatic increase in accounts receivable without an accompanying increase in sales may indicate a collection problem, and a dramatic decline without a reduction in sales may mean excessive write-offs.
- Inventories are divided by net sales rather than cost of goods sold (COGS). This was done since COGS is often not reported in our database and the definition of COGS is inconsistent across industries.

Variable transforms Once the variables are selected, they are transformed into a preliminary EDF value. Figure 4.4 presents the transformations used in the model. The horizontal axis is the percentile score of the ratio and the vertical axis is the default probability of that ratio in isolation (univariate). The percentile score gives the percentage of the database that had a ratio below that of the company (e.g., if ROA is in the 90th percentile that means that 90% of the sample had an ROA lower than that firm).

The shape of the transformation indicates how significantly a change in level impacts the EDF value. If the slope of the transform is steep, a small change will have a larger impact on risk than if the slope were flat.

- For the **Profitability** group, ROA and Change in ROA are included. ROA's transform is downward-sloping, but the slope becomes almost zero as ROA becomes large (Figure 4.4). Such a transform indicates that more profitable firms have lower default probabilities, but the impact diminishes as ROA increases. Change in ROA is "U-shaped" indicating that large increases or decreases in ROA increase the default likelihood. The actual transform shape indicates that large reductions in ROA increase the likelihood of default by a larger amount than large increases in ROA.
- For the **Leverage** group, retained earnings to current liabilities and LTD to the sum of LTD plus NW are used. Large values of retained earnings to current liabilities lower default probabilities while large values of LTD to the sum of LTD plus NW increase default probabilities (Figure 4.4).
- For the **Liquidity** group, Cash and Securities to Total Assets is downward-sloping, indicating that higher values of this ratio are associated with lower default probabilities (Figure 4.4).
- For the **Activity** group, three ratios are included. Inventories to Sales and Current Liabilities to Sales are both upward-sloping, indicating that high values of these ratios are associated with higher default probabilities (Figure 4.4). Change in Accounts Receivable Turnover is U-shaped, indicating that large positive values or large negative values are associated with higher default probabilities, while stable accounts receivable turnover is associated with lower default probabilities.
- The **Size** variable is Total Assets. This variable's transformation is downward-sloping, but the slope becomes almost zero as size becomes large (Figure 4.4). This indicates that larger firms have lower

default probabilities, but the impact of size on default probabilities is diminishing as firm size increases.

- The **Debt Coverage** variable is Cash Flow to Interest Expense. This variable is downward-sloping, indicating that large values of cash flow relative to interest expense lower the probability of default (Figure 4.4).
- The **Growth** variable is Sales Growth. It is U-shaped, indicating that large increases or decreases in sales are associated with higher default probabilities (Figure 4.4). The actual shape indicates that large increases in sales increase default probabilities by a larger amount than large decreases in sales.

4.1.2.2 Model weights

Importance The relative value of each variable used in calculating an EDF credit measure is important in understanding a company's risk. The non-linear nature of the model makes the weight of the variables more difficult to determine since the actual impact on the risk depends on the coefficient, the transformation shape, and the percentile ranking of the company. The model weights, therefore, are calculated based on the average EDF value for the transformation and its standard deviation. A variable with a flat transformation could have a low weight, even if the coefficient is large (Figure 4.4).

Calculation of weights To calculate the weighting of a variable, the EDF credit measure for a theoretical firm with all its variables at the average transformation values is computed. The variables are then increased one at a time by one standard deviation. The EDF change for each variable (in absolute value) is computed and added together. The relative weight of each variable is calculated as the EDF level changes for that variable as a percentage of the total change in EDF level. This gives the variable with the biggest impact on the EDF level the biggest weight, and the variable that has the smallest impact on the EDF level the smallest weight. Since the weights are a percentage of the total EDF value, they sum to 100%. The weight of each category is the sum of the weights of each variable in the category. Table 4.4 presents the weights in RiskCalc v1.0 NA and RiskCalc v3.1 US Leverage and profitability continue to be the most important categories while size has lessened. As more variables are included in the model, size becomes less important in determining default risk. Table 4.4 shows the risk drivers and their weights in RiskCalc v1.0 NA and RiskCalc v3.1.

Table 4.4 Risk drivers in RiskCalc v1.0 NA vs. RiskCalc v3.1 US*

RiskCalc v1.0 North America		RiskCalc v3.1 U.S.	
Risk drivers	Weight (%)	Risk drivers	Weight
Profitability	23	**Profitability**	27
Net income/assets		Cash flow/interest expense	
Net income growth		ROA (net income/assets)	
Interest coverage		Change in ROA	
Capital structure	21	**Capital Structure**	22
Retained earnings/assets		LTD/LTD plus net worth	
Liabilities to Assets		Retained earnings/ Current liabilities	
Liquidity	19	**Liquidity**	15
Cash/Assets		Cash/assets	
Quick ratio			
Size	14	**Size**	7
Assets		Assets	
Growth	12	**Growth**	10
Sales growth		Sales growth	
Activity	12	**Activity**	19
Inventories/COGS		Inventories/ sales	
		Current liabilities/ sales	
		Change in accounts receivable turnover	

*Note that the model weights for RiskCalc v1.0 sum to 101% due to rounding errors. LTD stands for long-term debt, and accounts receivable turnover is accounts receivable divided by sales. For a description of the variable selection process see Section 4.1.2.1. For a discussion of the procedure used to compute model weights see Section 4.1.2.2.

4.1.2.3 Industry adjustments

While the variables included in the RiskCalc model explain most of the risk factors, the relative importance of the variables can be different among industries. One important difference is inventories. For an industry that does not keep inventories, the inventory to sales ratio is zero. This occurs over 40% of the time in several of the industries in the US development sample (Table 4.5). Also, for the same set of financials, industries may have different default probabilities.

In the FSO mode of RiskCalc v3.1 US, the EDF value is adjusted for industry effects. Table 4.6 presents the increase in model power and accuracy from introducing industry controls into the FSO model. Both the power and the accuracy of the EDF credit measure increase as measured by the accuracy ratio and the gain in log likelihood. Table 4.7 presents the average EDF value by industry for the development

Table 4.5 Percentage of observations with zero inventories by sector

Sector	Percentage
Agriculture	28.1
Business products	9.8
Communications and Hi Tech	19.2
Construction	42.6
Consumer products	9.5
Mining, Transportation, Utilities and Natural resources	45.0
Services	49.9
Trade	15.1
Unassigned	35.9

Table 4.6 Increase in model power and accuracy from introducing industry controls

	1-year model		5-year model	
	Accuracy Ratio (%)	Relative increase in Log likelihood	Accuracy Ratio (%)	Relative increase in Log likelihood
FSO mode without industry controls	54.5		38.1	
FSO mode with industry controls	55.1	58.16***	38.8	99.8***

Note: In this table, and hereafter, Accuracy Ratio (or AR) is the measure of the model's ability to rank order credits. Increases in log likelihood measure the extent to which the model's EDF values match observed default rates. For further details, see Dwyer and Stein (2004), *Technical Document on RiskCalc v3.1 Methodology* (Technical Document).

Table 4.7 Average EDF credit measure in development sample by sector

	EDF (%)	
Sector	1-year	5-year
Agriculture	1.9	6.4
Business products	2.5	9.3
Communications and Hi Tech	2.8	9.0
Construction	1.4	5.2
Consumer products	2.9	10.0
Mining, Transportation, Utilities and Natural resources	2.2	7.5
Services	2.4	8.2
Trade	1.8	6.6
Unassigned	2.4	7.9

sample. The highest EDF values are in Consumer Products while the lowest are in Construction.

4.1.2.4 Credit cycle adjustment

EDF credit measures are impacted not only by the financials of a company, but also by the general credit cycle in the economy. To capture this effect, RiskCalc v3.1 US includes a CCA factor. The CCA is designed to incorporate the current credit cycle into the estimate of private firm default risk.

Selecting an adjustment factor The RiskCalc v3.1 model uses the distance-to-default (DD) calculation from the Moody's KMV public firm model. This measure is specifically designed to be a forward-looking indicator of default risk. It extracts signs of default risk from the stock market performance of individual firms (cf., Bohn and Crosbie, 2003). This measure was chosen because it is available for a large universe of industries and it has been extensively validated.

If the distance-to-default for public firms in an industry indicates a level of risk above the historical average for that industry, then the private firms' EDF values in that industry are adjusted upward by some factor. Conversely, if the level of risk is below the historical average, then the private firms' EDF values are adjusted downward. When the credit cycle adjustment factor is neutral, the CCA EDF coincides with the FSO EDF. For the Canadian and the US model, the distance-to-default factor is based on an aggregation of all public North American firms in the industry. In the event that a firm cannot be associated with a specific industry, the model uses a CCA that is based on an aggregation of all public North American firms.

Figure 4.5 presents the distance-to-default factor based on all public North American firms and contrasts that to the speculative grade default rate as measured by Moody's Investors Service default studies (Hamilton and Varma, 2003). For both recessions, the speculative default rate increases in advance of the recession so that a risk indicator that is *coincident* with the business cycle will not predict increases in risk. The distance-to-default factor anticipates both the recession and the increase in defaults measured by the speculative default rate. Therefore, it is a *forward-looking* measure of default risk in an industry. Table 4.8 shows that including the CCA factor increases both the power and the accuracy of the model.

The DD factor (grey line) is presented against the historical Speculative Bond Default Index (black line; the dotted black line indicates

Table 4.8 Power enhancements of the new RiskCalc v3.1 US model

	1-year model		1-year model	
	Accuracy Ratio (%)	Lead in Log likelihood*	Accuracy Ratio (%)	Lead in Log likelihood*
RiskCalc v3.1 model	57.0		35.7	
RiskCalc v1.0	49.5	403.6	30.7	196.7
Z-score	42.3	1356.5	24.7	803.3

*Presents the increase in log likelihood of RiskCalc v3.1 over the alternative model. Larger values indicate that levels of RiskCalc v3.1 are better-calibrated vis-à-vis the alternative model.

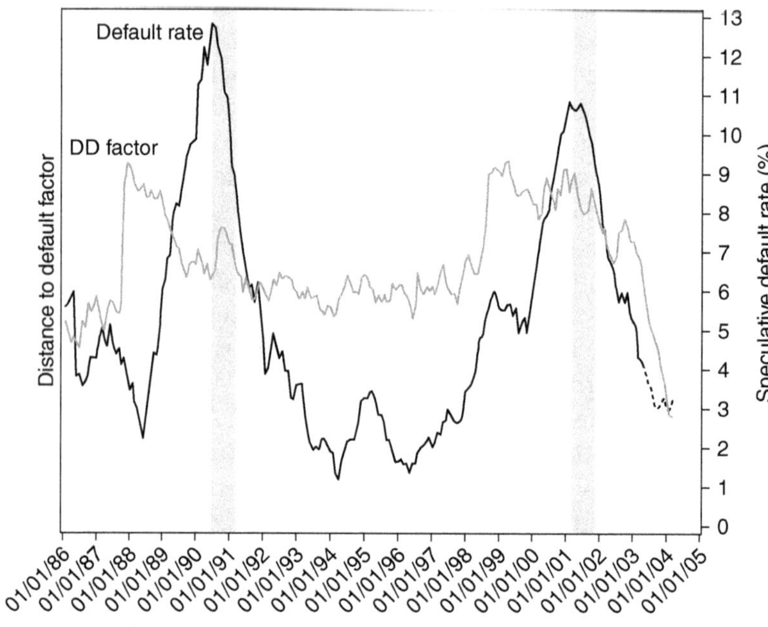

Figure 4.5 North American DD factor and the speculative default rate, 1986–2004

forecasted values). Grey vertical bars indicate periods of recession as defined by the NBER. Large values of the DD factor provided early warnings of increased default rates for both recessions.

4.1.3 Validation results

Once a model is developed, it must be shown to be effective in predicting defaults. There are a variety of tests of model power: those that test rank ordering (grouping credits from worst to best) and those that test the calibration of the model (level of EDF credit measure is correct).

The tests need to check not only the model effectiveness, but also its robustness and how well it works on data outside the sample. To do such out-of-sample testing, we performed walk-forward and k-fold analyses. In addition to the typical out-of-sample testing, we tested using data that became available after the model was finalized and in production.

The results of the testing show that the model is uniformly more powerful than other models across different time periods, sectors, and size classifications.

4.1.3.1 *Increase in overall model power and accuracy*

Table 4.8 presents the in-sample overall measures of power and likelihood for RiskCalc v3.1 versus alternative models. With the CCA, the model's performance improves by almost eight points of AR (Accuracy Ratio) at the 1-year horizon compared with RiskCalc v1.0. Relative to other available alternatives, the results were more dramatic. The new RiskCalc v3.1 US model outperformed the Z-score model (Altman *et al*, 1995) by more than ten points at both the 1-year and 5-year horizons. The FSO mode outperforms the old model by five points at both horizons.[7] RiskCalc v3.1 is also more accurate than alternative models as measured by the log likelihood differences.[8]

Figure 4.6 presents the cumulative accuracy profiles for the 1- and 5-year models corresponding to Table 4.8. The power improvements

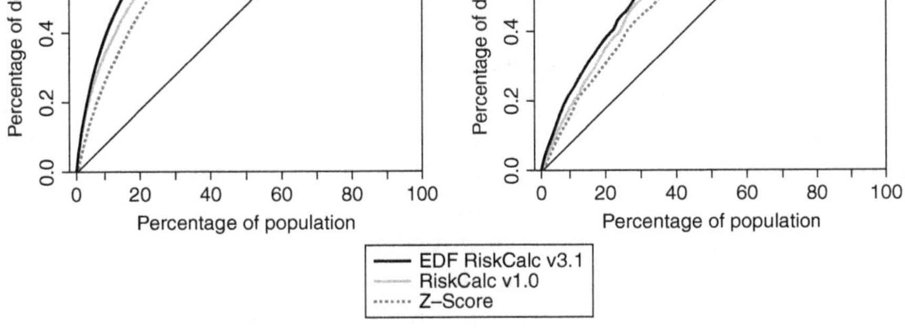

Figure 4.6 Power of alternative models (1- and 5-year) – US

Table 4.9 Correlations among the transformed input factors (Spearman rank)

LTD to LTD plus NW	1.0										
NI to Assets	0.173	1.0									
Sales Growth	−0.054	0.029	1.0								
Cash to Assets	0.212	0.190	−0.011	1.0							
Chg in AR turnover	−0.099	0.033	0.223	0.017	1.0						
Chg in ROA	−0.070	0.045	0.183	−0.054	0.107	1.0					
Inventory to Net Sales	−0.063	0.061	−0.031	0.223	−0.015	−0.073	1.0				
Cash Flow to Int. Exp.	0.166	0.443	0.077	0.252	0.082	0.009	0.131	1.0			
Ret. Earnings to Current Liab.	0.210	0.308	0.118	0.220	0.045	0.048	0.027	0.322	1.0		
Curr. Liab. to Sales	0.117	0.284	0.113	0.254	0.217	−0.031	0.150	0.266	0.434	1.0	
Total Assets	−0.125	−0.041	0.104	−0.087	0.019	0.194	−0.131	0.024	0.038	−0.197	1.0

are largely in the middle of the distribution relative to RiskCalc v1.0 (particularly for the 1-year model). This result implies that both very good and very poor credits are correctly identified by both RiskCalc v1.0 and RiskCalc v3.1. The added discriminatory power is assessing the credit quality of credits that fall in the middle range.

4.1.3.2 Correlations and variance inflation factors

In order to ensure model robustness, the model must be tested for excessive multicollinearity. This occurs if a number of the variables used in the model are highly correlated. Excessive multicollinearity can cause instability in parameter estimates. In order to check for this issue, the correlation coefficients (see Table 4.9) for the financial statement ratios in the model and the variance inflation factors (see Table 4.10) are computed on the transformed variables (see Figure 4.4).[9] The highest correlation coefficient is between [Cash Flow to Interest Expense] and [Net Income to Total Assets] (0.44). The next highest coefficient is between [Retained Earnings to Current Liabilities] and [Current Liabilities to Net Sales] (0.43). Such coefficients are well below what we would typically consider indications of multicollinearity, and this finding is also verified by the VIF (Variance Inflation Factors) analysis.

The VIF (see Table 4.10) for the financial statement variables represent how much of the variation in one independent variable can

Table 4.10 Variance inflation factors

Variable	VIF
Retained earnings to Current liabilities	1.53
Current liabilities to Net sales	1.48
Net income to Total assets	1.42
Cash flow to Total interest expense	1.33
Inventories to Net sales	1.29
LTD to LTD plus NW	1.26
Change in ROA	1.24
Change in Accounts receivable turnover	1.20
Cash and marketable securities to Total assets	1.20
Net sales growth	1.13
Total assets	1.14

be explained by all the other independent variables in the model. The correlation coefficient measured only the relationships between two variables. The estimated VIF values are notably below the threshold levels of 4 to 10 that are commonly used in VIF analysis when testing for presence of multicollinearity.[10] Therefore, the findings indicate that the model variables do not present any substantial multicollinearity.

4.1.3.3 Model power by industry and size groups

It is important to test the power of a model not only overall, but also among different industry segments and firm sizes.

Table 4.11 and Table 4.12 present the power comparisons by sector for the 1-year and 5-year models, respectively. RiskCalc v3.1 outperforms both RiskCalc v1.0 and Z-score in all sectors. The highest power in the 1-year model is found in Construction (66.5%) while the lowest is found in Agriculture (52.3%). At the 5-year horizon (Table 4.11) the highest power is in Agriculture (46.5%) and the lowest is in Business Products (27.6%).

Table 4.13 and Table 4.14 present the power comparisons by firm size for the 1-year and 5-year models, respectively. RiskCalc v3.1 outperforms both RiskCalc v1.0 and Z-score in all size groups. The highest power in the 1-year model is found in the largest firms – over $50 million in assets, and the lowest is in the smallest firms – under $500,000 in assets. This is because the quality of financial statements generally increases with firm size. For example, larger firms are more likely to have audited statements.

Table 4.11 Model power by industry, 1-year model

	Percentage of defaults	AR RiskCalc v3.1 (%)	AR RiskCalc v1.0 (%)	AR Z-score (%)
Agriculture	3.6	52.3	46.5	46.4
Business products	15.1	58.3	50.6	47.1
Communications and Hi Tech	5.9	58.7	52.1	49.7
Construction	9.2	66.5	56.9	51.1
Consumer products	10.5	61.7	56.4	47.2
Mining, Transportation, Utilities and Natural Resources	9.1	55.9	50.0	44.9
Services	20.2	56.1	46.9	34.9
Trade	26.4	55.2	46.5	36.8

Table 4.12 Model power by industry, 5-year model

	Percentage of defaults	AR RiskCalc v3.1 (%)	AR RiskCalc v1.0 (%)	AR Z-score (%)
Agriculture	4.3	46.5	39.4	35.4
Business products	14.7	27.6	25.3	24.1
Communications and Hi Tech	5.2	41.8	35.0	24.9
Construction	8.9	38.8	34.2	21.2
Consumer products	11.1	37.2	28.8	25.4
Mining, Transportation, Utilities and Natural Resources	9.4	40.2	37.9	28.5
Services	19.5	30.8	23.0	16.7
Trade	26.9	33.2	31.9	28.6

Table 4.13 Model power by size, 1-year model

Range	Percentage of defaults	AR RiskCalc v3.1 (%)	AR RiskCalc v1.0 (%)	AR Z-score (%)
<$500,000	4.8	49.7	43.1	43.6
$500,000 to $1 mm	9.1	47.6	43.3	41.1
$1 mm to $2mm	15.3	57.0	52.4	44.1
$2mm to $5mm	20.8	59.2	53.2	47.0
$5mm to $10mm	15.2	53.7	43.9	41.9
$10mm to $50mm	20.0	55.1	49.6	34.9
over $50mm	14.7	62.9	54.8	42.3

Table 4.14 Model power by size, 5-year model

Range	Percentage of defaults	AR RiskCalc v3.1 (%)	AR RiskCalc v1.0 (%)	AR Z-score (%)
<$500,000	6.8	36.7	29.0	28.5
$500,000 to $1 mm	11.2	42.0	39.3	33.4
$1 mm to $2mm	17.1	32.3	30.1	22.8
$2mm to $5mm	21.9	34.9	28.4	20.1
$5mm to $10mm	14.7	42.6	35.9	33.0
$10mm to $50mm	17.7	41.1	37.0	26.8
over $50mm	10.8	33.8	27.9	16.4

Table 4.15 Model power over time, 1-year horizon

Year	Percentage of defaults	AR RiskCalc v3.1 (%)	AR RiskCalc v1.0 (%)	AR Z-score (%)
1993	1.2	68.2	64.5	59.4
1994	3.3	57.4	55.4	52.5
1995	5.6	56.6	53.0	44.6
1996	7.1	60.5	60.1	53.0
1997	11.3	47.7	44.2	36.3
1998	20.8	38.9	35.0	28.3
1999	23.6	44.6	39.6	33.5
2000	19.8	49.0	43.6	36.0
2001	7.2	71.9	66.5	55.1

Table 4.16 Model power over time, 5-year horizon

Year	Percentage of defaults	AR RiskCalc v3.1 (%)	AR RiskCalc v1.0 (%)	AR Z-score (%)
1993	3.2	45.1	43.5	33.6
1994	6.7	44.7	43.2	34.9
1995	11.6	38.3	35.7	26.2
1996	16.2	36.1	31.5	22.0
1997	19.8	33.6	28.2	22.2
1998	19.0	37.4	31.1	26.2
1999	14.6	42.3	35.9	31.7
2000	8.8	48.5	40.9	34.8

4.1.3.4 *Power performance over time*

Since models are designed to be implemented at various points in a business cycle, power tests were conducted by year (see Table 4.15 and Table 4.16). These tests examine whether or not the model performance is excessively time dependent.

Table 4.15 and Table 4.16 present the results from this analysis at the 1- and 5-year horizons, respectively. The AR of RiskCalc v3.1 is compared with RiskCalc v1.0 and Z-score for each year. RiskCalc v3.1 consistently outperforms both RiskCalc v1.0 and Z-score by a considerable margin. The RiskCalc v1.0 consistently outperforms the Z-score model in 1999, 2000, and 2001. These years should be regarded as out-of-sample since RiskCalc v1.0 was released in early 2000 and the majority of the observations in 1999 are based on year-end financial statements and would not have been in the RiskCalc v1.0 development sample. This out-of-sample robustness demonstrates that RiskCalc v1.0 was not "over fit".

4.1.3.5 *Out-of-sample testing: k-fold tests*

The model exhibits a high degree of power in distinguishing good credits from bad ones (see Table 4.8), but whether this power is attributable to the overall model effectiveness or the impact of a particular subsample also needs to be tested. A standard test for evaluating this is the "k-fold test," which divides the defaulting and non-defaulting companies into k equally sized segments. This yields k equally sized observation subsamples that exhibit the identical overall default rate and are temporally and cross-sectionally independent. The model is then run on k-1 subsamples and these parameter estimates are used to score the k-th subsample. We repeat this procedure for all possible combinations, and put the k scored out-of-sample subsamples together and calculate an AR on this combined data set.

Table 4.17 summarizes the k-fold test results (with $k = 5$). The reported figures are the ARs by the corresponding sample and time horizons. The out-of-sample model consistently outperforms RiskCalc v1.0. Figure 4.7 presents the cumulative accuracy profiles associated

Table 4.17 RiskCalc v3.1 k-fold test results

	Out-of-sample AR (%)		RiskCalc v1.0 (%)	
	1-year AR	5-year AR	1-year AR	5-year AR
Subsample 1	51.5	38.3	45.7	36.1
Subsample 2	56.3	35.2	48.5	33.6
Subsample 3	54.8	36.0	46.5	31.1
Subsample 4	50.4	34.9	45.3	31.0
Subsample 5	54.7	35.9	47.3	34.0
k-fold overall	56.8	34.7	50.3	31.1
In-sample AR	57.5	35.7		

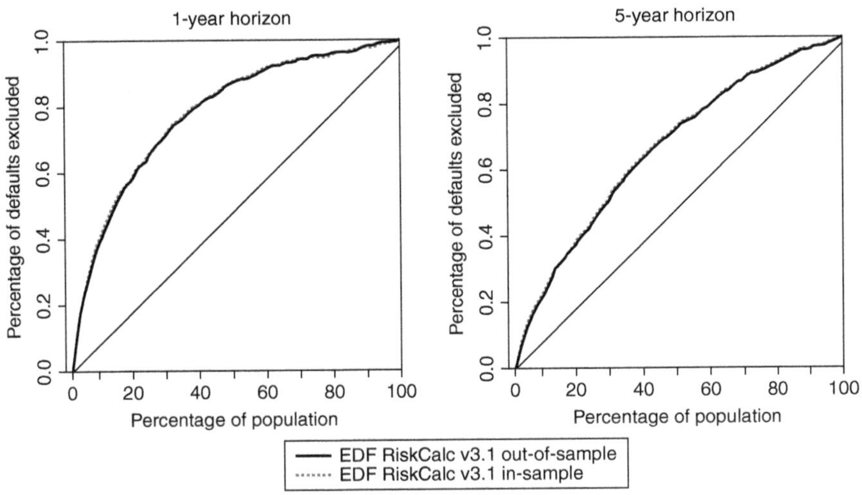

Figure 4.7 RiskCalc v3.1 US k-fold

with the overall out-of-sample results against the in-sample results. The model performance is maintained both in- and out-of-sample in the k-fold analysis. The difference in AR between the overall in-sample and out-of-sample results is not larger than one point in all cases. Further, RiskCalc v3.1 outperforms RiskCalc v1.0 in an out-of-sample context at both the 1- and 5-year horizons (Table 4.17).

The *k*-fold testing does not control for time dependence. Each of the *k* subsamples contains data from all periods. As a result, if there were a particularly high period of default rates, this would be included in each of the *k*samples. Such testing does not give a true sense of the how the model would have performed during these volatile periods because the model is estimated with full information on those time periods.

4.1.3.6 *Walk-forward tests*

An alternative out-of-sample test developed by Moody's KMV is a *walk-forward* analysis, which is designed along similar lines as the k-fold test, except that it controls for the effects of time. The model is estimated up to a certain year and the parameter estimates are used to score the observations in the *next* year. These model scores are *out-of-time*. The model is re-estimated including one more year of data and we repeat the analysis for the next year and continue until the end of the sample. These out-of-sample out-of-time scores are combined into a single prediction set and the AR and the power curve are calculated for the

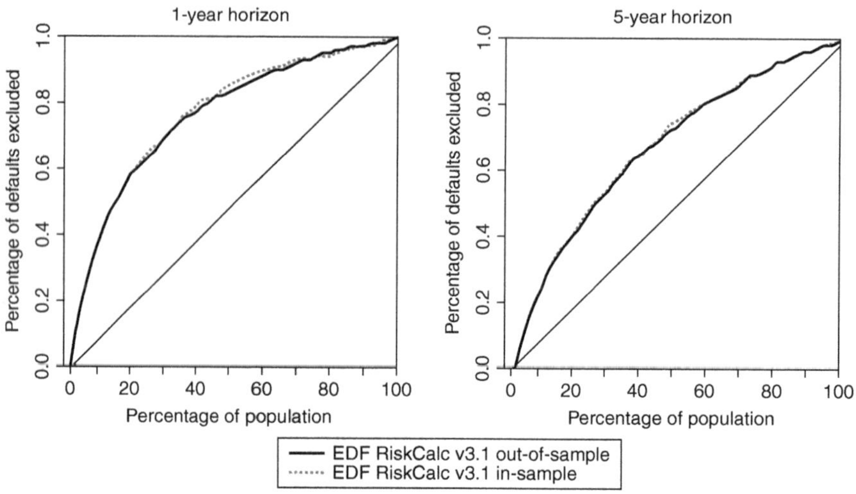

Figure 4.8 Out-of-sample performance (1- and 5-year) US walk-forward

combined set. This is then compared to the corresponding in-sample AR and power curve.

No data from a future period is used in fitting the model and only data from future periods is used for testing it. The parameter estimates are checked for stability across the different samples. Figure 4.8 presents the results from this analysis. The difference in AR between the in-sample and out-of-sample results is no more than one point in all cases. Further, RiskCalc v3.1 outperforms RiskCalc v1.0 in an out-of-time context at both the 1- and 5-year horizons.[11]

4.1.3.7 Out-of-sample test on newly received data

In addition to the other testing done on the model, the model was also tested on a dataset that only became available once the model was completed (i.e., a dataset that was not used for either development or calibration of the model or for any of the other validation tests). This data set included the most recent submissions from contributors to the CRD.

This holdout sample includes only firms that were never in the development or validation sample and includes more than 20,000 new usable observations and 500 new usable defaults. The holdout sample provides an ideal test of the variable selection process and the model's functional form, because it is not subject to a data snooping issue.[12]

Table 4.18 reports the results of the analysis. RiskCalc v3.1 outperforms RiskCalc v1.0 by 6.0 and 8.0 points in the 1-year and 5-year

Table 4.18 Out-of-sample performance of the new RiskCalc v3.1 model

	1-year model		5-year model	
	Accuracy Ratio (%)	Lead in Log likelihood*	Accuracy Ratio (%)	Lead in Log likelihood*
RiskCalc v3.1 model	60.8	0	36.4	
RiskCalc v1.0	54.8	193	28.4	330
Z-score	43.3	691	21.5	862

*Presents the increase in log likelihood of RiskCalc v3.1 over the alternative model. Larger values indicate that levels of RiskCalc v3.1 are better-calibrated vis-à-vis the alternative model.

horizons, respectively. While not directly comparable because they are based on different samples, the gains in power are very consistent with those observed in Table 4.8.[13] RiskCalc v1.0 continues to outperform the Z-score by a considerable margin. Finally, the likelihood gains of RiskCalc v3.1 over every other model remain substantial as well. This provides the strongest evidence of the robustness and accuracy of RiskCalc v3.1. While not always possible, such holdout testing is one of the best possible validation techniques for determining the robustness of a model.

4.1.3.8 Model calibration and implied ratings

To aid in the interpretation of an EDF credit measure, an EDF value is mapped to an.EDF rating (an EDF-implied rating). All RiskCalc v3.1 models to date have used the same mapping. The mapping is designed so that:

- there is a large range of EDF ratings (as required for economic and regulatory applications);
- no one rating contains too many credits (as required for economic and regulatory applications);
- the distribution of the 5-year ratings is approximately the same as the distribution of 1-year ratings (for consistency with rating-based analysis applications);
- the EDF value associated with an EDF rating is approximately the same as the observed historical default;
- the rate associated with a Moody's Bond Rating (for consistency with rating-based analysis applications).

Figure 4.9 shows the distribution of CRD observations by rating category in the development sample (for the CCA EDF credit measures over the full time period). Note that 13 categories between A1 and Caa/C

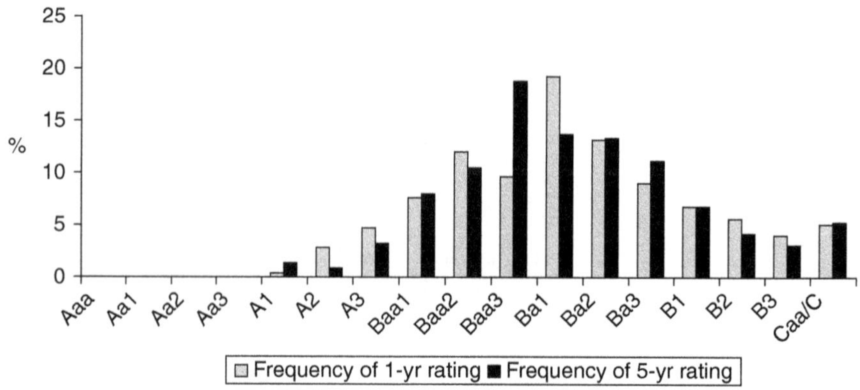

Figure 4.9 EDF-implied ratings for the 1- and 5-year models in the development sample

are utilized and that less than 20% of the observations are in any one category. A trace number of Aa3 EDF ratings are observed in the sample, but are not visible in the histogram. The 1-year distribution peaks at Ba1 and the 5-year distribution peaks at Baa3. While not reported here, other research has shown that the distribution of the CCA.EDF ratings changes over time with the credit cycle while the distribution of the FSO.EDF ratings remains relatively stable over time.

4.1.4 Further model improvements

For a detailed discussion of these enhancements, refer to the Technical Document. In this section, we will briefly outline some other enhancements to the model.

4.1.4.1 Continuous term structure

The previous version of the RiskCalc model provided the user with two discrete default probability estimates: a 1-year and a 5-year EDF. In this version, utilizing the two point estimates for 1- and 5-year estimates, we fit a Weibull function, and thus achieve a continuous term structure of EDF values for each credit. In other words, users of RiskCalc v3.1 US can now obtain EDF estimates for any point between 1 and 5 years. In addition, RiskCalc v3.1 provides EDF estimates for alternative definitions, such as the Forward EDF and the Annualized EDF (see Table 4.19).

Cumulative EDF A cumulative EDF credit measure gives the probability of default over that time period. For example, a 5-year cumulative EDF of 13.44% means that that company has a 13.44% chance of defaulting

Table 4.19 Term structure of EDF credit measures: an example

EDF	Cumulative	Forward	Annualized
Year 1	4.23	4.23	4.23
Year 2	7.00	2.90	3.57
Year 3	9.37	2.55	3.23
Year 4	11.49	2.34	3.01
Year 5	13.44	2.20	2.84

over that 5-year period. The second column of Table 4.19 provides an example of the cumulative 1- to 5-year credit measures produced by the model.

Forward EDF The forward EDF is the probability of default between t-1 and t conditional upon survival until t-1. In other words, the 4-year forward EDF is the probability that a firm will default between years 3 and 4 assuming the firm survived to year 3.[14] The third column of Table 4.19 displays the forward 1- to 5-year EDF credit measures that are derived from the forward EDF values.

Annualized EDF The annualized EDF credit measure is the cumulative EDF value for a given period, stated on a per year basis. For example, a company with a cumulative 5-year EDF of 13.44% would have a 5-year annualized EDF of 2.84%.[15] This means that the average default rate per year for a 13.44% cumulative default rate is 2.84%. The last column of Table 4.19 presents the annualized EDF credit measures for years 1 to 5 that are derived from the cumulative EDF values.

4.1.4.2 Central default tendency

Since most companies do not default, defaulting companies are relatively rare and thus more valuable in building a default prediction model. Much of the lack in default data is due to the data storage issues within financial institutions such as, defaulting companies being purged from the system after troubles begin, not all defaults being captured, or other sample errors. Also, if the date of default is uncertain the financial statement associated with the firm may be excluded from model development, depending on the severity of the problem. This can result in a sample that has lower default rates than occur in the general population. If the underlying sample is not representative, then it needs to be adjusted for the true central default tendency. When default definitions used in the data sample understate the defaulting population, as is the case with Italy, the central default tendency can be used to realign the default rates.

The estimate of long-run aggregate probabilities of default (or central default tendency) is important as an anchor for a model. The best estimation of default probability is a ratio that would reflect the number of obligors that defaulted in 1 year compared with the total obligors at the beginning of that year. Given the data problems surrounding the private middle-market company data, MKMV consulted prominent Italian financial institutions, as well as Moody's analysts. Based on these discussions and data review, 2.1% is used as the central tendency figure for the 1-year model.

Calculating a 5-year central default tendency There is a lack of publicly available data for direct calculation of the central tendency rate of a cumulative 5- year default probability. Based on extensive MKMV research, a 5-year cumulative default tendency is derived from the 1-year estimate. This research, combined with the information provided by the CRD, shows that the 5-year cumulative default rate is, on average, 4 times the level of the 1-year default rate. Therefore, 8.4% is used as the central default tendency for the 5-year model.

Central default tendency in FSO and CCA modes In the FSO model, the central default tendency remains constant over time. In CCA mode, the central default tendency is equal to the central default tendency of the FSO mode when the effects of the credit cycle are neutral. When the forward-looking prediction of the credit cycle indicates increasing default risk, the central default tendency of the CCA mode will be larger, and when the effects of the credit cycle indicate reducing default risk, the central default tendency will be smaller.

4.2 Business case: Fashionbyte

4.2.1 Introduction to Fashionbyte

Starting its base in the USA, Fashionbyte began operations in 2003 with the launch of its online multi-brand stores, Fashionbyte.com and Look.com, with the mission of becoming a global internet retailing partner for leading fashion and design brands.

Through the proprietary multi-brand and mono-brand online stores that Fashionbyte operates on behalf of fashion houses, it offers a rich assortment of high-quality fashion and homeware & design products to retail in 52 countries, most of them from globally recognized designers.

Over the years, Fashionbyte has developed enduring relationships with brand-owners and licensees. In certain cases, these relationships pertain to the supply of merchandise for sale through its proprietary online stores.

Fashionbyte refers to the companies that regularly supply products to them to sell through its proprietary online stores as its "Commercial Partners."

In certain other cases, they have developed collaborative relationships with fashion houses, for which they manage and operate brand-specific online stores. Fashionbyte refers to these brand-specific online stores as their "Online Flagship Stores" and to these fashion houses as their "Strategic Partners."

4.2.2 Business model and competitive advantages

Fashionbyte has organized its business into two separate business lines, as follows.

(i) The Multi-Brand Business Line, which includes activities related to the online stores, Fashionbyte.com and Look.com.

- Fashionbyte.com offers a vast array of quality clothing, footwear and accessories from well-known designers' collections from the corresponding season of the previous year, which are sold at reduced prices. To complement its offerings, it sells a selection of collections created exclusively for sale through Fashionbyte.com, vintage garments and special editions from trendy stylists and designers, as well as books, art and design objects.
- Look.com houses a selection of mini-shops under the same domain (so-called shops-in-a-shop) dedicated to the current collections of established brands and to exclusive or handcrafted items of clothing, all characterized by relatively limited distribution.

(ii) The Mono-Brand Business Line includes activities relating to the establishing and management of online flagship stores for some of the major fashion brands in the world, for which the Group serves as a strategic partner for the internet distribution channel. The products available at the online flagship stores are sold and invoiced directly by Fashionbyte to the final customers.

The Group operates according to a business model structured into the following business processes:

a. commercial planning and procurement;
b. marketing;
c. interactive services;
d. digital production;
e. retail management;
f. order processing and customer care.

Within this framework, the Group's technology function is active in a transversal manner in support of all its processes.

Fashionbyte believes that its competitive position is based on the following key strengths:

- the rich assortment of quality products the company is able to offer as a result of consolidated relationships with a number of prestigious international fashion and design companies for which the company represents an important commercial partner and/or strategic partner for the development of the online sales channel, one that is capable of understanding and maintaining the market positioning of each individual brand;
- the company's global geographical presence, which arises from the flexibility provided by the internet to simultaneously offer products in various markets, and which makes Fashionbyte a key point of reference for fashion houses with a global presence that want their brands to also be available online worldwide, thus reducing their dependence on specific geographical markets;
- the company's two different but synergic business lines: the Multi-Brand Business Line and the Mono-Brand Business Line;
- Fashionbyte's understanding of the needs of its customers, to whom the company offers an engaging purchasing experience, combining a welcoming environment with innovative content and high customer service standards;
- the company's organizational and strategic structure, supported by a scalable technology and logistics platform, which is capable of sustaining a consistent increase in volumes across both business lines in its existing and other potential geographic markets;
- the market's awareness of Fashionbyte as a "brand of brands," as confirmed by the international fashion business and other press.

The market in which the Company operates is highly competitive. The Company's principal competitors fall into the following categories:

(i) retailers, including traditional retail stores, which may or may not use the internet to grow their customer base;
(ii) e-commerce service providers.

Many of Fashionbyte's current and potential competitors have greater resources, longer operating histories, more customers, and greater brand recognition. They may secure better terms from vendors, adopt more aggressive pricing policies or devote more resources to technology, to fulfilling orders and to marketing.

In addition, new and enhanced technologies, including search services, web services, and digital services, may increase the competition that Fashionbyte faces.

Notwithstanding the fact that Fashionbyte has achieved a distinctive position in the market, the internet facilitates competitive entry and comparison-shopping and renders e-commerce inherently more competitive than other retail platforms. If competition continues to intensify, Fashionbyte may not have the resources it needs to respond effectively and in a timely manner, which could adversely affect its market share, operating results and financial status.

Despite the difficulty of identifying competitors that are directly comparable to Fashionbyte on the basis of the breadth of their product categories, their price bands, reference customer bases and their target markets, it has been possible to identify certain companies that, based on the criteria listed above, compete with the Group in specific segments of the market. These include:

(i) online retailers or online retail services providers: Net-à-porter (mainly in the U.K. and USA), Amazon.com (mainly in the USA), ASOS (mainly in the U.K.), eBags (mainly in the USA), Start Today (mainly in Japan), GSI Commerce (mainly in the USA), vente-privee.com (mainly in France and other European countries), Bluefly (mainly in the USA), overstock.com (mainly in the USA), dress-for-less (mainly in Germany) and Yoox.com (mainly in Italy);
(ii) traditional fashion retailers that have extended their activity to the online channel: Neiman Marcus Direct (mainly in the USA), Saks Fifth Avenue (mainly in the USA), and Nordstrom (mainly in the USA);

(iii) fashion houses that directly manage their own online stores: Hermès International, Gucci, Louis Vuitton Malletier and Polo Ralph Lauren.

In order to strengthen the company's competitive position in the online fashion market, and to continue to increase its profitability and improve its cash flows, the management intends to implement the following strategies:

- broadening and enhancing the collections available via its Multi-Brand Business Line by strengthening its relationships with its current commercial partners and selecting new commercial partners;
- taking advantage of the current window of opportunity in its Mono-Brand Business Line to select new strategic partners and develop solid relationships with them over the coming years;
- continuing to expand internationally by adopting a differentiated and balanced approach in each geographical area;
- increasing the size of its online customer base by strengthening its brand and continuing its investments into web marketing;
- continuing to improve the quality of its service and of its customers' online "shopping experience" in order to increase its conversion and retention rates;
- exploiting the scalability of its business model and synergies between its business lines in order to improve its cost structure and to increase the internal transfer and use of its accumulated know-how;
- continuing to strengthen and update its IT platform;
- attracting and retaining the best people.

4.2.3 Equity valuation

The Fashionbyte Income Statement, Balance Sheet and Cash Flow Statement are illustrated in Table 4.20, Table 4.21 and Table 4.22. (historical and forecasted data in US$ million).

The equity fair valuation is calculated using two approaches:

1) the discounted cash flow Method, as the first method;
2) the unlevered multiple approach as a control method.

4.2.3.1 Discounted cash flow methodology

The Enterprise Value is based on the present values of expected free cash flows in years$n+1$, $n+2$ and$n+3$ plus the terminal value computed

Table 4.20 Fashionbyte income statement

INCOME STATEMENT	n − 1	n	n + 1	n + 2	n + 3	n + 4
TOTAL REVENUES	257.8	362.9	479.3	623.4	800.1	1.021.2
COGS	(155.6)	(225.0)	(301.8)	(397.5)	(528.2)	(655.4)
GROSS PROFIT	**102.1**	**137.9**	**177.4**	**225.9**	**271.9**	**365.8**
Selling +Mktg	(55.4)	(78.2)	(94.8)	(115.5)	(139.5)	(166.6)
General +administrative	(23.4)	(32.0)	(41.7)	(49.3)	(61.0)	(72.0)
Other	(8.5)	(0.8)	(1.2)	(2.4)	(3.2)	(4.1)
EBITDA	**14.9**	**26.8**	**39.8**	**58.8**	**68.1**	**123.1**
Depreciation & provisions	(10.3)	(6.3)	(10.9)	(21.0)	(18.6)	(27.4)
EBIT	**4.6**	**20.6**	**28.9**	**37.8**	**49.6**	**95.7**
Net Financial Items	(2.5)	(0.3)	(1.5)	(0.8)	(0.8)	0.3
Non operating profits (losses)	10.3	2.0	0.0	0.0	0.0	(0.0)
Reported pre-tax profit	12.4	22.2	27.3	36.9	48.7	96.0
Tax	(5.4)	(9.8)	(13.4)	(19.0)	(28.5)	(38.4)
Net profit	**6.9**	**12.4**	**14.0**	**17.9**	**20.3**	**57.6**

Table 4.21 Fashionbyte balance sheet

BALANCE SHEET	n − 1	n	n + 1	n + 2	n + 3	n + 4
Cash and liquid assets	59.3	49.3	13.5	15.7	23.0	74.5
Trade receivables	71.3	127.9	139.5	144.9	159.0	147.4
Other	15.9	32.4	34.8	13.5	36.9	37.8
Inventory	89.6	129.0	156.1	184.9	226.1	255.0
Current assets	**236.1**	**338.6**	**344.0**	**359.1**	**445.0**	**514.7**
Intangibles	12.4	16.1	21.0	21.2	34.6	32.2
Other fixed assets	5.9	13.5	33.0	40.6	49.0	47.3
Fixed assets	**18.3**	**29.6**	**54.0**	**61.8**	**83.5**	**79.5**
Total assets	**254.4**	**368.2**	**398.0**	**420.9**	**528.5**	**594.2**
Interest bearing	81.7	162.6	160.7	147.3	149.1	139.6
Trade payables	46.2	63.0	58.1	75.2	142.2	166.0
Other	34.9	34.4	56.3	44.4	51.8	65.9
Total liabilities	**162.8**	**260.0**	**275.0**	**266.8**	**343.1**	**371.5**
Shareholders' equity	**91.6**	**108.2**	**122.9**	**154.1**	**185.4**	**222.7**
Total shareholders' equity + liabilities	**254.4**	**368.2**	**398.0**	**420.9**	**528.5**	**594.2**

Table 4.22 Fashionbyte cash flows

CASH FLOW STATEMENT	n − 1	n	n + 1	n + 2	n + 3	n + 4
Reported profit after tax	6.9	12.4	14.0	17.9	20.3	57.6
Non-cash items	13.2	12.2	16.3	22.9	18.5	27.4
Net Working capital	11.0	(18.6)	(20.5)	(10.2)	(14.4)	(18.6)
Operating Cash Flow	**31.2**	**6.0**	**9.8**	**30.6**	**24.4**	**66.4**
Capital expenditures	(4.9)	(20.8)	(39.8)	(27.1)	(33.9)	(33.9)
Other investments	1.4	1.4	0.0	0.0	0.0	0.0
Free Cash Flow	**27.6**	**(13.5)**	**(30.0)**	**3.5**	**(9.5)**	**32.5**
Shares	54.2	0.0	0.0	0.0	0.0	0.0
Other	(0.8)	(8.5)	(3.4)	(1.7)	0.0	0.0
Change in net debt	**80.9**	**(22.0)**	**(33.4)**	**1.9**	**(9.5)**	**32.5**

on the assumption that the *n*+4 free cash flow can be considered a perpetuity. The discount rate is equal to the weighted average cost of capital. The equity fair value is equal to the enterprise value less the net financial position at year end *n*.

The weighted average cost of capital is calculated on the following inputs:

- risk free rate on USA 10-year Government Bond rate, at 2.1%;
- equity beta for retail industry, equal to 1.05×;
- equity market risk premium estimate for the USA equity market, assumed to be equal to 5.15%;
- growth rate is 1%;
- cost of debt is 5%;
- tax rate is equal to 40.0%.

The cost of equity and the weighted average cost of capital is computed using the CAPM, as follows:

$$\textit{Cost of Equity} = \textit{Risk Free Rate} + \beta \cdot (\textit{Equity Risk Premium})$$

$$\textit{Cost of Equity}_{\textit{Fashionbyte}} = 2.1\% + 1.05 \times 5.15\% = 7.5\%$$

$$\textit{WACC} = \textit{Cost of Equity} \cdot \frac{\textit{Equity}}{\textit{Debt} + \textit{Equity}} + \textit{Cost of Debt} \cdot (1 - \textit{tax rate}) \cdot \frac{\textit{Debt}}{\textit{Debt} + \textit{Equity}}$$

$$\textit{WACC}_{\textit{Fashionbyte}} = 7.5\% \cdot 40\% + 5\% \cdot (1 - 40\%) \cdot 60\% = 4.95\%$$

The Enterprise Value (EV) is equal to the present value of free cash flows, as follows:

$$EV = -30.0 \times 1.0495^{-1} + 3.5 \times 1.0495^{-2} - 9.5 \times 1.0495^{-3} + \frac{32.5}{4.95\% - 1\%} \times 1.0495^{-3}$$

$$EV = US\$687.3MM$$

The equity fair value is equal to the EV less the net financial position, as follows:

$$\text{Equity Value} = \text{Enterprise Value} - \text{Financial Debt} + \text{Cash and liquid assets;}$$

$$\text{Equity Value} = 687,3MM - 162,6MM + 49,3MM;$$

$$\text{Equity Value} = US\$574MM.$$

4.2.3.2 Unlevered multiple approach

This approach is based on the determination of the EV/EBITDA ratios of comparable firms. As noted in Chapter 2, the identification of listed firms that are comparable with the private firm to be evaluated is usually a difficult task. In the case of Fashionbyte, the following multiples of comparable firms are individuated (see Table 4.23).

The preferred multiple is the EV/EBITDA and is on average equal to 12×; the expected average EBITDA is assumed to be equal to 55.5 million.

Table 4.23 Comparable firms

	PER		PCF		EF/Sales		EV/EBITDA		EV/EBIT	
	n+1	n+2	n+1	n+2	n+1	n+2	n+1	n+2	n+1	n+2
Luxury sector average	**72.7**	**19.7**	**16.0**	**14.2**	**3.1**	**2.8**	**12.7**	**11.1**	**15.6**	**13.4**
Bulgari	37.2	29.7	21.6	18.8	3.2	2.9	18.8	16.4	29.2	24.1
Burberry	21.8	19.0	14.6	12.9	3.0	2.5	11.8	10.1	14.8	12.6
Christian Dior	15.6	14.0	4.6	4.2	2.1	1.9	8.5	7.5	10.0	8.7
Hermes	38.5	34.6	31.5	28.6	6.9	6.3	21.6	19.5	24.3	21.7
Hugo Boss	18.1	16.2	13.2	12.0	2.3	2.0	10.6	9.3	13.4	11.8
LVMH	18.3	16.4	13.0	11.7	2.7	2.4	11.2	9.8	12.4	10.7
Richemont	17.8	15.3	14.7	12.5	2.7	2.4	11.2	9.4	12.8	10.6
Swatch	16.8	14.7	14.4	12.8	2.6	2.3	9.4	8.0	10.7	9.0
Tod's	20.4	17.8	16.0	14.2	2.9	2.6	11.1	9.6	13.1	11.3

Source: Bloomberg.

The equity fair value of Fashionbyte can be calculated as follow:

$$W = \left[\left(\frac{\text{EV}}{\text{EBITDA}}\right)_S \times \text{EBITDA}_T\right] - \text{Financial Debt}$$
$$+ \text{Cash and liquid assets;}$$
$$W = [12 \times 55.5] - 162.6 + 49.3 = \text{US\$ } 552.7 \text{ million}$$

In this evaluation process, the application of the DCF method and the use of the Comparables Approach (as a control method) for estimating Fashionbyte's equity fair value both produce similar values (US$ 574 million vs. US $ 552.7 million) and it would therefore seem that the result calculated using the second (control) method validates the estimate achieved using the first method. However, if Fashionbyte's credit risk is taken into consideration in the evaluation process, the result is very different.

4.2.4 The new approach

According to the Integrated Asset Pricing Model (IAPM), Fashionbyte's cost of equity is the maximum of either the risk premium calculated using the CAPM, or the risk premium determined following the FIA.

As shown in the previous paragraph, according to the CAPM calculation, Fashionbyte's cost of equity is equal to 7.5%.

Fashionbyte's cost of equity using the FIA (see Chapter 3), meanwhile, is estimated as follows:

1) probability of default valuation;
2) equity expected loss calculation;
3) equity risk premium determination.

Fashionbyte's probability of default is 1.57%, in other words there a 1.57% probability that its shareholders will lose all of their capital (recovery rate zero) (see Floor Theorem, Chapter 3); on the other hand, the probability of shareholders losing at least 1 US dollar is equal to 15% (see Cap Theorem, Chapter 3).

The combined rule to calculate the equity expected loss (EEL) is as follows:

$$\text{EEL} = \text{default probability} + (\text{probability of losing at least 1 US dollar}$$
$$- \text{default probability}) \ 50\%;$$
$$\text{EEL} = 1.57\% + (15\% - 1.57\%) \times 50\%;$$
$$\text{EEL} = 8.29\%.$$

The last step is to compute the equity risk premium based on the EEL and the probability of winning at least one US dollar. A rule-of-thumb approach is to define the size of "bet" that would need to be won in order to compensate shareholders for the EEL with a probability equal to "1 *minus* the probability of losing at least 1 US dollar", as follows:

$$\text{Probability of winning at least 1 US dollar} \times \text{Equity Risk Premium} = \text{Equity Expected Loss;}$$

$$\text{Equity Risk Premium} = \text{Equity Expected Loss} / \text{Probability of winning at least 1 US dollar;}$$

$$\text{Equity Risk Premium} = 8.29\% / (1 - 15\%);$$

$$\text{Equity Risk Premium} = 8.29\% / 85\%;$$

$$\text{Equity Risk Premium} = 9.74\%;$$

$$\text{Cost of Equity} = \text{Risk Free Rate} + \text{Equity Risk Premium;}$$

$$\text{Cost of Equity} = 2.1\% + 9.74\%;$$

$$\text{Cost of Equity} = 11.85\% \text{ (FIA).}$$

In this case the equity risk premium calculated using the FIA is higher than the equity risk premium based on the CAPM, and it is therefore advisable to use 11.85% as Fashionbyte's cost of equity.

If we assume that Fashionbyte's cost of equity is equal to 11.85%, the new weighted average cost of capital is 6.685%, as follows:

$$\text{WACC} = \text{Cost of Equity} \times \frac{\text{Equity}}{\text{Debt} + \text{Equity}} + \text{Cost of Debt} \times (1 - \text{tax rate}) \times \frac{\text{Debt}}{\text{Debt} + \text{Equity}}$$

$$\text{WACC}_{\text{Fashionbyte}} = 11.85\% \times 40\% + 5\% \times (1 - 40\%) \times 60\% = 6.685\%$$

The EV is equal to the present value of free cash flows, as follows:

$$\text{EV} = -30.0 \times 1.06685^{-1} + 3.5 \times 1.06685^{-2} - 9.5 \times 1.06685^{-3} + \frac{32.5}{6.685\% - 1\%} \times 1.06685^{-3}$$

$$\text{EV} = \text{US\$ } 438.22 \text{ million}$$

The equity fair value is equal to the EV less the net financial position, as follows:

$$\text{Equity Value} = \text{Enterprise Value} - \text{Financial Debt} + \text{Cash and liquid assets};$$

$$\text{Equity Value} = 438.22 - 162.6 + 49.3;$$

$$\text{Equity Value} = \text{US\$324.8 million}.$$

As we can see the two results – the first as shown in the previous paragraph and the second as presented in this paragraph – are very different: an underestimation of 4.35% in the cost of equity (11.85% FIA minus 7.5% CAPM) means an overestimation of 43.4% of Fashionbyte's equity fair value (US$ 574 million vs. US$ 324.8 million).

5
Integrated Pricing Model in Japan

5.1 RiskCalc Japan*

5.1.1 Data description

5.1.1.1 Data exclusions

Excluded companies The goal of the RiskCalc model is to provide an EDF credit measure for private Japanese companies in the middle market. The firms and industries covered in the model must have similar default characteristics. To create the most powerful model for Japanese middle-market companies, those that did not reflect the typical company characteristics in this market were eliminated. The following types of company are not included in the model development.

- **Small Companies** – For companies with assets of less than ¥12 million, their future success is often linked to the finances of the key individuals. For this reason, they are not reflective of a typical middle-market company and are excluded from the database.
- **Financial Institutions** – The balance sheets of financial institutions (banks, insurance companies, and investment companies) exhibit higher leverage than the typical private firm. The regulation and capital requirements of these institutions make them dissimilar to the typical middle-market company and, therefore, they are excluded from the database.
- **Real Estate Development Companies** – The annual accounts of real estate development and investment companies provide only a partial description of the dynamics of the firm and, therefore, its likelihood of default. This is because its financial health often hinges on a particular development.[1]
- **Public Sector and Non-profit Institutions** – Government-run companies' default risks are influenced by the states' or municipalities' unwillingness to allow them to fail. Therefore, their results are not

Table 5.1 Japanese private firm sample data

Japanese private firms	RiskCalc v3.1 Japan	RiskCalc v3.2 Japan	Credit research database growth (%)
Financial statements	699,000+	955,000+	**T37**
Unique number of firms	135,000+	201,000+	**T49**
Defaults	5,500+	12,000+	**T118**
Time period	1993–2002	1992–2005	**T + 4 years**

comparable to other private firms. Non-profit financial ratios are different from for-profit firms, particularly with regard to variables relating to net income, as they do not have a profit maximization objective.

Excluded financial statements The financial statements in the CRD are cleaned to eliminate highly suspect financial statements. Plausibility checks of financial statements are conducted, such as assets not equal to liabilities plus net worth, and financial statement covering a period of less than 12 months. If errors are detected, those statements are excluded from the analysis.

5.1.1.2 Descriptive statistics of the data

Overview of the data The extensive data on both non-defaulting and defaulting companies contained in Moody's CRD has increased substantially since RiskCalc v3.1.

Table 5.1 provides a summary of the data set used in development, validation, and calibration of the RiskCalc v3.2 Japan model. The number of financial statements, firms, and defaults utilized in the recent version is considerably larger than v3.1. There has been more than a 49% increase in the number of unique firms, and more than a 37% increase in the number of financial statements. In addition, there has been more than a 100% increase in the number of defaults. The current data set is also based on a longer time period.

Figure 5.1 presents the distribution of Japanese financial statements and defaults by year.

Robustness of the data When building a model, potential database weaknesses need to be examined. Not only does the database need to cover a large number of firms and defaults, but the defaults also need to be distributed among industries and company types covered. For example, if the database has significant numbers of small firms, or firms in one particular industry without sufficient defaults in those areas, the model

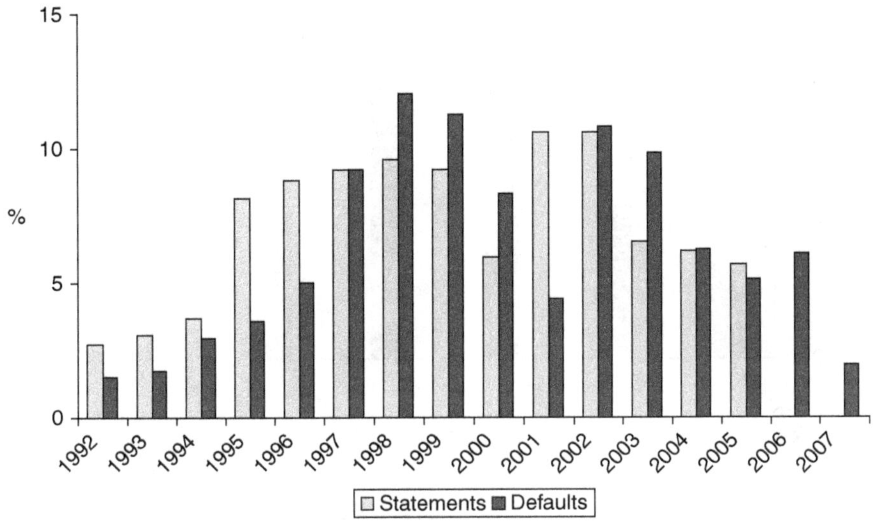

Figure 5.1 Date distribution of financial statements and default data

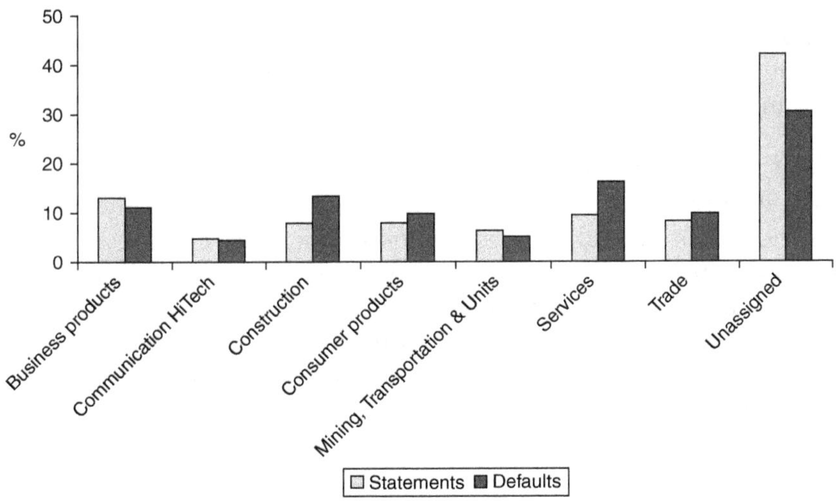

Figure 5.2 Distribution of defaults and firms by industry

may not be a good default predictor. The CRD used in developing the RiskCalc models has addressed both of these issues.

Figure 5.2 and Figure 5.3 present the distribution of defaults and firms by industry and size classification, respectively. These figures show that the proportion of defaults in any one size group or industry is comparable to the number of firms in these groupings. Firm

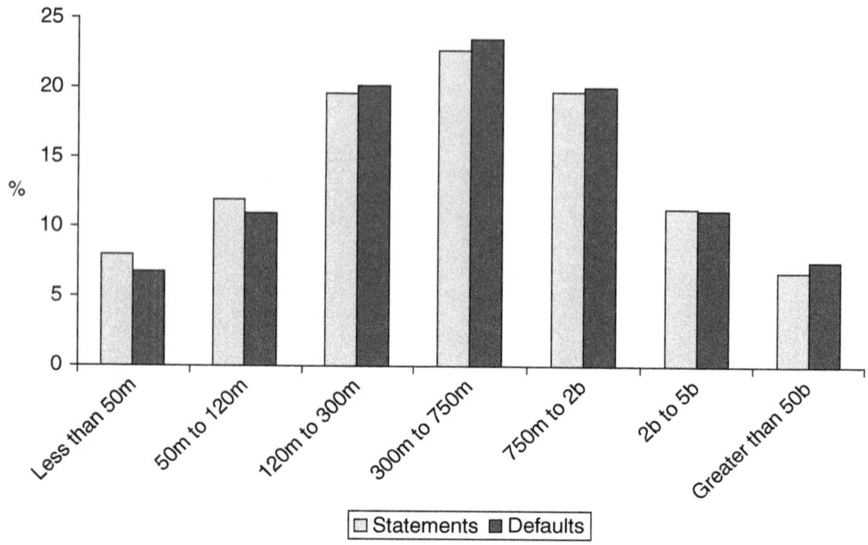

Figure 5.3 Statements and default distribution by size

size as measured by assets range from ¥12 million to over ¥5 billion (Figure 5.3), with the range between ¥120 million and ¥750 million accounting for approximately half of the sample.

5.1.1.3 Definition of default

RiskCalc provides assistance to institutions and investors for determining the risk of default, missed payments, or other credit events. The proposals for BIS II have stimulated debates about what constitutes an appropriate definition of default. RiskCalc applies the criteria used by most of the advanced economies in the world. The events which we defined as defaults include special attention, in danger of bankruptcy, and bankrupt/de facto bankrupt.

5.1.1.4 Central default tendency

Because most companies do not default, companies that do default are relatively rare and thus more valuable in building a default prediction model. Much of the lack in default data comes from data storage issues within financial institutions (e.g., defaulting companies being purged from the system after troubles begin), not all defaults being captured, or other sample errors. Also, if the date of default is uncertain, the financial statement associated with the firm may be excluded from model development, depending on the severity of the problem. This can result in a sample that has lower default rates than actually occur in the general population. If the underlying sample is not representative, then it needs to be adjusted for the true central default tendency (CDT). When default definitions used in the data sample may understate the defaulting population, as is the case with Japan, the CDT can be used to realign the default rates.

The estimate of long-run aggregate probabilities of default (i.e., CDT) is important as an anchor for a model. The best estimation of the default probability is a ratio that reflects the number of obligors that defaulted in one year compared with the total obligors at the beginning of that year. Often these types of data are not available.

The estimate of the CDT for Japan is based on several sources.

- loan loss provision data from the OECD.
- provisioning data gathered from financial statements of large Japanese banks.
- data for major city and regional banks gathered from the *Banking Statistics Supplement: Japan,* published by Moody's Investors Service.
- statistics on total credit charges from the Japanese Bankers Association.
- confirmation of the CDT exceeding the default rates observed in our development sample.

Based on these discussions and data review, 2.0% is used as the CDT figure. In calibrating RiskCalc v3.2 for Japanese private companies, a central tendency of 2.0% is used for the 1-year PD, The corresponding central tendency rate used for the 5-year is 7.7%.[2]

To test the 1-year mean default rate, bank loan provisions are used. Financial institutions make provisions for bad loans that are representative of their expectations for write-offs. From the volume of losses and the volume of loans, an average default rate can be calculated by making an assumption regarding LGD:

$$Volume\ of\ Losses = Volume\ of\ Loans \times Probability\ of\ Default \times LGD.$$

Therefore,

$$Probability\ of\ Default = \frac{Volume\ of\ Losses}{(Volume\ of\ Loans \times LGD)}$$

The foundation approach to capital allocation as described in Basel II uses a LGD rate of 50%, so this assumption can be used to calculate the implied default rates.

5.1.2 Model components

The RiskCalc v3.2 model incorporates several components to determine the EDF credit measure. The inputs to the model include selection of the financial ratios, transforms of those ratios, the inclusion of industry information, and the CCA.

The development of a RiskCalc model involves the following steps:

1. Choosing a limited number of financial statement variables for the model from a list of possible variables.[3]
2. Transforming the variables into interim probabilities of default using non-parametric techniques.
3. Estimating the preliminary weightings of the financial statement variables, using a probit model, combined with industry variables.
4. Creating a (non-parametric) final transform that converts the probit model score into an actual EDF credit measure.

In FSO mode, the models are based on the following functional form:

$$FSO\ EDF = F\left(\Phi\left(\sum_{i=1}^{N}\beta_i T_i(x_i) + \sum_{j=1}^{K}\gamma_j I_j\right)\right)$$

where

$x_1, \ldots, x_N$	are the input ratios;
$I_1, \ldots, I_K$	are indicator variables for each of the industry classifications;
$\gamma_1, \ldots, \gamma_K$	are estimated coefficients;
D	is the cumulative normal distribution;
F *and* $T_1, \ldots, T_N$	are non-parametric transforms;[4]
FSOEDF	is the financial statement only EDF credit measure.

The *T*s are the transforms of each financial statement variable, which capture the non-linear impacts of financial ratios on the default likelihood, as shown in Figure 5.4 and discussed in detail later in the document. We refer to *F* as the final transform (i.e., the final mapping). The final transform captures the empirical relationship between the probit model score and actual default probabilities. We describe the final transform as calibrating the model score to an actual EDF value. The difference between the FSO EDF and the CCA EDF credit measure is that in CCA mode the final transform is adjusted to reflect our assessment of the current stage of the credit cycle, while in FSO mode it remains constant.

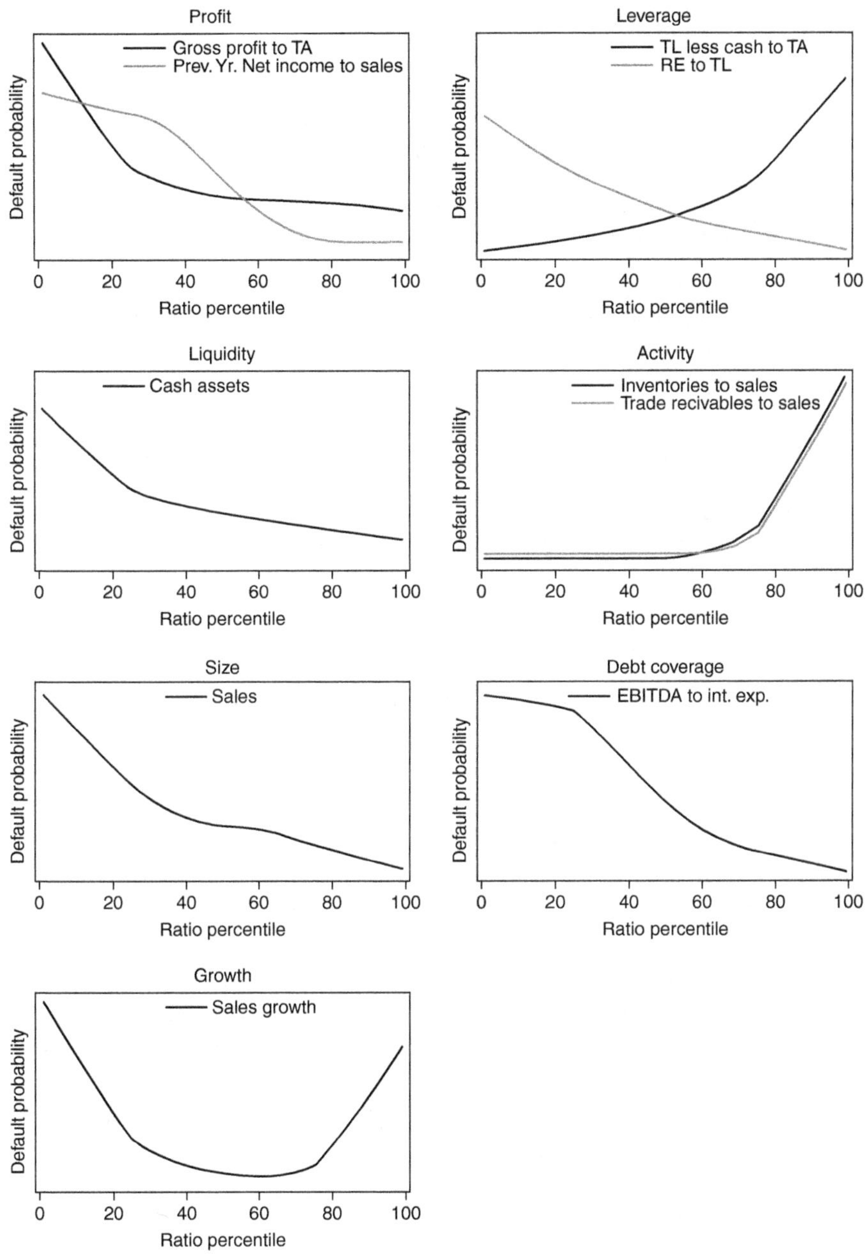

Figure 5.4 Transformations of financial statement variables in RiskCalc v3.2 Japan

Table 5.2 Groupings of financial statement ratios

Profitability ratios include net income, net income less extraordinary items, EBITDA, EBIT, and operating profit in the numerator; and total assets, tangible assets, fixed assets and sales in the denominator. *High profitability reduces the probability of default.*

Leverage ratios include liabilities to assets and long-term debt to assets. *High leverage increases the probability of default.*

Debt coverage is the ratio of cash flow to interest payments or some other measure of liabilities. *High debt coverage reduces probability of default.*

Growth variables are typically the change in ROA and sales growth. These variables measure the stability of a firm's performance. *Both rapid growth and rapid decline (negative growth) will increase a firm's default probability.*

Liquidity variables include cash and marketable securities to assets, the current ratio and the quick ratio. These variables measure the extent to which the firm has liquid assets relative to the size of its liabilities. *High liquidity reduces the probability of default.*

Activity ratios include inventories to sales and accounts receivable to sales. These ratios may measure the extent to which a firm has a substantial portion of assets in accounts that may be of subjective value. For example, a firm with a lot of inventories may not be selling its products and may have to write off these inventories. *A large stock of inventories relative to sales increases the probability of default; other activity ratios have different relationships to default.*

Size variables include sales and total assets. These variables are converted into a common currency as necessary and then are deflated to a specific base year to ensure comparability (e.g. total assets are measured in 2001 U.S. dollars). *Large firms default less often.*

5.1.2.1 *Financial statement variables*

Selecting the variables Our variable selection process starts with a list of possible financial statement variables addressing various risk factors. The working list of ratios is divided into groups that represent different underlying concepts regarding a firm's financial status (Table 5.2). A model is then built with at least one variable per group. When it is possible to enrich the scope of the model in a given category and increase model performance while maintaining model robustness, several variables from each group will be used in the model.

We ask the following questions when deciding which variables to include in the final model:

1. Is the variable readily available?
2. Are the definitions of the inputs to the variable unambiguous?
3. Is the meaning of the variable intuitive?
4. Does the variable predict default activity?
5. Is the variable not highly correlated with other variables in the model?

Table 5.3 Financial statement variables used in RiskCalc v3.2 Japan

Category	Variable
Activity	Inventory to Net sales Trade receivables to Net sales
Debt coverage	EBITDA to Interest expense
Growth	Net sales growth
Leverage	Total liabilities less Cash to Total assets Retained earnings to Total liabilities
Liquidity	Cash to Total assets
Profitability	Gross profit to Total Assets Previous year income to Previous year net
Sales Size	Real Net Sales

We chose the same set of variables as RiskCalc v3.1 Japan. Table 5.3 presents the variables used in the final version of RiskCalc v3.2 Japan. They differ from the variables chosen for RiskCalc Japan v1.0 in three important ways.

- Unlike v3.1, RiskCalc v3.2 Japan contains dynamic factors. As a result, we include two variables that require inputs from the previous year's financial statements: Net Sales Growth and Previous Year's Net Income to Sales. In our experience to date, Net Sales Growth acts as a two-sided indicator, where both declining sales and rapidly increasing sales increase the likelihood of default. Further, including Previous Year's Net Income to Sales controls for the stability of the firm's profits; consistent profitability lowers the probability of default. By including inputs from the previous year's financial statement, the new model uses more information than the previous model, which increases the model's power.
- For the debt coverage variable, we use EBITDA to Interest Expense instead of Gross Profit, as EBITDA is more representative of the firm's actual profitability.
- We include a new variable, Trade Receivables to Net Sales. This variable measures the extent to which the firm carries debt associated with product sales to its customers. A large ratio of trade receivables to sales could indicate a problem associated with collecting on these debts. Trade Receivables is the sum of accounts receivable and notes receivable. In Japan, the classification of trade receivables into one of these groups is somewhat arbitrary and differs by industry. Therefore, we combine accounts receivable and notes receivable in the construction of this ratio.

Variable transforms After the variables are selected, they are transformed into a preliminary EDF value; Figure 5.4 presents the transformations used in the model. The horizontal axis gives the percentile score of the ratio, and the vertical axis gives the default probability of that ratio in isolation (univariate). The percentile score represents the percentage of the database that had a ratio or level below that of the company (e.g., if ROA is in the 90th percentile, then 90% of the sample had an ROA lower than that firm).

The shape of the transformation indicates how significantly a change in level impacts the EDF value. If the slope of the transform is steep, a small change will have a larger impact on risk than if the slope were flat.

- For the **Profitability** group, we include Gross Profit to Total Assets and Previous Year Net Income to Sales. The Gross Profit to Total Assets transform is downward-sloping, and the slope becomes smaller as Gross Profit to Total Assets becomes large. This transform indicates that more profitable firms have lower default probabilities, but the impact of Gross Profit to Total Assets on default probabilities diminishes as Gross Profit to Total Assets increases. Previous Year Net Income to Previous Year's Sales has more of an S-shaped transform, implying that low levels of profitability in the previous year can increase default likelihood, and that a higher level of previous year profitability reduces the default likelihood. In addition, there is a range between the 40th–60th percentiles where the default likelihood is highly sensitive to the previous year's profitability.
- For the **Leverage** group, we include two variables: Total Liabilities less Cash to Total Assets and Retained Earnings to Total Liabilities. Large values of Retained Earnings to Total Liabilities lower default probabilities, while large values of Total Liabilities less Cash to Total Assets increase default probabilities.
- For the **Liquidity** group, Cash to Assets is downward-sloping, indicating that higher values of this ratio are associated with lower default probabilities.
- For the **Activity** group, the ratios are Inventories to Sales and Trade Receivables to Sales. Both are upward-sloping, indicating that high values of these ratios are associated with higher default probabilities. Both of these variables exhibit a threshold effect. Increases in these variables do not have significant impact on the likelihood of default until around the 60th percentile.
- The **Size** variable is Sales. This variable's transformation is downward-sloping.

- The **Debt Coverage** variable is EBITDA to Interest Expense. This variable is downward-sloping, indicating that large values of EBITDA relative to interest expense lower the probability of default.
- The **Growth** variable is Sales Growth. It is U-shaped, indicating that large increases or decreases in sales are associated with higher default probabilities.

5.1.2.2 Model weights

Importance Financial analysts are interested in the relative importance of different factors that comprise the model (e.g., profitability vs. liquidity, and leverage vs. debt coverage). Due to the non-linear nature of the model, describing the relative importance of different variables in the model is complicated. For example, the EDF value of a firm is very sensitive to Gross Profit to Total Assets if the firm has low levels of profitability. If the firm has high levels of Gross Profit to Total Assets, however, the sensitivity of its EDF to profitability is considerably smaller (Figure 5.4).

Calculation of weights We developed the following methodology to describe the relative importance of a variable in the model on average. After transforming the variables using the transforms in Figure 5.4, we compute the EDF value for a theoretical firm with all its variables at the average values. The variables are then increased one at a time by one standard deviation. The EDF level change for each variable (in absolute value) is computed. The relative weight of each variable is then calculated as this change divided by the sum of the changes for each variable. This gives the variable with the largest impact on the EDF level the largest weight, and the variable with the smallest impact on the EDF level the smallest weight. The weights of each variable sum to 100% by construction. The weight of each category is the sum of the weights of each variable in that category.

In developing the RiskCalc v3.2 Japan model, we keep the same variables and inputs as v3.1 after examining the robustness of each ratio's prediction power in the new data. The new model has been re-weighted according to the new data, reflecting the new credit environment that is beyond the coverage of the RiskCalc v3.1 Japan development data. As shown in Figure 5.1, the new model has an additional four years of data, including the period between 2003 and 2005.

Table 5.4 presents the weights in RiskCalc v3.1 Japan and RiskCalc v3.2 Japan. The most important categories continue to be Leverage and

Table 5.4 Risk factors: RiskCalc v3.1 Japan vs. RiskCalc v3.2 Japan

RiskCalc v3.1 Japan		RiskCalc v3.2 Japan	
Risk factors	Weight (%)	Risk factors	Weight (%)
Leverage Liabilities less cash to assets Retained earnings to total liabilities	26	**Leverage** Liabilities less cash to assets Retained earnings to total liabilities	28
Debt Coverage EBITDA to interest expense	22	**Debt coverage** EBITDA to interest expense	25
Activity Inventory to net sales Trade receivables to net sales	13	**Activity** Inventory to net sales Trade receivables to net sales	12
Liquidity Cash to total assets	16	**Liquidity** Cash to total assets	16
Profitability Gross profit to total assets Previous year's net income to sales	12	**Profitability** Gross profit to total assets previous year's net income to sales	11
Growth Net sales growth	8	**Growth** Net sales growth	9
Size Net sales	3	**Size** Net sales	3

Debt Coverage, whose importance increased, as did that of the Growth group.

The importance of Profitability, and Activity decreased, while Size and Liquidity remained approximately the same.

5.1.2.3 Industry adjustments

While the variables included in the RiskCalc model explain most of the risk factors, the relative importance of the variables can be different among industries. In the FSO mode of RiskCalc v3.2 Japan, the EDF value is adjusted for industry effects. Table 5.5 presents the increase in model power and accuracy from introducing industry controls into the FSO model. Both the power and the accuracy of the EDF credit measure increase, as measured by the AR and the gain in log likelihood. The significance of the gain in likelihood indicates that the industry controls are especially important in producing an accurate EDF credit

Table 5.5 Increase in model power and accuracy from introducing industry controls

	1-year model		5-year model	
	Accuracy Ratio (%)	P-value of relative gain in Log likelihood (%)	Accuracy Ratio (%)	P-value of relative gain in Log likelihood (%)
FSO mode without industry controls	59.6	—	47.3	—
FSO mode with industry controls	61.0	<0.0001	49.3	<0.0001

Table 5.6 Average EDF in development sample by sector

Sector	Average 1-year EDF (%)	Average 5-year EDF (%)
Business products	1.25	5.12
Construction	1.49	6.27
Consumer products	2.51	9.50
Communication and High Tech	1.87	7.80
Mining, transportation and utilities	1.51	6.07
Services	2.32	9.08
Trade	1.54	6.31
Unassigned	2.32	8.57

measure. Table 5.6 presents the average EDF value by industry for the development sample.

In this table, and hereafter, AR is the measure of the model's ability to rank order credits. Increases in log likelihood, on the other hand, measure the extent to which the model's EDF values match observed default rates.[5]

5.1.2.4 Credit cycle adjustment

The existence of a credit cycle is a known factor to market participants and can easily be observed by episodes of elevated default activity. Further, elevated rates of default activity are generally associated with recessions.

The CCA mode of the RiskCalc v3.2 Japan model includes a Credit Cycle Adjustment factor in addition to the FSO component. The CCA is designed to incorporate an assessment of the current stage of the credit cycle into our estimate of private firm default risk.

Selecting an adjustment factor Incorporating a CCA into the model is challenging for several reasons. There are many possible indicators of the credit cycle, but there is no conclusive evidence about which ones to choose. Further complicating this task is the fact that there are few credit cycles with which to test these indicators.

In building our CCA, we draw on the Moody's KMV public firm model to provide a forward-looking measure of default risk. For public firms throughout the world, our model provides an option-theoretic assessment of its default risk by calculating its distance-to-default (DD). This measure is specifically designed to be a forward-looking indicator of default risk. It extracts signs of default risk from the stock market performance of individual firms, and has been extensively validated.[6]

A calculation of DD measure necessitates the availability of equity prices at the firm level, so we cannot calculate it directly for private firms. Accordingly, we implement the CCA in the following way: if the level of DD for public firms in a given industry group increases, then private firms' EDF values in the industry are adjusted downward. Conversely, if the level of DD for the public firms in an industry decreases vis-à-vis the historical average for that industry, the private firms' EDF values in that industry are adjusted upward.

Adjustment factor used in the model To elaborate, the fitting of CCA is based on empirical data. For the RiskCalc v3.2 Japan model, the DD factor is based on an aggregation of all public Japanese firms in the corresponding industry. If a firm cannot be associated with a specific industry, the model uses a CCA that is based on an aggregation of all public Japanese firms.

When the CCA factor is neutral, the CCA EDF coincides with the FSO EDF. This relationship does not necessarily imply that the average of the CCA EDF on any particular sample will equal the average of the FSO EDF, as the relationship between CCA and FSO is non-linear, and the selected sample may not cover a sufficient historical window to contain a complete credit cycle.

Figure 5.5 presents the DD factor for public Japanese firms against the real GDP growth rates. The DD factor increases with the growth of GDP. Grey areas indicate business cycle peak-to-trough dates from ECRI.

Figure 5.6 presents the inverted DD factor against the median of the option-adjusted spreads on Japanese bonds. The DD factor has been inverted so that large positive factors are associated with elevated risk. The spreads generally coincide with the DD factor, but for 2006–9, the DD factor increases in anticipation of the spreads.

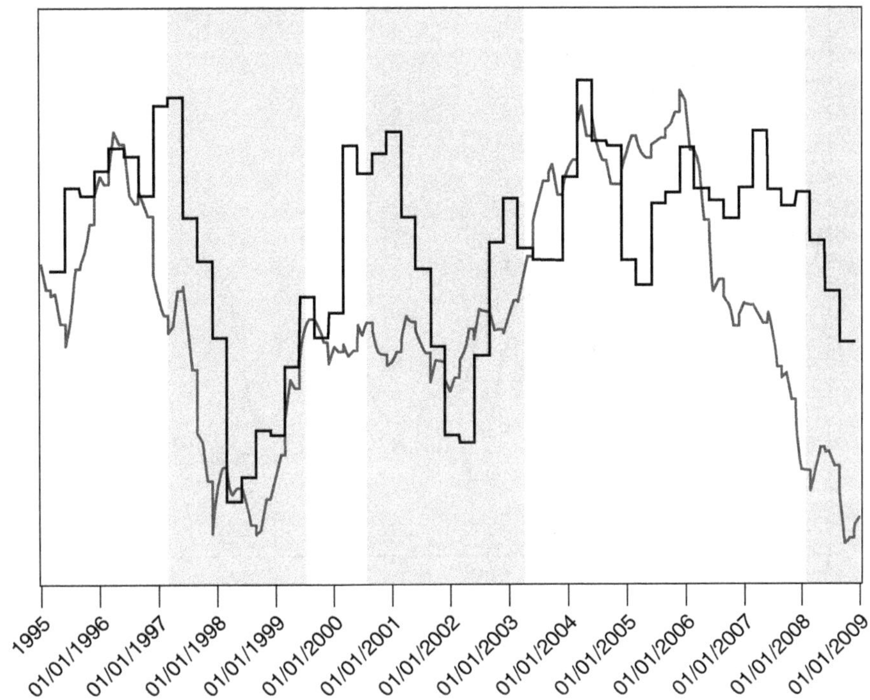

Figure 5.5 DD factor in Japanese firms and the GDP growth rates, 1995–2009

5.1.3 Validation results

In this section, we present test results on the model's ranking power, and the accuracy of its predicted EDF credit measure over two sets of samples: the new data sample and the overall full sample. We also present the results of Moody's KMV model robustness and stability tests. These tests examine the independent variable correlation matrices and Variance Inflation Factors (VIF) to ensure that the model does not contain excessive multicollinearity.

The results show that the model is uniformly more powerful than other models across different time periods, sectors, and size classifications.

5.1.3.1 Model power and accuracy

In Japan, we performed rank order validation of the model in both CCA and FSO modes. As in other countries, data issues can complicate the interpretation of AR differences between these modes. Therefore, we focus on whether the new model outperforms the old model and other benchmarks in both modes. Changes in the DD, the legal

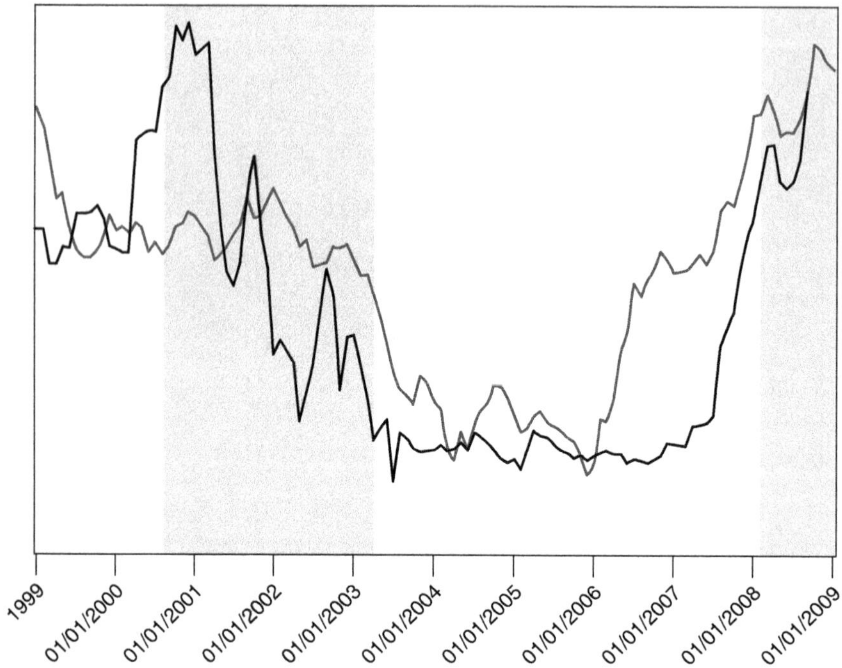

Figure 5.6 Inverted DD factor in Japanese & option-adjusted spreads on Japanese bonds, 1999–2009

environment, or simply the process of collecting defaults can skew AR difference between the two modes. Also, during 2001–5 in Japan, loans that had been performing poorly for an extended period were written off. We present the overall AR for the power tests across periods, sectors, and size classifications. We also present AR for the FSO model relative to RiskCalc v3.1 FSO and Z-score. Power comparisons by cut are often more robust to data issues described above when done in the FSO mode of the model.

Table 5.7 presents the in-sample overall measures of power for RiskCalc v3.2 Japan versus alternative models over the new data sample.[7] Table 5.7 also contains *p*-values for the statistical test showing how the difference between the AR from v3.2 and the benchmark is less than or equal to zero. A *p*-value of less than 0.05 indicates that we can reject the hypothesis that the difference in the ARs is less than or equal to zero with 95% confidence.

The new RiskCalc v3.2 model outperformed the Z-score model by more than 30 percentage points at the 1-year horizon, and 23 percentage points at the 5-year horizon.[8]

Table 5.7 Overall power of the new RiskCalc v3.2 Japan model – new data sample

	1-year model		5-year model	
Mode	Accuracy Ratio (%)	p-value of relative gain of v3.2 over alternatives	Accuracy Ratio (%)	p-value of relative gain of v3.2 over alternatives
RiskCalc v3.2	58.0	–	48.5	–
RiskCalc v3.1	56.6	<.0001	46.9	<.0001
RiskCalc v1.0	54.3	<.0001	44.4	<.0001
Z-score	27.2	<.0001	25.5	<.0001

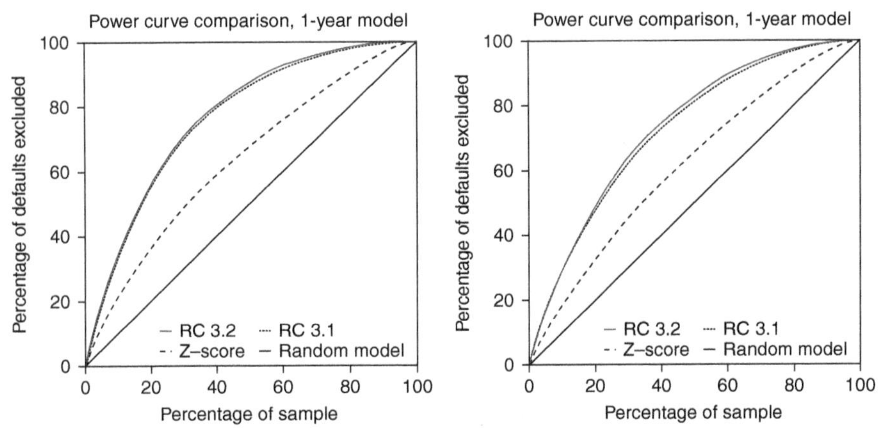

Figure 5.7 Power of alternative models (1- and 5-year) – Japan, new data sample

Figure 5.7 presents the cumulative accuracy profiles for the 1- and 5-year models corresponding to Table 5.7. It shows the power improvements of RiskCalc v3.2 FSO, RiskCalc v3.1, and the Z-score. These power improvements are uniformly significant across different regions of the distribution relative to Z-score.

Table 5.8 presents the in-sample overall measures of power for the RiskCalc v3.2 Japan model versus alternative models over the full sample. With the CCA, model performance improves by about one percentage point of AR at the 5-year horizon. However, compared with RiskCalc v3.2, there is approximately a one percentage point loss at the 1-year horizon. Table 5.8 also contains *p*-values for the statistical test showing how the difference between the AR from v3.2 and the benchmark is less than or equal to zero.

Table 5.8 Overall power of the new RiskCalc v3.2 Japan model – full sample

	1-year model		5-year model	
Mode	Accuracy Ratio (%)	p-value of relative gain of v3.2 in Log likelihood	Accuracy Ratio (%)	p-value of relative gain of v3.2 in Log likelihood
RiskCalc v3.2	61.0	–	49.3	–
RiskCalc v3.1	60.9	0.1152	47.7	<.0001
RiskCalc v1.0	59.0	<.0001	48.6	<.0001
Z-score	29.7	<.0001	24.7	<.0001

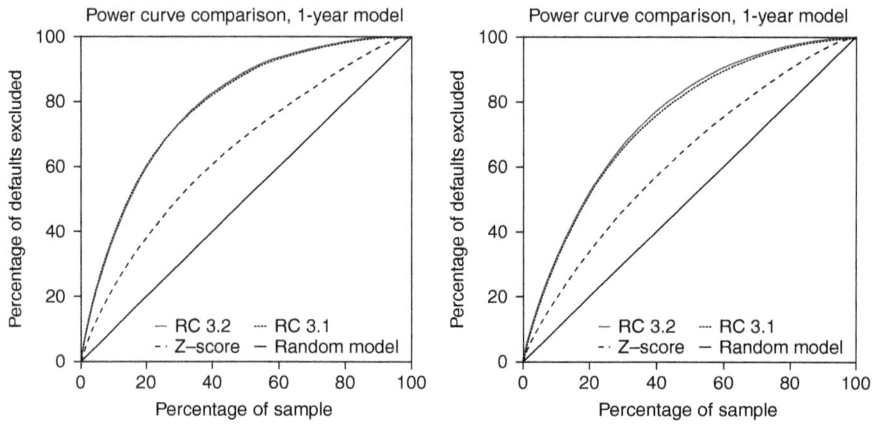

Figure 5.8 Power of alternative models (1- and 5-year) – Japan, full sample

For the overall sample, the new RiskCalc v3.2 model outperformed the Z-score model by more than 30 percentage points at the 1-year horizon, and 25 percentage points at the 5-year horizon.[9]

Figure 5.8 presents the cumulative accuracy profiles for the 1- and 5-year models corresponding to Table 5.8. It shows the power improvement of RiskCalc v3.2, RiskCalc v3.1, and the Z-score. These power improvements are uniformly significant across different regions of the distribution relative to Z-score.

5.1.3.2 Correlations and variance inflation factors

In this section, we present the correlation coefficients (Table 5.9) for the model ratios and the VIF (Table 5.10). These analyses check for excessive multicollinearity in the model.

Table 5.9 displays the Spearman Rank correlation coefficients computed on the transformed variables as they enter into the probit regression (Figure 5.4). The highest correlation coefficient is between

Table 5.9 Correlations among the transformed input factors (Spearman rank)

Inventory to net sales										
EBITDA to	1.00									
interest expense	0.18	1.00								
net sales growth										
Total liabilities less	0.13	0.17	1.00							
Cash to total assets	0.06	0.26	0.08	1.00						
Cash to total assets	0.06	0.12	0.02	0.61	1.00					
Gross profit to										
total assets	0.14	0.19	0.09	0.17	0.29	1.00				
Retained earnings to										
total liabilities	0.06	0.37	0.11	0.66	0.27	0.12	1.00			
Trade receivables to										
net sales	0.09	0.07	0.08	0.05	0.08	0.11	0.05	1.00		
Previous year net										
Income to net sales	0.06	0.33	0.06	0.22	0.07	0.02	0.34	0.04	1.00	
Real net sales	−0.02	0.21	0.14	0.30	0.27	0.12	0.30	0.02	0.00	1.00

Table 5.10 Variance inflation factors

Variable	VIF
Total liabilities less cash to total assets	2.78
Retained earnings to total liabilities	2.13
Cash to total assets	1.86
EBITDA to interest expense	1.35
Real net sales	1.33
Gross profit to total assets	1.26
Lag net income to lag net sales	1.24
Inventory to net sales	1.13
Net sales growth	1.07
Trade receivable to net sales	1.03

Retained Earnings to Total Liabilities and Total Liabilities less Cash to Total Assets. The correlation coefficient is 0.66. The second highest (0.34) is between Retained Earnings to Total Liabilities and Previous Year Net Income to Net Sales. Such coefficients are below what we would consider indications of multicollinearity that would typically cause concern. This is also verified by the VIF analysis below.

Table 5.10 presents the VIF for the financial statement variables in the model. The VIF values represent how much of the variation in one independent variable can be explained by all other independent variables in the model, which is in contrast to the pair-wise correlation coefficients in Table 5.9 that show how closely two variables move together. As Table 5.10 illustrates, in the case of all model variables

Table 5.11 Model power by industry, 1-year model

	Percentage of defaults	AR RiskCalc v3.2 (%)	AR RiskCalc v3.1 (%)	AR Z-score (%)
Business products	11.2	66.0	62.8	35.9
Construction	4.4	66.0	64.8	44.4
Consumer products	13.6	60.6	59.7	21.5
Communications and Hi Tech	10.1	63.1	61.5	30.4
Mining, Utilities and Transportation	5.3	64.5	62.1	31.0
Services	16.3	55.6	55.5	30.6
Trade	9.8	63.2	62.0	26.6

Table 5.12 Model power by industry, 5-year model

	Percentage of defaults	AR RiskCalc v3.2 (%)	AR RiskCalc v3.1 (%)	AR Z-score (%)
Business products	11.2	53.8	51.1	32.0
Construction	4.5	49.8	49.3	32.4
Consumer products	13.6	46.6	46.2	18.4
Communications and Hi Tech	10.3	47.3	46.1	25.4
Mining, Utilities and Transportation	5.2	53.0	52.3	28.8
Services	16.1	45.6	44.7	27.3
Trade	9.8	50.4	49.8	22.3

the estimated VIF values are notably below 4, thus below the commonly used threshold levels in VIF analysis when testing for presence of multicollinearity.[10] Thus, the findings strongly indicate that the model variables do not present any substantial multicollinearity.

5.1.3.3 *Model power by industry and size groups*

It is important to test the power of a model not only overall, but also among different industry segments and firm sizes. To address these issues, we conduct a series of model power tests by industry and size. We also include the power of Z-score for reference. The results are summarized for short- and long-term horizons in Table 5.11 through to Table 5.14.

Table 5.11 and Table 5.12 present the power comparisons by sector for the 1-year and 5-year models, respectively. At both horizons, RiskCalc v3.2 outperforms both RiskCalc v3.1 and Z-score across industries. The highest power in the 1-year model (see Table 5.11) is found in

Table 5.13 Model power by size (total assets in 2002 Japanese yen), 1-year model

Range	Percentage of defaults	AR RiskCalc v3.2 (%)	AR RiskCalc v3.1 (%)	AR Z-score (%)
<150mm	16.3	57.9	59.9	27.4
¥150-350mm	21.2	61.0	61.2	30.7
¥350-1 billion	28.3	62.6	61.6	31.8
¥1-2.5 billion	18.2	61.7	59.8	26.2
>¥2.5 billion	16.0	62.2	60.1	24.3

Table 5.14 Model power by size (total assets in 2002 Japanese yen), 5-year model

Range	Percentage of defaults	AR RiskCalc v3.2 (%)	AR RiskCalc v3.1 (%)	AR Z-score (%)
<150mm	17.5	44.9	44.0	20.8
¥150-350mm	22.0	49.1	47.2	23.0
¥350-1 billion	27.8	50.7	48.8	24.9
¥1-2.5 billion	18.0	52.5	50.1	27.9
>¥2.5 billion	14.6	53.3	51.3	29.1

Business Products and Construction (66.0%), while the lowest is found in Services (55.6%). At the 5-year horizon (see Table 5.12), the highest power is in Business Products (53.8%) and the lowest is in Services (45.6%).

Table 5.13 and Table 5.14 present the power comparisons by total assets (in 2002 Japanese yen) for the 1-year and 5-year models, respectively. At both horizons, RiskCalc v3.2 outperforms both RiskCalc v3.1 and Z-score in all size groups except the smallest one, with total assets less than ¥150 million. At both the 1-year and 5-year horizons, the highest power is found in the largest firms, and the lowest power is in the smallest firms under ¥150 million in assets. This finding is not surprising because the quality of financial statements generally increases with firm size. For example, larger firms are more likely to have audited statements.

Table 5.15 and Table 5.16 present the power comparisons by Net Sales (in 2002 Japanese yen) for the 1-year and 5-year models, respectively. Similar to the power comparisons by total assets, RiskCalc v3.2 outperforms both RiskCalc v3.1 and Z-score in all size groups except the smallest one, with net sales less than ¥150 million.

5.1.3.4 *Power performance over time*

Because models are implemented at various points in time in a business cycle, we conducted model power tests by year to examine whether

Table 5.15 Model power by size (net sales in 2002 Japanese yen), 1-year model

Range	Percentage of defaults	AR RiskCalc v3.2 (%)	AR RiskCalc v3.1 (%)	AR Z-score (%)
<150mm	22.0	54.3	56.2	22.3
¥150-350mm	19.9	62.1	63.1	27.9
¥350-1 billion	27.6	65.1	64.5	30.8
¥1-2.5 billion	17.1	62.1	60.1	30.7
>¥2.5 billion	13.3	61.1	58.0	32.6

Table 5.16 Model power by size (net sales in 2002 Japanese yen), 5-year model

Range	Percentage of defaults	AR RiskCalc v3.2 (%)	AR RiskCalc v3.1 (%)	AR Z-score (%)
<150mm	20.2	49.4	48.4	17.0
¥150-350mm	20.9	54.0	53.1	24.0
¥350-1 billion	27.9	55.2	53.8	26.9
¥1-2.5 billion	18.2	54.6	52.5	30.2
>¥2.5 billion	12.8	50.3	47.9	27.3

the model performance is excessively timedependent or exhibits big swings in power depending on time.

Table 5.17 and Table 5.18 present the results from this analysis at the 1- and 5-year horizons, respectively. The AR of RiskCalc v3.2 is compared with RiskCalc v3.1 and Z-score for each year. At the 1-year horizon, RiskCalc v3.2 outperforms RiskCalc v3.1 except during the period of 1997–2000. It outperforms Z-score by a sizeable margin for all years. At the 5-year horizon, RiskCalc v3.2 consistently outperforms both RiskCalc v3.1 and Z-score for all years.

5.1.3.5 Model calibration and implied ratings

- As many credit analysts are trained to differentiate credit quality in terms of letter grades, in order to assist the interpretation of an EDF, we map the EDF credit measures to.EDF ratings (an EDF-implied letter grade) utilizing Moody's bond default studies. All RiskCalc v3.1 models (or later versions) to date have used the same mapping. This mapping is designed with the following considerations:
- There is a large range of EDF ratings (as required for economic and regulatory applications).
- No one rating contains too many credits (as required for economic and regulatory applications).

Table 5.17 Model power over time, 1-year horizon

Year	Percentage of defaults	AR RiskCalc v3.2 (%)	AR RiskCalc v3.1 (%)	AR Z-score (%)
1992	0.5	65.8	65.8	26.3
1993	1.8	66.9	64.7	30.6
1994	2.3	66.0	64.9	30.8
1995	5.1	67.9	67.0	32.4
1996	7.2	62.6	62.2	30.9
1997	8.3	60.0	60.3	32.3
1998	7.8	64.0	65.2	35.3
1999	5.9	63.2	66.3	37.4
2000	5.9	58.9	61.8	30.5
2001	16.2	62.8	61.9	28.1
2002	14.2	60.6	59.7	26.9
2003	8.0	54.1	52.7	22.1
2004	8.3	52.5	50.6	24.8
2005	8.7	53.9	51.8	31.2

Table 5.18 Model power over time, 5-year model

Year	Percentage of defaults	AR RiskCalc v3.2 (%)	AR RiskCalc v3.1 (%)	AR Z-score (%)
1992	1.8	58.6	56.7	29.2
1993	2.6	56.9	54.9	26.6
1994	3.9	55.4	54.1	26.4
1995	8.6	55.9	54.9	28.8
1996	9.3	55.3	54.2	28.6
1997	9.5	53.4	52.3	30.7
1998	8.3	54.0	53.1	31.1
1999	6.5	53.2	51.9	31.6
2000	4.5	55.2	54.0	30.0
2001	13.7	55.9	54.5	24.6
2002	12.7	50.3	48.8	23.1
2003	8.1	44.3	41.4	19.6
2004	6.2	47.4	44.1	22.9
2005	4.3	54.3	51.0	28.8

- The distribution of the 5-year ratings is approximately the same as the distribution of 1-year ratings (for consistency with rating-based analysis applications).
- The EDF credit measure associated with an EDF rating is approximately the same as the observed historical default rate associated with a Moody's Bond Rating (for consistency with rating-based analysis applications).

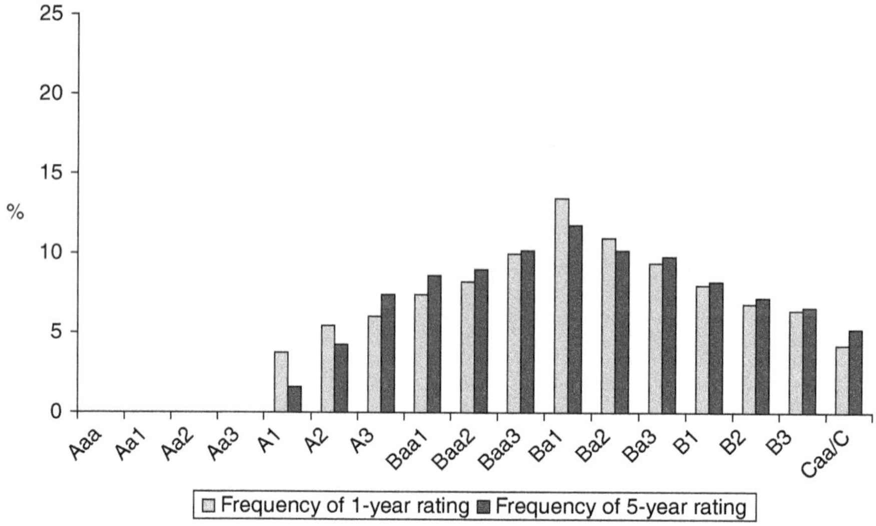

Figure 5.9 EDF-implied ratings for the 1- and 5-year models in the development sample

Table 5.19 Information on new private firm sample data

Japanese private firms	New data	RiskCalc v3.2 Japan
Financial statements	36,000+	955,000+
Unique number of firms	33,000+	201,000+
Defaults	420+	12,000+
Time period	2006–2008	1992–2005

Figure 5.9 shows the distribution of CRD observations by rating category in the development sample (for the CCA EDF values over the full time period). Note that 13 categories between A1 and Caa/C are utilized, and that less than 14% of the observations are in any one category. For both the 1-year and 5-year models, the distribution peaks at Ba1. While not reported here, other research has shown that the distribution of the CCA.EDF ratings changes over time with the credit cycle while the distribution of the FSO.EDF ratings remains relatively stable over time.

5.1.3.6 New data validation

Table 5.19 compares new data received in October 2008 with the RiskCalc v3.2 Japan development sample information.

Table 5.20 Overall power of the RiskCalc v3.2 Japan 1-year model—new data

Model	Accuracy Ratio (%)	p-value of relative gain over over v3.2 in Log likelihood
RiskCalc v3.2	59.5	–
RiskCalc v3.1	57.9	<.0001

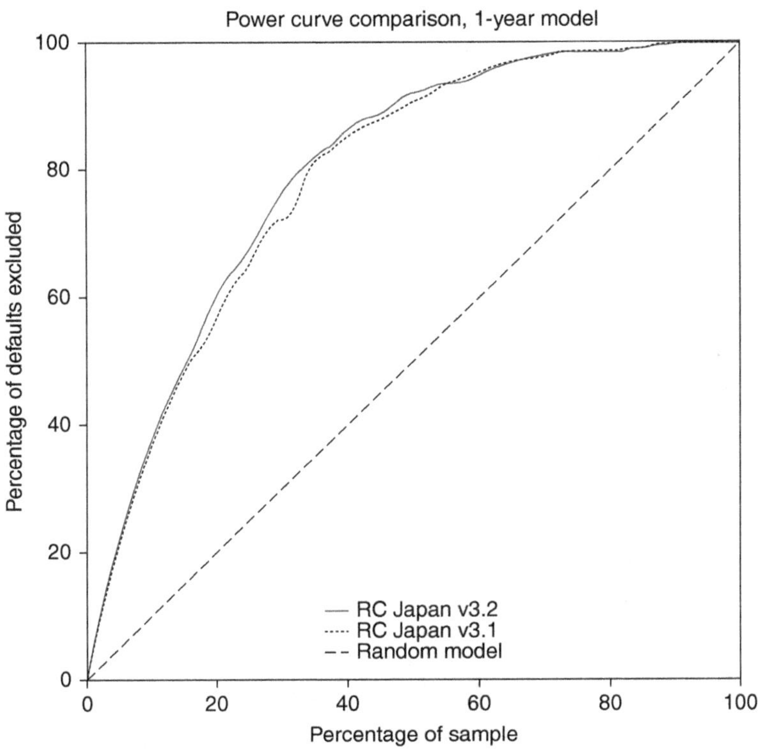

Figure 5.10 Power of alternative models (1 -year): new data

We ran the data through both RiskCalc Japan v3.2 and v3.1 in order to examine the performance of v3.2 versus v3.1. Table 5.20 and Figure 5.10 show the overall power performance of v3.2 versus v3.1. The new model has significant power gains over v3.1.

5.1.4 Further model improvements

In this section, we briefly outline some other improvements to the model.[11]

Table 5.21 Term structure of EDF credit measures: an example

EDF	Cumulative	Forward	Annualized
Year 1	4.23	4.23	4.23
Year 2	7.00	2.90	3.57
Year 3	9.37	2.55	3.23
Year 4	11.49	2.34	3.01
Year 5	13.44	2.20	2.84

5.1.4.1 Continuous term structure

The previous version of the RiskCalc model provided the user with two discrete default probability estimates: a 1- year and a 5-year EDF credit measure. In this version, utilizing the two point estimates for 1- and 5-year estimates we fit a Weibull function, and thus achieve a continuous term structure of EDF values for each credit. In other words, users of RiskCalc v3.2 Japan can now obtain EDF values for any point between 1 and 5 years. In addition, RiskCalc v3.2 provides EDF values for alternative definitions, such as the Forward EDF and the Annualized EDF (See Table 5.21).

Cumulative EDF credit measures A cumulative EDF credit measure gives the probability of default over that time period. For example, a 5-year cumulative EDF credit measure of 13.44% means that that company has a 13.44% chance of defaulting over that 5-year period. The second column of Table 5.21 provides an example of the cumulative 1- to 5-year credit measures produced by the model.

Forward EDF credit measures The forward EDF is the probability of default between t-1 and t, conditional upon survival until t-1. In other words, the 4-year forward EDF credit measure is the probability that a firm will default between years 3 and 4, assuming the firm survived to year 3.[12] The third column of Table 5.21 displays the forward 1- to 5-year EDF credit measures derived from the forward EDF values.

Annualized EDF credit measures The annualized EDF credit measure is the cumulative EDF value for a given period, stated on a per year basis. For example, a company with a cumulative 5-year EDF credit measure of 13.44% would have a 5-year annualized EDF of 2.84%.[13] This means that the average default rate per year for a 13.44% cumulative default rate is 2.84%. The last column of Table 5.21 presents the annualized EDF credit measures for years 1 to 5. These credit measures are derived from the cumulative EDF values.

5.1.4.2 New analytical tools

The RiskCalc v1.0 application provides users with an analytical tool to gauge the relative impact of each variable – as a deviation from the mean of each ratio. To equip users with further tools, we developed relative sensitivities (also known as sensitivity multiples), which exhibit the EDF sensitivity to each of the model variables at the point of evaluation. This feature is especially useful when addressing the topic of identifying variables to improve the EDF value of a company.

The relative sensitivity gives the impact of a small change in a variable on the EDF level of the company. It indicates which variables are most sensitive to an increase. A positive number means an increase in the variable will increase risk and a negative number will decrease risk. The percentile is the sensitivity of the variable relative to the average.

For example, a small increase in the activity ratio (Trade Receivables/Net Sales) will change the risk of the company. It is about 300% (1 year) as sensitive as the average variables (Figure 5.11).

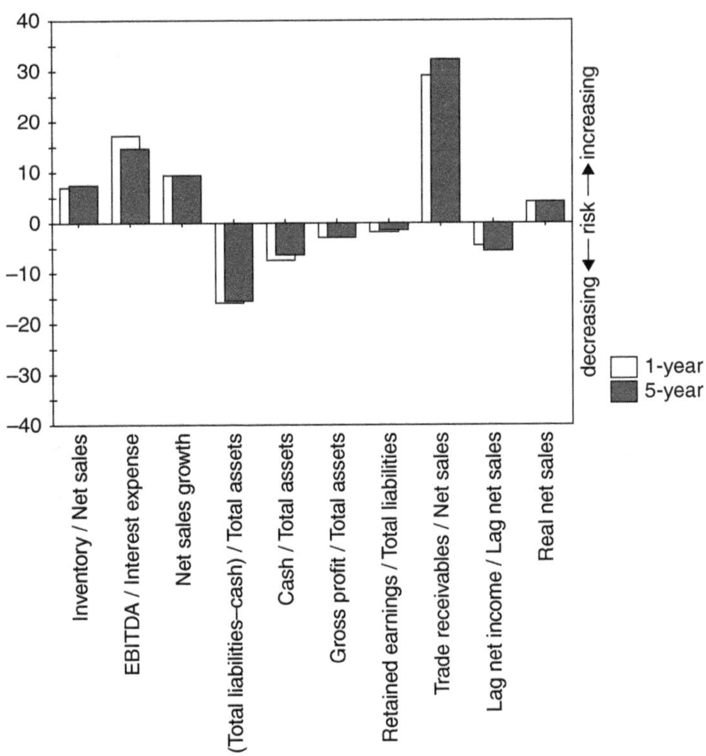

Figure 5.11 Relative sensitivities for the RiskCalc v3.2 Japan model

5.1.4.3 Asset value and volatility calculation

One of the features of the PFM model that is appreciated by users is an implied asset value and an estimate of the firm's volatility. This feature is useful for example in analysing IPO activities. In order to address this question, as an add-on to the model we estimate the asset volatility of the firm using its industry and size and a methodology that is very similar to the PFM model. We then use a structural model framework to solve for the implied asset value from the estimated EDF value, the estimated volatility, and the firm's liability structure.

5.1.4.4 Percentile map

The percentile map feature allows users to quickly isolate the problematic ratios for a given company. As shown in Figure 5.12, each horizontal bar represents a ratio that is labelled on the left (e.g., Lag Income to Lag Sales). The column on the right displays the actual value of the ratio. The percentage number within the horizontal bar graph represents the percentile of the ratio within the development sample (e.g., 92.6% of the development sample had a prior year Net Income to Sales ratio of less than 4.66%). The shading represents the risk level associated with the ratio: light grey is low risk, dark grey is high risk and grey is neutral risk. The variables shaded red to green represent "good" ratios

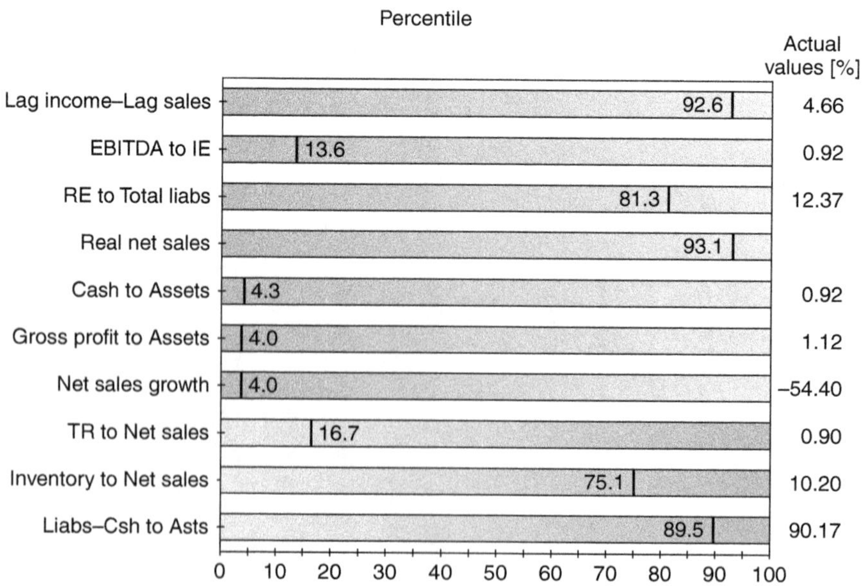

Figure 5.12 Ratio percentile analysis for the RiskCalc v3.2 Japan model

for which high values lower risk, while the variables shaded green to red represent "bad" ratios for which high values increase risk. Net Sales growth is shaded red to green to red. This demonstrates that both high and low values of sales growth indicate high risk, while moderate sales growth indicates low risk. For this hypothetical firm, the problematic ratios are EBITDA to Interest Expense, Cash to Assets, Gross Profits to Assets, Net Sales Growth, and Total Liabilities less Cash to Total Assets.

5.1.5 Conclusion

The RiskCalc v3.2 Japan is based on a substantially larger database than RiskCalc v3.1 Japan, with twice as many defaults, a 34% increase in the number of firms and a 9% increase in the number of financial statements. Furthermore, it has an additional four years of data. The model includes variables from the previous years' financial statements, which capture firm dynamics and improve model power. Improved data coverage has allowed us to further refine our financial statement model and achieve a very robust prediction model of private firm default behaviour.

RiskCalc v3.2 Japan represents a substantial advance in default prediction for private Japanese firms. The model is more powerful than any publicly available alternatives that we have tested. We demonstrated how the increase in power is consistent across industry sectors, size classifications, and regions, as well as for different time periods.

As with RiskCalc v3.1 Japan, the RiskCalc v3.2 model controls for differences in the default risk across industries in the FSO mode. In addition, it also adjusts the EDF level to reflect the current stage of the credit cycle in the given industry. If default risk in a given firm's industry is high, then the EDF level is adjusted upward. Likewise, when default risk in the industry is low, the EDF level is adjusted downward. This additional feature of the model increases the model power and precision and allows users to monitor their portfolios on a monthly basis.

In addition, the framework for RiskCalc v3.1 and v3.2 models offers further enhancements, such as a continuous term structure, providing EDF values for any point between 1 and 5 years, newer analytic tools, and the ability to calculate asset value and volatilities using a structural model framework.

This model is useful for financial institutions seeking to implement quantitative tools for originating loans, managing portfolio risk, and meeting regulatory requirements. It also provides a benchmark of the risk associated with a private firm, useful in securitizing middle-market debt. Finally, as an established objective external benchmark, RiskCalc will enable institutions to communicate between each other about their exposures.

5.2 Business case: Nippon Solar

5.2.1 Introduction to Nippon Solar

Nippon Solar is a big player in the photovoltaic (PV) solar modules manufacturing industry, and a premier provider of comprehensive PV solar systems.

Nippon Solar is one of the first companies to integrate non-silicon thin film technology into high-volume low-cost production.

The company has been able to attract customers through a competitive pricing strategy combined with a replicable low-cost manufacturing process. By continuing to expand its production and improve its technology and manufacturing process, the management believes that the company can further reduce manufacturing costs per watt and improve its cost advantage over traditional crystalline silicon solar module manufacturers.

The company's objective is to become one of the biggest solar module manufacturers within 5 years, capable of offering a solar electricity solution that competes on a non-subsidised basis with the price of retail electricity in East Asia.

5.2.2 Business model and competitive advantages

Nippon Solar Inc. was founded in 2001 to bring an advanced thin film semiconductor process into commercial production through the acquisition of predecessor technologies and the initiation of a research, development and production program that allowed the company to improve upon the predecessor technologies. It launched its commercial operations in January 2004. The company designs and manufactures solar modules using a proprietary thin film semiconductor technology that has enabled it to reduce its average solar module manufacturing costs.

Its products consist of solar modules, supported by:

- certifications;
- a solar module warranty;
- a recycling program.

In 2008, its average manufacturing costs were $1.60 per watt, significantly lower than those of manufacturers of traditional crystalline silicon solar modules.

By continuing to expand its production output and improve its technology and manufacturing process, the management believes that the company can further reduce its manufacturing costs per watt and improve its cost advantage over traditional crystalline silicon solar module manufacturers.

Nippon Solar manufactures its solar modules on high-throughput production lines using a fully automated, proprietary and continuous manufacturing process.

The company's net sales grew from $10 million in 2007 to $63 million in 2010. Strong market demand and a positive customer response to Nippon Solar's modules, together with its ability to expand its production with no raw material constraints, have meant that Nippon Solar has had the opportunity to rapidly expand its sales and thereby increase its market share.

Nippon Solar has long-term solar module supply contracts with 12 East Asian project developers and system integrators that in aggregate will allow a turnover of approximately $500 million between 2011 and 2015.

In order to satisfy its contractual requirements and address additional market demand, Nippon Solar is planning to expand its annual manufacturing capacity from 40MW to 180MW by the first half of 2013.

Nippon Solar is able to rely on a number of competitive strengths that have put the company in a good position to become one of the biggest players in the East Asian solar energy industry and compete in the broader electric power industry.

- **Cost-per-watt advantage:** proprietary thin film semiconductor technology allowed the company to achieve an average manufacturing cost of $1.60 per watt in 2008, one of the lowest in East Asia and significantly less than the per watt manufacturing cost of crystalline silicon solar modules.
- **Continuous and scalable production process:** Nippon Solar manufactures its solar modules on high-throughput production lines using an automated, proprietary, continuous process at every step in the manufacturing phase, from semiconductor deposition to final assembly and testing.
- **Replicable production facilities:** the company uses a systematic replication process to build new production lines with operating metrics that are comparable to the performance of existing production lines, taking advantage of economies of scale, accelerated

development cycles and leveraged operations, thus enabling further reductions in the manufacturing cost-per-watt of solar modules.

- **Stable supply of raw materials:** Nippon Solar is not currently constrained by, and does not foresee any shortage of, its semiconductor materials.
- **Pre-sold capacity through long-term supply contracts:** Long-term supply contracts provide predictable net sales and enable economies of scale to be rapidly achieved through expansion in capacity. By pre-selling the solar modules to be produced on future production lines, Nippon Solar is able to minimise the customer demand risk of its rapid expansion plans.

Global demand for electricity is expected to increase to 27.1 trillion kilowatt hours in 2025, according to the Energy Information Administration. Japan positions itself as the third largest market with 484MW, but is also showing important growth potential thanks to favourable political support.

However, supply constraints, rising prices, dependence on foreign countries for fuel feedstock and environmental concerns could limit the ability of many conventional sources of electricity to supply the rapidly expanding global demand.

These challenges are creating a unique growth opportunity for the renewable energy industry, including solar energy, which is the only source of renewable power with a large enough resource base to supply a significant percentage of the world's electricity needs.

The EPIA (European Photovoltaic Industry Association) revised its forecasts for 2010: the World PV Market could reach between 10.1GW and 15.5GW of new installations in 2010 under the Moderate scenario and the Policy-Driven scenario respectively, compared to 8.2GW to 12.7GW in the previous forecast. In the Policy-Driven scenario, the world annual PV market could reach up to 30GW in 2014 providing, of course, that favourable conditions are established by policy makers, regulators and the energy sector as a whole.

The annual market developed from less than 1GW in 2003 to more than 7.2GW in 2009, in spite of the difficult financial and economic circumstances. After a 160% increase in the CAGR (Compound Annual Growth Rate) from 2007 to 2008, the PV market continued to grow another 15% in 2009.

The solar energy and renewable energy industries are both highly competitive and continually evolving as participants strive to distinguish themselves within their markets and compete within the larger electric power industry.

Within the renewable energy industry, Nippon Solar's main sources of competition are: a) crystalline silicon solar module manufacturers, b) thin film solar module manufacturers and c) companies developing solar thermal and concentrated photovoltaic technologies.

Among photovoltaic module and cell manufacturers, the principal methods of competition are:

- price per watt;
- production capacity;
- conversion efficiency;
- reliability.

Nippon Solar competes favourably on all of these grounds.

Within the photovoltaic industry, Nippon Solar faces competition from crystalline silicon solar cell and module manufacturers, including BP Solar, Evergreen Solar, Kyocera, Motech, Q-Cells, Renewable Energy Corporation, Sanyo, First Solar, Schott Solar, Sharp, SolarWorld, Sunpower and Suntech, and expects to compete with future entrants to the photovoltaic industry that offer new technological solutions.

Some of Nippon Solar's competitors are larger and have greater financial resources, larger production capacities and greater brand name recognition than Nippon Solar enjoys and may, as a result, be better positioned to adapt to changes in the industry or the economy as a whole. A bigger competitor's greater size provides them with a competitive advantage in that they can often achieve economies of scale and purchase certain raw materials at lower prices.

Many of Nippon Solar's competitors also have greater brand name recognition, more established distribution networks, larger customer bases, and well-established relationships with current and potential distributors that have extensive knowledge of the target markets.

As a result of their greater size, some of Nippon Solar's competitors may be able to devote more resources to the research, development, promotion and sale of their products or to respond more quickly to evolving industry standards and changes in market conditions than the company is able to do.

5.2.3 Equity valuation

At year n, Nippon Solar presented the following balance sheet and income statements. The accounting forecasts from year $n+1$ to year $n+3$ are also reported (see Figure 5.13, Figure 5.14).

Income statement

US$ thousand	Fiscal Year n+3	n+2	n+1	n
Net sales	958,138	577,935	233,704	62,590
Cost of sales	*(573,745)*	*(363,350)*	*(167,123)*	*(37,436)*
Gross profit	384,394	214,584	66,581	25,154
Research and development	*(46,245)*	*(15,543)*	*(7,005)*	*(2,950)*
Sales, general and administrative	*(136,548)*	*(80,705)*	*(38,140)*	*(15,464)*
Production start-up	*(16,449)*	*(15,070)*	*(7,822)*	*(5,437)*
Operating income	**185,151**	**103,267**	**13,614**	**1,303**
Foreign currency (loss) gain	2,415	2,653	872	2,571
Interest income	586	490	231	1
Interest expense, net	(24,052)	(14,520)	(5,063)	(1,515)
Other income (expense), net	(1,384)	(433)	(565)	(371)
Income tax (expense) benefit	(84,382)	(53,535)	1,109	(2,414)
Net income	**78,333**	**37,922**	**10,197**	**(424)**

Figure 5.13 Nippon Solar income statements

Balance sheet

US$ thousand	n+3	n+2	n+1	n
Cash and cash equivalents	58,141	32,125	37,465	22,868
Marketable securities, current and noncurrent	58,602	48,969	23,071	150
Accounts receivable, net	155,184	178,613	108,423	92,577
Inventories, current and noncurrent	280,927	206,367	168,643	47,656
Property, plant and equipment, net	608,518	390,741	199,448	82,945
Project assets, current and noncurrent	71,099	-	-	-
Deferred tax assets, current and noncurrent	70,575	33,039	25,830	-
Other assets	259,848	90,684	73,024	**22,070**
Total assets	**1,562,894**	**980,537**	**635,905**	**268.267**
Long-term financial debt	1,202,616	725,284	428,849	75,747
Accrued solar module collection and recycling liability	43,033	16,341	6,065	1,727
Other liabilities				
Total liabilities	**1,245,649**	**741,625**	**434,914**	**77,474**
Total shareholders' equity	**317,246**	**238,912**	**200,990**	**190,793**
Total liabilities & Shareholders' equity	**1,562,894**	**980,537**	**635,904**	**268,267**

Figure 5.14 Nippon Solar balance sheets

As can be seen from the forecasted accounting data, the expansion of investments and sales is assumed to be financed by debt. In the negotiation process, two capital injections have been agreed in order to maintain a debt/equity ratio in the range 0.5–1.1. The first capital increase, amounting to US$ 250 million, will be made in year $n+2$, and the second capital increase of US$ 450 million will be made in year $n+3$.

The equity valuation process is carried out using two different approaches:

1) the present value of future earnings, net of both capital increases;
2) the NAV.

5.2.3.1 Discounted earnings methodology

The key inputs used in the estimation process are as follows:

- risk free rate as per the Japanese 10-years' Government Bond rate, about 1.1%;
- equity risk premium estimated for the Japanese Equity Market is 6.7%;
- equity beta for East Asia power generation industry is 1.09;
- growth rate is 2.5%;
- discount rates on the two capital increases are assumed to be equal to the risk free rate;
- the expected and normalized perpetual earnings are assumed to be the year $n+3$ earnings.

The cost of equity is determined using the CAPM as follows:

$$\text{Cost of Equity} = \text{Risk Free Rate} + \beta \cdot (\text{Equity Risk Premium})$$

$$\text{Cost of Equity}_{\text{Nippon Solar}} = 1.1\% + 1.09 \cdot (6.7\%) = 8.403\%$$

The equity fair value is calculated as the present value of future earnings, net of the present value of the two capital increases. The discount rate of future earnings is the cost of equity; the discount rate of capital injections is the risk free rate.

$$\begin{aligned} W = {} & 10.197 \times (1+0.08403)^{-1} + 37.922 \times (1+0.08403)^{-2} \\ & + \frac{78.333}{8.403\% - 2.5\%} \times (1+0.08403)^{-2} \\ & - 250 \times (1+0.011)^{-2} - 450 \times (1+0.011)^{-3} \end{aligned}$$

$$W = 1{,}170.957 - 680.060$$

$$W = US\$490.897\,\text{million}$$

5.2.3.2 Net Asset Value methodology

In order to express the NAV with embedded intangible assets (as the long-term value of the solar module supply contracts) the valuations below are carried out:

- revaluation of fixed assets: US$ 15 million;
- NPV of supply contracts: US$ 35 million;
- write-down on current assets: US$ 10 million;
- tax effect: US$ 12 million.

Nippon Solar's NAV is equal to US$ 228.99 million, as follows:

$$\begin{aligned}\text{NAV} &= \text{Equity Book Value} + \text{Revaluation of fixed assets} \\ &\quad + \text{NPV of Supply Contracts} - \\ &\quad \text{Write-down on current assets} - \text{Tax effect;} \\ \text{NAV} &= 200.99 + 15 + 35 - 10 - 12; \\ \text{NAV} &= US\$228.99 \text{ million}\end{aligned}$$

The Nippon Solar NAV estimate seems to be largely confirmed by the Earnings-Based Method, where the difference between US$ 490.868 million and US$ 228.99 million could be explained by the company's goodwill. However, if we replace the earnings-based method with the IAPM (Integrated Asset Pricing Model), a significantly different picture emerges of the value of Nippon Solar.

5.2.4 The new approach

According to the IAPM, Nippon Solar's cost of equity is the maximum of either the risk premium calculated using the CAPM, or the risk premium determined following the FIA.

As shown in the previous paragraph, Nippon Solar's cost of equity as based on the CAPM is equal to 8.403%.

Nippon Solar's cost of equity with the FIA (see Chapter 3) can be defined by carrying out the following calculations:

1. Probability of default valuation;
2. Equity Expected Loss (EEL) calculation;
3. Equity Risk Premium (ERP) determination.

Nippon Solar's probability of default is 1.88%, that is to say there is a 1.88% probability that shareholders will lose all of their capital (recovery rate zero) (see Floor Theorem, Chapter 3); on the other hand, the probability of shareholder losing at least 1 US dollar is equal to 16.5% (see Cap Theorem, Chapter 3).

The combined rule to calculate the EEL is as follows:

EEL = default probability + (probability of losing at least
1 US dollar – default probability) 50%;

EEL = 1.88% + (16.5% – 1.88%) 50%;

EEL = 9.19%.

The last step is to compute the ERP based on the EEL and the probability of winning at least 1 US dollar. A rule-of-thumb approach is to define the size of "bet" that would need to be won in order to compensate the shareholders for the EEL with a probability equal to "1 *minus* the probability of losing at least 1 US dollar", as follows:

Probability of winning at least 1 US dollar
× Equity Risk Premium = Equity Expected Loss;

Equity Risk Premium = Equity Expected Loss/
Probability of winning at least 1 US dollar;

Equity Risk Premium = 9.19%/(1 – 16.5%);

Equity Risk Premium = 9.19%/83.5%;

Equity Risk Premium = 11%;

Cost of Equity = Risk free rate + Equity Risk Premium;

Cost of Equity = 1.1% + 11%;

Cost of Equity = 12.1% (FIA).

In this case the ERP calculated with the FIA is higher than the ERP based on the CAPM, and it is therefore advisable to use 12.1% as Nippon Solar's cost of equity.

If we assume that Nippon Solar's cost of equity is equal to 12.1%, the equity fair value based on the present value of future earnings, net of the present value of the two capital increases, changes dramatically (we need to remember that the discount rate of future earnings is the cost of equity while the discount rate of capital injections is the risk free rate).

$$
\begin{aligned}
W &= 10.197 \times (1+0.121)^{-1} + 37.922 \times (1+0.121)^{-2} \\
&\quad + \frac{78.333}{12.1\% - 2.5\%} \times (1+0.121)^{-2} \\
&\quad - 250 \times (1+0.011)^{-2} - 450 \times (1+0.011)^{-3} \\
W &= 688.599 - 680.060 \\
W &= US\$8.539\,\text{million}
\end{aligned}
$$

As we can see the two results of using the earnings-based method, the first deriving from the CAPM and the second deriving from the FIA, are very different: Nippon Solar's equity value changes from US$ 490.897 million to US$ 8.539 million. Moreover, with regards the FIA cost of equity, there is no goodwill and the NAV will need to be reduced because there is a bad will value (US$ 228.99 million – US$ 8.539 million). In other words, based on the FIA cost of equity, Nippon Solar's value is almost zero if the buyer needs to inject US$ 700 million within two years.

6
Integrated Pricing Model in China

6.1 RiskCalc China*

6.1.1 Data description

The data source for the RiskCalc v3.1 China model is the Moody's Analytics CRD, which acquired the financial statement data of Chinese firms from data vendors. The default data are manually collected from publicly available channels.

6.1.1.1 Definition of default

In general, when building RiskCalc models, we seek to collect all credit events where economic loss occurred. We also include all defaults that are consistent with the Basel definitions, provided that the information is available on these defaults. However, when building a specific PD or internal rating model, for various reasons we probably cannot collect all possible types and all possible cases of defaults. The RiskCalc China v3.1 model was built with publicly available default information. The default data is comprised mostly of bankruptcy cases, with a small number of non-bankruptcy, missing-payment type defaults. We have made a number of modelling choices to reflect default types beyond bankruptcies and missing-payments that are not captured in our data at this time.

6.1.1.2 Data exclusions

Excluded companies As in other RiskCalc v3.1 models, we exclude certain types of companies because the financial statements or characteristics of these firms differ from the typical firms in our development sample. The following types of companies are not included in the data:

- **Firms without complete financial statements** – We require that a financial statement has a non-missing net income number and positive total assets and sales numbers. The sample includes all firms large enough to produce financial statements in compliance with local accounting standards. Less than 1% of the sample firms have assets smaller than US$100,000.

- **Financial Institutions** – The balance sheets of financial institutions (banks, insurance companies, and investment companies) exhibit higher leverage than the typical firm. The regulation and capital requirements of these institutions differentiate them from other firms. Therefore, they are excluded from the database.
- **Real Estate Development Companies** – The annual accounts of real estate development and investment companies provide only a partial description of the dynamics of these firms and, therefore, their likelihood to default. This is because their financial health often hinges on a particular development.[1]
- **Public sector and non-profit institutions** – Government agencies' default risks are influenced by the states' or municipalities' unwillingness to allow them to fail. As a result, their financial results are not comparable to other private firms. Non-profit financial ratios are different from for-profit firms, particularly with regard to variables relating to net income.

Excluded financial statements We conducted plausibility checks of financial statements, such as assets not equal to liabilities plus net worth, and financial statements covering a period of less than 12 months. If errors are detected, those statements are excluded from the analysis.

6.1.1.3 Descriptive statistics of the data

Overview of the data Table 6.1 presents the data counts. The sample covers 809,776 financial statements for 304,830 firms, and 2094 defaults. Figure 6.1 presents the distribution of financial statements and defaults by year in the development sample. The sample covers the time period ranging from 2003 to 2009.

Robustness of the data When building a model, we need to examine potential database weaknesses. Not only does the database need to cover a large number of firms and defaults, but the defaults also need

Table 6.1 Information on sample data

Period	Number of firms	Number of defaults	Number of statements
2003–2009	304,830	2,094	809,776

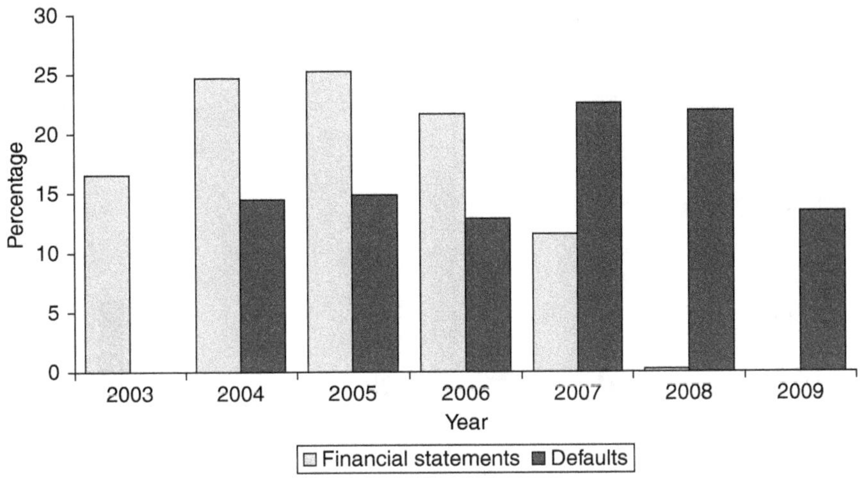

Figure 6.1 Distribution of statements and defaults by year

to be distributed among industries and company size. For example, if the database has few firms in a particular size range without sufficient defaults in those groups, the model may not produce good default risk measurements.

The RiskCalc China model assigns firms to 12 sectors by their Standard Industrial Classification (SIC) code. Firms without industry information are grouped into a category labelled Unassigned. Compared with the sector classification used in other v3.1 models, we separate CommHiTech into Communication and High Tech. We split Mining-TransUtility into three sectors: Mining, Transportation, and Utilities. We also add one new sector: Automobiles. We use the following two criteria when determining the sector classifications.

- The classification is economically meaningful.
- We have enough statements and defaults in each sector.

Figure 6.2 presents the distributions of the sample firms by industry and the proportion of defaults in each industry. Business Products and Consumer Products are the two largest sectors in our sample, consistent with the fact that industrial firms are the major components of Chinese economy. Figure 6.3 presents the distributions by firm size measured[2] as assets in US dollars. Our sample includes both large firms and small firms.

We then examine the geographic coverage of the sample. The sample covers financial statements and defaults from all 31 mainland

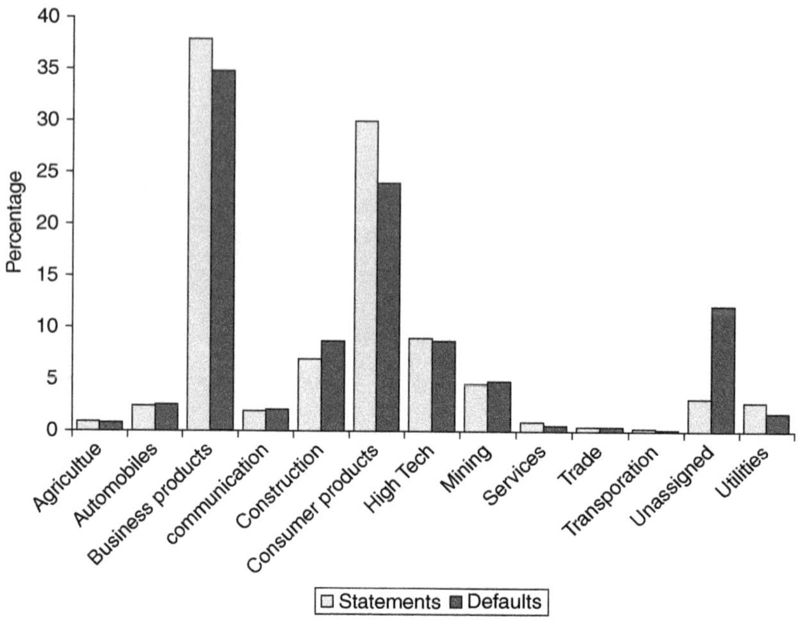

Figure 6.2 Distribution of statements and defaults by industry

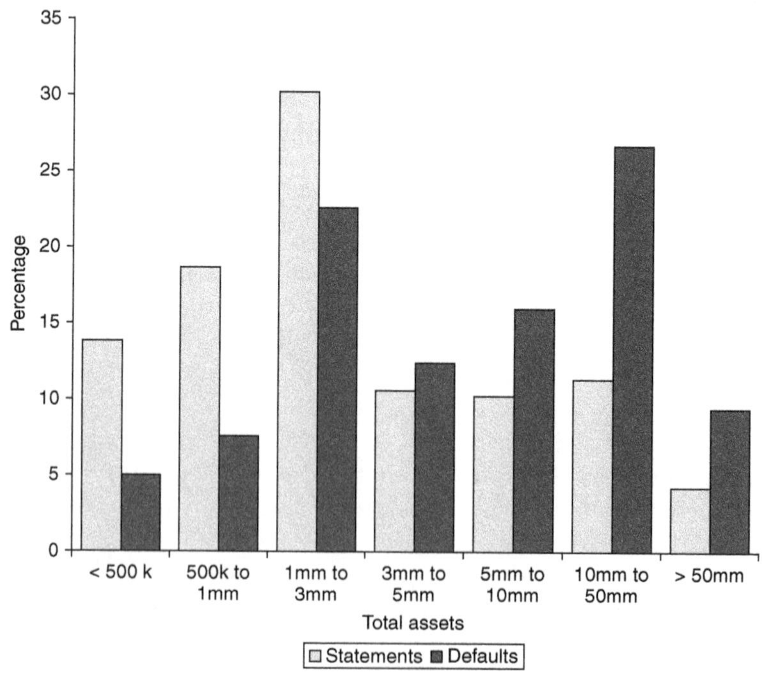

Figure 6.3 Distribution of statements and defaults by size (assets in USD)

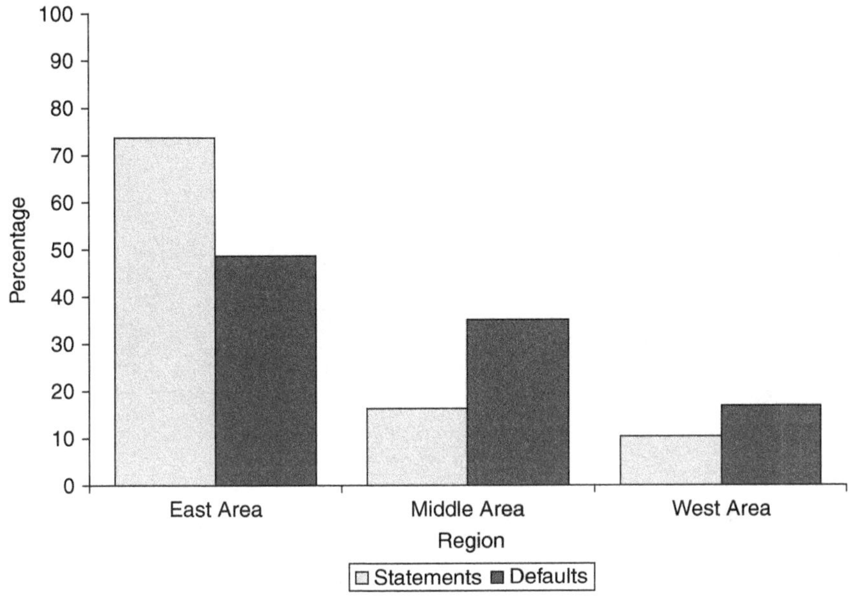

Figure 6.4 Distribution of statements and defaults by region

provinces and municipalities. We follow a classification method from the National Bureau of Statistics of China to classify the 31 provinces and municipalities into east, middle, and west areas. In China, the east area is generally more developed than the middle and west areas.

Figure 6.4 shows the distribution of the statements and defaults by region. The east area accounts for about 70% of the statements and 50% of the defaults in our sample. We compared the sample statement distribution to the GDP distribution across regions. The east area accounts for a large portion of the total GDP.[3]

We also examine the ownership types of the sample firms. The ownership structure and legal status of Chinese companies have been evolving with the progress of the legal, market, and economic development in China. Before the economic reform starting in 1978, state-owned companies dominated all other legal forms. With the sweep of the reform, other types of ownership structures have become more important. Our sample firms fall into dozens of legal forms, which we put into three categories: privately owned firms, partially or wholly state-owned firms, and partially or wholly overseas-owned firms.

Figure 6.5 presents the sample distribution over ownership structures. The state-owned firms represent less than 10% of the statements,

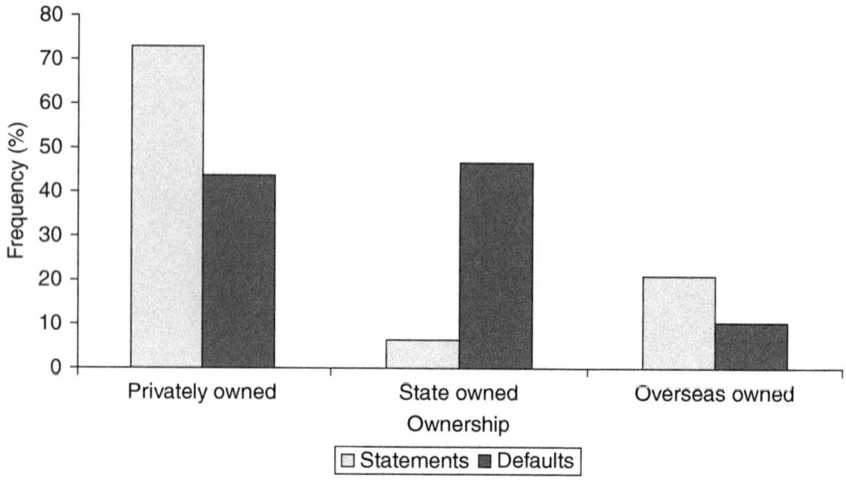

Figure 6.5 Distribution of statements and defaults by ownership type

but around 45% of defaults. One explanation is that state-owned firms were, in many cases, established during China's planned economy era, when there was no clear market exit mechanism. Many of the non-performing state-owned firms continued to operate with the support of the government and state-owned banks. During our sample period (2003–9), with the proposal and passage of the first Bankruptcy Law in China, more state-owned firms were put into bankruptcy. Later in the document we will discuss how the model performs separately for firms with different ownership structures.

6.1.1.4 Central default tendency

Because most companies do not default, companies that do default are relatively rare and thus more valuable in building a default risk model. The lack of default data may arise from data collection issues (e.g., not all defaults were captured). Also, if the date of default is uncertain, the financial statement associated with the firm may be excluded from model development, depending on the severity of the problem. This can result in a sample with lower default rates than occur in the general population. If the underlying sample is not representative, then it needs to be adjusted for the central default tendency (CDT). The CDT is an estimation of the true average PD of the development sample. When default definitions used in the data sample understate the defaulting population, the CDT can be used to realign the default rates.

The estimate of long-run aggregate probabilities of default (i.e., CDT) is important as an anchor for a model. The best estimation of default probability is a ratio that reflects the number of obligors that defaulted in one year compared with the total obligors at the beginning of that year. Often these types of data are not available.

The estimate of the CDT of the RiskCalc China v3.1 model is based on two sources.

- Confirmation of the CDT exceeding the default rates observed in our development sample by a significant margin. Because the sample default rates vary significantly with region and ownership types, we ensure that the CDT is above the sample default rate across samples cut by region and ownership types.
- Loan loss provision data from local banks. We collected loan loss provision data from 13 national banks and 16 city commercial banks.

The multiple sources of external data led us to an estimate of 3% as the CDT figure for the 1-year model.

Calculating a 5-year CDT There is a lack of publicly available data for direct calculation of the CDT of a cumulative 5-year default probability. We pick a 5-year CDT so that forward EDF values on average line up with realized EDF values. The figure used as the CDT for the 5-year model is 11.5%.

Central default tendency in CCA modes The CDT in CCA mode is equal to the CDT of the FSO mode when the effects of the credit cycle are neutral. When the forward-looking prediction of the credit cycle indicates increasing default risk, the CDT of the CCA mode will be larger, and when the effects of the credit cycle indicate decrease in default risk, CDT will be smaller.

6.1.2 Model components

The RiskCalc v3.1 model incorporates various components to determine the EDF credit measure. The inputs to the model include a selection of the financial ratios, transforms of those ratios, the inclusion of industry information, and the CCA.

The development of a RiskCalc model involves the following steps.

1. Choosing a limited number of financial statement variables for the model from a list of possible variables.[4]
2. Transforming the variables into interim probabilities of default using non-parametric techniques.

3. Estimating the weightings of the financial statement variables using a probit model, combined with industry variables.
4. Creating a (non-parametric) final transform that converts the probit model score into an actual EDF credit measure. In FSO mode, the models are based on the following functional form.

$$FSO\,EDF = F\left(\Phi\left(\sum_{i=1}^{N}\beta_i T_i(x_i) + \sum_{j=1}^{K}\gamma_j I_j\right)\right)$$

where

$x1, \ldots, xN$	are the input ratios;
$I1, \ldots, IK$	are indicator variables for each of the industry classifications;
$\gamma 1, \ldots, \gamma K$	are estimated coefficients;
D	is the cumulative normal distribution;
F and $T1, \ldots, TN$	are non-parametric transforms;
$FSO\,EDF$	is the financial statement only EDF credit measure.

The Ts are the transforms of each financial statement variable, which capture the non-linear impacts of financial ratios on the default likelihood, as is shown in Figure 6.6 and discussed in detail later. F is the final transform (i.e., the final mapping). The final transform captures the empirical relationship between the probit model score and actual default probabilities. The final transform is described as calibrating the model score to an actual EDF credit measure. The difference between the FSO EDF and the CCA EDF is that in CCA mode the final transform is adjusted to reflect our assessment of the current stage of the credit cycle, while in FSO mode it remains constant.

6.1.2.1 *Financial statement variables*

Selecting the variables Our variable selection process starts with a long list of possible financial statement variables. The working list of ratios is divided into groups that represent different underlying concepts regarding a firm's financial status (Table 6.2). A model is then built with at least one variable per group. When it is possible to increase model performance and maintain model robustness, several variables from each group will be used in the model (Table 6.3).

By non-parametric, we mean that the $T(x_i)$ is a continuous function of x not requiring a specification of a closed (i.e., parametric) functional form. We estimate these transforms using a variety of local regression and density estimation techniques.

Table 6.2 Groupings of financial statement ratios

Ratio	Description
Activity ratios	Measure a firm's operating efficiency. They typically involve working capital items such as inventory, accounts receivable, or accounts payable. A large stock of inventories relative to sales may indicate operation difficulties and high probability of default; other activity ratios have different relationships to default.
Debt coverage	The ratio of cash flow to interest payments or some other measure of liabilities. High debt coverage reduces the probability of default.
Growth variables	Typically include sales growth. These variables measure the stability of a firm's performance. Growth variables often behave like a double-edged sword: both rapid growth and rapid decline (negative growth) tend to increase a firm's default probability.
Leverage ratios	Include liabilities to assets or debt to assets. High leverage increases the probability of default.
Liquidity variables	Include cash and marketable securities to assets or liabilities, the current ratio, and the quick ratio. These variables measure the extent to which the firm has liquid assets relative to the size of its assets or liabilities. High liquidity reduces the probability of default.
Profitability ratios	Include net income, net income less extraordinary items, profit before tax, and operating profit in the numerator; and total assets, tangible assets, fixed assets and sales in the denominator. High profitability reduces the probability of default.
Size	Measured by total assets or sales deflated to a specific base year to ensure comparability. Large firms default less often.

Table 6.3 Financial statement variables in RiskCalc v3.1 China*

Category	Definition
Activity	Inventory/Sales
	Accounts
	Receivable/sales
	Sales/assets
Debt coverage	EBITDA to interest expense
Growth	Sales growth
Leverage	Net worth/total liabilities
Liquidity	Current assets/current liabilities
Profitability	Return on Assets (ROA)
	Change in operating profit margin
Size	Total sales

*EBITDA is defined as the following: Operating Profit (or Loss) + Amortization and Depreciation.

We ask the following questions when deciding which variables to include in the final model:

- Is the variable readily available?
- Are the definitions of the inputs to the variable ambiguous?
- Is the meaning of the variable intuitive?
- Does the variable help to measure default risk?
- Is the variable generally not correlated with other variables in the model?

Variable transforms After the variables are selected, they are transformed into a preliminary EDF value. Figure 6.6 presents the transformations used in the model. The horizontal axis gives the percentile score of the ratio, and the vertical axis gives the default probability of that ratio in isolation (univariate). The percentile score represents the percentage of the database that had a ratio below that of the company (e.g., if ROA is in the 90th percentile, then 90% of the sample had a lower ROA than that firm).

The shape of the transformation indicates how significantly a change in level impacts the EDF value. If the slope of the transform is steep, a small change will have a larger impact on risk than if the slope were flat.

- For the Activity group, the transforms for Accounts Receivable to Sales and Inventory to Sales are downward-sloping (Figure 6.6). When inventories and accounts receivables pile up it can indicate financial or operational troubles. The transform for Sales to Asset ratio is upward-sloping. Inability to generate sales is associated with higher default probabilities.
- For the Debt Coverage group, the transform for EBITDA to Interest Expense is downward-sloping (see Figure 6.6). This indicates that firms with large EBITDA relative to Interest Expense have lower default probabilities.
- For the Growth group, the transform of Sales Growth (see Figure 6.6) is downward-sloping, indicating that large decreases in sales are associated with higher default probabilities. On average, the sample Chinese firms have higher sales growth rate than firms in more developed markets such as the US In more developed markets, we often observe that sales growth has a U-shaped relationship with default probabilities (i.e., both sharp declines and rapid increases in sales are associated with high default risk). In building the China

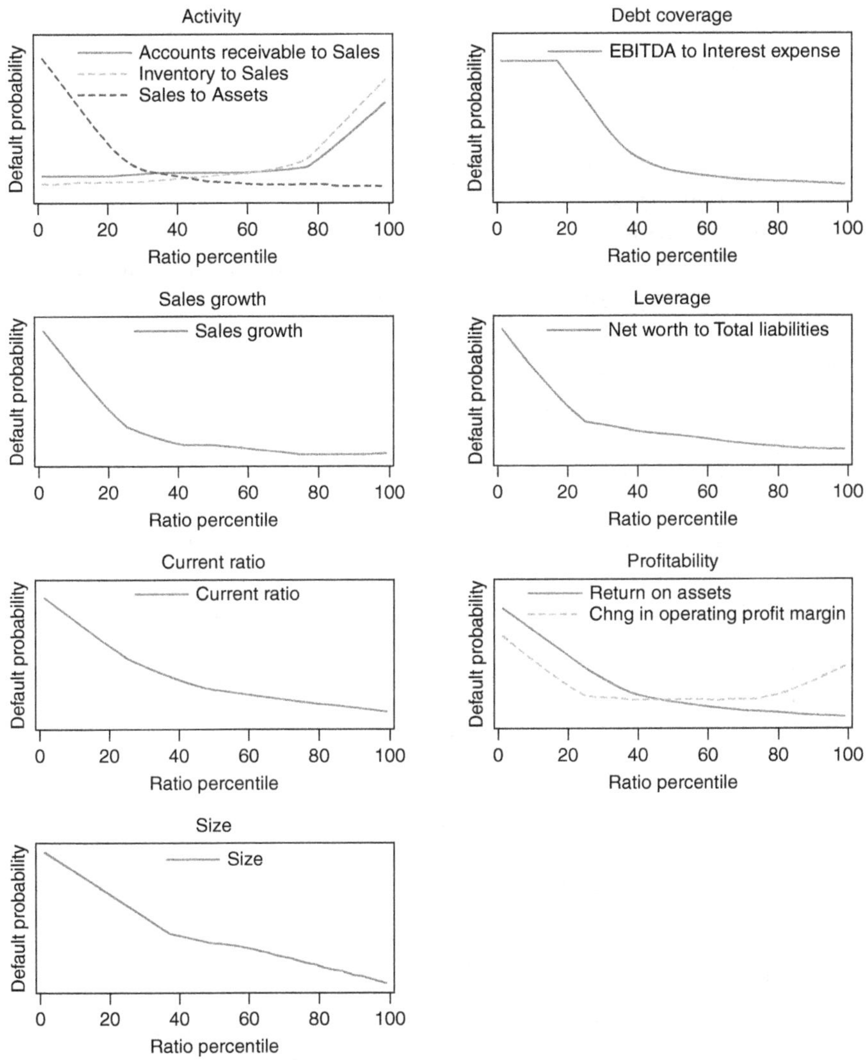

Figure 6.6 Transformations of financial statement variables in RiskCalc v3.1 China

model, we did not observe such a U-shaped relationship. Higher sales growth indicates lower default risk, although the relationship becomes flatter for high sales growth firms. The high sales growth and its association with lower default risk are consistent with the fast development of the Chinese economy during the sample period (2003–9).

- For the Leverage group, the transform for the NetWorth to Total Liabilities ratio is downward-sloping (see Figure 6.6). This indicates that firms with more leverage have higher default probabilities.
- For the Liquidity group, the transform of Current Assets to Current Liabilities is downward-sloping (see Figure 6.6), indicating that firms with more current assets to cover their current liabilities are associated with lower default probabilities.
- For the Profitability group, the transform of ROA is downward-sloping (see Figure 6.6). This indicates that firms with large ROA have lower default probabilities. The transform of Change in Operating Profit Margin is U-shaped. Very large increase or decrease in operating profit margin indicates high default probability. A sharp decline in operating profit margin can indicate that the firm has a significant increase in operating expenses relative to sales. A sudden increase in operating profit margin may come from different sources. A large increase in sales without corresponding increase in expenses can indicate financial statement manipulation, or the firm may have experienced significant changes in its core business.
- For the Size group, the transform of Size is downward-sloping (see Figure 6.6), indicating that larger firms have lower default probabilities.

6.1.2.2 Model weights

Importance The relative value of each variable used in calculating an EDF credit measure is important in understanding a company's risk. The non-linear nature of the model makes the weight of the variables more difficult to determine, because the actual impact on the risk depends on the coefficient, the transformation shape, and the percentile ranking of the company. The model weights, therefore, are calculated based on the average EDF value for the transformation and its standard deviation. A variable with a flat transformation could have a low weight, even if the coefficient is large (see Figure 6.6).

Calculation of weights To calculate the weighting of a variable, the EDF credit measure is computed for a theoretical firm with all its variables at the average transformation values. The variables are then increased one at a time by one standard deviation. The EDF change for each variable (in absolute value) is computed and added together. The relative weight of each variable is then calculated as the EDF level change for that variable as a percentage of the sum of EDF level changes across all variables. This gives the variable with the largest impact on the EDF

Table 6.4 Risk drivers in RiskCalc v3.1 China

Category	Weights: 1-year (%)	Weights: 5-year (%)
Activity	22.07	27.89
Debt coverage	11.42	12.36
Growth	4.89	1.55
Leverage	22.81	19.68
Liquidity	10.6	9.23
Profitability	23.32	23.95
Size	4.89	5.34

level the largest weight, and the variable with the smallest impact on the EDF level the smallest weight. Since the weights are a percentage of the total change in EDF levels, they sum to 100%. The weight of each category is the sum of the weights of each variable in that category.

Table 6.4 presents the weights in the RiskCalc v3.1 China model. The most important category is Profitability, with a weight of 23.32% at the 1-year horizon. Activity (with three ratios) is the most important category at the 5-year horizon.

6.1.2.3 *Industry adjustments*

For the same set of financials, different industries may have different default probabilities. The EDF value is adjusted for industry effects. RiskCalc v3.1 China has 13 industries: Agriculture, Automobile, Business Products, Communication, Construction, Consumer Products, High Tech, Mining, Services, Trade, Transportation, Utilities, and Unassigned. Firms without industry classification information or those that cannot be classified into the other 12 industries are put into Unassigned. Trade takes a coefficient that increases default risk, while Utilities takes a coefficient that decreases default risk. Given the same set of financial ratios, the Trade industry coefficient typically moves the EDF up by about one to two rating notches (e.g., from Baa1 to Baa3), and the Utilities industry coefficient typically moves the EDF down by about two to three rating notches (e.g., from Baa1 to A1). In most other RiskCalc models, industries other than Trade and Utilities also affect EDF values. In the China model, we only include these two, because they are the only two industries with significant and intuitive coefficients. This may be due to the data limitation; we will continue to research and update the model when we have enough evidence.

Table 6.5 presents the increase in model power and accuracy from introducing industry controls. The ARof the model increases slightly. The gain in log likelihood is large and statistically significant. A large

Table 6.5 Increase in model power and accuracy from introducing industry controls

FSO mode	1-year model Accuracy Ratio (%)	1-year model P-value of relative gain in Log likelihood	5-year model Accuracy Ratio (%)	5-year model P-value of relative gain in Log likelihood
Without industry controls	59.6	—	47.3	—
With industry controls	61.0	< 0.0001	49.3	< 0.0001

gain in likelihood indicates that the industry controls are important in producing an accurate EDF credit measure.

In this table and hereafter, AR is the measure of the model's ability to rank order credits. Log likelihood measures the extent to which the model's EDF values better match observed default rates.[5]

6.1.2.4 Credit cycle adjustment

EDF credit measures are impacted not only by the financials of a company, but also by the general credit cycle in the economy. To capture this effect, the RiskCalc v3.1 suite of models includes a credit cycle adjustment (CCA) factor. The CCA is designed to incorporate the current credit cycle into the estimate of private firm default risk.

Selecting an adjustment factor The RiskCalc v3.1 models use the DD calculation from the Moody's Analytics Public EDF model. This measure is specifically designed to be a forward-looking indicator of default risk. It extracts signals of default risk from the stock market performance of individual firms. This measure was chosen because it is available for a large universe of industries and has been extensively validated.

If the DD factor for public firms in an industry indicates a level of risk above the historical average for that industry, then the private firms' EDF values in that industry are adjusted upward. Conversely, if the level of risk is below the historical average for that industry, then the private firms' EDF values are adjusted downward. When the credit cycle adjustment factor is neutral, the CCA EDF value coincides with the FSO EDF value.

Adjustment factor used in the model For the China model, the DD factor is based on an aggregation of all publicly listed Chinese firms in the industry. Every month, the DD factor is calculated for each of the 13 industries.[6] Three industries – Agriculture, Communication, and Unassigned – do not have enough firms to calculate a meaningful DD

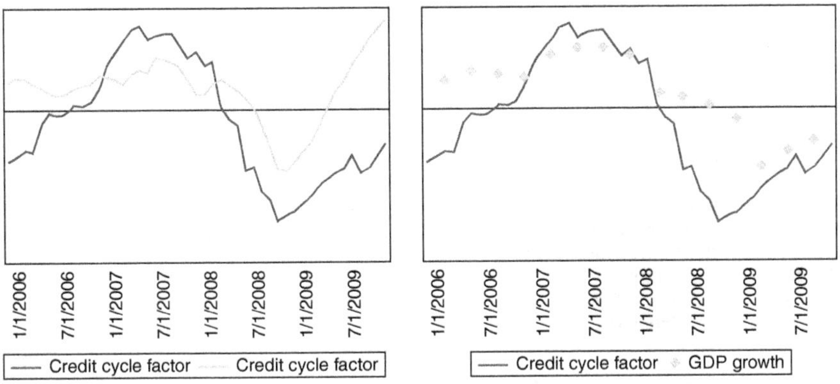

Figure 6.7 DD factor and macroeconomic indicators

factor; for these industries the model uses a CCA based on all publicly listed Chinese firms across industries.

Figure 6.7 presents the DD factor based on all publicly listed Chinese firms, and compares that to the GDP growth rate of China and the Economy Leading Index as published by the Statistics Bureau of China. The Credit Cycle factor is in line with the Economy Leading Index and the GDP growth rate. Note that the DD factor series start from 2006. Before 2006, the CCA factor does not line up well with the macroeconomic indicators. We set CCA EDF values equal to FSO EDF values before 2006.

6.1.3 Validation results

After a model is developed, it must be proven effective in measuring default risk. In this section, test results are presented on the model's ranking power (i.e., the model's ability to sort credits from worst to best).

The tests need to check not only the model effectiveness, but also its robustness and how well it works on data outside the sample. We conducted k-fold analyses for out-of-sample testing. The results of the testing showed that in general, the model is more powerful than other models across different time periods, regions, sectors, and size classifications. We also verify that the model performs effectively across different ownership types.

6.1.3.1 Overall model power and accuracy

Table 6.6 presents the in-sample overall measures of power for the RiskCalc v3.1 China model versus Altman's Z-score-China.[7] The model outperforms Z-score-China at both 1-year and 5-year horizons.

Table 6.6 Power performance of the RiskCalc v3.1 China model

	1-year model		5-year model*	
Model	Accuracy Ratio (%)	p-value	Accuracy Ratio (%)	p-value
RiskCalc China	67.8	—	64.9	—
Z-score	60.7	< .0001	55.5	< .0001

*Note that the Accuracy Ratios at the 5-year horizon are close to the Accuracy Ratios at the 1-year horizon. This is due to the short time-series of the development sample, compared with the development sample of other RiskCalc models. The 5-year model was estimated using the oldest statements prior to defaults within a five-year window. In theory, 2007 defaults should be linked to a 2002 statement when available. However, in our sample it can only be linked to a 2003 statement.

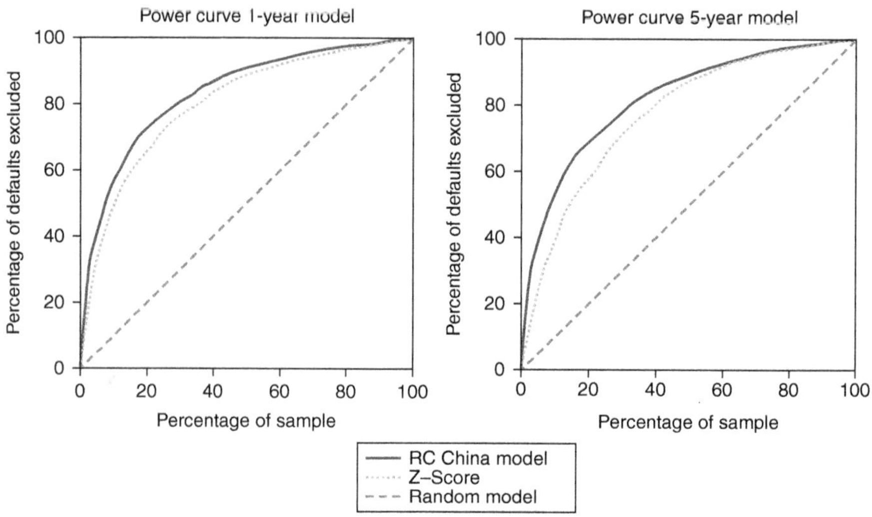

Figure 6.8 Power of alternative models (1- and 5-year): China model

Table 6.6 also contains *p*-values for the statistical test to display whether the difference between the ARs from the China model and the benchmark is equal to zero. A *p*-value of less than .05 indicates that we can reject the hypothesis that the difference in the ARs is equal to zero with 95% confidence.

Figure 6.8 presents the cumulative accuracy profiles for the 1- and 5-year models corresponding to Table 6.6. The power improvements are uniformly significant across different regions of the distribution relative to Z-score-China.

6.1.3.2 *Correlations and variance inflation factors*

To ensure model robustness, the model must be tested for excessive multicollinearity, which occurs if a number of the variables used in

Table 6.7 Correlations among the transformed input factors (Spearman rank)

Inventory/Sales	1.00									
Accounts receivable/Sales	0.24	1.00								
Sales/Assets	0.40	0.51	1.00							
EBITDA to interest expense	0.14	0.27	0.31	1.00						
Sales growth	0.14	0.18	0.20	0.17	1.00					
Net worth/Total liabilities	0.10	0.17	0.08	0.31	0.06	1.00				
Current assets/Current liabilities	−0.08	0.00	0.18	0.23	0.03	0.48	1.00			
Return on Assets (ROA)	0.17	0.34	0.39	0.71	0.21	0.34	0.25	1.00		
Change in operating profit margin	0.09	0.11	0.24	0.16	0.18	0.03	0.07	0.21	1.00	
Total sales	0.19	0.18	0.23	0.22	0.23	0.07	0.05	0.23	0.08	1.00

the model are highly correlated. Excessive multicollinearity can cause instability in parameter estimates. To check for this issue, the correlation coefficients in Table 6.7 for the financial statement ratios in the model and the variance inflation factors (VIF) in Table 6.8 are computed on the transformed variables in Figure 6.6.

The VIF levels for the financial statement variables in Table 6.8 represent how much of the variation in one independent variable can be explained by all other independent variables in the model. The correlation coefficient, however, measures only the relationships between two variables. The highest VIF level is 2.29, indicating that the collinearity between the variables is low.[8] The two ratios with the highest correlation are EBITDA to Interest Expense and ROA in Table 6.7.

6.1.3.3 *Power performance by industry and size groups*

It is important to test the power of a model not only overall, but also among different industry segments and firm sizes.

Table 6.9 and Table 6.10 present the power comparisons by sector for the 1-year and 5-year models, respectively. The highest power in the 1-year horizon (see Table 6.9) is found in Automobile (85%), while the lowest is found in Trade (44%). Business Products and Consumer Products are the two largest sectors in the development sample, and the model performs well on these two sectors (AR is 70.7% for Business

Table 6.8 Variance inflation factors

Variable	VIF
Return on Assets (ROA)	2.29
Sales/Assets	2.09
EBITDA to interest expense	2.05
Accounts receivable/Sales	1.60
Net worth/Total liabilities	1.51
Current assets/Current liabilities	1.47
Inventory/Sales	1.29
Total sales	1.14
Sales growth	1.13
Change in operating profit margin	1.10

Table 6.9 Power by industry 1-year, China model

Sector	Percentage of defaults	AR China model	AR Z-score	Diff p-value
Agriculture	0.9	47.3	45.0	0.71
Automobile	2.9	85.0	80.3	0.05
Business products	35.0	70.7	64.1	0.00
Communication	2.0	68.5	54.5	0.00
Construction	9.0	63.5	54.4	0.00
Consumer products	23.8	65.0	59.0	0.00
High Tech	10.2	70.3	66.8	0.05
Mining	4.1	58.1	54.0	0.14
Services	0.8	61.1	47.6	0.03
Trade	0.8	44.4	43.8	0.93
Transportation/Utilities	2.2	46.4	33.8	0.00
Unassigned	8.2	66.5	58.1	0.00

Table 6.10 Power by Industry 5-year: China Model

Sector	Percentage of defaults	AR China model	AR Z-score	Diff p-value
Agriculture	0.9	45.0	39.2	0.07
Automobile	2.7	76.1	71.4	0.00
Business products	34.7	67.2	58.3	0.00
Communication	2.0	64.8	53.2	0.00
Construction	8.5	58.0	47.2	0.00
Consumer products	23.4	62.9	54.9	0.00
High Tech	10.1	64.7	58.1	0.01
Mining	4.0	64.2	56.9	0.02
Services	0.8	52.7	33.1	0.55
Trade	0.8	31.7	26.5	0.96
Transportation/Utilities	2.1	40.0	24.9	0.00
Unassigned	10.0	66.5	56.8	0.07

Table 6.11 Power by size (total assets in US dollars), 1-year China model

Range	Percentage of defaults	AR China model (%)	AR Z-score (%)	Diff p-value
Less Than $500k	4.9	54.0	45.1	0.01
$500k to 1 MM	7.0	61.3	54.3	0.00
$1 MM to 3 MM	20.2	62.4	56.1	0.00
$3 MM to 5 MM	12.7	65.7	58.8	0.00
$5 MM to 10MM	16.2	71.4	65.3	0.00
$10MM to 50MM	25.5	70.1	63.0	0.00
Greater than $50MM	13.5	62.4	60.3	0.10

Table 6.12 Power by size (total assets in US dollars), 5-year China model

Range	Percentage of defaults	AR China model (%)	AR Z-score (%)	Diff p-value
Less Than $500k	5.2	53.9	47.2	0.01
$500k to 1 MM	7.1	59.1	53.1	0.00
$1 MM to 3 MM	20.1	64.2	58.0	0.00
$3 MM to 5 MM	13.0	63.2	57.5	0.00
$5 MM to 10MM	16.4	68.4	60.1	0.00
$10MM to 50MM	24.9	66.5	57.1	0.00
Greater than $50MM	13.3	47.7	40.4	0.00

Products and 65.0% for Consumer Products). Similar observations can be made at the 5-year horizon (see Table 6.10).

Table 6.11 and Table 6.12 present the power comparisons by firm size (Assets in US dollars) for the 1-year and 5-year models, respectively. The model performs well across size cuts.

6.1.3.4 Power performance over time

Because models are implemented at various points in a business cycle by design, power tests by year were conducted to examine whether the model performance is excessively time dependent.

Table 6.13 and Table 6.14 present the results from this analysis at the 1- and 5-year horizons, respectively. The AR of the RiskCalc v3.1 China model is compared with Z-score for each year. In building the model we require that the financial statements used to measure default risk are at least 1.5 years prior to the default date. Therefore, 2007 statements can only be used to measure year 2009 default risk in our sample. For this reason, 2007 is only associated with 2.3% of the total defaults used in the sample. The model performs consistently well across the sample period, and ARs are higher than that of Z-score-China for all years.

Table 6.13 Power over time: 1-year horizon, China model

Year	Percentage of defaults	AR China model (%)	AR Z-score (%)	Diff p-value
2003	30.0	60.1	53.3	0.00
2004	29.8	62.9	54.9	0.00
2005	25.3	64.0	58.5	0.00
2006	12.7	66.5	64.5	0.07
2007	2.3	60.0	51.0	0.01

Table 6.14 Power over time: 5-year horizon, China model

Year	Percentage of defaults	AR China model (%)	AR Z-score (%)	Diff p-value
2003	38.3	59.3	52.6	0.00
2004	29.9	57.9	51.1	0.00
2005	19.9	63.5	58.5	0.00
2006	10.0	66.4	64.5	0.07
2007	1.8	59.2	51.0	0.02

6.1.3.5 Power performance by region and ownership structure

Table 6.15 and Table 6.16 present the power comparison results by region. The development sample covers financial statements and defaults from all the 31 mainland provinces and municipalities. We put the sample into east, middle, and west areas, using the classification method from the National Bureau of Statistics of China. The east area is more developed than the rest of the country, accounting for 60% of the GDP. In the development sample, we also observed that the sample default rate is lower in the east area than in the middle and west areas. Given the imbalance of economic development across regions in China, it is important to ensure that the model performs well in different regions. As shown in Table 6.15 and Table 6.16, the AR of the model is high in all three regions, and consistently outperforms the benchmark model.

We also look at power comparison by ownership structure. Before the economic reform that began in the late 1970s, almost all enterprises in China were state-owned. With China's march into a market-oriented economy and the Open Door Policy, privately-owned and overseas-owned companies have become important forces of the economy. In Table 6.17 and Table 6.18, we present the results by ownership forms. The model performs well for different ownership forms.

Table 6.15 Power by area: 1-year horizon, China model

Area	Percentage of defaults	AR China model (%)	AR Z-score (%)	Diff p-value
East	48.7	63.7	56.0	0.00
Middle	32.9	68.2	61.1	0.00
West	18.4	74.3	67.3	0.00

Table 6.16 Power by area: 5-year horizon, China model

Area	Percentage of defaults	AR China model (%)	AR Z-score (%)	Diff p-value
East	48.6	62.2	53.4	0.00
Middle	33.5	67.4	58.2	0.00
West	18.0	73.4	62.1	0.00

Table 6.17 Power by ownership structure: 1-year horizon, China model

Ownership	Percentage of defaults	AR China model (%)	AR Z-score (%)	Diff p-value
Privately owned	43.1	58.5	50.3	0.00
State-owned	46.3	55.0	47.7	0.00
Overseas-owned	10.5	57.8	53.6	0.00

Table 6.18 Power by ownership structure: 5-year horizon, China model

Ownership	Percentage of defaults	AR China model (%)	AR Z-score (%)	Diff p-value
Privately owned	42.8	57.6	49.5	0.00
State-owned	46.6	53.6	40.2	0.00
Overseas-owned	10.5	49.5	44.8	0.00

6.1.3.6 Out-of-sample testing: k-fold tests

The model exhibits a high degree of power in distinguishing good credits from bad ones (Table 6.6), but whether this power is attributable to the overall model effectiveness or the impact of a particular subsample also needs to be tested. A standard test for evaluating this is the k-fold test, which divides the defaulting and non-defaulting companies into k equally sized segments. This yields k equally sized observed subsamples that exhibit the identical overall default rate and are temporally and cross-sectionally independent. The model is then run on $k-1$ subsamples and these parameter estimates are used to score the

k-th subsample. This procedure is repeated for all possible combinations, and the k scored out-of-sample subsamples are put together to calculate an AR on this combined data set.

Table 6.19 summarizes the k-fold test results (with $k = 5$) for the development sample. The reported figures are the ARs by the corresponding sample. The out-of-sample model consistently outperforms Z-score. Figure 6.9 presents the cumulative accuracy profiles associated with the overall out-of-sample results against the in-sample results. The model performance is maintained both in- and out-of-sample in the k-fold analysis.

Results The in- and out-of-sample plots are virtually indistinguishable at both the 1- and 5-year horizons in Figure 6.9. The difference in

Table 6.19 RiskCalc v3.1 China model k-fold test results

	Out-of-sample AR (%)		Z-score China (%)	
	1-year AR	5-year Ar	1-year AR	5-year AR
Subsample 1	62.8	62.8	50.8	51.1
Subsample 2	66.6	64.0	55.3	52.2
Subsample 3	66.6	64.4	55.4	52.9
Subsample 4	66.4	64.0	55.5	54.6
Subsample 5	63.0	62.7	52.9	51.2
k-Fold Overall	66.9	64.5	55.1	51.7
In-sample AR	67.8	64.9		

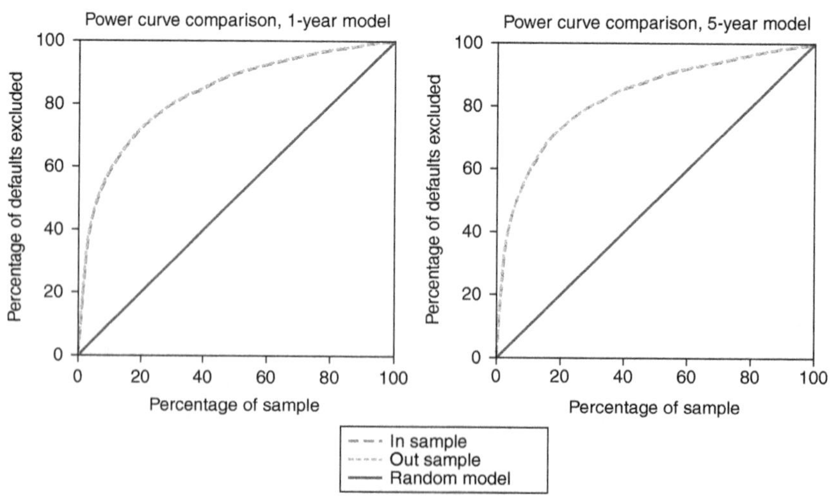

Figure 6.9 Out-of-sample performance (1- and 5-year): China model k-fold

AR between the overall in-sample and out-of-sample results is small for the 1-year and the 5-year. Furthermore, the RiskCalc v3.1 China model outperforms the Z-score-China in an out-of-sample context at both the 1- and 5-year horizons (see Table 6.19).

6.1.3.7 Model calibration and implied ratings

To help interpret EDF credit measures, the model maps an EDF value to an EDF-implied rating. All RiskCalc v3.1 models to date have used the same mapping. This mapping is designed with the following considerations:

- There is a large range of EDF-implied ratings (as required for economic and regulatory applications).
- No one rating contains too many credits (as required for economic and regulatory applications).
- The distribution of the 5-year ratings is approximately the same as the distribution of 1-year ratings (for consistency with rating-based analysis applications).
- The EDF value associated with an EDF rating is approximately the same as the observed historical default rate associated with a Moody's bond rating (for consistency with rating-based analysis applications).

Figure 6.10 shows the distribution of the observations by rating category in the development sample for the FSO EDF credit measures over the full time period. Note that less than 15% of the observations are in any one category. The distributions peak at Ba1 for both the 1-year and the 5-year ratings. While not reported here, other research has shown that the distribution of the CCA EDF-implied ratings changes over time with the credit cycle, while the distribution of the FSO EDF-implied ratings remains relatively stable over time.

6.1.3.8 Other robustness tests

Performance of the model in predicting special treatment for publicly listed firms

Special treatment (ST) is a unique early warning mechanism used in the Chinese stock market. A publicly listed firm will be labelled as an ST firm if it meets certain conditions, such as having negative earnings for two consecutive years. This constitutes a message from the regulator (China's Securities Regulatory Commission, CSRC) to the investors that a firm may have financial difficulties. Once the firm is categorized as ST, it is required to put the label "ST" in front of its stock name.

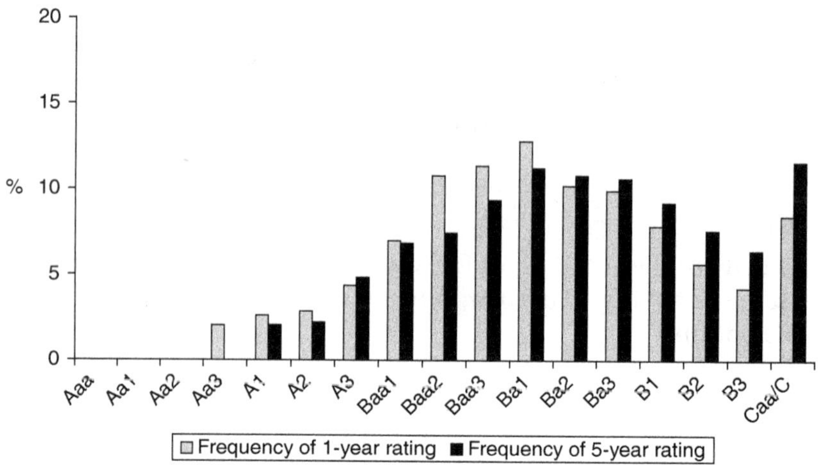

Figure 6.10 EDF-implied ratings for the 1- and 5-year models in the development

There are also special trading limitations and auditing requirements imposed on ST firms. If an ST firm cannot improve its financials, it will be labelled as "Particular Transfer," which is a prelude to delisting.

Using ST listing as a proxy of financial distress for publicly listed firms, we tested how well the model can predict ST. Between the years 2003 and 2008, we identified 150 firms listed as ST, out of a total of about 1800 publicly listed firms. The AR of the model in predicting ST firms is 63%.

Comparing the EDF level to bond spread-implied EDF To get a sense of how the EDF outputs compare to the spread-implied EDF for corporate bonds, we collected about 80 firms with bonds outstanding and bond price data available from Bloomberg. These 80 firms are also in our development sample, and therefore have RiskCalc China EDF scores.

Spreads were computed based on the yield curve of CFIF China Fixed Rate Government Bonds. The curve is composed of China Inter-Bank traded Yuan-denominated China Government Bonds. We then estimate the spread-implied EDF value using the following simplified method.

$$CSI\,EDF = N\left(N^{-1}(CQDF) - \lambda\sqrt{R^2 D}\right)$$

where

$CQDF = 1 - (1 - QDF)^D$;

D is the duration of the bond;

$QDF = Spread/LGD$.

As a rough estimation, we assume the market Sharpe ratio, to be 0.56 and R^2, the correlation estimate, to be 0.3. For LGD, the loss given default parameter, we assume 40%. The CSI EDF (cumulative spread-implied EDF) is then annualized to approximate spread-implied EDF at the 1-year horizon. As a caveat, the parameter assumptions here are based on Moody's Analytics extensive research in more developed markets (e.g., US bond markets), and the method is simplified. The bond market in China has grown exponentially during the past few years and has its own unique institutional features. A careful study on how to impute spread-implied EDF values for bonds issued in China is a promising research topic on its own. Nevertheless, it is not the focus of this study.

The results show that the RiskCalc EDF values are, on average, consistent with spread-implied EDF. The mean RiskCalc EDF under the CCA mode is 1.53%, compared with the mean spread-implied EDF of 1.49%. On the other hand, RiskCalc EDF values are more spread-out. For those 80 firms with bond data, the standard deviation of the RiskCalc EDF is 4.4%, almost five times larger than the standard deviation of the spread-implied EDF values (0.96%). In other words, the spread-implied EDF values are more clustered, which indicates that the spreads are clustered as well. RiskCalc provides more granular measures of default risk.

6.2 Business case: Daijin

6.2.1 Introduction to Daijin

Daijin Power Generation Limited has installed capacity of around 11.3 GW, making it one of China's emerging major multi-energy power generating companies. It is also enjoying double-digit growth in its power production business, which uses renewable energy sources to generate power from hydro, tidal, wind and geo-thermal energy.

The company operates 27 renewable energy source (RES) plants, including:

- five power stations in the south-east of China, which between them have total installed capacity of more than 43,339 MW;
- a geo-thermal power plant in northern China.

Daijin undertakes scientific and other research, planning, surveying and engineering services, and has links with retail power supply companies.

6.2.2 Business model and competitive advantages

Daijin's activities are geared towards the implementation of the state's energy policy, especially in the sphere of the hydropower sector, which is aimed at creating appropriate conditions for the efficient functioning of the wholesale electric energy market. It is also engaged in the efficient maintenance and centralized process management of hydropower facilities, the implementation of a uniform strategy to support an investment programme, the raising of capital funds to assist with the general development of the hydropower sector, the development and implementation of the state's scientific and technical policy and the implementation of new advanced types of machinery and technologies, including the development of renewable sources of electric power.

The company's key spheres of activity, which have been assigned top priority ever since its inception, are as follows:

- activities relating to electric power generation and/or capacity;
- activities relating to the supply (sale) of electric power and capacity, including supplies to commodity exchanges authorized to organize trade exchanges of electric power and capacity in the wholesale market;
- activities relating to the buying-in (purchase) of electric power and capacity in the wholesale electric power market (capacity);
- ensuring the maintenance of power supplies in compliance with the normative requirements by undertaking timely and high-quality repairs, together with the technical re-fitting and upgrading of power facilities;
- maintenance of power facilities that do not figure on the company's own balance sheet, under the terms of agreements with the owners of such power facilities;
- training personnel and testing their understanding of the rules, standards and instructions that apply to its operations, to occupational health, industrial safety and fire safety;
- introduction of energy-saving ways of operating the company's power plants and the observance of power supply modes in accordance with agreements;
- assimilation of new machinery and technologies that ensure the efficiency, safety and environmental friendliness of the company's facilities;
- focusing its scientific and technical know-how and its production potential on the development and assimilation of new state-of-the-art types of machinery, technologies and materials;

- development and implementation of programmes targeted at the use of renewable sources of electric power;
- exercising the powers of executive bodies in joint stock companies and other companies pursuant to the procedure provided for by the legislation and agreements in place.

The company aims to become a multi-national, vertically integrated holding and a world leader in the development of renewable energy sources. The company is keen to be:

- seen as a diversified engineering complex capable of securing the competitive and highly efficient development of renewable energy engineering in China and elsewhere;
- seen as a well-developed retail power supply business ensuring a high-quality consumer service and uninterrupted supply;
- seen as having a well-balanced business portfolio reflecting the maximum worth of the company;
- being amongst the first to introduce innovations relating to engineering and technological solutions as well as to control systems.

The company is a key agent of the state when it comes to the implementation of hydropower development projects in compliance with China's Energy Strategy for the period up until 2020. It also serves as a platform for the consolidation of the hydropower industry of the People's Republic of China.

Daijin's Strategic Plan between now and 2015 and onwards to 2020 sets a wide array of strategic lines for the company's development, on the basis of which the company's management has defined certain medium-term strategic initiatives.

Adjustments in the strategic objectives for the period up until 2015 and shifts in its strategic development priorities have been necessitated by changes in external conditions, including:

- developments in the domestic energy industry which is now focused on the dynamic growth of renewable energy: the forecast target for renewable energy development will account for 2.1% and 5.2% of total power supply production by 2015 and 2020 respectively;
- the development of an electrical energy/power supply marketing model to enhance the investment appeal of related projects;
- the trend towards industry consolidation: this will necessitate a large-scale investment programme to be implemented by industrial

entities if the prerequisites for a consolidated management system are to be created. International experience in hydropower management proves that hydropower plants controlled by large companies are contributing to the operation and sustainable development of the hydropower industry as well as the electric power industry overall.

The company has certain unique advantages:

- the generation of environmentally friendly electrical power: renewable and ecologically clean sources of energy production;
- energy-efficient production: hydropower is one of the guarantors of decreasing the dependence of the cost of electrical energy on changes in fossil fuel costs in the People's Republic of China, due to the absence of a fuel factor in the production of hydroelectric power;
- its ability to spearhead innovations in renewable energy engineering: its priority focus on technological renovation, giving an impetus to scientific and technological developments and to industrial applications of new generation technologies based on renewable energy sources;
- state-of-the-art management underpinned by in-depth experience in the construction and management of hydropower assets, both on the domestic and foreign markets.

Table 6.20 presents information about the existing principal and potential competitors of the company by core activity.

At present, the company has no foreign competitors.

Under its international strategy, Daijin should seek to become a company investing in RES generation facilities and be actively involved in their development, design, construction and subsequent operation in various geographical markets, depending on how promising they are, including pursuing such activities abroad.

In this connection the company expects to find itself in competition with the following overseas companies in the future: EdF, Statkraft, Iberdrola, Enel, Eon, Lahmeyer International, Mott MacDonald, SNC-Lavalin, Hindustan Construction Co (HCC), VA TECH Hydro, RusHydro, North American Hydro, GE Energy, Electricité du Laos, Electricité du Vietnam, NHPC and NTPC.

Table 6.20 Summary of competitive analysis

Main competitors	Description	Competitive field
Energoatom Concern OJSC	**Competitor's strengths:** considerable installed capacity of power facilities concentrated in European Russia; close to optimal load. **Competitor's weaknesses:** low flexibility and the resulting low effect from the balancing market; not represented in Siberia and the Far East.	As regards sales, competition may only occur in extreme surplus conditions. As regards development, struggle for state financing resources.
Heat-generating companies (OGK, TGK)	**Competitor's strengths:** wide territorial spread, primary generating capacities located in Russia (70%), possibility of submitting price bids to DAM and priority heating cycle load. **Competitor's weaknesses:** comparatively low flexibility, dependence of generated power prices on fuel prices.	As regards power sales, competition for amounts at specific hours of the day in heating cycle.

The company's competitive capacity factors are listed below, together with a description of how these may affect the competitiveness of its products/services:

1. environmental friendliness of power generation, since water resources are renewable and the most eco-friendly energy source, helping to reduce thermal power plant emissions and preserve hydrocarbon fuel reserves;
2. high flexibility – HPPs constitute the most flexible facilities, capable, if need be, of increasing their output considerably within a matter of minutes to cover peak loads;
3. absence of the fuel component from the cost of production, which not only provides independence from energy carrier price variations, but consequently offers long-term guarantees of the best prices for consumers.

All of the factors listed above have an equally considerable impact on the company's competitiveness.

6.2.3 Equity valuation

The company's valuation process is based on DCF Methodology, using relative valuation multiples (EV/EBITDA and Price-to-Book Value) as a "control methodology".

Daijin's balance sheet and income statements for years n, $n+1$, $n+2$ and $n+3$ are shown below (see Figure 6.11 and Figure 6.12).

The equity valuation of Daijin is determined using two approaches:

1) the unlevered earnings-based methods;
2) the NAV.

Unlevered earnings-based method

In order to estimate the weighted average cost of capital, the key inputs are used as follows:

Income statement	US$ Million			
	n	n+1	n+2	n+3
Total revenue	1,332.8	1,540.5	1,664.8	1,835.1
Operating costs	(882.8)	(962.7)	(1,022.1)	(1,144.1)
R&D	(12.6)	(23.7)	(20.0)	(14.4)
Lease payments	0.0	0.0	0.0	0.0
Other operating profit/(expense)	(18.3)	(16.2)	(15.5)	(21.1)
EBITDA	**419.1**	**537.9**	**607.2**	**655.5**
Depreciation & amortisation	(180.2)	(247.6)	(301.3)	(305.8)
EBIT	**238.9**	**290.3**	**305.9**	**349.7**
Net interest income/(expense)	(122.6)	(140.2)	(140.2)	(140.2)
Associates	(10.9)	11.5	40.1	18.3
Pretax profits	**105.4**	**161.6**	**205.8**	**227.8**
Income tax	(89.2)	(101.0)	(124.1)	(123.5)
Net income	**16.2**	**60.6**	**81.6**	**104.3**

Figure 6.11 Daijin income statements

Balance sheet US$ Million	
	N
Assets:	
Cash & equivalents	55.1
Accounts receivable	449.6
Inventory	512.8
Other current assets	120.7
Total current assets	**1,138.2**
Net PP&E	4,090.9
Net intangibles	0.0
Total investments	291.8
Other long-term assets	250.3
Total assets	**5,771.3**
Liabilities:	
Accounts payable	220.2
Short-term debt	529.7
Other current liabilities	39.8
Total current liabilities	**789.8**
Long-term debt	1,923.3
Other long-term liabilities	408.9
Total long-term liabilities	**2,332.2**
Total liabilities	**3,122.0**
Total shareholders equity	**2,649.3**
Total liabilities & equity	**5,771.3**

Figure 6.12 Daijin balance sheet

- Risk Free Rate is 3.63%, benchmark on 10-years China Government Bonds;
- Equity Beta is estimated equal to 0.8;
- Equity Market Premium for China is 13.4%;
- Credit Spread is equal to 3.5%;
- Tax Rate is 33%;
- Cost of Debt is 7.13%;
- Chinese RES Power Generation Industry stable growth rate is 2.5%.

Daijin's cost of equity is determined using the CAPM, as follows:

$$\text{Cost of Equity} = \text{Risk Free Rate} + \beta \cdot (\text{Equity Risk Premium})$$
$$\text{Cost of Equity}_{\text{Daijin}} = 3.63\% + 0.8 \cdot (13.4\%) = 14.35\%$$

Daijin's WACC is calculated as follows:

$$\text{WACC}_{\text{Daijin}} = \text{cost of equity}_{\text{Daijin}} \cdot \frac{\text{Equity}}{\text{Debt} + \text{Equity}} + \text{cost of debt}_{\text{Daijin}} \cdot (1 - t_{\text{China}}) \cdot \frac{\text{Debt}}{\text{Debt} + \text{Equity}}$$

$$\text{WACC}_{\text{Daijin}} = 14.35\% \cdot 52\% + 7.13\% \cdot (1 - 33\%) \cdot 48\% = 9.75\%$$

According to the Unlevered Earnings-Based method, the EV is equal to the present value of future EBITDA, discounted with the WACC, and the Equity Value is equal to the EV less the Net Financial Debt. Assuming an average expected and normalized Daijin EBITDA of US$ 600.2 MM, in formula we have:

$$W = \frac{EBITDA}{wacc - g} + \text{Cash} - \text{Financial Debt}$$

$$\text{W} = \frac{600.2}{9.75\% - 2.5\%} + 55.1 - 2,453$$

$$W = 8,278.621 + 55.1 - 2,453$$

$$W = US\$5,880.7MM$$

Net Asset Value methodology

In order to express Daijin's NAV it is necessary to evaluate the fixed assets at US$ 3,700 MM, with a tax effect of US$ 402.93 MM, is necessary.

The Daijin's NAV is equal to US$ 5,946.4 MM, as follows:

$$NAV = Equity\,Book\,Value + Revaluation\,of\,fixed\,assets\,Tax\,effect$$

$$NAV = 2,649.3 + 3,700 - 402.9$$

$$\text{NAV} = \text{US\$}\,5,946.4\,\text{MM}.$$

The Dijin's NAV estimate is higher than the equity value based on unlevered earnings and it is necessary to adjust the NAV for the bad will of US$ 65.7 million (US$ 5,946.4 million – US$ 5,880.7 million). In the next section the IAPM is applied in order to verify the impact on the Daijin's equity value.

6.2.4 The new approach

According to the IAPM, Daijin's cost of equity is the maximum either of the risk premium calculated using the CAPM, or the risk premium determined following the FIA.

As shown in the previous section, according to the CAPM, Daijin's cost of equity is equal to 14.35%.

Daijin's cost of equity using the FIA (see Chapter 3), meanwhile, is estimated as follows:

1. Probability of default valuation;
2. Equity Expected Loss calculation;
3. Equity Risk Premium determination.

Daijin's probability of default is 1.5%, in other words there is a 1.5% probability that its shareholders will lose all of their capital (recovery rate zero) (see Floor Theorem, Chapter 3); on the other hand, the probability of shareholders losing at least 1 US dollar is equal to 12.5% (see Cap Theorem, Chapter 3).

The combined rule to calculate the EEL is loss as follows:

$$\text{EEL} = default\,probability + (probability\,of\,losing\,at\,least\,1\,US\,dollar - default\,probability)\,50\%$$

$$\text{EEL} = 1.5\% + (12.5\% - 1.5\%)\,50\%$$

$$\text{EEL} = 7\%.$$

The last step is to compute the Equity Risk Premium based on the EEL and the probability of winning at least 1 US dollar. A rule-of-thumb approach is to define the size of "bet" that would need to be won in order to compensate shareholders for the EEL with a probability equal to "1 minus the probability of losing at least one US dollar", as follows:

$$\textit{Probability of winning at least one US dolla} \times \textit{Equity Risk Premium} = \textit{Equity Expected Loss}$$

$$\textit{Equity Risk Premium} = \frac{\textit{Equity Expected Loss}}{\textit{Probability of winning at least one US dollar}}$$

$$\textit{Equity Risk Premium} = \frac{7\%}{(1 - 12.5\%)}$$

$$\textit{Equity Risk Premium} = \frac{7\%}{87.5\%}$$

$$\textit{Equity Risk Premium} = 8\%$$

$$\textit{Cost of Equity} = \textit{Risk free rate} + \textit{Equity Risk Premium}$$

$$\textit{Cost of Equity} = 3.63\% + 8\%$$

$$\textit{Cost of Equity} = 11.63\% \, (\textit{FIA}).$$

In this case the equity risk premium calculated using the FIA is lower than the equity risk premium based on the CAPM, and it is therefore advisable to use 14.35% as Daijin's cost of equity. This means that no new equity value calculation is needed: the results of the previous section can be considered acceptable.

7
Integrated Pricing Model in Russia

7.1 RiskCalc Russia*

7.1.1 Unique features of the Russian market

The unique institutional features of Russian firms and the market environment raise questions that must be addressed during the modelling process. In this section, we review features that, in our opinion, are relevant to the default risk modelling process. To date, the lack of data has been another obstacle to building credit risk assessment models in Russia. We discuss the data used in developing the RiskCalc Russia v3.1 model in Section 7.4.

Unique institutional features of the Russian economy include the following.

- **Fast economic growth and the rising economic significance of Russia** – Between 1999 and 2008, the Russian economy grew at more than 7%, on average. This high growth attracted massive capital inflows that continued through 2007. Russian firms are also becoming more international, often buying stakes in foreign companies. The financial system has grown significantly with a boom in both retail and corporate lending.[1] The rapid growth in Russia results in the Sales Growth variable being treated differently than in RiskCalc country models intended for more mature economies, as discussed in Section 5.1.
- **Close ties between economic growth and energy prices** – Russia's economy relies heavily on oil and gas exports.[2] Oil price changes have been an important factor behind the economic growth and the recent downturn. As firms typically update financial statements annually or quarterly, it takes time for the impact of exogenous shocks such as oil price changes to materialize in financial reporting. This delay creates a challenge for a financial information-based

model such as RiskCalc. The model includes an option for adjusting outputs with a credit cycle factor. This factor incorporates the forward-looking information included in the stock prices of Russian listed firms. Section 5.4 discussed the adjustment details.

- **Transitioning accounting standards** – Russian accounting standards are evolving toward the international standards.[3] Nonetheless, according to a 2010 International Monetary Fund (IMF) report important differences between international financial accounting standards (IFRS) and Russian standards still exist.[4] The Russian accounting reform is an ongoing process, and the accounting standards are still heavily influenced by tax authority requirements.[5] The transitioning feature of accounting standards emphasizes the importance of building the model with local datasets. A model developed under a different accounting regime would be difficult to use in Russia. Further, such a model would likely be sub-optimal. We conduct various checks on financial statement quality, and exclude problematic statements and items during model development. We select generic ratios that can be populated from different accounting systems.
- **High default rate** – We observe a relatively elevated sample default rate in the development sample. The loan loss provision data collected from 132 Russian banks between 1999 and 2008 confirm that banks' expected loss estimation is also at a high level.

7.1.2 Data description

We use Moody's Analytics CRD as the data source for the RiskCalc v3.1 Russia model. The CRD acquired Russian firm financial statement data from data vendors. The default data were collected both manually and from public sources.

7.1.2.1 Definition of default

In general, when building RiskCalc models, we seek to collect all credit events where economic loss occurred. We also include all defaults consistent with the Basel definitions, provided the information is available. However, when building a specific PD or internal rating model, for various reasons, it is impossible to collect all default types and cases. The RiskCalc Russia v3.1 model was built with data acquired from data vendors and supplemented with defaults manually collected from publicly available sources. The default data primarily consists of liquidations, together with a small number of bankruptcies and miss-payment type defaults. We made a number of modelling choices that reflect default types beyond liquidations, bankruptcies, and miss-payments not captured in our data at this time.

7.1.2.2 Data exclusions

Excluded companies As in other RiskCalc v3.1 models, we exclude the following types of companies, because the financial statements or characteristics of these firms differ from the typical firms in our development sample.

- **Firms without complete financial statements** – We require that financial statements have a non-missing net income number and positive total assets and sales numbers. The sample includes all firms large enough to produce financial statements in compliance with local accounting standards. In particular, our development sample is restricted to all firms with inflation-adjusted assets greater than US $100,000.
- **Financial Institutions** – The balance sheets of financial institutions (banks, insurance companies, and investment companies) exhibit higher leverage than the typical firm. The regulation and capital requirements of these institutions differentiate them from other firms. Therefore, they are excluded from the database.
- **Real Estate Development Companies** – The annual accounts of real estate development and investment companies provide only a partial description of firm dynamics and, therefore, their likelihood to default. This occurs because their financial health often hinges on a particular development.[6]
- Government Agency and Not-for-profit Institutions – Government agency default risks are influenced by the states' or municipalities' unwillingness to allow them to fail. As a result, their financial results are not comparable to other private firms. Not-for-profit financial ratios differ from for-profit firms, particularly with regard to variables relating to net income.

Excluded financial statements We conducted plausibility checks of financial statements, such as Assets not equal to Liabilities plus Net Worth, and financial statements covering a period of less than 12 months. If errors are detected, those statements are excluded from the analysis. We also excluded statements missing Sales Growth, thus restricting the sample to firms with at least two financial statements.[7]

Table 7.1 Information on sample data

Period	Number of firms	Number of defaults	Number of statements
2002–2009	295,264	22,185	802,947

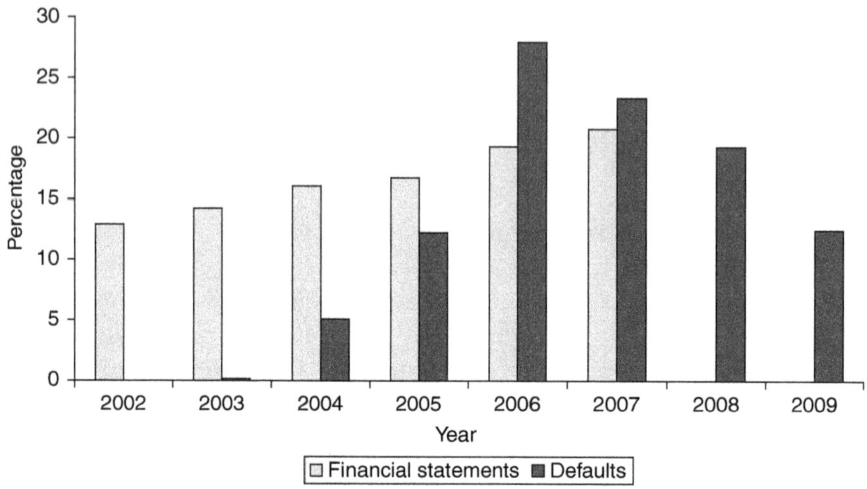

Figure 7.1 Distribution of statements and defaults by year

7.1.2.3 Descriptive statistics of the data

Overview of the data Table 7.1, Table 7.2 and Figure 7.2 present the data counts. The sample covers 802,947 financial statements for 295,264 firms, and 22,185 defaults. Figure 7.1 presents the distribution of financial statements and defaults by year in the development sample. The sample covers the time period ranging from January 2002–October 2009.

To ensure the model works well on both small and large companies, we place more weight on large firms in the regression analysis. Firms with sales greater than or equal to $10 million are weighted ten times those with sales less than $10 million.[8] The distributions by firm size, year, and industry are presented for both the whole sample and the weighted sample.

Robustness When building a model, we examine potential database weaknesses. Not only must the database cover a large number of firms and defaults, but the defaults also need to be distributed among industries and company size. For example, if the database has few firms in a particular size range without sufficient defaults in those groups, the model may not produce good default risk measurements.

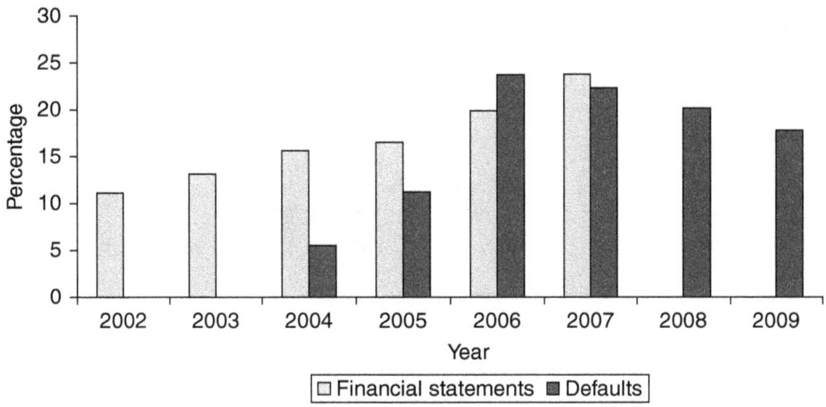

Figure 7.2 Weighted distribution of statements and defaults by year data

The Russia model follows standard RiskCalc sector classification and assigns firms to nine sectors: Agriculture, Business Products, Communications & Hi-Tech, Construction, Consumer Products, Mining Transportation & Utilities, Services, Trade, and Unassigned. Firms without industry information are grouped into the Unassigned category. We use the following two criteria when determining the sector classifications.

- The classification is economically meaningful;
- We possess enough statements and defaults in each sector.

Figure 7.3 presents the distributions of the sample firms by industry and the proportion of defaults in each industry. Trade, Construction, and Agriculture account for more than 60% of the sample, with fewer firms in High Tech and Consumer Products.

In weighted distribution, the three largest industries are Trade, Construction, and Mining Transportation & Utilities, shown in Figure 7.4.

Figure 7.5 presents the distributions by firm size, measured by assets in 2008 US dollars. Our sample includes both large firms and small firms. However, 88% of the firms in the sample have assets below $5 million, and 80% of the firms in the sample have sales below $5 million. We also found that smaller firms had more distressed-looking financial statements than larger firms.

Figure 7.6 shows the distribution by size after we applied the weights. With this weighting scheme the firms greater than $5 million constitute 42% of the sample. The distribution by industry, when we weight

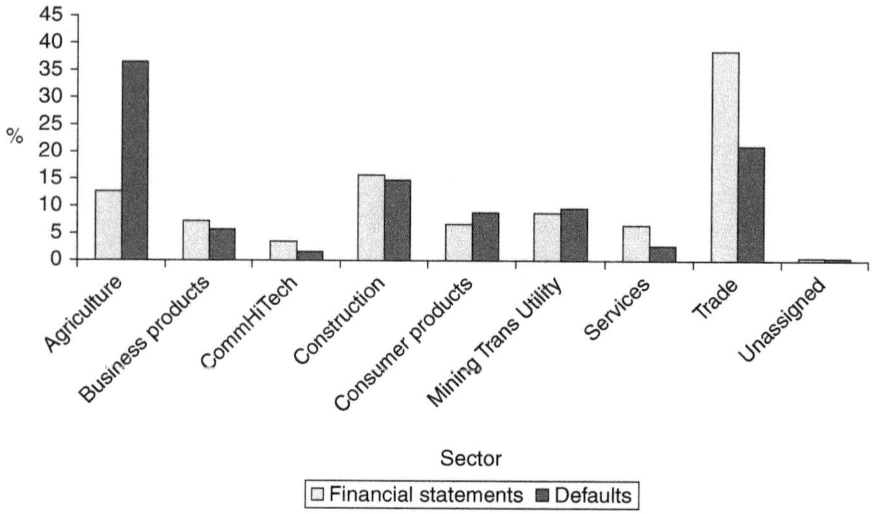

Figure 7.3 Distribution of statements and defaults by industry

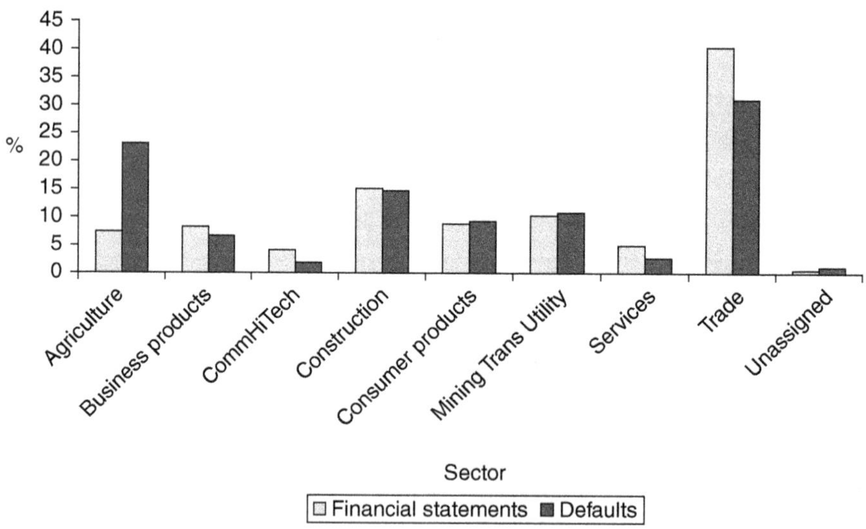

Figure 7.4 Weighted distribution of statements and defaults by industry

large firms more, is similar to the original one with the overall number of firms in Agriculture decreased.

Weighted distribution of statements and defaults by year is also similar to the original, shown in Figure 7.2.

We then examine the geographic coverage of the sample. The sample covers financial statements and defaults from all 83 federal subjects.

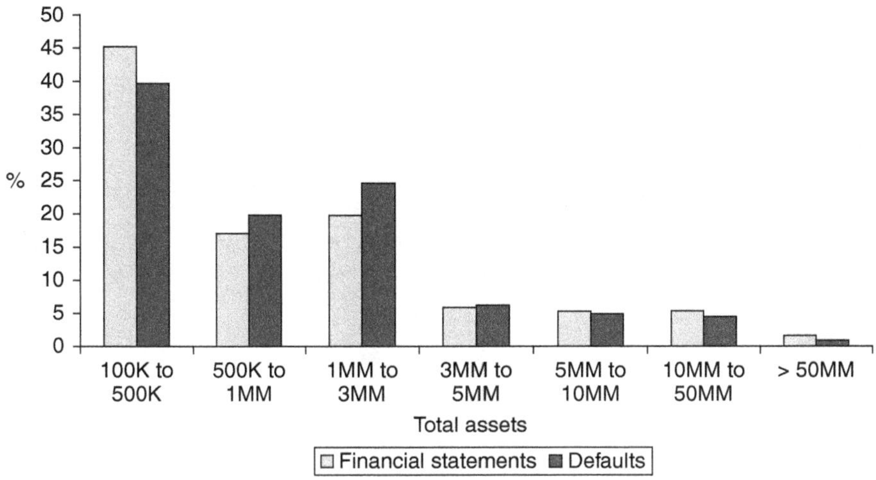

Figure 7.5 Original distribution of statements and defaults by size (assets in USD)

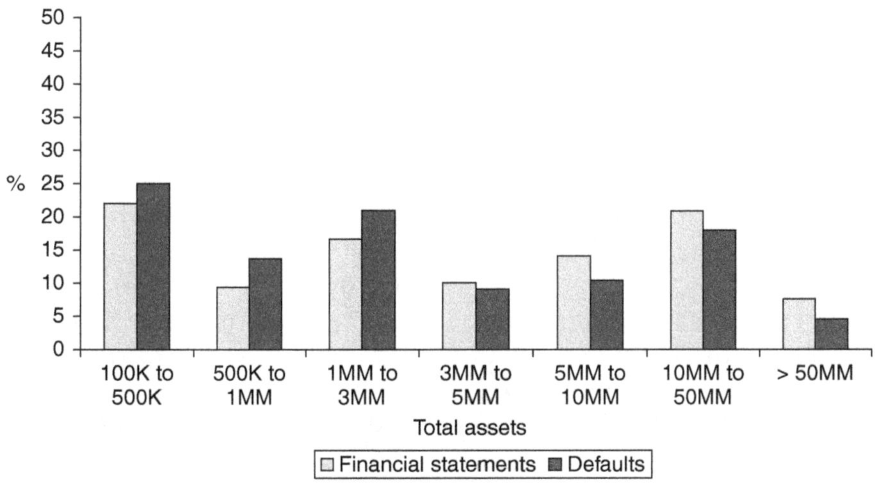

Figure 7.6 Distribution of statements and defaults by weighted size (assets in USD) used in the model

We follow the official classification to divide the sample into Central, Northwest, South (includes the North-Caucasian district), Volga, Urals, Siberia, and Far East federal districts (Okrugs). In Russia, the Central, Volga, and Urals districts are more economically developed than other regions.

Figure 7.7 shows the distribution of the statements and defaults by region. The grey bars in the figure correspond to the colours on the

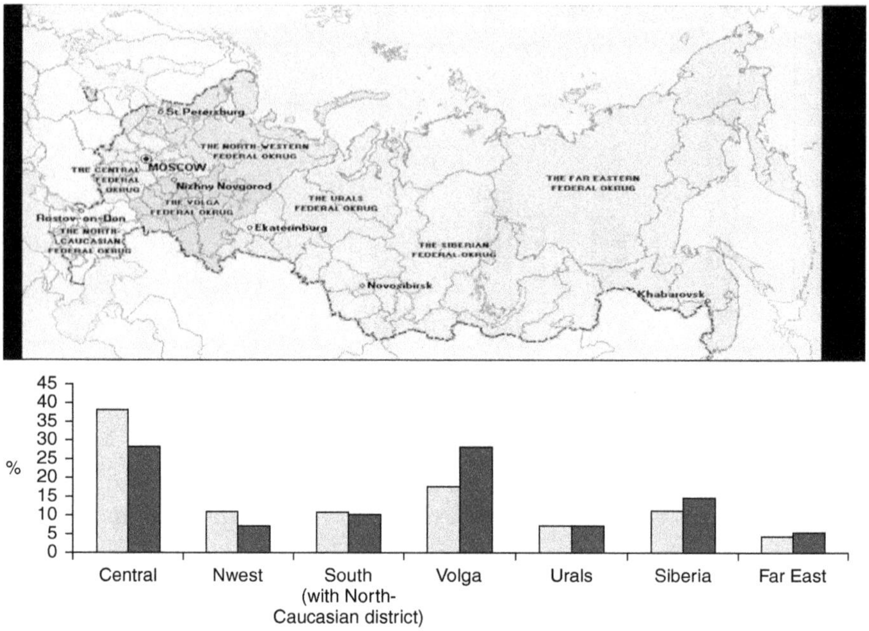

Figure 7.7 Distribution of financial statements and defaults by federal districts (Okrugs)

map and represent the percentage of financial statements; the black bars represent the percentage of defaults in the respective districts.[9] The Central district accounts for about 38% of the statements and 28% of the defaults in our sample. The Volga district is the second largest in terms of the number of financial statements (17.6%), and accounts for almost the same number of defaults as the Central district. The distribution of the number of statements and defaults by region are consistent with the Gross Regional Product (GRP) distribution across regions.[10]

Weighted distribution in Figure 7.8 is similar to the original in Figure 7.7.

7.1.2.4 Central default tendency

Because most companies do not default, companies that do default are relatively rare and thus more valuable when building a default risk model. The lack of default data may arise from data collection issues (for example, not all defaults were captured). Also, if the date of default is uncertain, the financial statement associated with the firm may be

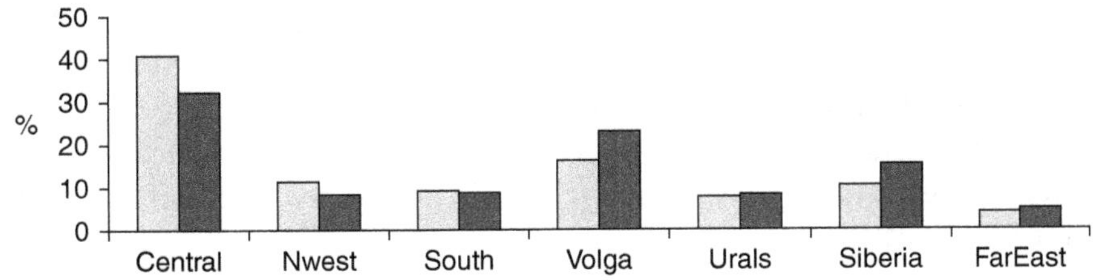

Figure 7.8 Weighted distribution of financial statements and defaults by federal districts (Okrugs)

excluded from model development, depending on the severity of the problem. This exclusion can result in a sample with lower default rates than actually occurs in the general population. If the underlying sample is not representative, then it needs to be adjusted for the central default tendency (CDT).

The CDT is an estimation of the true average PD of the development sample. When default definitions used in the data sample understate the defaulting population, the CDT can be used to realign the default rates.

The estimate of long-run aggregate probabilities of default (i.e., CDT) is important as an anchor for a model. The best estimation of default probability is a ratio that reflects the number of obligors that defaulted in one year compared with the total obligors at the beginning of that year. Often, these types of data are not available.

The estimate of the CDT in the RiskCalc Russia v3.1 model is based on two sources.

- The CDT was confirmed to exceed the default rates observed in our development sample.
- Loan loss provision data from local banks. We collected loan loss provision data from 132 local Russian banks. The multiple sources of external data led us to an estimate of 4.8% as the CDT figure for the 1-year model.

Calculating a 5-year CDT There is a lack of publicly available data for direct calculation of the CDT of a cumulative 5-year default probability. We pick a 5-year CDT so that forward EDF values, on average, line up with realized EDF values. We used 16.9% as the CDT for the 5-year model.

Central default tendency in CCA modes The CDT in CCA mode is equal to the CDT of the FSO mode when the effects of the credit cycle are neutral. When the forward-looking prediction of the credit cycle indicates increasing default risk, the CDT of the CCA mode will be larger, and when the effects of the credit cycle indicate decrease in default risk, CDT will be smaller.

7.1.3 Model components

The RiskCalc v3.1 model incorporates various components to determine the EDF credit measure. Model components include a selection of financial ratios, transforms of those ratios, specific industry information, and CCA.

RiskCalc model development involves the following steps.

1. Choose a limited number of financial statement variables for the model from a list of possible variables.[11]
2. Transform the variables into interim probabilities of default using non-parametric techniques.
3. Estimate financial statement variable weights using a probit model, combined with industry variables.
4. Create a (non-parametric) final transform that converts the probit model score into an actual EDF credit measure.

In FSO mode, the models are based on the following functional form:

$$FSO\ EDF = F\left(\Phi\left(\sum_{i=1}^{N}\beta_i T_i(x_i) + \sum_{j=1}^{K}\gamma_j I_j\right)\right)$$

where

$x1, \ldots, xN$	are the input ratios;
$I1, \ldots, IK$	are indicator variables for each of the industry classifications;
$\gamma 1, \ldots, \gamma K$	are estimated coefficients;
D	is the cumulative normal distribution;
F *and* $T1, \ldots, TN$	are non-parametric transforms;[12]
FSO EDF	is the financial statement only EDF credit measure.

The *T*s are the transforms of each financial statement variable, which capture the non-linear impacts of financial ratios on the default likelihood, shown in Figure 7.9 and discussed in detail later. *F* is the final transform (i.e., the final mapping). The final transform captures the

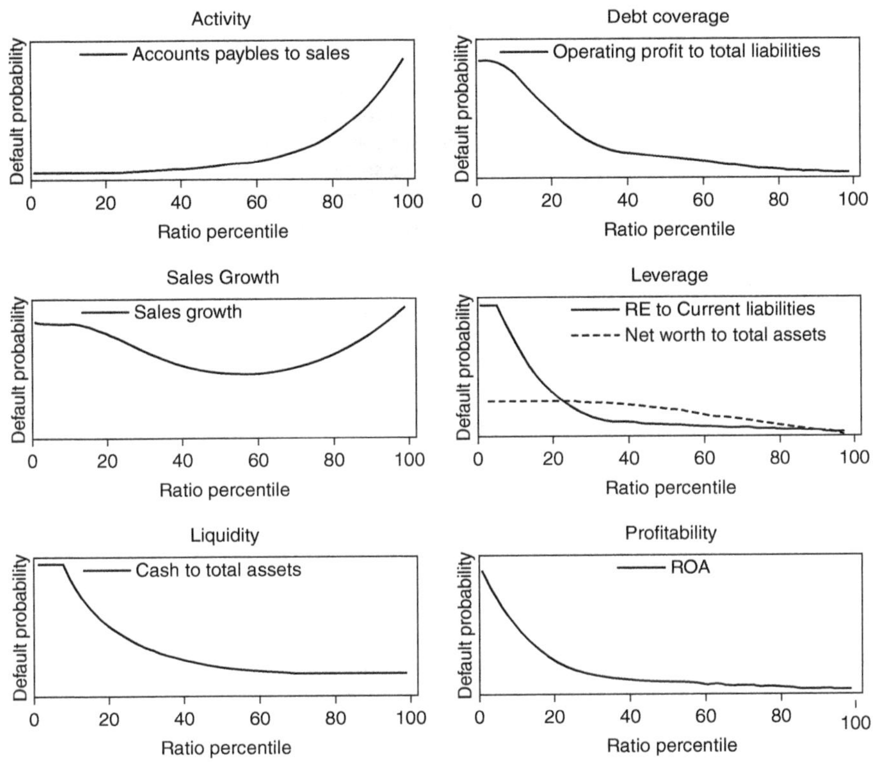

Figure 7.9 Transformations of financial statement variables in RiskCalc v3.1 Russia

empirical relationship between the probit model score and the actual default probabilities. The final transform is described as calibrating the model score to an actual EDF credit measure. The difference between the FSO EDF and the CCA EDF is that, in CCA mode, the final transform is adjusted to reflect our assessment of the current stage of the credit cycle, while in FSO mode, it remains constant.

7.1.3.1 Financial statement variables

Selecting the variables Our variable selection process begins with a long list of possible financial statement variables. The working list of ratios is divided into groups that represent different underlying concepts regarding a firm's financial status, shown in Table 7.2. We then construct a model with at least one variable per group. When it is possible to increase model performance and maintain model robustness, we use several variables from each group.

Table 7.2 Financial statement ratios groupings

Ratio	Description
Activity ratios	Measure a firm's operating efficiency. They typically involve working capital items such as inventory, accounts receivable, or accounts payable. A large stock of inventories relative to sales may indicate operation difficulties and high probability of default; other activity ratios have different relationships to default.
Debt coverage	The ratio of cash flow to interest payments or some other measure of liabilities. High debt coverage reduces the probability of default.
Growth variables	Typically include sales growth. These variables measure the stability of a firm's performance. Growth variables often behave like a double-edged sword: both rapid growth and rapid decline (negative growth) tend to increase a firm's default probability.
Leverage ratios	Include liabilities to assets or debt to assets. High leverage increases the probability of default.
Liquidity variables	Include cash and marketable securities to assets or liabilities, the current ratio, and the quick ratio. These variables measure the extent to which the firm has liquid assets relative to the size of its assets or liabilities. High liquidity reduces the probability of default.
Profitability ratios	Include net income, net income less extraordinary items, profit before tax, and operating profit in the numerator; and total assets, tangible assets, fixed assets and sales in the denominator. High profitability reduces the probability of default.
Size	Measured by total assets or sales deflated to a specific base year to ensure comparability. Large firms default less often.

We ask the following questions when deciding which variables to include in the final model:

- Is the variable readily available?
- Are the definitions of the variable inputs ambiguous?
- Is the meaning of the variable intuitive?
- Does the variable help measure default risk?
- Is the variable generally not correlated with other variables in the model?

Table 7.3 lists the financial variables selected in the RiskCalc Russia model. Most RiskCalc models include a size variable. While developing the Russian model, we observed that small firms tend to have much worse financial performance (as measured by basic financial ratios) than relatively large firms. Consequently, it was unnecessary to include

Table 7.3 Financial statement variables in RiskCalc v3.1 Russia

Category	Definition
Activity	Accounts payables/Sales
Debt coverage	Operating profit/Total liabilities
Growth	Sales growth
Leverage	Net worth/Total assets
	Retained earnings/Current liabilities
Liquidity	Cash & equivalents/Total assets
Profitability	Return on Assets (ROA)

a size variable to account for the higher observed default rates among the smaller firms.

Variable transforms After selecting the variables, the model transforms them into a preliminary EDF value. Figure 7.9 presents the transformations used in the model. The horizontal axis gives the percentile score of the ratio, and the vertical axis gives the default probability of that ratio in isolation (univariate). The percentile score represents the percentage of the database that has a ratio below that of the company (for example, if ROA is in the 90th percentile, then 90% of the sample has a lower ROA than that firm).

The shape of the transformation indicates how significantly a change in level impacts the EDF value. If the slope of the transform is steep, a small change will impact risk more than if the slope were flat.

- For the Activity group, the transform for Accounts Payable to Sales is upward-sloping (see Figure 7.9). Increase in Accounts Payable relative to Sales is associated with higher default probabilities.
- For the DebtCoverage group, the Operating Profit to Total Liabilities transform is downward-sloping (see Figure 7.9). This indicates that firms with a large Operating Profit relative to Total Liabilities have lower default probabilities.
- For the Growth group, the Sales Growth (see Figure 7.9) transform is U-shaped, indicating that a large increase or decrease in Sales is associated with higher default probabilities, while stable Sales year-upon-year decreases the probability of default. In emerging markets, and Russia in particular, firms tend to have higher growth rates than in mature markets. The transform becomes upward-sloping at approximately 60%, indicating that only firms with extremely high growth rate would be associated with elevated default risk.
- For the Leverage group, the Net Worth to Total Assets and Retained Earnings to Current Liabilities transforms are downward-sloping

(see Figure 7.9), indicating that firms with less leverage have lower default probabilities.

- For the Liquidity group, the Cash and Equivalents to Total Assets transform is downward-sloping (see Figure 7.9), indicating that firms with more liquid assets are associated with lower default probabilities.
- For the Profitability group, the ROA transform is downward-sloping (see Figure 7.9). This indicates that firms with large ROA have lower default probabilities.

7.1.3.2 Model weights

Importance The relative value of each variable used in calculating an EDF credit measure is important in understanding a company's risk. The non-linear nature of the model makes the variable weights more difficult to determine, because the actual impact on risk depends on the coefficient, the transformation shape, and the percentile ranking of the company. The model weights, therefore, are calculated based on the average EDF value for the transformation and its standard deviation. A variable with a flat transformation could have a low weight, even if the coefficient is large, as shown in Figure 7.9.

Calculation of weights To calculate the weight of a variable, we compute the EDF credit measure for a theoretical firm, including all its variables, at the average transformation values. Next, we increase the variables one at a time by one standard deviation, and then compute and add together the EDF change for each variable (in absolute value). We then calculate the relative weight of each variable as the EDF level change for that variable as a percentage of the sum of EDF level changes across all variables. This methodology gives the variable with the largest impact on the EDF level the largest weight, and the variable with the smallest impact on the EDF level the smallest weight. Since the weights are a percentage of the total change in EDF levels, they sum to 100%. Each category's weight is the sum of the weights of each variable in that category.

Table 7.4 presents the weights in the RiskCalc v3.1 Russia model. The most important category is Leverage (with two ratios) at both the 1-year and 5-year horizons.

7.1.3.3 Industry adjustments

For the same set of financials, different industries may have different default probabilities. The EDF value is adjusted for industry effects.

Table 7.4 Risk drivers in RiskCalc v3.1 Russia

Category	Weights: 1-year (%)	Weights: 5-year (%)
Activity	18.16	19.15
Debt coverage	10.83	13.55
Growth	2.00	2.86
Leverage	33.7	25.18
Liquidity	14.10	14.9
Profitability	21.23	14.97

All industry coefficients in our regression are statistically significant. When we add industry into regression, the power for the 1-year model increases by 2.4%, and the power for 5-year model increases by 2.7%, indicating industry controls are important in producing an accurate EDF credit measure.

7.1.3.4 Credit cycle adjustment

EDF credit measures are impacted not only by the financials of a company, but also by the general economic credit cycle. To capture this effect, the RiskCalc v3.1 model suite includes a credit cycle adjustment (CCA) factor. The CCA is designed to incorporate the current credit cycle into the estimate of private firm default risk.

Selecting an adjustment factor The RiskCalc v3.1 models use the Distance-to-Default (DD) calculation from the Moody's Analytics Public EDF model. This measure is specifically designed to be a forward-looking indicator of default risk, and it extracts signs of default risk from the stock market performance of individual firms. We chose DD because it is available for a large universe of industries, and it has been validated extensively.

If the DD factor for public firms in an industry indicates a level of risk above the historical average for that industry, then the private firm EDF values in that industry are adjusted upward. Conversely, if the level of risk falls below the historical average for that industry, then the model adjusts private firm EDF values downward. When the credit cycle adjustment factor is neutral, the CCA EDF value coincides with the FSO EDF value.

Adjustment factor used in the model For the Russian model, the DD factor is based on an aggregation of all publicly listed Russian firms within a specific industry. Each month, we calculate the DD factor for each of the nine industries.[13] We then use a combination of the industry

DD factor and the DD factor based on all publicly listed Russian firms (overall DD factor).

Not all industries possess enough observations, however. For those industries without enough observations, we place more weight on the overall DD factor. As the number of observations in the industry increases, so does the weight we place on the industry-specific DD factor.

We use a Bayesian approach to assign the weight of the industry DD factor and the overall DD factor. If an industry has ten firms in a specific month, we put 50% weight on the overall DD factor, with the remainder on the industry DD factor. If the number of firms exceeds 40, we place more than 80% of the weight on the industry factor. For the "Unassigned" industry, the model uses a CCA based solely on the overall DD factor. During our sample period, the number of publicly listed firms in Russia increased. Using the Bayesian method, we can place more weight on the overall factor, when the number of firms in an industry is too small to impute its own CCA factor, and then gradually increase the weight of the industry-specific factor when the number of firms increases.[14]

Figure 7.10 presents the DD factor based on all publicly listed Russian firms and compares it with the Russian GDP growth rate and the Russian Sovereign CDS spread.[15] The CCA factor is in line with the CDS spread (increase in spread signals worsening credit quality) and anticipates the GDP growth rate. We set CCA EDF measures equal to FSO EDF measures before 2003.

As one of the world's largest oil and gas exporters, the Russian economy depends heavily on energy prices. Not surprisingly, considering the sharp decline in oil prices, Russia was among the hardest-hit

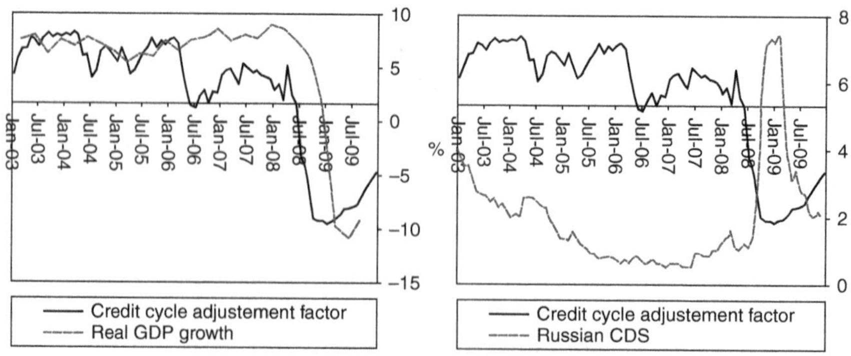

Figure 7.10 Comparison of DD factor with GDP growth rate and CDS spreads

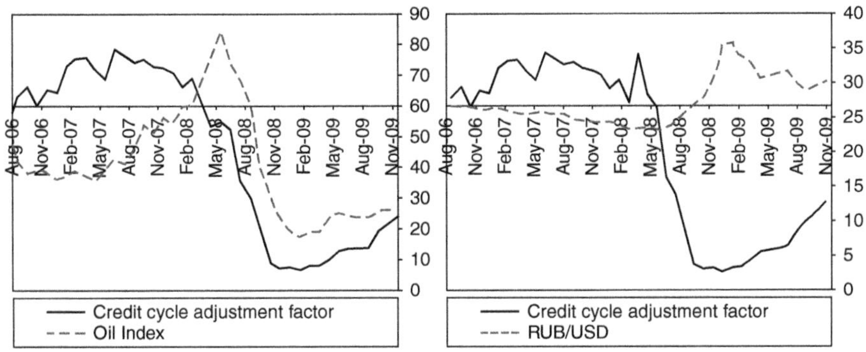

Figure 7.11 Comparison of DD factor with oil index and RUB/USD exchange rate

economies during the recent economic crisis. We plot the DD factor series against an oil index in Figure 7.11.[16] The DD factors lead the drop in the oil index by several months. DD factors also lead the increase in the RUB/USD exchange rate that followed the drop in oil prices.

7.1.4 Validation results

After a model is developed, it must prove effective in measuring default risk. In this section, we present test results on the model's ranking power (i.e., the model's ability to sort credits from worst to best).

The tests must check not only model's effectiveness, but also its robustness and how well it works on data outside the sample. We conducted k-fold analyses and walk-forward tests for out-of-sample testing. Results show the model is, in general, more powerful than other models across different time periods, sectors, and size classifications.

7.1.4.1 Overall model power and accuracy

Table 7.5 presents the in-sample overall measures of power for the RiskCalc v3.1 Russia model versus Altman's Z-score model.[17] The model outperforms the Z-score at both the 1-year and 5-year horizons.[18]

Table 7.5 also contains *p*-values for the statistical test to display whether or not the difference between the ARs from the Russian model and the benchmark is equal to zero. A *p*-value less than.05 indicates that we can reject the hypothesis that the difference in the ARs is equal to zero, with 95% confidence.

Figure 7.12 presents the cumulative accuracy profiles for the 1- and 5-year models corresponding to Table 7.5. The power improvements

Table 7.5 Power performance of the RiskCalc v3.1 Russia model

Model	1-year model		5-year model	
	Accuracy Ratio (%)	p-value	Accuracy Ratio (%)	p-value
RiskCalc Russia	63.7	–	54.3	–
Z-score	48.3	<.0001	33.9	<.0001

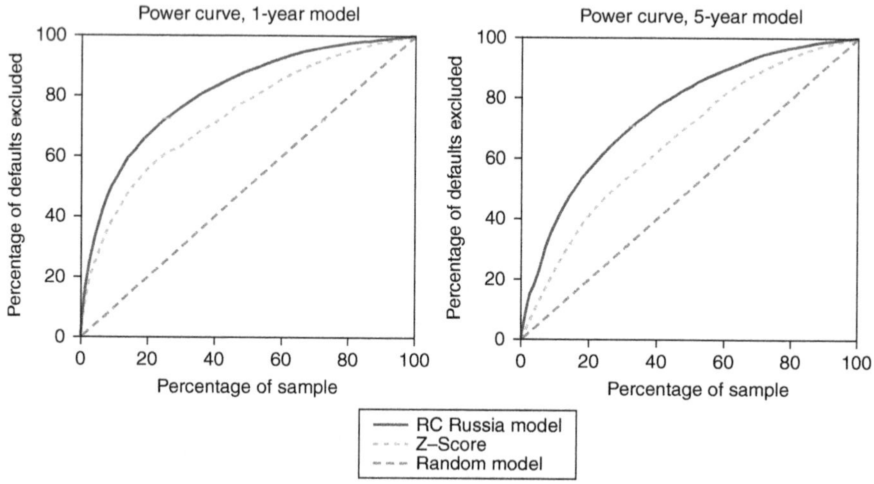

Figure 7.12 CAP plots (1- and 5-year): Russian model and Z-Score

are uniformly significant across different regions of the distribution relative to the Z-score.

7.1.4.2 Correlations and variance inflation factors

To ensure model robustness, the model must be tested for excessive multicollinearity, which occurs if a number of the variables used are highly correlated. Excessive multicollinearity can cause instability in parameter estimates. To check for this issue, we compute the correlation coefficients in Table 7.6 for the model's financial statement ratios and the variance inflation factors (VIF) in Table 7.7 on the transformed variables in Figure 7.9.

The VIF levels for the financial statement variables in Table 7.7 represent how much the variation in one independent variable can be explained by all the other independent variables in the model. However, the correlation coefficient measures only the relationships between two variables. The highest VIF level is 2.51, indicating that the collinearity between the variables is low.[19] Shown in Table 7.7, the

Table 7.6 Correlation among transformed inputs

Accounts payables/Sales	1.00						
Operating profit/Total liabilities	0.43	1.00					
Sales growth	0.25	0.23	1.00				
Net worth/Total assets	0.29	0.19	0.16	1.00			
Retained earnings/Current liabilities	0.32	0.54	0.10	0.16	1.00		
Assets	0.25	0.23	0.08	0.01	0.23	1.00	
Return on Assets (ROA)	0.32	0.73	0.20	0.20	0.57	0.18	1.00

Table 7.7 Variance inflation factors

Variable	VIF
Operating profit/Total liabilities	2.51
Return on Assets (ROA)	2.44
Retained earnings/Current liabilities	1.68
Accounts payables/Sales	1.43
Net worth/Total assets	1.30
Cash/Total assets	1.18
Sales growth	1.11

two ratios with the highest correlation are Operating Profit to Total Liabilities and ROA.

7.1.4.3 Power performance by industry and size groups

It is important to test a model's power not only overall, but also among different subsamples, such as industry segments and firm sizes.

Table 7.8 and Table 7.9 present the power comparisons by sector for the 1-year and 5-year models, respectively.[20] The Russian model outperforms the alternative model (Z-score) across all sectors. As shown in Table 7.8, the highest power in the 1-year horizon is found in Business Products (67%), while the lowest is found in Services (36%). Agriculture has the largest percentage of defaults in the sample and the model performed very well there. The model also performed well in Construction, which had an AR of 63%, Consumer Products (AR 66%) and MiningTransUtility (AR 62%). We see similar observations at the 5-year horizon, shown in Table 7.9.

Table 7.8 Power by industry: 1-year horizon, RiskCalc Russia

Sector	Percentage of defaults	AR Russian model (%)	AR Z-score (%)	Diff p-value
Agriculture	38.8	61.3	55.4	<0.0001
Business products	5.6	67.4	55.8	<0.0001
CommHighTech	1.4	55.6	42.1	<0.0001
Construction	14.5	62.7	53.5	<0.0001
Consumer products	8.7	65.9	54.9	<0.0001
Mining, Trans, Utility	9.5	62.0	52.9	<0.0001
Services	2.5	35.8	25.5	<0.0001
Trade	18.6	40.7	33.1	<0.0001
Unassigned	0.4	39.3	35.3	0.4050

Table 7.9 Power by industry: 5-year horizon, RiskCalc Russia

Sector	Percentage of defaults	AR Russian model (%)	AR Z-score (%)	Diff p-value
Agriculture	36.4	53.4	42.2	<0.0001
Business products	5.5	56.4	40.6	<0.0001
CommHighTech	1.5	44.4	31.4	<0.0001
Construction	14.6	46.9	38.1	<0.0001
Consumer products	8.7	46.1	37.3	<0.0001
Mining, Trans, Utility	9.5	47.7	38.8	<0.0001
Services	2.6	29.1	22.7	0.0001
Trade	20.8	33.3	30.2	<0.0001
Unassigned	0.4	37.3	31.2	0.2051

Table 7.10 Power by size (total assets in US dollars): 1-year horizon, RiskCalc Russia

Range	Percentage of defaults	AR Russian model (%)	AR Z-score (%)	Diff p-value
Less Than $500k	37.2	65.1	55.0	<0.0001
$500k to 1 MM	20.3	66.6	49.6	<0.0001
$1 MM to 3 MM	25.6	63.8	42.2	<0.0001
$3 MM to 5 MM	6.5	57.1	40.0	<0.0001
$5 MM to10MM	4.9	59.9	44.9	<0.0001
$10MM to50MM	4.6	53.3	41.3	<0.0001
Greater Than 50MM	0.8	45.0	30.0	<0.0001

Table 7.10 and Table 7.11 present the power comparisons by firm size (Assets in US dollars) for the 1-year and 5-year models, respectively. The model performs well across size cuts. The Russian Model outperforms the Z-score in all size categories.

Table 7.11 Power by size (total assets in US dollars): 5-year horizon, RiskCalc Russia

Range	Percentage of defaults	AR Russian model (%)	AR Z-score (%)	Diff p-value
Less Than $500k	34.8	47.4	37.7	<0.0001
$500k to 1 MM	19.8	57.8	36.8	<0.0001
$1 MM to 3 MM	28.9	59.8	30.4	<0.0001
$3 MM to 5 MM	6.7	54.1	25.0	<0.0001
$5 MM to10MM	5.1	49.3	30.8	<0.0001
$10MM to50MM	4.0	46.5	31.9	<0.0001
Greater Than 50MM	0.7%	38.1	27.5	<0.0001

Table 7.12 Power over time: 1-year horizon, RiskCalc Russia

Year	Percentage of defaults	AR Russian model (%)	AR Z-score (%)	Diff p-value
2002	7.5	63.7	50.7	<0.0001
2003	18.5	64.2	57.9	<0.0001
2004	29.6	69.4	52.0	<0.0001
2005	20.6	69.9	44.8	<0.0001
2006	15.2	51.3	38.2	<0.0001
2007	8.6	46.3	34.3	<0.0001

Table 7.13 Power over time: 5-year horizon, RiskCalc Russia

Year	Percentage of defaults	AR Russian model (%)	AR Z-score (%)	Diff p-value
2002	63.3	60.2	36.1	<0.0001
2003	15.4	44.3	32.0	<0.0001
2004	9.6	43.7	32.0	<0.0001
2005	5.3	36.3	29.5	<0.0001
2006	4.6	38.5	32.1	<0.0001
2007	1.9	40.3	35.6	0.0055

7.1.4.4 Power performance over time

Because models are implemented at various points in a business cycle by design, we conduct power tests by year to examine whether or not model performance is excessively time dependent.

Table 7.12 and Table 7.13 present the results from this analysis at the 1- and 5-year horizons, respectively. We compare the RiskCalc v3.1 Russia model AR with the Z-score for each year. In building the model, we require that the financial statements used to predict defaults are at least one year prior to the default date. Therefore, we use only statements

Table 7.14 Power by regions: 1-year horizon, RiskCalc Russia

District	Percentage of defaults	AR Russian model (%)	AR Z-score (%)	Diff p-value
Central	29.0	63.6	48.8	<0.0001
North-West	6.9	57.7	45.3	<0.0001
South	10.3	61.9	52.3	<0.0001
Volga	30.3	66.5	46.0	<0.0001
Urals	7.5	62.1	52.5	<0.0001
Siberia	15.4	62.1	47.5	<0.0001
Far-East	5.1	59.9	51.9	<0.0001

dated 2007 or earlier to predict 2009 defaults in our sample.[21] The Russian model outperforms the Z-score by a large margin.

7.1.4.5 Power performance by regions

Table 7.14 presents power comparison results by region. The development sample covers financial statements and defaults from all 83 federal subjects. We divide the sample into Central, Northwest, South (which includes the North-Caucasian district), Volga, Urals, Siberia, and the Far East federal districts (Okrugs), using the official classification.

The largest areas, both in terms of manufacturing and GRP, are the Central and Volga districts, which also have the highest default rate in our development sample. The Central district accounted for 36.7% of GRP in 2007. It also boasts the highest concentration of Services and Trade compared with other regions. The Volga and the Urals regions' economies are predominately manufacturing-based and accounted for 15.5% and 15.1% of GRP respectively. The Northwest, South, and the Far East districts represent the lowest tier in terms of economic development. The Far East region has the lowest population – 5% of the total population of Russia. Given the differences in economic development, it is important to ensure that the model performs well in different regions.

As shown in Table 7.14 and Table 7.15, the model's AR is high in all seven regions, consistently outperforming the benchmark model.

7.1.4.6 Out-of-sample testing: k-fold tests

The Russian model exhibits a high degree of power in distinguishing good credits from bad ones (shown in Table 7.5), but whether this power is attributable to overall model effectiveness or the impact of a particular subsample needs to be tested. A standard test for evaluating

Table 7.15 Power by regions: 5-year horizon, RiskCalc Russia

District	Percentage of defaults	AR Russian model (%)	AR Z-score (%)	Diff p-value
Central	29.4	63.5	47.6	<0.0001
North-West	7.5	54.9	43.2	<0.0001
South	10.5	62.7	51.6	<0.0001
Volga	29.2	68.4	46.5	<0.0001
Urals	7.5	61.6	51.9	<0.0001
Siberia	15.3	62.4	47.2	<0.0001
Far-East	5.4	59.1	50.5	<0.0001

Table 7.16 RiskCalc v3.1 Russia model k-fold test results

	Out-of-sample AR (%)		Z-score Russia (%)	
	1-year AR	5-year AR	1-year AR	5-year AR
Subsample 1	64.12	60.79	44.82	38.62
Subsample 2	64.57	60.28	46.51	39.23
Subsample 3	64.91	61.07	46.69	39.36
Subsample 4	62.43	59.10	43.16	37.15
Subsample 5	63.65	60.11	44.69	38.30
k-fold overall	64.93	56.22	48.19	33.82
In-sample AR	64.96	56.26		

this discrepancy is the k-fold test, which divides the defaulting and non-defaulting companies into *k* equally sized segments. This demarcation yields *k* equally sized observed subsamples that exhibit the identical overall default rate and are temporally and cross-sectionally independent. We then run the model on *k*-1 subsamples, and these parameter estimates are used to score the *k*-th subsample. This procedure is repeated for all possible combinations, and the *k* scored out-of-sample subsamples are put together to calculate an AR on this combined data set.

Table 7.16 summarizes the k-fold test results (with k=5) for the development sample. The reported figures are the ARs by corresponding sample and time horizons. The out-of-sample model consistently outperforms the Z-score.

Figure 7.13 presents the cumulative accuracy profiles associated with the overall out-of-sample results against the in-sample results. The model performance is maintained both in- and out-of-sample in the k-fold analysis.

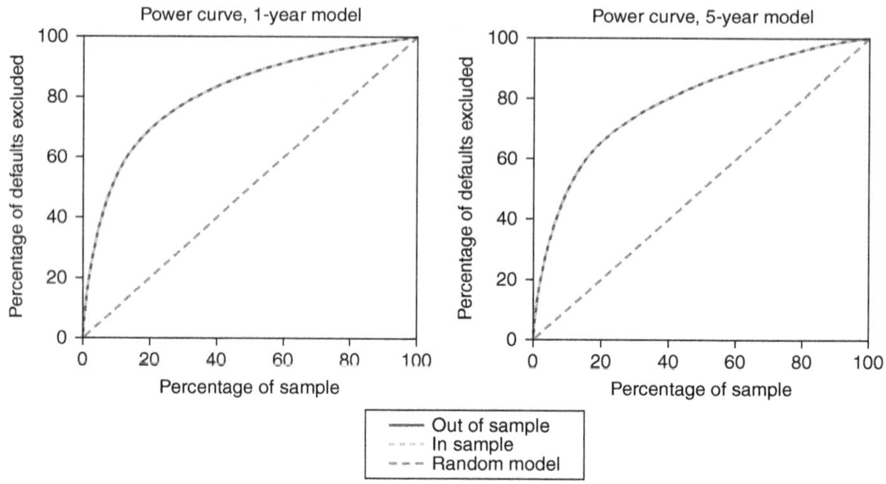

Figure 7.13 Out-of-sample performance (1- and 5-year): Russian model k-fold

Results The in- and out-of-sample plots are virtually indistinguishable at both the 1- and 5-year horizons in Figure 7.13. The difference in AR between the overall in-sample and out-of-sample results is small for both the 1-year and the 5-year horizons. Furthermore, the RiskCalc v3.1 Russia model outperforms the Z-score in an out-of-sample context at both the 1- and 5-year horizons (Table 7.16).

7.1.4.7 Walk-forward tests

Moody's Analytics also developed an alternative out-of-sample test, a walk-forward test, designed along similar lines to the k-Fold test, except that it controls for the effects of time. We estimate the model up to a certain year, and the parameter estimates are then used to score the observations in the next year. These model scores are out-of-time. We then re-estimate the model including one more year of data. We repeat the analysis for the next year, and continue until the end of the sample. These out-of-sample out-of-time scores are combined into a single prediction set, so that we can calculate the AR and the power curve for the combined set. We then compare the out-of-sample AR to the corresponding in-sample AR and power curve.

We do not use data from a future period in fitting the model, and use only data from future periods for testing it. We check the parameter estimates for stability across the different samples. Due to the length of the time series, we only perform the test for the 1-year model.

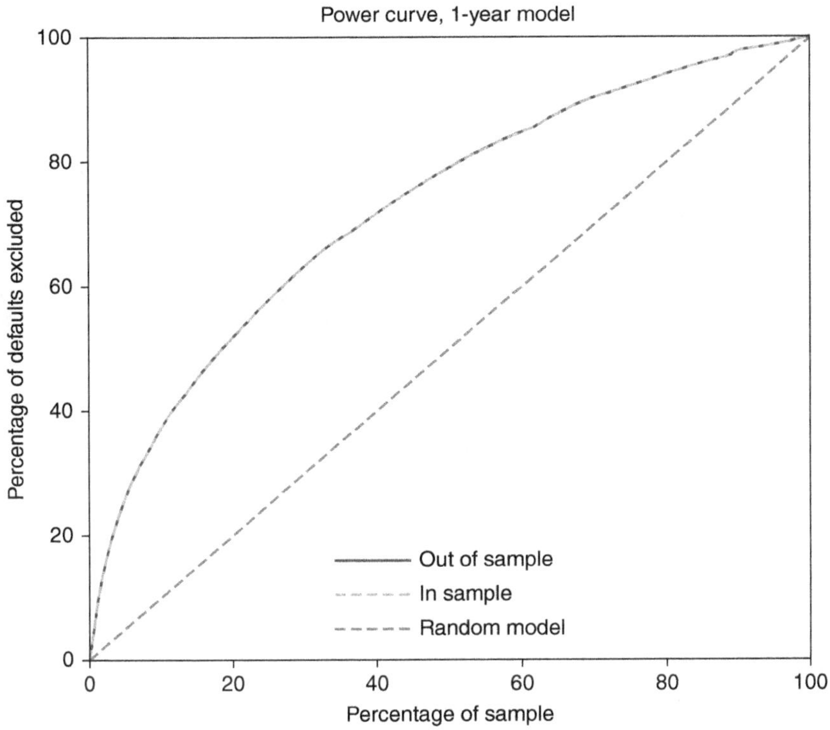

Figure 7.14 Out-of-sample performance (1-year): Russian model walk-forward

Table 7.14 presents the results from this analysis. In the walk-forward test, the out-of-sample ARs are smaller than the in-sample ARs, as shown in Figure 7.14. However, the difference is small: 0.5%.

7.1.4.8 Model calibration and implied ratings

To help interpret EDF credit measures, the model maps an EDF value to an EDF-implied rating. All RiskCalc v3.1 models to date use the same mapping. This mapping is designed with the following considerations.

- There is a large range of EDF-implied ratings (as required for economic and regulatory applications).
- No one rating contains too many credits (as required for economic and regulatory applications).
- The distribution of the 5-year ratings is approximately the same as the distribution of the 1-year ratings (for consistency with ratings-based analysis applications).

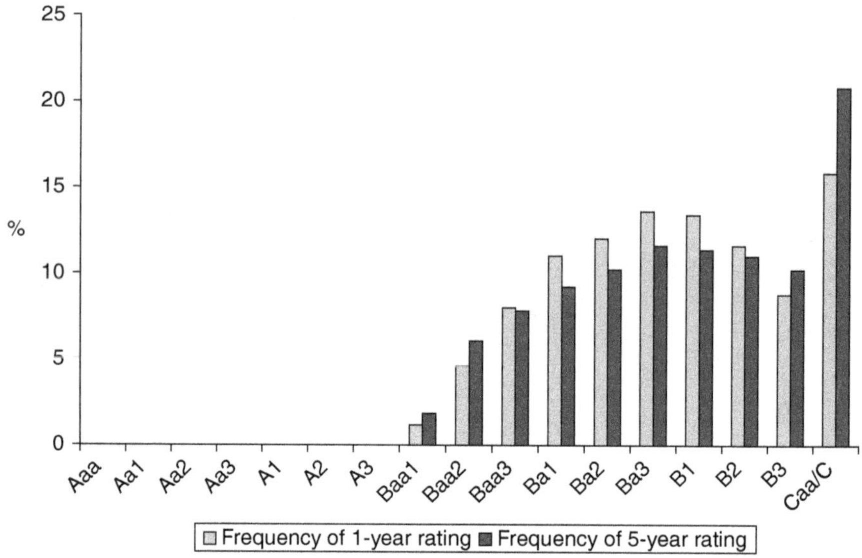

Figure 7.15 EDF-implied ratings for the 1- and 5-year models in the development sample

- The EDF value associated with an EDF rating is approximately the same as the observed historical default rate associated with a Moody's bond rating (for consistency with rating-based analysis applications).

Figure 7.15 shows the distribution of the observations by rating category in the development sample for the FSO EDF credit measures over the full time period. Note that less than 25% of the observations fall into any one category. The distributions peak at Baa3 for the 1-year rating and for the 5-year rating. While not reported here, other research shows that the distribution of the CCA EDF-implied ratings changes over time with the credit cycle, while the distribution of the FSO EDF-implied ratings remains relatively stable over time.

7.2 Business case: Ural Fashion

7.2.1 Introduction to Ural Fashion

Ural Fashion Limited is a private company based in Saint Petersburg within the Russian Federation.

Ural Fashion started its garment manufacturing operations in May 1997, but its trademark was only registered in 1999 by Delta Fashion, a company wholly owned by the family of the founder.

Ural's current business is the design and sale of casual menswear fashions. Ural Fashion Limited is a leading design-driven casual menswear fashion company in Russia and its branded products are ranked among the best in the Russian casual menswear fashion market. Its retail sales in 2010 constituted a 6.2% share of the market.

The company's products are designed in-house and sold under the Ural brand. It offers a wide range of products, including men's casual clothing, footwear and lifestyle accessories, primarily targeted at urban males between the ages of 20 and 40 who prefer stylish clothing that represents a sophisticated lifestyle.

7.2.2 Business Model and competitive advantage

The company has one of the top designer teams in Russia and more than 10 years of experience in the industry.

The company's marketing strategy focuses on promoting an overall brand image that embodies a lifestyle of "fashionable elegance", rather than individual products.

Unlike many of its competitors, Ural Fashion does not rely on large-scale, blanket television advertising, but instead adopts a targeted multi-channel marketing strategy through its sponsorship of selective public events and activities, participation at major fashion shows and exhibitions, and national advertising campaigns through television, the internet, magazines and newspapers.

The company outsources the production of most of its products to selected contract manufacturers, although most of its exclusive and high fashion items are produced in its own secure production facility in St. Petersburg Province in order to retain maximum control over quality and to prevent the unauthorized disclosure of new collections before their scheduled launch.

Products are sold through an extensive distribution network covering all of Russia's provinces and centrally administered municipalities, as well as through the company's direct stores.

Its products are primarily sold to customers through retail stores operated by its own distributors and their sub-distributors, all of which are operated under the Ural brand and are required to sell only the company's products.

As part of its expansion strategy, in April 2007, Ural Fashion began building up direct stores in selected cities where it already had an established presence and it believes that there is still potential for additional growth.

The strengths that differentiate Ural Fashion from its competitors may be summed up by the following key points:

- Strong focus on design and product innovation;
- Established and leading designer brand for fashion casual menswear in Russia;
- Creative multi-channel brand marketing strategies;
- Extensive and well-managed nationwide distribution network;
- Socially aware corporate culture supported by an experienced management team.

To further strengthen its position as a leading casual menswear fashion brand in Russia the company intends to pursue the following strategy:

- To open additional retail and flagship stores across Russia;
- Continue to raise the profile of the Ural brand through enhanced advertising and promotional activities;
- Expand and build on its design and product development capabilities;
- Expand and diversify its product offerings.

The company operates in a highly competitive industry and competes intensively with various domestic brands with similar business models and target markets.

The company also competes with a growing number of international brands trying to expand their market share in Russia so as to take advantage of rising consumer spending on casual menswear fashion.

International brands traditionally dominate the high-end market, but domestic brands have advantages in terms of price and distribution and are increasingly competitive in the mid-to high-end markets.

In addition, certain formal menswear brands have been seeking to expand into the casual menswear market, and if they are successful that could further intensify competition within the casual menswear fashion market in which the company operates.

The company's major competitors include, amongst others, the most important international brands, against which the company needs to compete in terms of brand image, design and concept, product mix, quality, price, customer service, and the breadth of its retail network.

Some of Ural's competitors may have greater financial, management, human, distribution, development, marketing or other resources, or better brand recognition than the company enjoys. It also faces a variety of competitive challenges, including:

- strong brand recognition among many competitors;
- relatively low entry barriers to the menswear industry;
- competitive pricing strategies of competitors;
- established relationships between competitors and their distributors;
- expansion by existing competitors;
- innovative sales methods adopted by competitors.

7.2.3 Equity valuation

At year *n*, Ural Fashion Limited presented the balance sheet, income statement and cash flow statement as shown in Figure 7.16, Figure 7.17 and Figure 7.18. (historical data and forecast data in thousands US$).

The financial position is very good, since the financial current liabilities are US$ 18.5 million in year *n*. Ural Fashion is an investment grade company.

The equity valuation process is carried out with two different approaches:

1) the present value of future earnings;
2) the Comparable Approach as a control method.

Discounted earnings methodology

The key inputs used for the estimation process are as follows:

- Risk free rate per Russian 10 years Government Bond rate is 4.86%;
- Equity Risk Premium estimated for the Russian Equity Market is 9.8%;
- Equity Beta for Ural Fashion (based on comparable companies) is 0.9;
- Growth rate is 3%;
- The expected and normalized perpetual earnings is assumed to be the year *n* earnings.

The Cost of Equity is determined using the CAPM as follows:

$$\text{Cost of Equity} = \text{Risk Free Rate} + \beta \cdot (\text{Equity Risk Premium})$$
$$\text{Cost of Equity}_{\text{Ural Fashion}} = 4.86\% + 0.9 \cdot (9.8\%) = 13.7\%$$

Balance sheet		(thousands US$)		
	n-3	**n-2**	**n-1**	**n**
Non-current assets				
Property, plant and equipment	446	382	305	433
Deferred offering cost	-	-	-	652
Total non-current assets	**446**	**382**	**305**	**1,085**
Current assets				
Inventories	7,554	1,243	2,602	3,868
Trade and other receivables	15,410	21,229	32,203	47,021
Prepayments	3,377	-	360	269
Fixed deposits–pledged	-	882	325	116
Cash and cash equivalents	3,533	10,553	21,160	35,645
Total current assets	**29,874**	**33,908**	**56,650**	**86,919**
Total assets	**30,320**	**34,290**	**56,955**	**88,004**
Total current liabilities	**11,694**	**15,570**	**15,232**	**27,079**
Assets net of current liabilities	**18,626**	**18,720**	**41,723**	**60,925**

Figure 7.16 Ural Fashion balance sheet

Income statement			(thousands US$)	
	n-3	n-2	n-1	N
Revenues	64,923	89,410	103,568	122,339
Cost of sales	(39,192)	(53,143)	(61,440)	(71,901)
Gross profit	**25,730**	**36,267**	**42,128**	**50,437**
Other income	57	266	134	121
Selling and distribution expenses	(4,924)	(7,422)	(7,975)	(8,812)
Administrative expenses	(1,898)	(2,775)	(3,314)	(5,557)
Finance costs	(34)	(54)	(152)	(1,208)
Profit before taxation	**18,931**	**26,283**	**30,821**	**34,981**
Income tax expense	(5,271)	(6,456)	(7,824)	(9,535)
Profit after taxation	**13,659**	**19,827**	**22,997**	**25,447**

Figure 7.17 Ural Fashion income statement

The equity fair value is calculated as the present value of future earnings, as follows:

$$W = 25,447 \times \frac{1}{13.7\% - 3\%}$$

$$W = US\$237,822.$$

Comparable approach

A sensitivity analysis to growth rate and comparable beta is performed in order to assess the volatility in the earnings multiplier. The growth rate is assumed to be in the range 2.5–3.5% and the Ural beta is assumed to be in the range 0.8–1. Figure 7.19 summarizes the volatility of earnings multipliers.

The Ural Fashion earnings multiplier is in the range 8.2–10.84 and is consistent with the price/earnings of listed companies that are

Cash flow statement	(thousands US$)			
	n-3	n-2	n-1	N
Net cash generated from operating activities	7,956	26,118	6,167	6,937
Net cash generated from/(used in) investing activities	(58)	(42)	35	107
Net cash generated from/(used in) financing activities	(8,219)	(19,054)	4,399	7,652
Cash and cash equivalents at period end	**3,533**	**10,553**	**21,155**	**35,636**

Figure 7.18 Ural Fashion cash flows

Comparable beta		0.8	0.9	1
Growth rate	2.5%	9.78	8.92	8.2
	3%	10.28	9.34	8.55
	3.5%	10.84	9.79	8.9

Figure 7.19 Ural earnings multiplier

comparable with Ural (8.5–10.5). The equity fair value of Ural Fashion can be estimated as being US$237,822.

7.2.4 The new approach

According to the IAPM, Ural Fashion's cost of equity is the maximum of either the risk premium calculated using the CAPM, or the risk premium determined following the FIA.

As shown in the previous section, Ural Fashion's cost of equity is equal to 13.7% based on the CAPM.

Ural Fashion's cost of equity using FIA (see Chapter 3) can be estimated as follows:

1) Probability of default valuation;
2) Equity Expected Loss calculation;
3) Equity Risk Premium determination.

Ural Fashion's probability of default is 0.22%, that is to say there is a 0.22% probability that shareholders will lose all of their capital (recovery rate zero) (see Floor Theorem, Chapter 3); on the other hand, the probability of the shareholders of losing at least 1 US dollar is equal to 5.2% (see Cap Theorem, Chapter 3).

The combined rule to calculate the EEL is as follows:

$$\text{EEL} = \text{default probability} + (\text{probability of losing at least 1 US dollar} - \text{default probability}) \times 50\%;$$

$$\text{EEL} = 0.22\% + (5.2\% - 0.22\%)\ 50\%;$$

$$\text{EEL} = 2.7\%.$$

The last step is to compute the Equity Risk Premium based on the EEL and the probability of winning at least 1 US dollar. A rule-of-thumb approach is to define the size of "bet" that needs to be won in order to compensate shareholders for the EEL with a probability equal to "1 *minus* the probability of losing at least a US dollar", as follows:

$$\text{Probability of winning at least 1 US dollar} \times \text{Equity Risk Premium} = \text{Equity Expected Loss};$$

$$\text{Equity Risk Premium} = \text{Equity Expected Loss} / \text{Probability of winning at least 1 US dollar};$$

$$\text{Equity Risk Premium} = 2.7\%/(1 - 5.2\%);$$

$$\text{Equity Risk Premium} = 2.7\%/94.8\%;$$

$$\text{Equity Risk Premium} = 2.86\%;$$

$$\text{Cost of Equity} = \text{Risk free rate} + \text{Equity Risk Premium};$$

$$\text{Cost of Equity} = 4.86\% + 2.86\%;$$

$$\text{Cost of Equity} = 7.72\%\ (\text{FIA}).$$

In this case the equity risk premium calculated using the FIA is lower than the equity risk premium based on the CAPM, and it is therefore advisable to use 13.7% as Ural Fashion's cost of equity.

The Russian company is an investment grade company (the annual probability of default is 0.22%) and it is not surprising that the best method for computing the cost of equity is the CAPM.

8
Integrated Pricing Model in India

8.1 RiskCalc emerging markets*

8.1.1 Data description

This section describes the data used to build the Emerging Markets model.

8.1.1.1 Construction of the development sample and validation sample

We use two data sources to build the Emerging Markets model. Moody's Analytics Credit Research Database (CRD™) provides the private firm data for Mexico, Korea, China, Russia, Ukraine, and South Africa. We obtain public firm financial statement data from vended sources and public firm defaults from Moody's Analytics default database. We refer to public firms as those with listed equity. The sample includes data from the following 24 countries or regions.

- Asia – China, India, Indonesia, Israel, Korea, Malaysia, Pakistan, Philippines, Taiwan, Thailand;
- Europe – Czech Republic, Hungary, Poland, Russia, Slovakia, Ukraine;
- The Americas – Argentina, Brazil, Chile, Colombia, Mexico, Peru, Venezuela;
- Africa – South Africa.

The combined dataset from these 24 markets contains a vast number of financial statements and defaults. Moreover, this "raw" sample contains more data from select countries such as China and Russia than other countries. In addition, the actual defaults captured in different countries vary. Therefore, we have more default data for some countries than others. If we utilized the raw datasets, the sample would be dominated by a couple of countries. Instead, we employ the following sampling method to build a more balanced development sample.

Sampling method For countries with public firm data, we retain all the default events and the defaulted firms'[1] financial statements. For each default event, we randomly choose 24 statements of non-defaulted firms. The process generates a sample default rate of 4%, also the average PD level we apply on the development sample.

For each of the six countries with private firm data (Mexico, Korea, China, Russia, Ukraine, and South Africa), we randomly sample half the number of defaults as in the previous step. Similarly, for each default, we randomly select 24 statements of non-defaulted firms. We then combine the sampled public firms and private firms. The private firm data from the CRD comprises three quarters of the sample, with each of the six countries accounting for an eighth. The public firm data comprises one quarter of the sample. The sample has a relatively balanced representation from the four continents, with 46% of statements from Asia, 26% from Europe, 14% from the Americas, and the remaining 14% from Africa. Table 8.1 presents the data composition. The sample covers a long time period (1992–2009) and includes firms of different size categories and from different industries.

We also construct a separate validation sample. From each data source, we randomly select the same number of financial statements as in the development sample. In the validation sample, we do not restrict the sample default rate to 4%. Rather, we include the default events associated with the randomly selected statements. Therefore, the validation sample's default rate for each country is close to the default rate of the original sample. We estimate the model on the development

Table 8.1 Sample data information

Country/Sub-region		Number of statements	Number of defaults
Asia	China	9,155	403
	Korea	12,993	514
	Rest of Asia	6,409	345
Africa	South Africa	9,475	363
Europe	Russia	9,496	351
	Ukraine	9,400	351
	Rest of Europe	405	15
The Americas	Mexico	8,359	323
	Rest of the Americas	1,553	65

sample and test the model performance on both the development sample and the validation sample.

8.1.1.2 *Definition of default*

When building RiskCalc models, we generally seek to collect all credit events where economic loss occurred. We also include all defaults consistent with the Basel definitions, provided information is available on these defaults. This model uses default types ranging from 90 days past due to bankruptcy. Specifically, the sample covers the following default types:

- 90 days past due;
- unlikely to pay;
- non-accrual;
- loan loss provision created;
- loss;
- charge-off;
- distressed exchange offer;
- bankruptcy/liquidation.

8.1.1.3 *Data exclusions*

Excluded companies As in other RiskCalc v3.1 models, we exclude the following types of companies because the financial statements or characteristics of these firms differ from the typical firms in our development sample.

- **Firms without complete financial statements** – We require that a financial statement contains positive total assets, non-negative total sales, and non-negative total liabilities. The sample includes all firms large enough to produce financial statements in compliance with local accounting standards. About 8% of the sample firms have assets less than 100,000 USD.
- **Financial Institutions** – Financial institution balance sheets (banks, insurance companies, and investment companies) usually exhibit higher leverage than the typical firm. The regulatory and capital requirements of these institutions differentiate them from other firms. Therefore, we exclude them.
- **Real Estate Development Companies** – Real estate development and investment companies' annual accounts provide only a partial description of the dynamics of these firms and, therefore, their

likelihood to default, as their financial health often hinges on one particular development.[2]

- **Government Agency and Not-for-profit Institutions** – Government agencies' default risks are influenced by the states' or municipalities' unwillingness to allow them to fail. As a result, their financial results do not compare well with other private firms. Not-for-profit financial ratios also differ from for-profit firms, particularly with regard to variables relating to net income.

Excluded financial statements We conduct plausibility checks of financial statements, such as assets not equal to liability plus equity, negative current liabilities or negative current assets, and financial statements covering a period of less than 12 months. If we detect errors, we exclude those statements from the analysis.

8.1.1.4 Data descriptive statistics

Figure 8.1 presents the distribution of financial statements and defaults by year in the development sample. We classify the financial statements based on their fiscal year and defaults based on which year the default date falls into. The sample covers 1992 through 2009.

When building a model, we must examine potential database weaknesses. Not only should the database cover a large number of firms

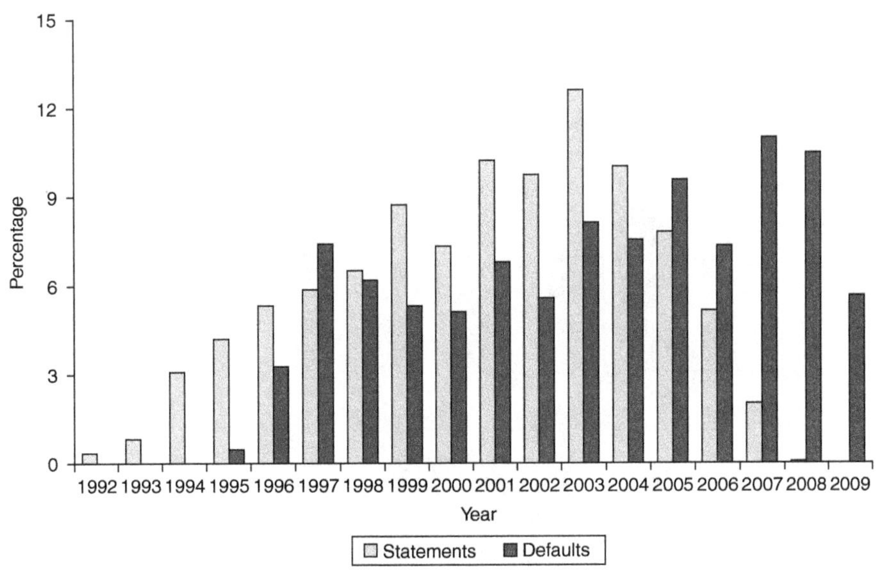

Figure 8.1 Distribution of statements and defaults by year

and defaults, but the defaults should also be distributed among industries and company size. For example, if the database has few firms in a particular size range without sufficient defaults in those groups, the model may not produce good default risk measurements.

The RiskCalc Emerging Markets model assigns firms to eight sectors by their Standard Industrial Classification (SIC) code, NACE code, or their local industry classification codes. We group firms without industry information into a category labelled Unassigned. When determining the sector classifications, we use the following two criteria.

- The classification is economically meaningful;
- We have enough statements and defaults in each sector.

Figure 8.2 presents the sample firms' distributions by industry and the proportion of defaults in each industry. Consumer Products and Trade are the two largest sectors in our sample.

Figure 8.3 presents the distributions by firm size as measured in Assets in US dollars. Our sample includes both large firms and small firms.

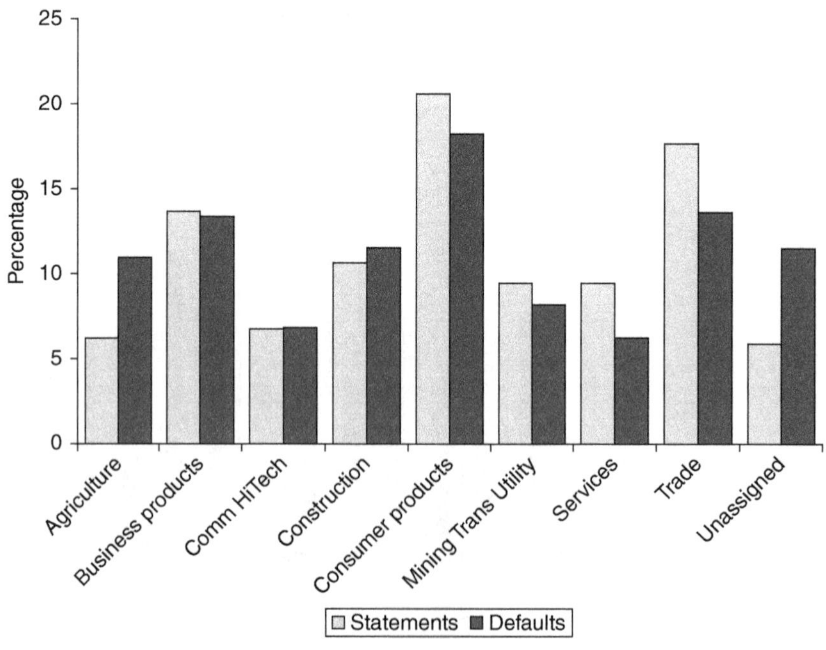

Figure 8.2 Distribution of statements and defaults by industry

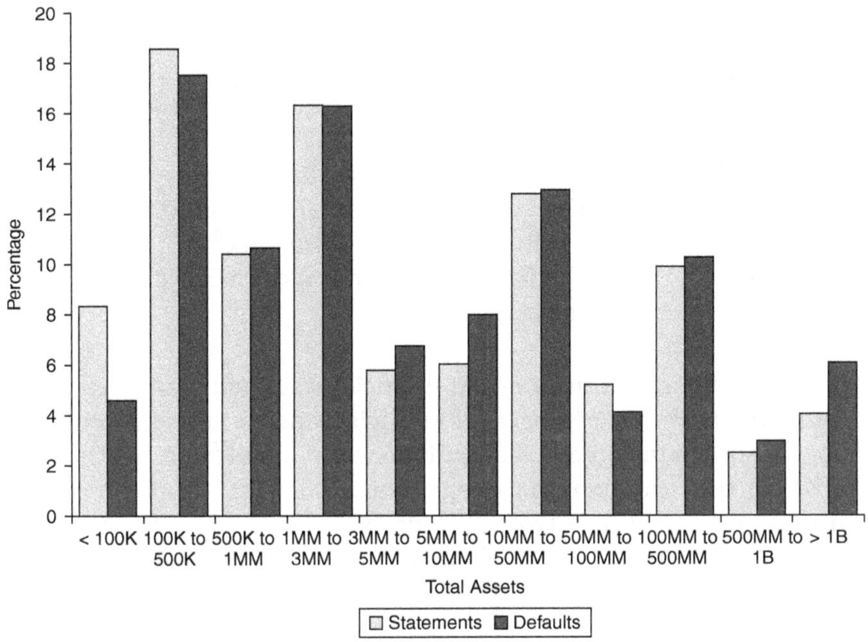

Figure 8.3 Distribution of statements and defaults by size

8.1.2 Model components

The RiskCalc v3.1 model incorporates various components to determine the EDF credit measure. Model inputs include selection of the financial ratios, transforms of those ratios, inclusion of industry information, and the CCA.

RiskCalc model development involves the following steps.

1. Choose a limited number of financial statement variables for the model from a list of possible variables[3]
2. Transform the variables into interim probabilities of default using non-parametric techniques
3. Estimate the weightings of the financial statement variables using a probit model, combined with industry variables
4. Create a (non-parametric) final transform that converts the probit model score into an actual EDF credit measure We base the models on the following functional form:

$$FSO\,EDF = F\left(\Phi\left(\sum_{i=1}^{N}\beta_i T_i(x_i) + \sum_{j=1}^{K}\gamma_j I_j\right)\right)$$

where

$x1, \ldots, xN$	are the input ratios;
$I1, \ldots, IK$	are indicator variables for each of the industry classifications;
$\gamma 1, \ldots, \gamma K$	are estimated coefficients;
D	is the cumulative normal distribution;
F *and* $T1, \ldots, TN$	are non-parametric transforms;[4]
FSO EDF	is the financial statement only EDF credit measure.

The *T*s are the transforms of each financial statement variable, which capture the non-linear impacts of financial ratios on the default likelihood, as shown in Figure 8.4 and discussed in detail later. *F* is the final transform (i.e., the final mapping). The final transform captures the empirical relationship between the probit model score and the actual default probabilities. The final transform is described as calibrating the model score to an actual EDF credit measure. This version of the model does not provide Credit Cycle Adjusted EDF (CCA EDF). We will consider adding this feature in future versions depending on user feedback.

8.1.2.1 Financial statement variables

Selecting the variables Our variable selection process begins with a long list of possible financial statement variables. We divide the working list of ratios into groups that represent different underlying concepts regarding a firm's financial status, shown in Table 8.2. We then build a model with at least one variable per group. When we can increase model performance and maintain model robustness, we use several variables from each group in the model.

We ask the following questions when deciding which variables to include in the final model. Note that this model is designed for multiple countries. Hence, the following criteria apply to all the countries covered in the development sample.

- Is the variable readily available?
- Are the definitions of the inputs to the variable ambiguous?
- Is the variable meaning intuitive?
- Does the variable help to measure default risk?
- Is the variable generally not correlated with other variables in the model?

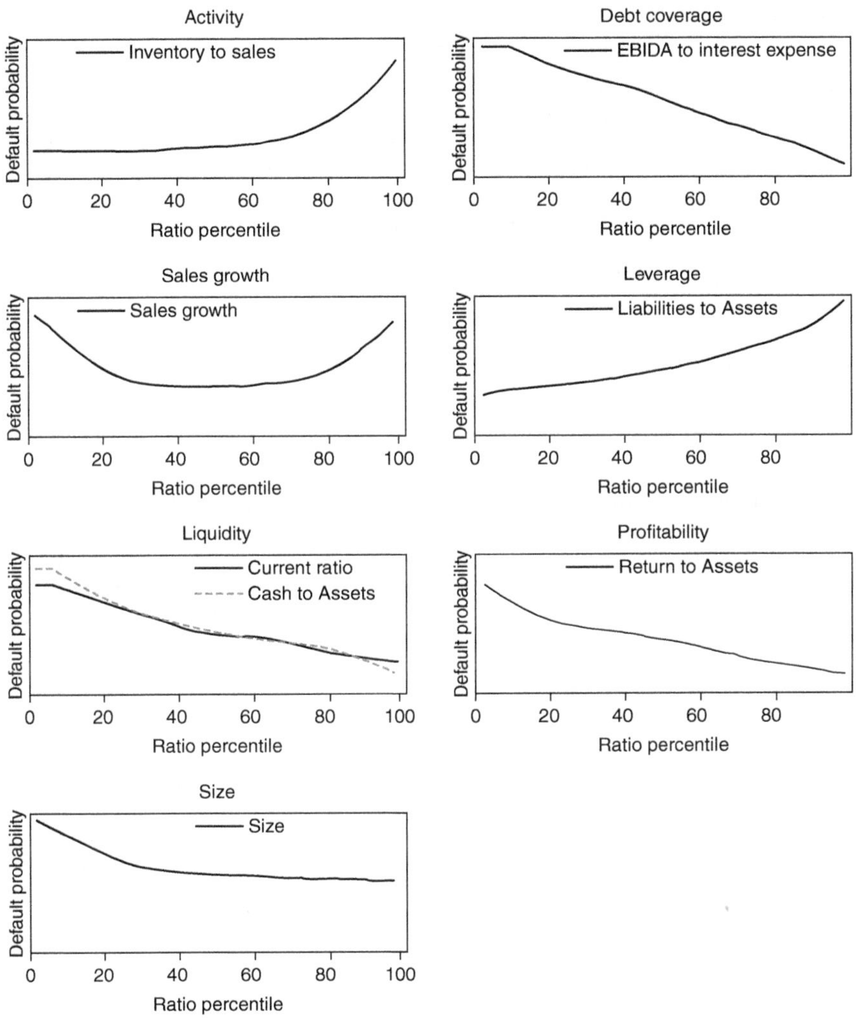

Figure 8.4 Transformations of financial statement variables in RiskCalc v3.1 emerging markets

Table 8.3 lists the financial statement variables in the RiskCalc v3.1 Emerging Markets model.

Variable transforms After we select the variables, we transform them into a preliminary EDF value. Figure 8.4 presents the transformations we use in the model. The horizontal axis gives the percentile score of the ratio, and the vertical axis gives the default probability of that ratio in isolation (univariate). The percentile score represents the percentage

Table 8.2 Groupings of financial statement ratios

Ratio	Description
Activity ratios	Measure a firm's operating efficiency. They typically involve working capital items such as inventory, accounts receivable, or accounts payable. A large stock of inventories relative to sales may indicate operation difficulties and high probability of default; other activity ratios have different relationships to default.
Debt coverage	The ratio of cash flow to interest payments or some other measure of liabilities. High debt coverage reduces the probability of default.
Growth variables	Typically include sales growth. These variables measure the stability of a firm's performance. Growth variables often behave like a double-edged sword: both rapid growth and rapid decline (negative growth) tend to increase a firm's default probability.
Leverage ratios	Include liabilities to assets or debt to assets. High leverage increases the probability of default.
Liquidity variables	Include cash and marketable securities to assets or liabilities, the current ratio, and the quick ratio. These variables measure the extent to which the firm has liquid assets relative to the size of its assets or liabilities. High liquidity reduces the probability of default.
Profitability ratios	Include net income, net income less extraordinary items, profit before tax, and operating profit in the numerator; and total assets, tangible assets, fixed assets and sales in the denominator. High profitability reduces the probability of default.
Size	Measured by total assets or sales deflated to a specific base year to ensure comparability. Large firms default less often.

Table 8.3 Financial statement variables in RiskCalc v3.1 emerging markets

Category	Definition
Activity	Inventory/Sales
Debt coverage	EBITDA to interest expense*
Growth	Sales growth
Leverage	Total liabilities/Total assets
Liquidity	Current assets/Current liabilities
	Cash and marketable securities/Total assets
Profitability	Return on Assets (ROA)
Size	Total sales (inflation-adjusted)

*EBITDA is defined as the following: Operating Profit (or Loss) + Amortization and Depreciation.

of the database with a ratio below that of the company. For example, if ROA is in the 90th percentile, then 90% of the sample had a lower ROA than that firm.

The shape of the transformation indicates how significantly a change in level impacts the EDF value. If the slope of the transform is steep, a small change has a larger impact on risk than if the slope is flat.

- For the Activity group, the transforms for Inventory to Sales is upward-sloping (see Figure 8.4). When inventories pile up, they can indicate financial or operational troubles.
- For the Debt Coverage group, the transform for EBITDA to Interest Expense is downward-sloping (see Figure 8.4). This indicates that firms with large EBITDA relative to Interest Expense have lower default probabilities.
- For the Growth group, the transform of Sales Growth (see Figure 8.4) is U-shaped, indicating that large increases or decreases in sales are associated with higher default probabilities. For emerging markets, the right-hand side of the U-shaped relationship is flatter than that for a developed economy such as the US. This finding is consistent with the higher average sales growth in emerging markets.
- For the Leverage group, the transforms for the Total Liabilities to Total Assets ratio is upward-sloping (see Figure 8.4), indicating that firms with more leverage have higher default probabilities.
- For the Liquidity group, the transform of Current Assets to Current Liabilities and Cash and Marketable Securities to Total Assets are downward-sloping (see Figure 8.4), indicating that firms with more current assets to cover their current liabilities, or with more cash, are associated with lower default probabilities.
- For the Profitability group, the transform of ROA is downward-sloping (see Figure 8.4), indicating that firms with large ROA have lower default probabilities.
- For the Size group, the transform of Size is downward-sloping (see Figure 8.4), indicating that larger firms have lower default probabilities.

8.1.2.2 Model weights

Importance The relative value of each variable used in calculating an EDF credit measure is important in understanding a company's risk. The non-linear nature of the model makes the weight of the variables more difficult to determine, because the actual impact on the risk depends on the coefficient, the transformation shape, and the percentile ranking of the company. Therefore, we calculate the model weights based on the average EDF value for the transformation and its standard deviation. A variable with a flat transformation could have a low weight, even if the coefficient is large, as shown in Figure 8.4.

Calculation of weights To calculate the weighting of a variable, we compute the EDF credit measure for a theoretical firm with all its variables at the average transformation values. We then increase the variables one at a time by one standard deviation. The EDF level change for each variable (in absolute value) is computed and added together. The relative weight of each variable is then calculated as the EDF level change for that variable as a percentage of the sum of EDF level changes across all variables. This gives the variable with the largest impact on the EDF level the largest weight and the variable with the smallest impact on the EDF level the smallest weight. Since the weights are a percentage of the total change in EDF levels, they sum to 100%. The weight of each category is the sum of the weights of each variable in that category.

Table 8.4 presents the weights in the RiskCalc v3.1 Emerging Markets model. The weights are relatively balanced across categories, with no single category accounting for more than 20%. Activity, Debt Coverage, Leverage, Liquidity, and Profitability are more important than Growth and Size.

8.1.2.3 Industry adjustments

For the same set of financials, different industries may have different default probabilities. The EDF value is adjusted for industry effects. RiskCalc v3.1 Emerging Markets has nine industries: Agriculture, Business Products, CommHiTech, Construction, Consumer Products, MiningTransUtility, Services, Trade, and Unassigned. We place firms without industry classification information or those that cannot be classified into the other eight industries into Unassigned.

Table 8.4 Risk drivers in RiskCalc v3.1 emerging markets

Category	Weights: 1-year (%)	Weights: 5-year (%)
Activity	11.71	19.31
Debt coverage	18.61	17.34
Growth	9.45	8.99
Leverage	18.69	17.41
Liquidity	18.71	17.79
Profitability	19.14	15.58
Size	3.70	3.58

Table 8.5 Increase in model power and accuracy from introducing industry controls

Industry controls	1-year model		5-year model	
	Accuracy Ratio (%)	Increase in Log likelihood	Accuracy Ratio (%)	Increase in Log likelihood
Without industry controls	48.5	—	38.5	—
With industry controls	49.4	131.2***	39.5	197.5***

***Indicates significance at the 1% level.

Agriculture takes a coefficient that increases default risk, while Consumer Products takes a coefficient that decreases default risk. Given the same set of financial ratios, the Agriculture industry coefficient typically moves the EDF level up by about one notch (e.g., from Ba3 to B1), and the Consumer Products industry coefficient typically moves the EDF level down by about one rating notch (e.g., from Baa1 to A3). Other industry coefficients also affect EDF values.

Table 8.5 presents the model power increase and accuracy from introducing industry controls. The AR of the model increases slightly. The gain in log likelihood is large and statistically significant. A large gain in likelihood indicates that the industry controls are important in producing an accurate EDF credit measure.

In this table, and hereafter, AR is the measure of the model's ability to rank order credits. Log likelihood measures the extent to which the model's EDF values better match observed default rates.[5]

8.1.3 Validation results

After we develop a model, it must prove effective in measuring default risk. In this section, we present test results on the model's ranking power (i.e., the model's ability to sort credits from worst to best).

The tests must check not only model effectiveness, but also its robustness and how well it works on data outside the sample. We examine model performance on a separate validation sample. We also conduct k-fold analyses for out-of-sample testing. The results show that the model is, in general, more powerful than other models across different markets, sectors, time periods, and size classifications.

8.1.3.1 Overall model power and accuracy

Table 8.6 presents the in-sample overall measures of power for the RiskCalc v3.1 Emerging Markets model versus the RiskCalc v3.1 US model. The Emerging Markets model outperforms the RiskCalc v3.1 US model at both 1-year and 5-year horizons.

Table 8.6 Power performance of the RiskCalc v3.1 emerging markets model

Model	1-year model		5-year model	
	Accuracy Ratio (%)	p-value	Accuracy Ratio (%)	p-value
RiskCalc Emerging Markets	49.4%	—	39.5%	—
RiskCalc v3.1 US	45.4%	< .0001	33.8%	< .0001

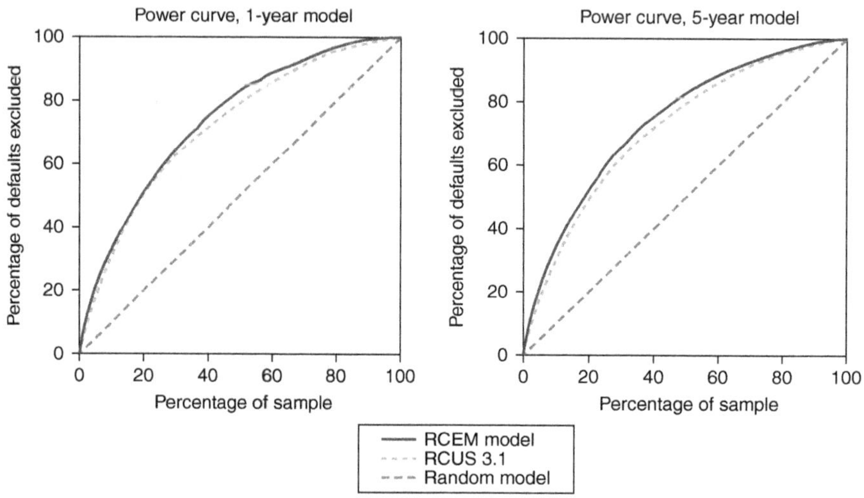

Figure 8.5 Power of alternative models (1- and 5-year): emerging market model

Table 8.6 also contains *p*-values for the statistical test to display whether the difference between the ARs from the Emerging Markets model and the benchmark equals zero. A *p*-value of less than.05 indicates we can reject the hypothesis that the difference in the ARs equals zero with 95% confidence.

Figure 8.5 presents the cumulative accuracy profiles for the 1- and 5-year models corresponding to Table 8.6. The power improvements are uniformly significant across different regions of the distribution relative to RiskCalc v3.1 US.

8.1.3.2 Correlations and variance inflation factors

To ensure model robustness, we must test the model excessive multicollinearity, which occurs if a number of the variables used in the model are highly correlated. Excessive multicollinearity can cause instability in parameter estimates. To check for this issue, we compute the correlation coefficients for the financial statement ratios in the

Table 8.7 Correlations among the transformed input factors (Spearman rank)

Inventory to sales	1.00							
EBITDA to interest expense	0.20	1.00						
Sales growth	0.15	0.23	1.00					
Liabilities to assets	−0.03	0.42	0.14	1.00				
Current assets to Current liabilities	−0.09	0.38	0.08	0.54	1.00			
Cash to assets	0.23	0.27	0.12	0.15	0.25	1.00		
Return on assets	0.21	0.73	0.21	0.38	0.37	0.23	1.00	
Total sales	0.26	0.18	0.21	−0.03	−0.01	0.37	0.13	1.00

Table 8.8 Variance inflation factors

Variable	VIF
EBITDA to interest expense	2.39
Return on Assets (ROA)	2.27
Liabilities to assets	1.65
Current assets to Current liabilities	1.65
Total sales	1.41
Cash to assets	1.35
Inventory to sales	1.34
Sales growth	1.12

model (Table 8.7) and the variance inflation factors (VIF) (Table 8.8) on the transformed variables in Figure 8.4.

The VIF levels for the financial statement variables in Table 8.8 represent how much the variation in one independent variable can be explained by all other independent variables in the model. The correlation coefficient, however, measures only the relationships between two variables. The highest VIF level is 2.39, indicating that the collinearity between the variables is low.[6] The two ratios with the highest correlation are EBITDA to Interest Expense and ROA in Table 8.7.

8.1.3.3 Power performance by region and country

Table 8.9 and Table 8.10 present the power comparison results by region. The development sample covers financial statements and defaults from 24 countries in four continents. We divide the sample into Asia, Africa, Europe, and the Americas. Given the imbalance of economic development across regions and countries, it is important to ensure that the Emerging Markets (EM) model performs well in different regions. As shown in Table 8.9 and Table 8.10, the model's ARs

Table 8.9 Power by region: 1-year horizon, emerging markets model

Region	Country/Sub-region	Percentage of defaults	AR EM model (%)	AR U.S. Model (%)	Diff p-value
Asia	China	11	60.1	41.1	0.00
	Korea*	23	40.4	38.3	0.13
	Rest of Asia	17	71.2	68.2	0.01
Africa	South Africa	11	44.7	48.6	0.02
Europe	Russia	11	62.5	53.5	0.00
	Ukraine	11	57.6	45.6	0.00
	Rest of Europe	1	77.8	72.4	0.15
The Americas	Mexico	11	38.1	26.5	0.00
	Rest of the Americas	3	42.6	36.7	0.02

*Korea data includes both audited and unaudited financial statements. Audited statements are of better quality and therefore have better predictive ability of defaults.

Table 8.10 Power by region: 5-year horizon, emerging markets model

Region	Country/Sub-region	Percentage of defaults	AR EM model (%)	AR U.S. Model (%)	Diff p-value
Asia	China	12	51.3	27.6	0.00
	Korea	21	34.9	31.2	0.00
	Rest of Asia	15	41.2	39.7	0.31
Africa	South Africa	12	39.6	47.2	0.00
Europe	Russia	13	54.4	42.1	0.00
	Ukraine	12	45.3	32.9	0.00
	Rest of Europe	1	53.0	53.6	0.91
The Americas	Mexico	10	36.4	24.1	0.00
	Rest of the Americas	3	19.5	17.7	0.54

outperform the benchmark AR in all regions and countries except for South Africa, where we have a country-specific RiskCalc model.

8.1.3.4 Power performance by industry and size groups

It is important to test the power of a model not only overall, but also among different industry segments and firm sizes.

Table 8.11 and Table 8.12 present the power comparisons by firm size (Assets in US dollars) for the 1-year and 5-year models, respectively. The model performs well across size cuts. At the 1-year horizon, the new model's AR is larger than that of the benchmark model for most of the size cuts. The difference in AR is larger for firms with assets smaller than US$500MM. Similar results can be found for the 5-year horizon.

Table 8.13 and Table 8.14 present the power comparisons by sector for the 1-year and 5-year models, respectively. As shown in Table 8.13, the highest power in the 1-year horizon is found in Business Products

Table 8.11 Power by size (total assets in US dollars), 1-year emerging markets model

Range	Percentage of defaults	AR EM model (%)	AR U.S. Model (%)	Diff p-value
Less Than $100k	3	47.7	34.5	0.00
$100k to 500k	14	46.4	39.4	0.00
$500K to 1MM	10	41.2	32.8	0.00
$1MM to 3MM	15	34.6	28.3	0.00
$3MM to 5MM	6	49.8	44.0	0.02
$5MM to 10MM	8	49.	43.1	0.01
$10MM to 50MM	13	62.7	55.9	0.00
$50MM to 100MM	6	67.4	63.8	0.03
$100MM to 500MM	12	62.3	55.7	0.00
$500MM to 1B	5	65.7	65.2	0.85
Greater than $1B	8	57.7	58.5	0.69

Table 8.12 Power by size (total assets in US dollars), 5-year emerging markets model

Range	Percentage of defaults	AR EM model (%)	AR U.S. Model (%)	Diff p-value
Less Than $100k	3	52.5	39.2	0.00
$100k to 500k	15	44.5	39.1	0.00
$500K to 1MM	11	41.7	29.0	0.00
$1MM to 3MM	16	37.6	28.7	0.00
$3MM to 5MM	6	43.2	43.3	0.98
$5MM to 10MM	7	45.3	37.9	0.01
$10MM to 50MM	12	55.3	49.2	0.00
$50MM to 100MM	6	49.3	48.1	0.55
$100MM to 500MM	12	38.0	36.5	0.37
$500MM to 1B	5	42.9	46.6	0.24
Greater than $1B	6	45.2	43.5	0.49

Table 8.13 Power by industry, 1-year emerging markets model

Sector	Percentage of defaults	AR EM model (%)	AR U.S. Model (%)	Diff p-value
Agriculture	10	53.0	51.4	0.31
Business products	14	60.0	52.9	0.00
CommHiTech	8	56.4	55. 8	0.71
Construction	13	41. 3	40.6	0.68
Consumer products	18	56.6	53.4	0.01
Mining,Trans, Utility	8	45.2	45.4	0.90
Services	6	48.0	48.6	0.77
Trade	13	40.6	38.9	0.30
Unassigned	10	35.2	35.0	0.94

Table 8.14 Power by industry, 5-year emerging markets model

Sector	Percentage of defaults	AR EM model (%)	AR U.S. Model (%)	Diff p-value
Agriculture	11	48.1	43.8	0.03
Business products	14	47.0	37.3	0.00
CommHiTech	7	44.3	41.6	0.27
Construction	12	25.8	24.6	0.52
Consumer products	18	43.5	37.1	0.00
Mining,Trans, Utility	8	36.0	38.9	0.18
Services	6	30.7	34.2	0.24
Trade	13	32.9	31.3	0.42
Unassigned	10	32.4	37.6	0.03

(AR is 60%), while the lowest is found in Unassigned (35%). Consumer Products is the largest sector in the development sample, and the model performs well on it (AR is 57%). Similar observations can be made at the 5-year horizon. At the 5-year horizon, Agriculture gives the highest power (48%), while the lowest is found in Construction (26%). Consumer Products continues to do well (AR is 44%) and outperforms the benchmark significantly, shown in Table 8.14.

8.1.3.5 *Power performance over time*

Because we implement models at various points in a business cycle by design, we conduct power tests by year to examine whether or not the model performance is excessively time dependent.

Table 8.15 and Table 8.16 present the results from this analysis at the 1- and 5-year horizons, respectively. We compare the AR of the RiskCalc v3.1 EM model with the RiskCalc v3.1 US model for each year. In building the model, we require that the financial statements used to measure default risk are issued at least half a year prior to the default date. The model performs consistently well across the sample period, and ARs are higher than that of RiskCalc v3.1 US for most years. Emerging Markets has a slightly lower 1-year AR than that of the US model in 2007, but that difference is not significant (p-value = 0.57).

8.1.3.6 *Out-of-sample testing: validation sample test*

To build the validation sample, we randomly select data from the same sources as we do for the development sample. However, we do not impose the 4% sample default rate on the validation sample. Therefore, the validation sample has a similar default rate as in the original data sources. Table 8.17 and Table 8.18 present the power comparison results by region for the 1- and 5-year horizons, respectively. The

Table 8.15 Power over time: 1-year horizon, emerging markets model

Year	Percentage of defaults	AR EM model (%)	AR U.S. Model (%)	Diff p-value
1994	3	31.7	27.8	0.43
1995	6	42.3	37.4	0.03
1996	8	43.5	39.2	0.03
1997	6	49.1	45.1	0.07
1998	6	56.8	55.3	0.44
1999	7	54.3	51.2	0.04
2000	7	49.	47.2	0.12
2001	7	42.0	41.	0.58
2002	10	36.7	35.8	0.60
2003	9	46.1	44.1	0.25
2004	10	57.6	46.9	0.00
2005	10	56.9	46.6	0.00
2006	9	50.2	37.6	0.00
2007	3	41.7	43.2	0.57

Table 8.16 Power over time: 5-year horizon, emerging markets model

Year	Percentage of defaults	AR EM model (%)	AR U.S. Model (%)	Diff p-value
1994	4	39.2	36.7	0.37
1995	6	34.7	34.6	0.96
1996	8	38.9	31.7	0.00
1997	7	48.1	40.6	0.00
1998	6	51.7	46.9	0.00
1999	7	49.8	43.5	0.00
2000	7	42.1	35.0	0.00
2001	7	44.6	36.8	0.00
2002	11	49.2	39.3	0.00
2003	10	53.5	44.0	0.00
2004	11	53.4	39.8	0.00
2005	8	53.8	38.9	0.00
2006	5	49.7	30.6	0.00
2007	2	41.0	40.2	0.79

EM model outperforms the benchmark model in most sub-regions or countries.

8.1.3.7 Out-of-sample testing: k-fold country test

We design our model for all emerging markets for which there is currently no RiskCalc country model. The model exhibits sizable power in distinguishing good credits from bad ones for both the development

Table 8.17 Power by region for validation sample: 1-year horizon, emerging markets model

Region	Country/Sub-region	Percentage of defaults	AR EM model (%)	AR U.S. Model (%)	Diff p-value
Asia	China	1.2	61.8	54.8	0.11
	Korea	22.0	35.8	36.3	0.61
	Rest of Asia	4.5	60.4	56.4	0.05
Africa	South Africa	2.9	42.7	43.0	0.90
Europe	Russia	8.1	65.5	55.4	0.00
	Ukraine	10.7	52.4	40.9	0.00
	Rest of Europe	0.2	45.7	44.8	0.92
The Americas	Mexico	48.3	31.2	22.1	0.00
	Rest of the Americas	0.2	73.8	72.3	0.84

Table 8.18 Power by region for validation sample: 5-year horizon, emerging markets model

Region	Country/Sub-region	Percentage of defaults	AR EM model (%)	AR U.S. Model (%)	Diff p-value
Asia	China	1.8	53.2	42.0	0.00
	Korea	27.0	33.5	34.7	0.19
	Rest of Asia	4.7	52.1	49.1	0.12
Africa	South Africa	3.3	38.4	39.0	0.84
Europe	Russia	13.4	54.7	43.0	0.00
The Americas	Ukraine	13.7	46.4	34.5	0.00
	Rest of Europe	0.1	40.4	42.4	0.80
	Mexico	35.0	28.9	22.1	0.00
	Rest of the Americas	0.3	70.3	69.1	0.78

sample and the validation sample. The sample covers 24 emerging markets from Asia, Europe, America, and Africa. Nevertheless, it does not cover every emerging market. A natural question arises: would the model perform effectively on a country not contained in the sample?

To address this question, we adapt the standard k-fold test to a country level out-of-sample test. We divide the sample into seven cuts by country. China, Russia, Ukraine, Mexico, Korea, and South Africa count as one cut each, with the remaining countries in the last cut. We then run the model on six subsamples, and we use the parameter estimates to score the seventh subsample. For example, we exclude China and estimate the model on the rest of the sample; the accuracy ratio on this sample is the in-sample AR. We then apply the parameter estimates on the China data and compute the accuracy ratio, which is the out-of-sample AR. We repeat the exercise for each of the seven cuts.

Table 8.19 RiskCalc v3.1 emerging markets model k-fold country test results

	Out-of-sample AR (%)		RiskCalc U.S. model AR (%)	
	1-year AR	5-year AR	1-year AR	5-year AR
China	60.5	50.9	31.0	27.6
Russia	57.1	47.9	49.5	42.2
Ukraine	55.9	45.6	42.8	32.8
Mexico	42.1	37.9	24.5	23.
Korea	40.3	34.7	38.2	31.1
South Africa	44.8	38.8	49.1	47.1
Other Countries	66.8	39.2	62.8	37.2
k-fold Overall	49.1	39.9	45.4	34
In-sample AR	53.2	43.0	—	—

Table 8.19 reports the ARs by the corresponding sample. The out-of-sample AR is consistently high across country cuts and outperforms the benchmark score in most of the cuts. This exercise shows that the model estimated on a sample of multiple countries would work well on a country not used in the estimation sample.

8.1.4 Model calibration and the adjustment factor

8.1.4.1 Central default tendency

Central Default Tendency (CDT) intends to capture the actual default probability of a given market segment over a specific period of time. If we have all the default events on this segment, we can estimate the CDT directly. However, it is difficult to collect data on all default events. Therefore, we must infer the CDT indirectly from different information sources.

We estimate the CDT for the EM model based on information from multiple countries. We collect loan loss provision data on 23 emerging markets between 1999 and 2009. Loan loss provision data reflect banks' estimates of the expected loss on loan portfolios. With assumptions of LGD ranging from between 40% to 50%, we estimate that the PD level across the 23 markets falls into a range around 4%. We select 4% as the representative CDT across emerging markets. Section 8.1.4.3 discusses how to adjust the model outputs to reflect different PD levels across markets.

The CDT estimation process for the EM model differs from that of a typical RiskCalc country model. For a RiskCalc country model, we infer the CDT with information on the local PD level.

There is a lack of publicly available data for direct calculation of the CDT of a cumulative 5-year default probability. We choose a 5-year

CDT so that forward EDF values, on average, line up with realized EDF values. We use 15.3% as the CDT for the 5-year model.

8.1.4.2 Model calibration

To help interpret EDF credit measures, the model maps an EDF value to an EDF-implied rating. All RiskCalc v3.1 models to date use the same mapping. We design this mapping with the following considerations.

- Large range of EDF-implied ratings (as required for economic and regulatory applications);
- No one rating contains too many credits (as required for economic and regulatory applications);
- The distribution of the 5-year ratings is approximately the same as the distribution of the 1-year ratings (for consistency with rating-based analysis applications).

Figure 8.6 shows the distribution of the observations by rating category in the development sample for the EDF credit measures over the full time period. Note that any one category contains less than 17% of the observations. The distributions peak at B1 for both the 1-year and the 5-year ratings.

8.1.4.3 The adjustment factor

We calibrate the EM model's development sample to a CDT of 4%. Given the heterogeneity across markets, one model calibration may

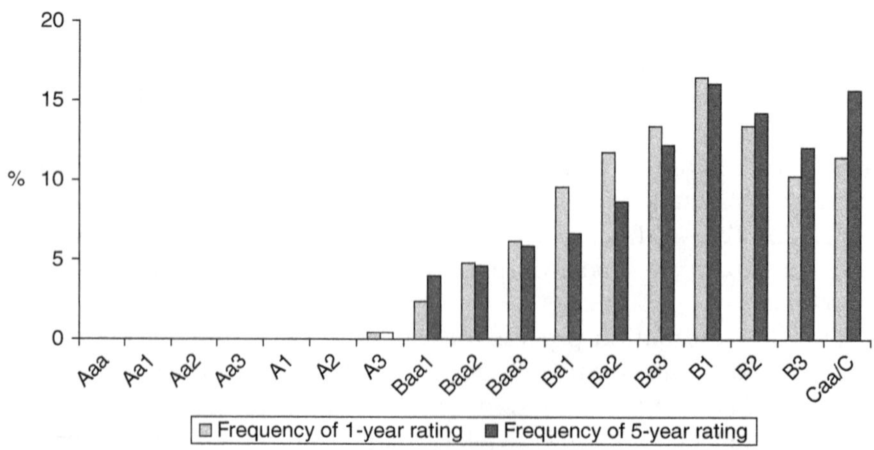

Figure 8.6 EDF-implied ratings for the 1- and 5-year models in the development

Table 8.20 An example of the adjustment factor table

Country	Model	Multiplier
Country B	Emerging market model	1.5
Country C	Emerging market model	1.3

not work for all countries and regions. Some markets may have a higher average PD level or country risk than the others. Therefore, in this model, we allow the users to apply an adjustment factor to the EDF outputs.

The account administrator at the user end maintains an adjustment factor table. Table 8.20 provides an example. In this specific case, the institution has exposures in Country B and Country C, and it determines that the adjustment factor for Country B exposure is 1.5, and the adjustment factor for Country C is 1.3. The institution runs the portfolio through the RiskCalc EM model to get the EDF measures. The adjusted PD values then equal the EDF outputs from the model times the corresponding adjustment factor.

We can use different methods to infer the adjustment factors. Moody's Analytics works with individual users on the set of multipliers most suitable for their portfolios. For more detailed information on the adjustment factor, please see the FAQ on this topic.[7] If the user has three or four years of default experience in a particular segment, they can set a multiplier so that the adjusted PD level is consistent with the sample default rate of the segment. The statistics on default rates or loan loss rates published by the regulators or other agencies also shed light on the proper PD level. Loan loss provision data is another good information source, typically available in major banks' financial statements or statutory filings.

With certain LGD assumptions, one can infer the PD estimates from loan loss provision ratios. Furthermore, to take into account country risk, users can utilize sovereign risk measurements as a benchmark to determine whether the PD level on local firms is appropriate. Sovereign risk measures include agency sovereign ratings and CDS-implied sovereign ratings. In all cases, it is important to observe whether or not the information used to infer adjustment factors comes from an economic downturn or expansion. If the available information covers mostly an expansionary period, it is appropriate to set a multiplier higher than the information suggests.

8.2 Business case: Rabbas

8.2.1 Introduction to Rabbas

Rabbas is a leading global ethanol and sugar company with low-cost, large-scale and integrated operations in India, and is one of the largest exporters of sugar in the world.

The company's production is based on sugar cane, a competitive and viable feedstock for ethanol, sugar and energy as a result of its low production cost/high energy efficiency ratio compared to other sources of ethanol, such as corn and sugar beet.

Rabbas operates mills, refineries and port facilities and has numerous warehouses. Its management team has experience in running large-scale facilities, as well as a track record of acquiring, improving and integrating additional companies and extracting operational synergies.

The company has significantly expanded its businesses bases through a series of acquisitions and organic growth, thus increasing its crushing capacity.

In this section the equity valuation methods traditionally used for private companies will be compared with the new approach.

8.2.2 Business model and competitive advantages

Rabbas is focused on increasing production capacity through an expansion of its existing facilities, the development of greenfield projects and a programme of acquisitions as and when opportunities arise.

The company is also continuing to invest in the co-generation of electricity, which not only allows it to be energy self-sufficient but also represents a potential additional source of future cash flow.

The company's overall objectives are to achieve sustainable and profitable growth, further reduce its operating costs and build on its competitive strengths in order to expand its leadership with a view to becoming a global company with a worldwide platform in the ethanol and sugar markets.

The company's strategy is focused on:

- enhancing its leadership position in the Indian and global ethanol and sugar markets by taking advantage of both the future export opportunities likely to emerge from the liberalisation of trade barriers that have traditionally limited access to some major markets, and of mandatory blending requirements to use ethanol as an additive to gasoline;

- establishing new commercial and distribution partnerships with international players within the industry so as to expand and diversify its client base;
- pursuing selective acquisitions and partnerships in India and internationally;
- continuing to expand its existing facilities and building additional large-scale facilities, featuring technological improvements and enhanced logistics.

Rabbas wants to pursue organic growth opportunities in order to meet expected demand by:

- pursuing expansion initiatives in order to capitalize on the growing global demand for ethanol and sugar.
- increasing its production capacity through an expansions of existing facilities and the development of greenfield projects.
- considering other greenfield ethanol projects in India to further increase its production capabilities.

As the same time, the company wishes to further improve the efficiency and productivity gains of its operations through investments in the development of new varieties of sugarcane, more efficient agricultural, industrial and logistic processes, expanded satellite monitoring of sugar cane development in the region, increased mechanisation of harvests, an emphasis on employee training programs and improvements in information flows and internal control systems.

Through its 3-year business plan, Rabbas plans to increase its investments in the co-generation of energy and the mechanisation of its harvests, which would not only be cost-efficient in the long-term but would also reduce the company's emission levels and reduce the burning of sugar cane fields prior to their manual harvest.

The risk factors faced by the management of the business include the following:

- in this industry demand and market prices for the company's products are cyclical and are affected by general economic conditions in India and throughout the world;
- ethanol prices are directly correlated to the price of sugar but are also becoming closely correlated to the price of oil, which means that a decline in sugar prices will adversely affect both the ethanol and the sugar businesses and a decline in the price of oil may adversely affect its ethanol business;

- competition is very significant and may adversely affect the company's market share and profitability;
- the implementation of the company's expansion strategy in new regions of India and on international markets is very challenging;
- the company's financial performance may be materially adversely affected by a reduction in market demand for ethanol or a change in the governmental policies requiring that ethanol be added to gasoline;
- substantial costs may be incurred if environmental regulations are to be complied with; if the company fails to comply with these regulations, however, it may be exposed to sanctions;
- adverse weather conditions may reduce the amount of sugar cane that the company can cultivate and buyin during a given harvest and may also have a negative impact on the sucrose content of that particular crop;
- seasonality can affect the company's results, which could in turn have a materially adverse effect on the company's quarterly financial results.

Being a low-cost, large-scale producer with well-established integrated operations and long-standing relationships with key customers and suppliers, the company's aim is to capitalize on favourable trends in the ethanol and sugar industries – especially by leveraging its competitive strengths, which are:

- Low-costs: the company's existing mills and other facilities are strategically located and its operations are also positioned in close proximity to customers, proprietary sugarcane fields and growers, as well as to port terminals and other transportation infrastructure and warehouses. These factors all help the company to manage its operating costs. Increasing mechanisation of agricultural processes and improvements in its industrial operations, combined with the fact that the company is energy self-sufficient, should enable it to continue reducing its operating costs.
- Leading market position. The company's market position as one of the largest global producers and exporters of ethanol and sugar means it has certain competitive advantages over its main competitors, particularly in terms of cost-efficiencies, greater pricing power and integrated logistics.
- Integrated platform. The company is engaged in both the agricultural and industrial aspects of ethanol and sugar production. Rabbas

not only cultivates and harvests its own crops, it also buys in and processes sugar cane from other growers. The company produces approximately 75% of its sugar cane requirements on land it either owns or leases and purchases most of the remaining 25% from third parties under long-term contracts.

- Innovative approach to business. The company is developing innovative products, production techniques and distribution methods to ensure that it continues to be at the forefront of technological improvements and standards relevant to the industry.
- Production flexibility. The company produces virtually every type of ethanol and sugar consumed by the Indian and international markets. Its facilities allow the company to switch its production between ethanol and sugar, as well as between different types of ethanol and sugar, so as to respond promptly to changes in customer demand and market prices at any point during the crushing process.
- Financial resources. The company has a good balance sheet and a solid track record of sales growth.

The company faces significant competition, which may adversely affect its market share and profitability in the future years.

The ethanol and sugar industries are highly competitive. In the international arena, the company is competing with such global ethanol and sugar producers as Aventine Renewable Energy, Inc., Archer-Daniels-Midland Company, Cargill, Inc. and A.E. Staley Manufacturing Company (a subsidiary of Tate & Lyle, PLC). Also, some of Rabbas' competitors are divisions of larger enterprises that have greater financial and marketing resources, larger customer bases and broader product ranges.

In India, the company also competes with numerous small- to medium-size producers. Despite increased consolidation, the Indian ethanol and sugar industries remain highly fragmented.

Many factors influence Rabbas' competitive position, including the availability, quality and cost of fertiliser, energy, water, chemical products and labour.

Both international and Indian ethanol and sugar markets are benefiting from trends that represent opportunities for the company's future growth and greater profitability, such as:

- the increasing global demand for ethanol;
- strong Indian demand for ethanol;
- increasing market opportunities for sugar at a global level as a result of increased sugar consumption due to (1) population growth, (2)

migration from rural to urban areas, (3) increasing purchasing power in many countries, and (4) greater consumption of processed foods;
- sizeable Indian market for sugar.

8.2.3 Equity valuation

Figure 8.7, Figure 8.8 and Figure 8.9 show Rabbas' balance sheet and income statement for the last two years (year $n-1$ and year n) (per million US$).

Assets	n-1	n
Current assets	**533**	**995**
Cash & equivalents	178	58
Accounts receivable	90	380
Inventories	167	315
Other current assets	98	242
Non-current assets	**175**	**252**
Permanent assets	**1.184**	**2.133**
Property, plant & equipment, net	793	1.447
Other permanent assets	391	686
Total assets	**1.893**	**3.380**

Figure 8.7 Rabbas assets in year n-1 and year n

Liabilities	**n-1**	**n**
Current liabilities	**407**	**748**
Loans and financing	273	504
Accounts payable	69	112
Other current liabilities	65	133
Non-current liabilities	**739**	**1.346**
Loans and financing	437	1.094
Other operating liabilities	302	252
Shareholders' equity	**747**	**1.286**
Total liabilities	**1.893**	**3.380**

Figure 8.8 Rabbas liabilities in year n-1 and year n

In year *n* a capital increase was necessary in order to restore the company to financial health and sustain its future income performance. Earnings in year *n* can be assumed to be a perpetual indicator of profitability. The equity valuation is based on the following two methods:

1. Earnings-based method, i.e. the present value of future earnings;
2. Comparables approach, based on the average EV/EBITDA of its global peers, estimated using relative performance indicators (growth, return and WACC).

Income statement	n-1	n
Net revenues	**1.022**	**2.892**
COGS (excl. depreciation)	(814)	(2.351)
SG&A expenses (excl. amortization)	(123)	(259)
EBITDA	**85**	**281**
Depreciation & amortization	(102)	(170)
EBIT	**(17)**	**111**
Net interest income (expense)	(130)	71
Other non-operating income	(1)	62
Pre-tax profit	**(147)**	**245**
Income tax	51	(65)
Net income	**(96)**	**180**

Figure 8.9 Rabbas income statements in year n-1 and year n

Earnings-based method

In order to calculate the present value of future normalized earnings, the key variables are as follows:

- expected and normalized future earnings: US$ 180 million;
- risk free rate: equal to Indian 10-years Government Bond rate, 8.8%;
- equity beta for the Indian farming and agricultural industry: 1.1;
- equity risk premium for the Indian equity market is 3.4%;
- growth rate: 5%.

The Rabbas' cost of equity is determined using the CAPM:

$$\text{Cost of Equity} = \text{Risk Free Rate} + \beta \cdot (\text{Equity Risk Premium})$$
$$\text{Cost of Equity}_{\text{Rabbas}} = 8.80\% + 1.1 \cdot (3.4\%) = 12.54\%.$$

The equity value based on the present value of future and normalized earnings is calculated as follows:

	Growth rate %	4.5	5	5.5
Risk free rate	7.8	2,557	2,752	2,980
	8.8	2,239	2,387	2,557
	9.8	1,991	2,108	2,239

Figure 8.10 Sensitivity analysis on growth rate and risk free rate

$$W = \frac{180}{ke - g};$$

$$W = \frac{180}{12.54\% - 5\%};$$

$$W = US\$2,387MM$$

In order to establish the magnitude of the sensitivity of Rabbas' equity value to key variables, a scenario analysis is performed based on the range of a variation in the growth rate between 4.5% and 5.5% and the range of variation in the risk free rate between 7.8% and 9.9% (see Figure 8.10).

As shown in Figure 8.10, the equity value of Rabbas is within a range of variation of between US$ 1,991 million and US$ 2,980 million.

8.2.3.1 Comparables approach

The EV/EBITDA multiple is the ratio between the total market value of the company and earnings before interests, taxes, deprecations and amortizations.

The list of key inputs used to estimate Rabbas' equity value in accordance with the comparables approach is as follows:

- average EV/EBITDA multiple for the Indian farming and agriculture industry is equal to 11;
- expected Rabbas EBITDA is US$ 281 million;
- cash &equivalent in year n is US$ 58 million;
- financial debt in year n is equal to US$ 1.598 million.

$$W = \left[\left(\frac{\text{EV}}{\text{EBITDA}}\right)_{\text{Sample}} \times \text{EBITDA}_{\text{Rabbas}}\right]$$

$$- \text{Financial Debt} + \text{Cash and Equivalents}$$

$$W = [11 x 281] - 1,598 + 58 = \text{US\$}\,1,551\,\text{MM}.$$

The Rabbas equity value based on the comparables approach is materially lower than the Rabbas equity value based on the present value of future and normalized earnings.

8.2.4 The new approach

According to the IAPM, Rabbas' cost of equity is the maximum of either the risk premium calculated using the CAPM, or the risk premium determined following the FIA.

As shown in the previous section, the Rabbas' cost of equity is equal to 12.54% when calculated using CAPM.

Rabbas' cost of equity determined using the FIA (see Chapter 3) is estimated as follows:

1. probability of default valuation;
2. equity expected loss calculation;
3. equity risk premium determination.

Rabbas' probability of default is 1.86%, that is to say there is a 1.86% probability that the shareholders will lose all of their capital (recovery rate zero) (see Floor Theorem, Chapter 3); on the other hand, the probability of shareholders losing at least a US dollar is equal to 14.7% (see Cap Theorem, Chapter 3).

The combined rule to calculate the EEL is as follows:

$$\text{EEL} = \text{default probability} + (\text{probability of losing at least one US dollar} - \text{default probability})\ 50\%;$$

$$\text{EEL} = 1.86\% + (14.7\% - 1.86\%)50\%;$$

$$\text{EEL} = 8.28\%.$$

The last step is to compute the equity risk premium based on the EEL and the probability of winning at least 1 US dollar. A rule-of-thumb approach is to define the size of "bet" that would need to be won in order to compensate the shareholders for the EEL with a probability equal to "1 *minus* the probability of losing at least 1 US dollar", as set out below:

$$\text{Probability of winning at least 1 US dollar} \times \text{Equity Risk Premium} = \text{Equity Expected Loss};$$

$$\text{Equity Risk Premium} = \text{Equity Expected Loss} \,/\, \text{Probability of winning at least 1 US dollar};$$

Equity Risk Premium = 8.28% / (1 – 14.7%);

Equity Risk Premium = 8.28% / 85.3%;

Equity Risk Premium = 9.7%.

Cost of Equity = Risk free rate + Equity Risk Premium;

Cost of Equity = 8.8% + 9.7%;

Cost of Equity = 18.5% (FIA).

In this case the equity risk premium calculated using the FIA is higher than the equity risk premium based on the CAPM, and it is therefore advisable to use 18.5% as Rabbas' cost of equity.

If we assume a Rabbas' cost of equity equal to 18.5%, the new equity value based on the present value of future and normalized earnings is as follows:

$$W = \frac{180}{ke - g};$$

$$W = \frac{180}{18.5\% - 5\%};$$

$$W = US\$1,333MM.$$

In this case, it is easy to verify that the Rabbas' equity value based on the present value of future and normalized earnings (US$ 1,333 million) is more in line with the Rabbas' equity value determined using the comparables approach, which suggests that the market price of listed companies incorporates a higher cost of equity than the CAPM cost of equity.

9
Integrated Pricing Model in Italy

9.1 RiskCalc Italy*

9.1.1 Data description

In the development of a RiskCalc model, the first step is the collection of a large and appropriate database. In addition, data needs to be "cleaned" so that it is representative of the actual risk of the firms covered. MKMV has developed techniques for cleaning the database to improve the model results.

9.1.1.1 Overview of the data

The extensive data on both non-defaulting and defaulting companies contained in Moody's CRI has increased substantially since RiskCalc v1.0 was developed. In addition to the increase in time-series data, there has been an increase in the number of participants in the CRI.

Figure 9.1 presents the distribution of Italian financial statements and defaults by year in the CRI. Table 9.1 summarizes the data used in the development, validation, and calibration of the RiskCalc v3.1 Italy model.

9.1.1.2 Robustness of the data

In building a model, potential database weaknesses need to be examined. Not only does the database need to cover a large number of firms and defaults, but the defaults also need to be distributed among industries and company types covered. For example, if the database has significant numbers of small firms or firms in one particular industry, and there are not sufficient defaults in those areas, the model may not be a good default predictor. The CRD used in developing the RiskCalc models has addressed both of these issues.

Figure 9.2 presents the distributions of Italian defaults and firms by industry and the proportion of defaults in each industry. Figure 9.3 and

Table 9.1 Information on Italian private firm sample data

Italian private firms	RiskCalc v1.0 Italy	RiskCalc v3.1 Italy	Credit research database growth (%)
Financial statements	124,000+	510,000+	**T311**
Unique number of firms	52,000+	116,000+	**T123**
Defaults	950+	6,600+	**T594**
Time period	1995–1999	1993–2002	**T5 additional years**

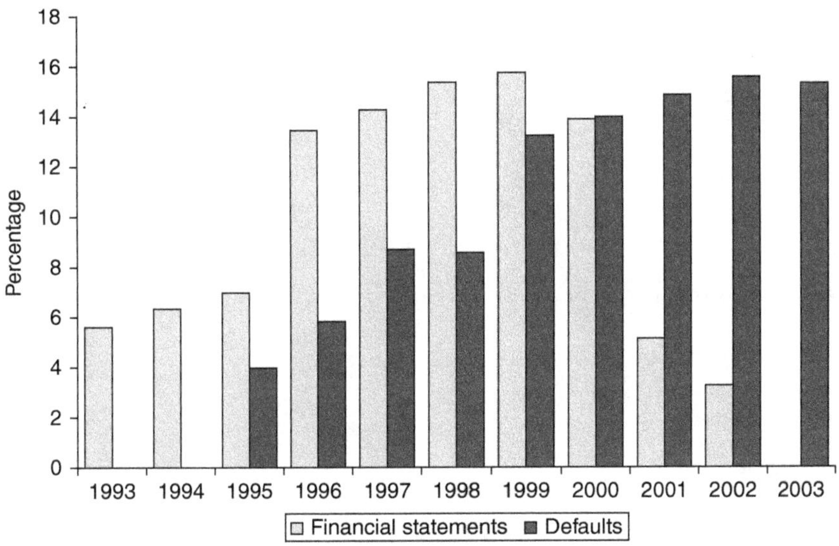

Figure 9.1 Date distribution of Italian financial statements and default data

Figure 9.4 present similar distributions by the size of firms measured as real total assets and real net sales in 2002 euros, respectively. These figures demonstrate that the proportion of defaults in any one size group or industry group is comparable to the proportion of firms in these groupings. The size distribution shows that the majority of firms (65%) hold between 1 and 10 million euro in assets. The proportion of firms between 1 and 10 million euro in sales is 79% (where firms with less than 500,000 euro in sales are excluded from the sample).

9.1.2 Model components

The RiskCalc v3.1 model incorporates various components to determine the EDF credit measure. The inputs to the model include selection of the financial ratios and transforms of those ratios, the inclusion of industry information, and the CCA.

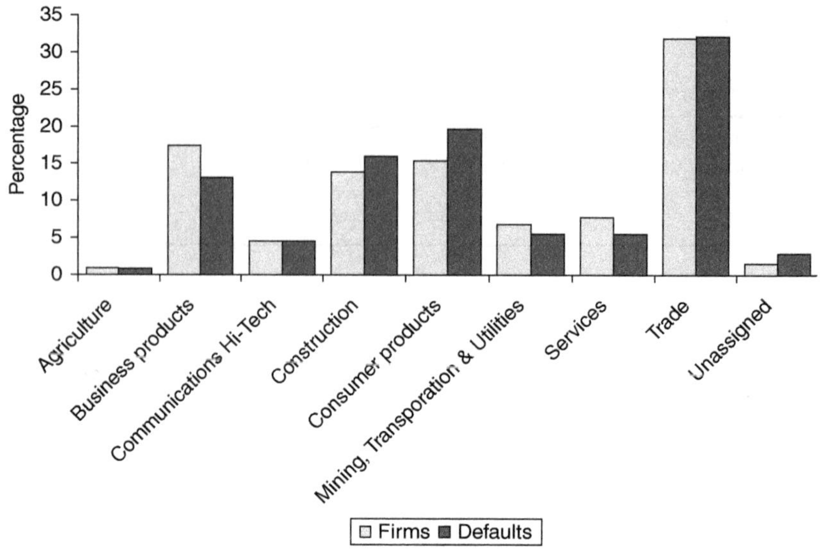

Figure 9.2 Distribution of Italian defaults and firms by industry

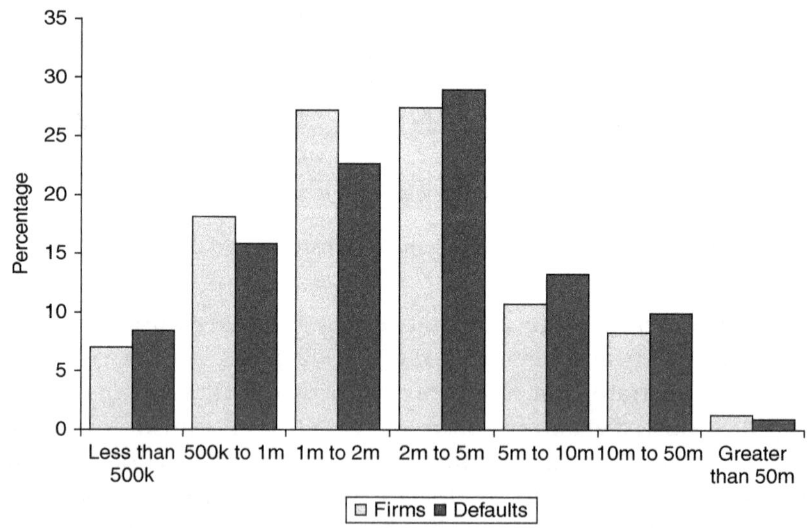

Figure 9.3 Size (as total assets) distribution of defaults and firms

The development of a RiskCalc model involves the following steps:

1. Choosing a limited number of financial statement variables for the model from a list of possible variables.
2. Transforming the variables into interim probabilities of default using non-parametric techniques.

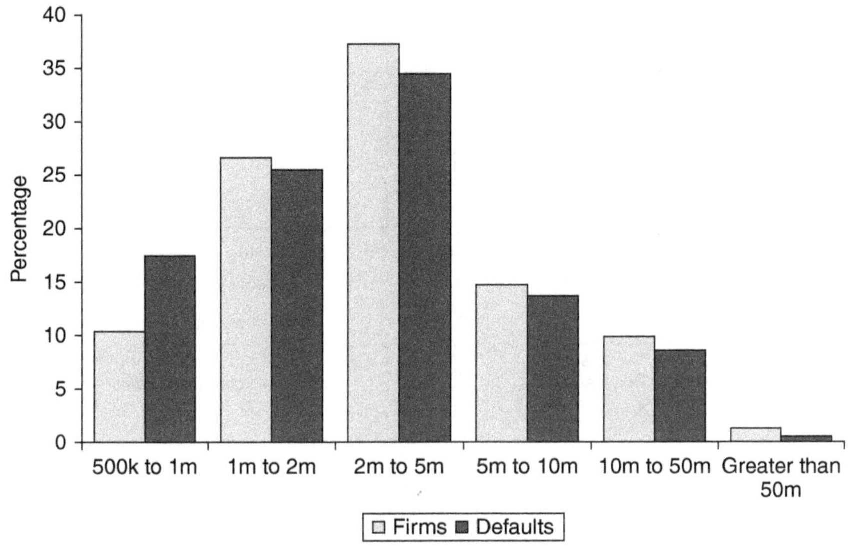

Figure 9.4 Size (as net sales) distribution of defaults and firms

3. Estimating the weightings of the financial statement variables, using a probit model, combined with industry variables.
4. Creating a (non-parametric) final transform that converts the probit model score into an actual EDF credit measure.

In FSO mode, the models are based on the following functional form:

$$FSO\ EDF = F\left(\Phi\left(\sum_{i=1}^{N}\beta_i T_i(x_i) + \sum_{j=1}^{K}\gamma_j I_j\right)\right)$$

where

$x1, \ldots, xN$	are the input ratios;
$I1, \ldots, IK$	are indicator variables for each of the industry classifications;
$\gamma 1, \ldots, \gamma K$	are estimated coefficients;
D	is the cumulative normal distribution;
F *and* $T1, \ldots, TN$	are non-parametric transforms;
FSO EDF	is the financial statement only EDF credit measure.

The *T*s are the transforms of each financial statement variable, which capture the non-linear impacts of financial ratios on the default

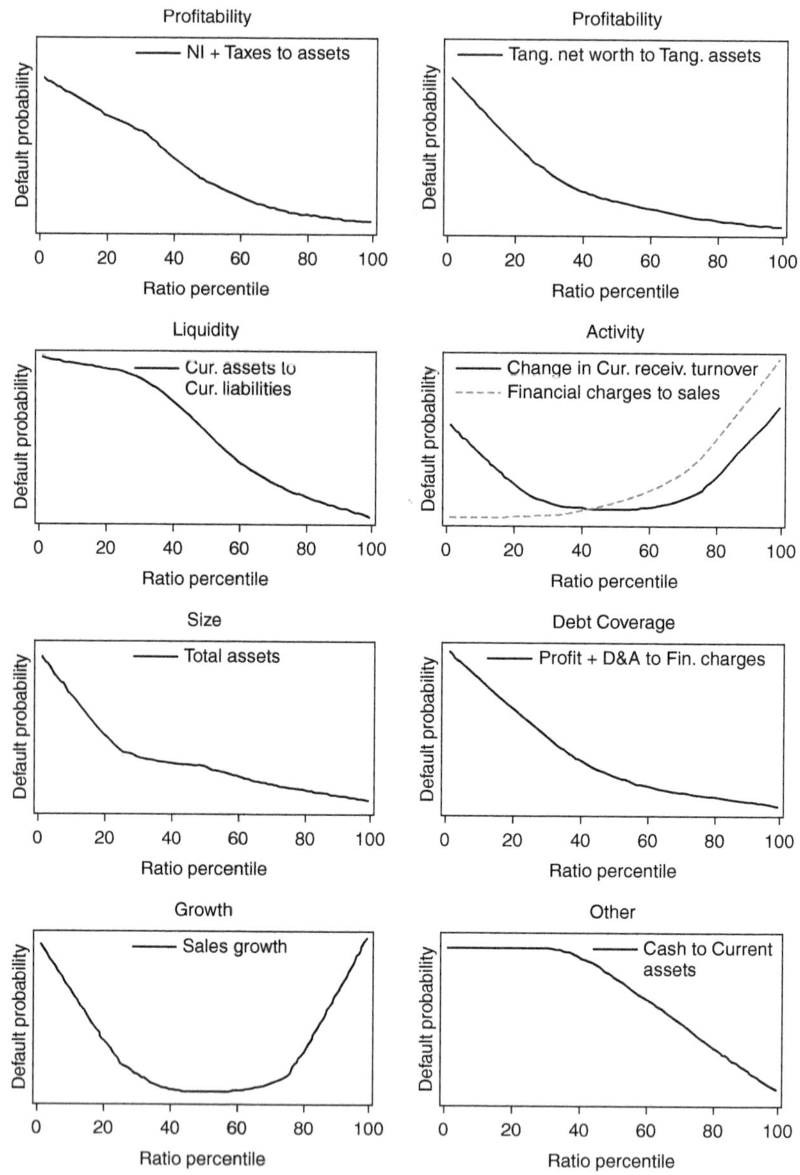

Figure 9.5 Transformations of financial statement variables used in the model

likelihood. (This is shown in Figure 9.5 and discussed in detail later in the document.) *F* is the final transform (i.e. the final mapping). The final transform captures the empirical relationship between the probit model score.

These variables are often ratios, but not always. For example, one measure of profitability is Net Income to Total Assets, which is a ratio, and one measure of size is Inflation-Adjusted Total Assets, which is not a ratio.

By non-parametric, we mean that $T(x_i)$ is a continuous function of x not requiring a specification of a specific closed (or parametric) functional form. We estimate these transforms using a variety of local regression and density estimation techniques and actual default probabilities. We describe the final transform as calibrating the model score to an actual EDF credit measure. The difference between the FSO EDF and the credit cycle adjusted EDF is that in CCA mode the final transform is adjusted to reflect our assessment of the current stage of the credit cycle, while in FSO mode it remains constant.

9.1.2.1 Financial statement variables

Selecting the variables Our variable selection process starts with a long list of possible financial statement variables. The working list of ratios is divided into groups that represent different underlying concepts regarding a firm's financial status (see Table 9.2). A model is then built with at least one variable per group. When it is possible to increase model performance while maintaining model robustness, several variables from each group will be used in the model. Criteria that must be met for variables to be included in the final model are:

- Is the variable readily available?
- Are the definitions of the inputs to the variable unambiguous?
- Is the meaning of the variable intuitive?
- Does the variable predict default activity?
- Is the variable not highly correlated with other variables in the model?

Variable transforms Once the variables are selected, they are transformed into a preliminary EDF value. Figure 9.5 presents the transformations used in the model. The horizontal axis gives the percentile score of the ratio and the vertical axis gives the default probability of that ratio in isolation (univariate). The percentile score represents the percentage of the database that had a ratio below that of the company (e.g., if ROA is in the 90th percentile that means that 90% of the sample had an ROA lower than that firm).

The shape of the transformation indicates how significantly a change in level impacts the EDF value. If the slope of the transform is steep,

Table 9.2 Groupings of financial statement ratios

Examples of ratios in the **profitability** group include: net income, net income less extraordinary items, EBITDA, EBIT and operating profit in the numerator; and total assets, tangible assets, fixed assets and sales in the denominator. *High profitability reduces the probability of default.*

Examples of ratios in the **leverage (or gearing)** group include liabilities to assets and long-term debt to assets. *High leverage increases the probability of default.*

Debt coverage is the ratio of cash flow to interest payments or some other measure of liabilities. *High debt coverage reduces the probability of default.*

Growth variables are typically the change in ROA and sales growth. These variables measure the stability of a firm's performance. *Growth variables behave like a double-edged sword: both rapid growth and rapid decline (negative growth) will tend to increase a firm 's default probability.*

Liquidity variables include cash and marketable securities to assets, the current ratio, and the quick ratio. These variables measure the extent to which the firm has liquid assets relative to the size of its liabilities. *High liquidity reduces the probability of default.*

Activity ratios include inventories to sales and accounts receivable to sales. These ratios may measure the extent to which a firm has a substantial portion of assets in accounts that may be of subjective value. For example, a firm with a lot of inventories may not be selling its products and may have to write off these inventories. *A large stock of inventories relative to sales increases the probability of default; other activity ratios have different relationships to default.*

Size variables include sales and total assets. These variables are converted into a common currency as necessary and then are deflated to a specific base year to ensure comparability (e.g., total assets are measured in 2002 Euros). *Large firms default less often.*

Table 9.3 Financial statement variables used in RiskCalc v3.1 Italy*

Category	Variable
Activity	Change in Current Receivables Turnover
	Financial charges to sales
Debt coverage	Ordinary profit + Depreciation & amortization to financial charges
Growth	Sales growth
Leverage	(Net worth – Intangible assets) to (Assets – Intangible assets)
Liquidity	Current assets to Current liabilities
Profitability	(Net income + Taxes) to Assets
Other	Cash to Current assets
Size	Total assets

*Current Receivables Turnover is the ratio of receivables due within one year to sales.

a small change will have a larger impact on risk than if the slope were flat.

- For the Profitability group, the transform for NI + Taxes to Assets is downward-sloping, but the slope becomes almost zero as profitability becomes large (see Figure 9.5). Such a transform indicates that more profitable firms have lower default probabilities, but the impact diminishes as profitability increases.

- For the Leverage group, the transform for Tangible Net Worth to Tangible Assets is downward-sloping since leverage increases as the ratio decreases. Large leverage corresponds to low levels of Tangible Net Worth to Tangible Assets and high default risk. The slope becomes less negative as the ratio increases, which implies that a small increase in leverage, when leverage is high (and equity is low), will increase the default likelihood by a larger amount than when leverage is low (and equity is high) (see Figure 9.5).
- For the Liquidity group, the transform for Current Assets to Current Liabilities is downward-sloping and backwards "S shaped". The largest changes in default probability occur when moving upward or downward from the median of the distribution (see Figure 9.5).
- For the Activity group, two ratios are included. Financial Charges to Sales are upward-sloping indicating that high values of these ratios are associated with higher default probabilities. However, the slope is almost zero until the 30th percentile of the ratio and begins to increase rapidly after that point (see Figure 9.5). Change in Current Receivables Turnover is "U-shaped," indicating that large positive values or large negative values are associated with higher default probabilities, while stable current receivables turnover is associated with lower default probabilities.
- The Size variable is Total Assets. This variable's transformation is downward-sloping, but the slope becomes almost zero as size becomes large (see Figure 9.5). This indicates that larger firms have lower default probabilities, but the impact of size on default probability is diminishing as firm size increases.
- The Debt Coverage variable is Ordinary Profit + Depreciation & Amortization to Financial Charges. This variable is downward-sloping indicating that large values of cash flow relative to interest expense lower the probability of default. The slope becomes almost zero as debt coverage increases (see Figure 9.5).
- The Growth variable is Sales Growth. It is "U-shaped," indicating that large increases or decreases in sales are associated with higher default probabilities, while stable sales year-upon-year decreases the probability of default (see Figure 9.5).
- The Other variable is Cash to Current Assets, which measures the "quality" of current assets. The slope is zero for low values of the ratio and becomes downward-sloping as the ratio increases

(see Figure 9.5). This indicates that until Cash dips below a certain percentage level of Current Assets the probability of default is unaffected.

9.1.2.2 Model weights

Importance The relative value of each variable used in calculating an EDF credit measure is important in understanding a company's risk. The non-linear nature of the model makes the weight of the variables more difficult to determine since the actual impact on the risk depends on the coefficient, the transformation shape, and the percentile ranking of the company. The model weights, therefore, are calculated based on the average EDF value for the transformation and its standard deviation. A variable with a flat transformation could have a low weight, even if the coefficient is large (see Figure 9.5).

Calculation of weights To calculate the weighting of a variable, the EDF credit measure for a theoretical firm with all its variables at the average transformation values is computed. The variables are then increased one at a time by one standard deviation. The EDF change for each variable (in absolute value) is computed and added together. The relative weight of each variable is then calculated as the EDF level changes for that variable as a percentage of the total change in EDF level. This gives the variable with the biggest impact on the EDF level the biggest weight, and the variable that has the smallest impact on the EDF level the smallest weight. Since the weights are a percentage of the total EDF value, they sum to 100%. The weight of each category is the sum of the weights of each variable in that category. Table 9.4 presents the weights in RiskCalc v3.1 Italy.

9.1.2.3 Industry adjustments

While the variables included in the RiskCalc model explain most of the risk factors, the relative importance of the variables can be different among industries. In the FSO mode of RiskCalc v3.1 Italy, the EDF value is adjusted for industry effects. Table 9.5 presents the increase in model power and accuracy from introducing industry controls into the FSO model. Both the power and the accuracy of the EDF credit measure increase, as measured by the AR and the gain in log likelihood. The large gain in log likelihood indicates that the industry controls are especially important in producing an accurate EDF. Table 9.6 presents the average EDF value by industry for the development sample in April of 2003.

Table 9.4 Risk drivers in RiskCalc v3.1 Italy

Risk drivers	Weight (%)
Profitability	11
(Net income + Taxes)/Assets	
Leverage	26
Tangible net worth to Tangible assets	
Debt Coverage	19
Ordinary profit + Depreciation & amortization/Financial charges	
Activity	19
Financial charges/Sales	
Change in Current Receivables Turnover	
Growth	6
Sales growth	
Other	8
Cash/Current assets	
Liquidity	5
Current assets/Current liabilities	
Size	6
Total asset	

Table 9.5 Increase in model power and accuracy from introducing industry controls

	1-year model		5-year model	
	Accuracy Ratio (%)	Relative increase in Log likelihood	Accuracy Ratio (%)	Relative increase in Log likelihood
FSO mode without industry controls	73.9		59.0	
FSO mode with industry controls	74.2	203.1***	59.7	492.4***

*** Indicates a P-value of less than 0.01 percent.
In this table, and hereafter, Accuracy Ratio (or AR) is the measure of the model's ability to rank order credits. Increases in log likelihood measure the extent to which the model's EDF values match observed default rates. For further details, see Dwyer and Stein (2004), Technical Document on RiskCalc v3.1 Methodology (Technical Document).

Table 9.6 Average EDF credit measure in April 2003 by sector

Sector	1-year (%)	5-year (%)
Agriculture	1.96	7.58
Business products	1.82	6.01
Communications and Hi Tech	2.49	7.82
Construction	1.87	6.93
Consumer products	3.18	10.90
Mining, Transportation, Utilities and Natural resources	1.49	5.49
Services	1.79	5.96
Trade	2.37	7.68

9.1.2.4 Credit cycle adjustment

EDF credit measures are impacted not only by the financials of a company, but also by the general credit cycle in the economy. To capture this effect, RiskCalc v3.1 Italy includes a CCA factor. The CCA is designed to incorporate the current credit cycle into the estimate of private firm default risk.

Selecting an adjustment factor The RiskCalc v3.1 model uses the DD calculation from the Moody's KMV public firm model. This measure is specifically designed to be a forward-looking indicator of default risk. It extracts signals of default risk from the stock market performance of individual firms (cf., Bohn and Crosbie, 2003). This measure was chosen because it is available for a large universe of industries and it has been extensively validated.

If the DD for public firms in an industry indicates a level of risk above the historical average for that industry, then the private firms' EDF values in that industry are adjusted upward. Conversely, if the level of risk is below the historical average, then the private firms' EDF values are adjusted downward. When the credit cycle adjustment factor is neutral, the CCA EDF value coincides with the FSO EDF value.

Adjustment factor used in the model For the Italian model, the DD factor for each industry is a weighted average of two indices. The average is based on the aggregation of DD for all Italian and continental European firms in each industry.[1] The weight on the Italian factor is industry specific and determined by the value (assets) of Italian firms in each industry relative to all of continental Europe. In the event that a firm cannot be associated with a specific industry, the model uses a CCA based on an aggregation of all public Italian and continental European firms.

Figure 9.6 presents the evidence of the Italian DD factor and insolvency levels in Italy. The DD factor is inverted when graphed so that higher values on the graph indicate higher probabilities of default for Italian public firms. The DD tracks insolvency levels in a forward-looking manner throughout the period. Data on insolvency levels is compiled by Creditreform (2004).

Figure 9.7 provides evidence of the relationship between the DD factor and public default rates in continental Europe as measured by Moody's KMV.[2] Similar to private firm defaults, the factor is a forward-looking measure of the probability of default for public European firms. Overall, the private and public default evidence shows that the distance-to-default factor is a strong predictor of economic conditions

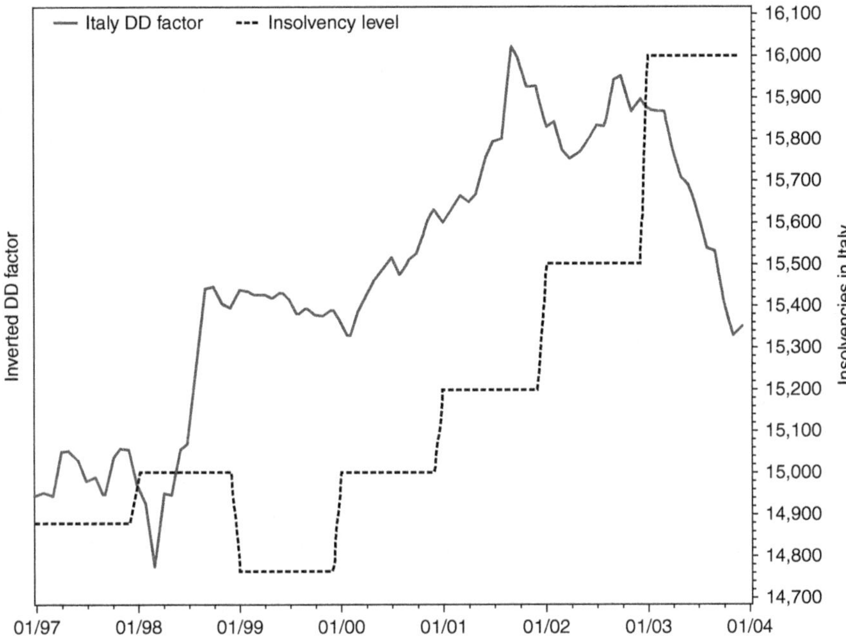

Figure 9.6 Italian DD factor and insolvencies in Italy, 1997–2003

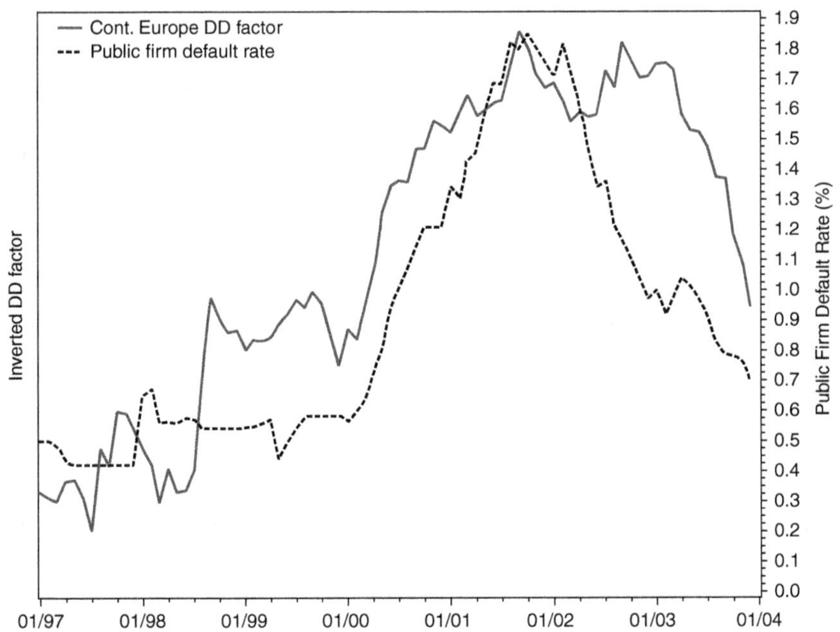

Figure 9.7 Continental Europe DD factor and public default rates, 1997–2003

Table 9.7 Power enhancements of the new RiskCalc v31 Italy model

	1-year model		5-year model	
	Accuracy Ratio (%)	Lead in Log likelihood*	Accuracy Ratio (%)	Lead in Log likelihood*
RiskCalc v3.1 Model	74.5%	–	59.7%	–
RiskCalc v3.1 Model - FSO	73.9%	106	59.6%	420
RiskCalc v1.0	71.8%	990	55.2%	985
Z-score	52.8%	9725	28.7%	4915

*Presents the increase in log likelihood of RiskCalc v3.1 Italy over the alternative model. Larger values indicate that levels of RiskCalc v3.1 are better-calibrated vis-à-vis the alternative model.

in each industry and will adjust the probability of default to reflect the position in the credit cycle. Table 9.7 shows that including the CCA factor increases both the power and the accuracy of the model.

Figure 9.6 gives the DD factor against the historical insolvencies levels in Italy. The DD factor increases in anticipation of the increase in default activity. Insolvency data is compiled by Creditreform (2004).

Figure 9.7 gives the DD factor against the historical public bond default rate for continental Europe. The DD factor increases in anticipation of the increase in default activity.

9.1.3 Validation results

Once a model is developed, it must be shown to be effective in predicting defaults. In this section, we present test results of the model's ranking power (the model's ability to sort credits from worst to best) and the accuracy of its predicted EDF credit measure (the model's ability to estimate the level of EDF correctly).

The tests need to check not only the model effectiveness, but also its robustness and how well it works on data outside the sample. To do out-of-sample testing, we performed walk-forward and k-fold analyses. The results of the testing show that the model is uniformly more powerful than other models across different time periods, sectors, and size classifications.

9.1.3.1 Increase in overall model power and accuracy

Table 9.7 presents the in-sample overall measures of power and likelihood for RiskCalc v3.1 Italy versus alternative models. With the CCA, the model's performance improves by almost three percentage points of AR at the 1-year horizon and over four percentage points at the 5-year horizon compared with RiskCalc v1.0 Italy. Relative to other available alternatives, the results were more dramatic. The new

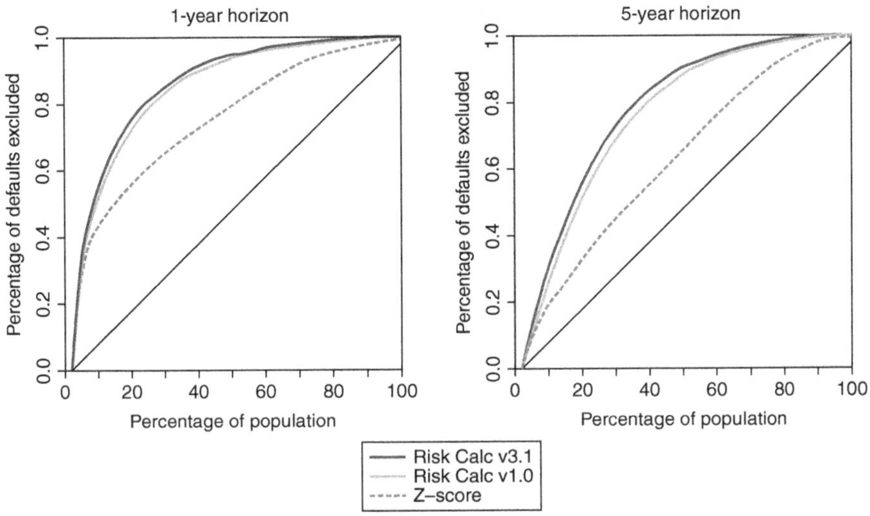

Figure 9.8 Power of alternative models (1- and 5-year) – Italy

RiskCalc v3.1 model outperformed the Z-score model (Altman *et al.*, 1995) by more than 20 percentage points at both the 1-year and 5-year horizons. The FSOmode outperforms the old model by two percentage points at the 1-year horizon and four percentage points at the 5-year horizon. RiskCalc v3.1 Italy is also more accurate than alternative models as measured by the log likelihood differences.[3]

Figure 9.8 presents the cumulative accuracy profiles for the 1- and 5-year models corresponding to Table 9.7. The power improvements are largely in the middle of the distribution relative to RiskCalc v1.0 (particularly for the 1-year model). This result implies that both very good and very poor credits are correctly identified by both RiskCalc v1.0 and RiskCalc v3.1. The added discriminatory power is in assessing the credit quality of credits that fall in the middle range.

9.1.3.2 Correlations and variance inflation factors

To ensure model robustness, the model must be tested for excessive multicollinearity, which occurs if a number of the variables used in the model are highly correlated. Excessive multicollinearity can cause instability in parameter estimates. In order to check for this issue, the correlation coefficients (see Table 9.8) for the financial statement ratios in the model and the VIF (see Table 9.9) are computed on the transformed variables (see Figure 9.5).[4]

Table 9.8 Correlations among the transformed input factors (Spearman rank)

Ordinary Profit + Depreciation & Amortization to Financial Charges	1.0								
(Net Income + Taxes) to Assets	0.734	1.0							
Financial Charges to Sales	0.636	0.419	1.0						
Tangible Net Worth to Tangible Assets	0.439	0.456	0.244	1.0					
Current Assets to Current Liabilities	0.314	0.360	0.310	0.602	1.0				
Sales Growth	0.145	0.131	0.106	0.112	0.069	1.0			
Total Assets	−0.028	−0.061	−0.255	0.163	0.076	0.036	1.0		
Change in Current Receivables Turnover	0.104	0.100	0.177	0.063	0.031	0.294	−0.053	1.0	
Cash to Current Assets	0.289	0.257	0.338	0.186	0.171	0.041	−0.116	0.077	1.0

Table 9.9 Variance inflation factors

Variable	VIF
Ordinary profit + Depreciation & amortization to financial charges	2.7
(Net income + Taxes) to assets	2.3
Financial charges to Sales	1.7
(Net worth – Intangible assets) to (Assets – Intangible assets)	1.7
Current assets to Current liabilities	1.5
Sales growth	1.2
Total assets	1.2
Change in Current Receivables Turnover	1.2
Cash to Current assets	1.1

Model results The highest correlation coefficient is between [Ordinary Profit + Depreciation & Amortization to Financial Charges] and [Net Income + Taxes to Total Assets] (0.73). The next highest coefficient is between [Ordinary Profit + Depreciation & Amortization to Financial Charges] and [Financial Charges to Sales] (0.64). Such coefficients are below what we would typically consider indications of multicollinearity, and this finding is also verified by the VIF analysis.

The VIF (Table 9.9) for the financial statement variables represent how much the variation in one independent variable can be explained by all the other independent variables in the model. The correlation coefficient, however, measures only the relationships between two variables. As shown in Table 9.9, the estimated VIF values in

Table 9.10 Model power by industry, 1-year model

	Percentage of defaults*	AR RiskCalc v3.1 (%)	AR RiskCalc v1.0 (%)	AR Z-score (%)
Agriculture	0.6	62.2	56.4	44.4
Business products	13.6	81.1	80.3	65.2
Communications and Hi Tech	4.7	79.8	77.9	65.2
Construction	17.1	70.1	66.5	47.5
Consumer products	21.8	77.1	74.5	54.4
Mining, Transportation, Utilities and Natural Resources	5.3	79.6	76.6	54.2
Services	4.5	70.1	68.7	54.4
Trade	32.3	69.7	65.6	46.8

the Italy model are notably below the threshold levels of 4 to 10 that are commonly used in VIF analysis when testing for presence of multicollinearity.[5] These findings indicate that the model variables do not present any substantial multicollinearity.

Further tests were performed to ensure that multicollinearity is not a problem in the Italian model. Tests for the usual effect of multicollinearity, which is model parameter instability, show that the model parameters are stable across random subsamples. In other words, re-estimating the model on small random subsamples of the data does not produce economically meaningful differences in the model's coefficients.

9.1.3.3 Model power by industry and size groups

It is important to test the power of a model not only overall, but also among different industry segments and firm sizes. Table 9.10 and Table 9.11 present the power comparisons by sector for the 1-year and 5-year models, respectively.

RiskCalc v3.1 Italy outperforms both RiskCalc v1.0 Italy and Z-score in all sectors. The highest power in the 1-year model is found in Business Products (81.1%) while the lowest is found in Agriculture (62.2%). At the 5-year horizon (Table 9.11) the highest power is in Business Products (66.0%) and the lowest is in Trade (55.7%).

Table 9.12 and Table 9.13 present the power comparisons by firm size for the 1-year and 5-year models, respectively. RiskCalc v3.1 Italy out performs both RiskCalc v1.0 Italy and Z-score in all size groups. The highest power in the 1-year model is found in the largest firms – over €50 million in assets – and the lowest is in the smallest firms – under €500,000 in assets. A similar relationship is often found between model

Table 9.11 Model power by industry, 5-year model

Sector	Percentage of defaults	AR RiskCalc v3.1 (%)	AR RiskCalc v1.0 (%)	AR Z-score (%)
Agriculture	0.7	58.6	46.5	22.4
Business products	13.3	66.0	64.0	40.4
Communications and Hi Tech	4.7	62.3	58.1	31.3
Construction	16.6	54.9	49.4	21.5
Consumer products	21.0	59.2	55.8	25.5
Services	5.2	58.2	54.2	34.0
Services	5.2	58.2	54.2	34.0
Trade	32.7	55.7	50.4	27.0

Table 9.12 Model power by size, 1-year model

Range	Percentage of defaults	AR EDF RiskCalc v3.1 (%)	AR RiskCalc v1.0 (%)	AR Z-score (%)
<€500,000	6.0	49.6	49.2	39.5
€500,000 to €1 mm	12.4	64.5	62.9	44.3
€1 mm to €2mm	22.9	75.0	73.6	51.4
€2mm to €5mm	31.0	76.5	73.4	51.3
€5mm to €10mm	15.1	77.4	75.4	55.9
€10mm to €50mm	11.6	77.9	76.8	55.9
over €50mm	1.2	78.9	78.9	62.5

Table 9.13 Model power by size, 5-year model

Range	Percentage of defaults	AR EDF RiskCalc v3.1 (%)	AR RiskCalc v1.0 (%)	AR Z-score (%)
<€500,000	6.4	38.9	36.6	21.3
€500,000 to €1 mm	12.2	51.8	48.7	26.2
€1 mm to €2mm	22.9	63.4	59.6	31.4
€2mm to €5mm	31.1	64.1	60.8	33.2
€5mm to €10mm	15.3	63.0	61.2	35.9
€10mm to €50mm	10.9	64.0	61.8	33.7
over €50mm	1.2	71.4	69.7	38.1

power and size in other countries. Such performance improvements are likely to reflect the higher quality of financial statements among larger firms.

9.1.3.4 Power performance over time

Since models are implemented at various points in a business cycle by design, power tests by year (Table 9.14 and Table 9.15) were conducted

Table 9.14 Model power over time, 1-year horizon

Year	Percentage of defaults	AR RiskCalc v3.1 (%)	AR RiskCalc v1.0 (%)	AR Z-score (%)
1993	6.8	68.9	67.4	39.8
1994	7.4	71.2	70.0	49.1
1995	8.0	75.6	75.2	53.4
1996	14.3	73.0	71.1	48.7
1997	16.7	73.9	70.9	48.0
1998	17.5	74.3	72.2	49.1
1999	16.9	71.4	68.9	47.7
2000	12.4	67.8	65.7	41.9

Table 9.15 Model power over time, 5-year horizon

Year	Percentage of defaults	AR RiskCalc v3.1 (%)	AR RiskCalc v1.0 (%)	AR Z-score (%)
1993	9.0	60.6	58.4	26.4
1994	8.9	62.7	60.6	32.8
1995	9.8	64.6	62.5	37.8
1996	18.8	63.7	60.3	35.0
1997	20.3	64.0	60.0	34.5
1998	19.0	65.7	63.2	39.2
1999	14.2	67.3	64.7	41.8

to examine whether or not the model performance is excessively time dependent.

Table 9.14 and Table 9.15 present the results from this analysis at the 1- and 5-year horizons, respectively. The AR of RiskCalc v3.1 Italy is compared with RiskCalc v1.0 Italy and Z-score for each year. As shown in these tables, RiskCalc v3.1 consistently outperforms both by a considerable margin.

9.1.3.5 Out-of-sample testing: k-fold tests

The model exhibits a high degree of power in distinguishing good credits from bad ones (in Table 9.7), but whether this power is attributable to the overall model effectiveness or the impact of a particular subsample also needs to be tested. A standard test for evaluating this is the k-fold test, which divides the defaulting and non-defaulting companies into *k* equally sized segments. This yields *k* equally sized observation subsamples that exhibit the identical overall default rate and are temporally and cross-sectionally independent. The model is then run on *k-1* subsamples and these parameter estimates are used to score the *k-th* subsample. We repeat this procedure for all possible combinations,

Table 9.16 RiskCalc v3.1 Italy k-fold test results

	Out-of-sample AR (%)		RiskCalc v1.0 (%)	
	1-year AR	5-year AR	1-year AR	5-year AR
Subsample 1	72.2	62.6	70.4	59.2
Subsample 2	72.7	62.6	70.5	58.9
Subsample 3	72.9	64.6	70.0	60.4
Subsample 4	73.5	63.7	70.8	60.1
Subsample 5	73.3	63.8	70.8	60.0
k-fold overall	75.1	59.1	72.5	53.3
In-sample AR	75.3	59.2		

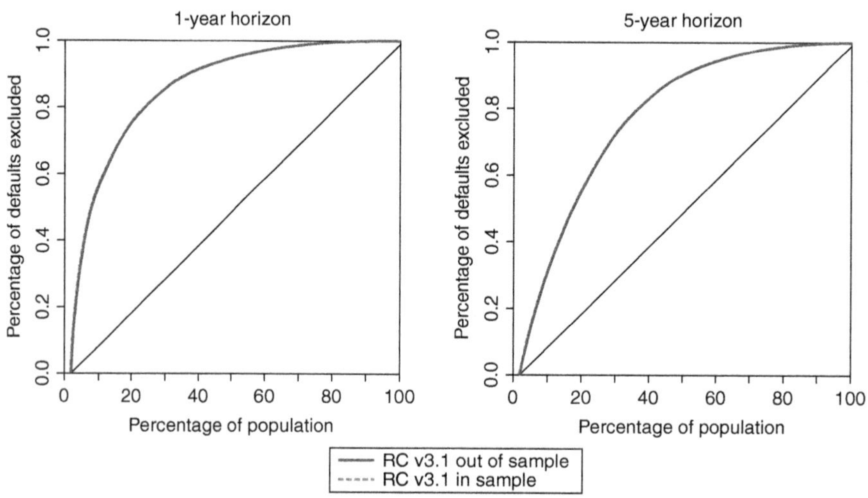

Figure 9.9 RiskCalc v3.1 Italy k-fold

and put the *k* scored "out-of-sample" subsamples together to calculate an AR on this combined data set.

Table 9.16 summarizes the k-fold test results (with k=5). The reported figures are the ARs by the corresponding sample and time horizons. The out-of-sample model consistently outperforms RiskCalc v1.0 Italy. Figure 9.9 presents the cumulative accuracy profiles associated with the overall out-of-sample results against the in-sample results. The model performance is maintained both in- and out-of-sample in the k-fold analysis.

Results The in- and out-of-sample plots are virtually indistinguishable at both the 1- and 5-year horizons in Figure 9.9. The difference in AR between the overall in-sample and out-of-sample results is not larger than 20 basis points in both cases. Furthermore, RiskCalc v3.1 Italy outperforms RiskCalc v1.0 Italy in an out-of-sample context at both the 1- and 5-year horizons (Table 9.16).

The k-fold testing does not control for time dependence. Each of the *k* subsamples contains data from all periods. As a result, if there were a particularly high period of default rates, this would be included in each of the *k* samples. Such testing does not give a true sense of how the model would have performed during those volatile periods because the model is estimated with full information on those time periods.

9.1.3.6 Walk-forward tests

An alternative out-of-sample test developed by Moody's KMV is a walk-forward analysis, which is designed along similar lines as the k-fold test, except that it controls for the effects of time. The model is estimated up to a certain year and the parameter estimates are then used to score the observations in the *next* year. These model scores are *out-of-time*. The model is re-estimated including one more year of data and we repeat the analysis for the next year and continue until the end of the sample. These out-of-sample out-of-time scores are combined into a single prediction set so that the AR and the power curve can be calculated for the combined set. The out-of-sample AR is then compared to the corresponding in-sample AR and power curve.

No data from a future period is used in fitting the model and only data from future periods is used for testing it. The parameter estimates are checked for stability across the different samples. Figure 9.10 presents the results from this analysis.

Results Similar to the k-fold results, the in- and out-of-sample plots for the walk-forward results are virtually indistinguishable at both the 1- and 5-year horizons in Figure 9.10. The difference in AR between the in-sample and out-of-sample results is no more than 30 basis points in both cases. Furthermore, RiskCalc v3.1 Italy outperforms RiskCalc v1.0 Italy in an out-of-time context at both the 1- and 5-year horizons.[6]

9.1.3.7 Model calibration and implied ratings

To aid in the interpretation of an EDF credit measure, an EDF value is mapped to an EDF rating (an EDF0-implied rating). All RiskCalc v3.1 models to date have used the same mapping. This mapping is designed so that:

- There is a large range of EDF ratings (as required for economic and regulatory applications);

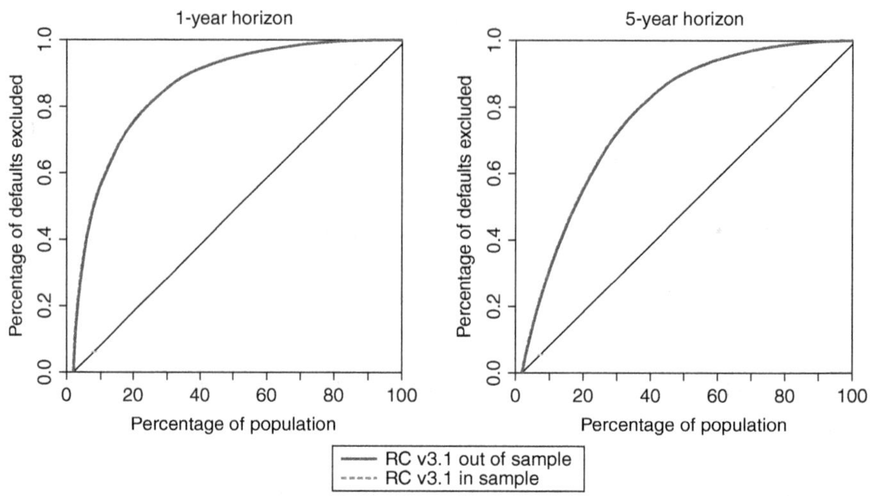

Figure 9.10 Out-of-sample performance (1- and 5-year) Italy walk-forward

- No one rating contains too many credits (as required for economic and regulatory applications);
- The distribution of the 5-year ratings is approximately the same as the distribution of the 1-year ratings (for consistency with rating-based analysis applications);
- The EDF value associated with an EDF rating is approximately the same as the observed historical default rate associated with a Moody's Bond Rating (for consistency with rating-based analysis applications).

These out-of-sample ARs are 2.5 and 6.1 points higher than RiskCalc v1.0 Italy, for the 1- and 5-year models respectively.

Figure 9.11 shows the distribution of CRD observations by rating category in the development sample (for the CCA EDF credit measures over the full time period). Note that 14 categories between Aa3 and Caa/C are utilized and that less than 15% of the observations are in any one category. The 1-year and 5-year distributions peak at Ba1. While not reported here, other research has shown that the distribution of the CCA EDF-implied ratings changes over time with the credit cycle while the distribution of the FSO EDF-implied ratings remains relatively stable over time.

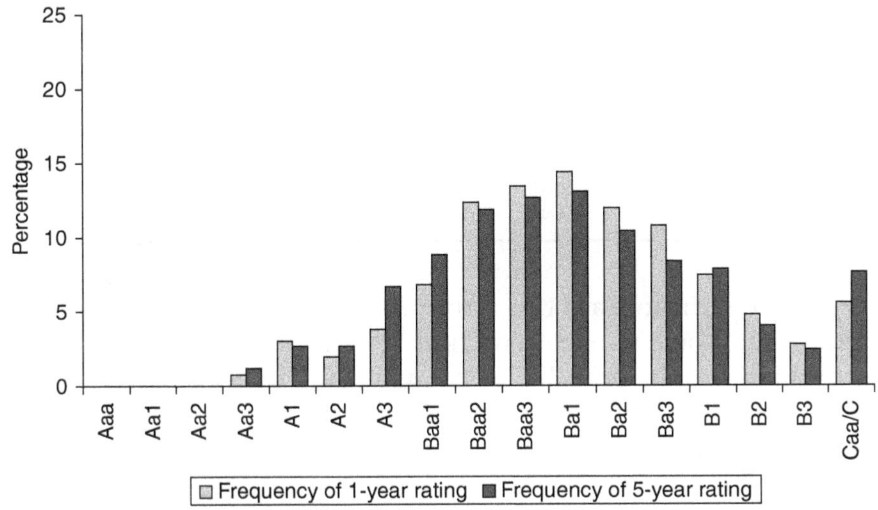

Figure 9.11 EDF-implied Ratings for the 1- and 5-year models in the development sample

9.1.4 Further model improvements

For a detailed discussion of these enhancements, refer to the Technical Document. In this section, we will briefly outline some other enhancements to the model.

9.1.4.1 Continuous term structure

The previous version of the RiskCalc model provided the user with two discrete default probability estimates: a 1-year and a 5-year EDF. In this version, utilizing the two point estimates for 1- and 5-year estimates, we fit a Weibull function, and thus achieve a continuous term structure of EDF values for each credit. In other words, users of RiskCalc v3.1 Italy can now obtain EDF estimates for any point between 1 and 5 years. In addition, RiskCalc v3.1 provides EDF estimates for alternative definitions, such as the Forward EDF and the Annualized EDF (see Table 9.17).

Cumulative EDF A cumulative EDF credit measure gives the probability of default over that time period. For example, a 5-year cumulative EDF of 13.44% means that that company has a 13.44% chance of defaulting over that 5-year period. The second column of Table 9.17 provides an example of the cumulative 1- to 5-year credit measures produced by the model.

Table 9.17 Term structure of EDF credit measures: an example

EDF	Cumulative	Forward	Annualized
Year 1	4.23	4.23	4.23
Year 2	7.00	2.90	3.57
Year 3	9.37	2.55	3.23
Year 4	11.49	2.34	3.01
Year 5	13.44	2.20	2.84

Forward EDF The forward EDF is the probability of default between *t*-1 and *t*, conditional upon survival until *t*-1. In other words, the 4-year Forward EDF is the probability that a firm will default between years 3 and 4 assuming the firm survived to year 3.[7] The third column of Table 9.17 displays the forward 1- to 5-year EDF credit measures that are derived from the cumulative EDF values.

Annualized EDF The annualized EDF credit measure is the cumulative EDF value for a given period, stated on a per year basis. For example, a company with a cumulative 5-year EDF of 13.44% would have a 5-year annualized EDF of 2.84%.[8] This means that the average default rate per year for a 13.44% cumulative default rate is 2.84%. The last column of Table 9.17 presents the annualized EDF credit measures for years 1 to 5,derived from the cumulative EDF values.

9.2 Business case: Sintesi Farmaceutica

9.2.1 Introduction to Sintesi Farmaceutica

Sintesi Farmaceutica SpA is a company engaged in the manufacturing, marketing & trading of pharmaceuticals formulations under its own brand names in the OTC (Over the Counter), Generic and Herbal Remedy market segment.

Sintesi Farmaceutica started life as a marketing company that used to outsource its finished product requirements (under its own brand and drug licence) from other formulation manufacturing facilities based in central Italy. In 2006 the company set up a state-of-the-art manufacturing facility at Deruta, in the Umbria region.

These days Sintesi continues to outsource some of its finished product requirements, having a purchase and sale agreement with these companies whereby the supplier manufactures Sintesi's products to Sintesi's own specifications and quality control requirements, but under the terms of which Sintesi controls the quality of the raw materials and their sourcing by the supplier, as well as manufacturing operations at its supplier's facilities.

The goods manufactured for Sintesi are sold in return for the pre-agreed order prices for each formulation product thus manufactured.

In order to cater for varied and increased demand the company also decided to set up its own pharmaceutical manufacturing facilities, and opened a manufacturing facility at San Marino in the State of San Marino, a tax free and duty free zone.

9.2.2 Business model and competitive advantages

The company's main sources of competitive advantages are:

- Multi-product capability – Sintesi has licences to manufacture various formulations. Sintesi routinely manufactures 200 to 250 types of formulations based on market demand and limited formulation lines. However, Sintesi also has versatile manufacturing facilities, capable of producing multiple products using a combination of processes. The flexible manufacturing infrastructure helps Sintesi to vary its product mix in response to changes in market demand. Sintesi also has a complete infrastructure in place for the development of new formulations including a pilot production plant and facilities for carrying out validation studies. It is therefore able to develop efficient and cost-effective specialized processes at short notice.
- Established client relationships – Sintesi has established client relationships in domestic markets through which it receives orders on a continuous basis. Sintesi believes that its existing relationship with its clients represents a competitive advantage in gaining new clients and growing its business.
- Compliance with environmental standards – Sintesi has already set up systems as a part of its existing business that not only meet the present environmental standards but that are also geared to meet even stricter environmental requirements, thereby enabling it to leverage newer business opportunities.
- Locational advantage – Sintesi's manufacturing facilities are located in central Italy, which enables it to take advantage of a good road network, locally available manpower (skilled manpower is readily available in and around the area in which the Sintesi plant is situated, which means the company is able to fulfil its staffing requirements) and plentiful availability of water in the region (one of the basic requirements of any pharmaceutical company). Water is extracted via tube wells.

	(values in US$)		
	n-2	n-1	n
Net sales	**6,126,370**	**10,956,157**	**12,081,321**
Other income	3,771	7,542	2,055
Material consumed	1,522,051	2,210,724	2,327,557
Finished goods purchased	2,444,446	5,768,238	6,668,976
Manufacturing & other expenses	1,401,427	1,783,191	1,804,998
EBITDA	**762,218**	**1,201,546**	**1,281,844**
Interest and finance charges	190,074	574,632	673,809
Depreciation	179,081	390,144	406,524
Preliminary exp. W/Off	2,055	3,192	4,170
Deferred revene expenditure W/Off	30,924	30,924	30,924
Net profit before tax and extra-ordinary items	**660,083**	**802,653**	**866,417**
Current tax	78,887	102,629	101,751
Deffered tax	15,921	(54,107)	0
Fringe benefit tax	17,677	22,884	10,414
Net profit before extra-ordinary items	**547,598**	**731,248**	**754,252**
Extra-ordinary items	0	0	(6,544)
Net income	**547,598**	**731,248**	**747,708**

Figure 9.12 Sintesi Farmaceutica income statement

The pharmaceutical industry is highly fragmented with a large number of players in both its organized and unorganized sectors. Any certified pharmaceutical formulator that has spare capacity and that complies with Italian Law is a potential competitor. In order to meet the competition, Sintesi is proposing an expansion of its business activity so as to achieve a diverse product portfolio, economies of scale and cost competitiveness.

9.2.3 Equity valuation

Sintesi Farmaceutica's accounting data are illustrated in Figure 9.12 and Figure 9.13.

	(values in US$)		
	n-2	**n-1**	**n**
A Fixed Assets			
Gross block	3,076,961	3,834,206	3,964,706
Depreciation	260,382	650,526	1,046,057
Net block	2,816,579	3,183,680	2,918,649
Capital work in progress	649,070	74,797	-
Net Block after adjustment for Revaluation Reserve and intangible assets (A)	**3,465,649**	**3,258,477**	**2,918,649**
B Investment(B)	738	738	738
C Current assets, loans and advances	-	-	-
Inventories	1,435,907	2,205,841	2,420,974
Sundry debtors	3,143,319	4,885,371	5,683,894
Cash and bank balances	8,599	31,503	28,929
Other current assets	20,151	-	-
Loans and advances	160,547	97,242	1,080,932
Total(C)	**4,768,522**	**7,219,956**	**9,214,729**
D Liabilities and provisions	-	-	-
M/L term loans	3,517,148	4,662,562	4,482,004
Short term loans	1,009,766	1,900,843	2,204,100
Deffered tax liabilities	54,107	-	-
Current liabilities & provisions	1,769,126	766,821	1,199,601
Total(D)	**6,350,147**	**7,330,226**	**7,885,705**
	-	-	-
E Net worth (A+B+C-D)	**1,884,762**	**3,148,945**	**4,248,411**

Figure 9.13 Sintesi Farmaceutica balance sheet

As at year *n* the Financial Debt/EBITDA ratio is 5.2 and the company needs a capital increase in order to reduce the economic risk. The credit rating of Sintesi Farmaceutica is speculative grade ("B+" with 4.5% annual probability of default). A capital increase of 2 million US dollars will reduce the financial debt and the Sintesi Farmaceutica's credit rating could become "BB" (an annual probability of default of 1.8%).

The equity valuation process is carried out with two different approaches:

1) The present value of future earnings, net of the capital increase;
2) The NAV.

9.2.3.1 Discounted earnings methodology

The key inputs used in the estimation process are as follows:

- risk free rate as per Italian 10-years' Government Bond rate, 5%;
- equity risk premium estimate for Italian Equity Market is 4.5%;
- equity beta for Italian power generation industry is 1.1;
- growth rate is 2%;
- capital increase is assumed to be immediately executed by the buyer;
- the expected and normalized perpetual earnings is assumed to be the year *n* earnings.

The cost of equity is determined using the CAPM as follows:

$$\text{Cost of Equity} = \text{Risk Free Rate} + \beta \cdot (\text{Equity Risk Premium})$$

$$\text{Cost of Equity}_{\text{Sintesi Farmaceutica}} = 5\% + 1.1 \cdot (4.5\%) = 9.95\%.$$

The equity fair value is calculated as the present value of future earnings, net of the present value of the capital increases. The discount rate of future earnings is the cost of equity; the discount rate of capital injections is the risk free rate.

$$W = \frac{747,708}{9.95\% - 2\%} - 2,000,000$$

$$W = 9,405,132 - 2,000,000$$

$$W = US\$7,405,132.$$

9.2.3.2 Net Asset Value methodology

In order to express the NAV with embedded intangible assets (such as R&D and licences) the following valuations are carried out:

- revaluation of fixed assets: US$ 2,500,000;
- cost of R&D and licences: US$ 3,000,000;
- tax effect: US$ 1,650,000.

The Sintesi Farmaceutica's NAV is equal to US$ 8,098,411, as follows:

$$\text{NAV} = \text{Equity Book Value} + \text{Revaluation of fixed assets}$$
$$+ \text{NPV of R\&D and licences} - \text{Tax effect}$$
$$\text{NAV} = 4,248,411 + 2,500,000 + 3,000,000 - 1,650,000;$$
$$\text{NAV} = US\$8,098,411.$$

Providing the capital increase is taken into account in the NAV methodology, the Sintesi Farmaceutica NAV estimate seems to be confirmed by the Earnings-Based Method.

9.2.4 The new approach

According to the IAPM, Sintesi Farmaceutica's cost of equity is the maximum of either the risk premium calculated using the CAPM, or the risk premium determined following the FIA.

As shown in the previous section, Sintesi Farmaceutica's cost of equity is equal to 9.95% based on CAPM.

Sintesi Farmaceutica's cost of equity using FIA (see Chapter 3) can be estimated as follows:

1. Probability of default valuation;
2. Equity Expected Loss calculation;
3. Equity Risk Premium determination.

After the capital increase, Sintesi Farmaceutica has a 1.8% probability of default, that is to say there is a 1.8% probability that shareholders will lose all of their capital (recovery rate zero) (see Floor Theorem, Chapter 3); on the other hand, the shareholders' probability of losing at least 1 US dollar is equal to 17.5% (see Cap Theorem, Chapter 3).

The combined rule to calculate the EEL is as follows.

$$\text{EEL} = \text{default probability} + (\text{probability of losing at least}$$
$$1 \text{ US dollar} - \text{default probability})\ 50\%;$$
$$\text{EEL} = 1.8\% + (17.5\% - 1.8\%)50\%;$$
$$\text{EEL} = 9.65\%.$$

The last step is to compute the equity risk premium based on the EEL and the probability of winning at least 1 US dollar. A rule-of-thumb approach is to define the size of "bet" that would need to be won in order to compensate shareholders for the EEL with a probability equal to "1 *minus* the probability of losing at least 1 US dollar", as follows.

Probability of winning at least 1 US dollar × Equity Risk Premium

= Equity Expected Loss

Equity Risk Premium = Equity Expected Loss/

Probability of winning at least one US dollar

Equity Risk Premium = 9.65% / (1 – 17.5%)

Equity Risk Premium = 9.65% / 82.5%

Equity Risk Premium = 11.7%.

Cost of Equity = Risk free rate + Equity Risk Premium

Cost of Equity = 5% + 11.7%

Cost of Equity = 16.7% (FIA).

In this case the equity risk premium using the FIA is higher than the equity risk premium based on CAPM, and it is therefore advisable to use 16.7% as Sintesi Farmaceutica's cost of equity.

If we assume that Sintesi Farmaceutica's cost of equity is equal to 16.7% after the capital increase, the equity fair value based on the present value of future earnings, net of the present value of the capital injection, changes substantially.

$$W = \frac{747,708}{16.7\% - 2\%} - 2,000,000$$

$$W = 5,086,449 - 2,000,000$$

$$W = US\$3,086,449.$$

As we can see, the two results using the earnings-based method, the first deriving from the CAPM and the second the FIA, are very different: Sintesi Farmaceutica's equity value changes from US$ 7,405,132 to US$ 3,086,449. Moreover, with the FIA cost of equity, there is no goodwill and the NAV must be reduced not only for the capital increase, but also because the expected earnings are weak; in other words, there is not enough profitability in R&D activities and licences-related investments and the badwill is equal to US$ 3,011,962, as follows.

NAV before capital injection:	*US*\$8,098,411
– Capital increase:	*US*\$2,000,000
– Equity value based on earnings NPV:	*US*\$3,086,449
= Badwill	*US*\$3,011,962.

In other words, according to the cost of equity established using the FIA, Sintesi Farmaceutica's equity value is less than half the estimated equity value based on the CAPM.

Appendix: Term Structure of Probability of Default and State-Dependent Transition Matrix

Term Structure of Probability of Default

The effects of grade migration over a period of time create a term structure of Probability of Defaults (PDs). For example, an AAA rated borrower cannot improve its rating over time and so, on average, the rating is likely to deteriorate. However, a CCC credit rating, if the company survives, can only improve. Only when longer term (more than 5 years) and consistent time-series data becomes available might internal migration matrices prove robust enough for use in the pricing model.

Observed Term Structures

The observed term structure for S&P rated companies is shown in Figure A1.1. As will be observed, higher quality credits tend to deteriorate over time while low quality credits tend to improve.

Marginal, Forward and Cumulative Probability of Default

The PDs for each year shown in Figure A.1 are *forward* PDs, that is to say they are the PD that would be expected for that year expressed as a percentage of companies that have survived. The number of companies that survive can be determined from the *cumulative* default rate. To illustrate these concepts, let us consider the following simple example in Table A.1:

There are three different questions for consideration here. What is the probability that:

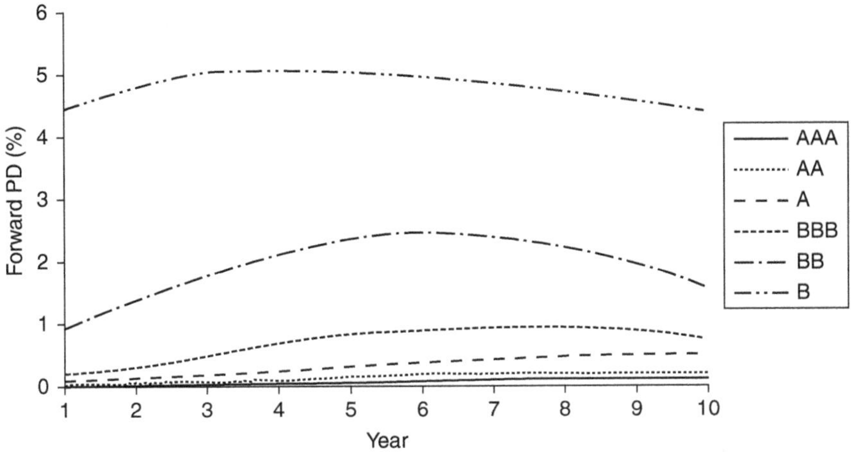

Figure A.1 Observed term structure of S&P rated companies (based on 1-year forward PD)

Table A.1 Example of default data

Year	Number of companies at start of year	Defaults per year	Cumulative defaults
1	100	1	1
2	99	2	3
3	97	3	6
4	94	4	10
5	90	5	15

1. a company will default over a 4 year period?
2. a company in year 4 will default over the next year?
3. a company will default in the 4th year of a facility?

The answers require different combinations of the numbers shown below:

1. 10 out of 100 companies default in the first 4 years: the *Cumulative Default Rate* in year 4 is 10%;
2. 4 out of the 94 companies that survived until year 4 will default in year 4: the *Forward Default Rate* in year 4 is 4.2%;
3. 4 out of 100 companies lent to default in the 4th year of their life: the *Marginal Default Rate* in year four is 4%.

The pricing model requires both the cumulative PD and the forward PD for the discounted cash flow calculation. The cumulative PD is required to determine the probability that revenues and costs are being incurred

Table A.2 Calculating marginal PDs from the migration matrix

Marginal PD Year n+1		1-year Migration Matrix			Marginal PD Year n
		AAA	...	CCC	
AAA	X	AAA		X	AAA
AA+		AA+			AA+
AA		AA			AA
AA–		AA–			AA–
A+		A+			A+
A		A			A
A–		A–			A–
BBB+	=	BBB+		X	BBB+
BBB		BBB			BBB
BBB–		BBB–			BBB–
BB+		BB+			BB+
BB		BB			BB
BB–		BB–			BB–
B+		B+			B+
B–		B–			B–
CCC		CCC			CCC

Source: Author's estimate on industry best practice computation methods.

in any given year (i.e. to account for survivorship), while the forward PD is required to calculate the expected loss.

Mapping PD Ratings to Observed Term Structures

Once the marginal PDs have been calculated, it is then possible to calculate the forward PDs using the equation set out below:

$$PD_{forward,\,year\,n} = \frac{PD_{marginal,\,year\,n}}{1 - \sum_{year=0}^{n} PD_{Marginal}}.$$

Transition Matrix State-Dependent Pricing Model

In the previous chapters we carried out an analysis that was indifferent to the phases of the economic cycle. Here we present an approach to the production of transition matrices that depends on the different phases of the cycle itself.

- Downgrading probabilities are, on average, increasing from Recovery to Hard Landing.

Table A.3 Transition matrix throughout the economic cycle

	Recovery	Overheat	Hard landing	Soft landing
Large corporate	√	√	√	√
Corporate	√	√	√	√
SME corporate	√	√	√	√
SME retail	√	√	√	√

Table A.4 Large corporate transition matrices (%)

	Recovery	Overheat	Hard landing	Soft landing
Stability	**77.17**	**75.13**	**73.80**	**75.97**
Downgrading	**13.46**	**18.59**	**19.12**	**15.97**
Upgrading	**14.55**	**13.69**	**12.53**	**13.79**

- Upgrading probabilities are decreasing from Recovery (greater probabilities) to Hard Landing.

Table A.5 Large corporate – recovery

	1c AAA	1c AA+	1c AA	1c AA–	1c A+	1c A	1c A–	1c BBB+	1c BBB	1c BBB–	1c BB+	1c BB	1c BB–	1c B+	1c B	1c B–	1c CCC	1c@ Default
AAA	83.9	3.3	6.2	1.7	2.5	1.7	0.8	0.0	0.0	0.0	0.0	0.0	0.0	0.0	0.0	0.0	0.0	0.0
AA+	2.0	92.1	3.3	2.6	0.0	0.0	0.0	0.0	0.0	0.0	0.0	0.0	0.0	0.0	0.0	0.0	0.0	0.0
AA	0.0	1.1	82.2	11.2	4.5	0.0	0.7	0.4	0.0	0.0	0.0	0.0	0.0	0.0	0.0	0.0	0.0	0.0
AA–	0.2	0.2	2.4	80.5	12.7	3.0	0.8	0.0	0.2	0.0	0.0	0.0	0.0	0.0	0.0	0.0	0.0	0.0
A+	0.1	0.1	0.0	2.4	87.6	7.4	1.3	1.1	0.0	0.0	0.0	0.0	0.0	0.0	0.0	0.0	0.0	0.0
A	0.0	0.0	0.1	0.3	3.2	82.7	9.8	2.9	0.9	0.0	0.1	0.0	0.0	0.0	0.0	0.0	0.0	0.0
A–	0.0	0.2	0.0	0.0	1.3	8.8	78.9	7.1	2.3	0.9	0.4	0.0	0.0	0.0	0.0	0.0	0.0	0.0
BBB+	0.0	0.0	0.1	0.0	0.0	1.1	7.7	79.4	8.1	2.6	0.3	0.1	0.1	0.3	0.0	0.0	0.0	0.0
BBB	0.0	0.0	0.0	0.1	0.1	0.4	1.6	6.2	80.8	7.5	1.6	0.4	0.5	0.6	0.1	0.1	0.0	0.0
BBB–	0.0	0.0	0.0	0.0	0.6	0.0	0.8	2.4	9.5	75.7	5.0	3.1	1.6	0.1	0.7	0.4	0.1	0.0
BB+	0.0	0.0	0.0	0.0	0.2	0.0	0.4	0.7	2.0	9.0	73.5	6.8	4.5	1.6	0.9	0.2	0.0	0.4
BB	0.0	0.0	0.0	0.0	0.2	0.4	0.2	0.9	0.9	2.9	12.0	70.2	5.6	1.1	2.9	1.3	1.3	0.0
BB–	0.0	0.0	0.0	0.0	0.0	0.1	0.1	0.0	0.4	0.3	1.8	8.8	73.9	5.1	6.1	1.6	0.4	1.3
B+	0.1	0.0	0.0	0.0	0.1	0.4	0.1	0.1	0.6	0.1	0.1	3.0	8.8	72.9	5.1	4.7	1.6	2.2
B	0.0	0.0	0.0	0.0	0.0	0.0	0.2	0.0	0.0	0.0	0.4	1.3	2.9	9.4	67.7	9.6	5.4	3.1
B–	0.0	0.0	0.2	0.0	0.0	0.0	0.0	0.2	0.2	0.2	0.0	0.6	0.6	5.8	7.3	65.2	9.6	10.0
CCC	0.0	0.0	0.0	0.0	0.0	0.0	0.0	0.0	0.0	0.0	0.6	0.0	0.6	0.6	1.5	6.8	68.5	21.4

Table A.6 Large corporate – overheat

	1c AAA	1c AA+	1c AA	1c AA−	1c A+	1c A	1c A−	1c BBB+	1c BBB	1c BBB−	1c BB+	1c BB	1c BB−	1c B+	1c B	1c B−	1c CCC	1c@ Default
AAA	86.6	3.9	8.7	0.0	0.0	0.8	0.0	0.0	0.0	0.0	0.0	0.0	0.0	0.0	0.0	0.0	0.0	0.0
AA+	2.6	77.6	2.0	17.1	0.7	0.0	0.0	0.0	0.0	0.0	0.0	0.0	0.0	0.0	0.0	0.0	0.0	0.0
AA	1.8	4.3	79.1	11.0	1.2	2.5	0.0	0.0	0.0	0.0	0.0	0.0	0.0	0.0	0.0	0.0	0.0	0.0
AA−	0.0	0.0	1.2	86.4	6.5	4.3	1.0	0.5	0.0	0.0	0.0	0.0	0.2	0.0	0.0	0.0	0.0	0.0
A+	0.0	0.0	0.4	3.2	81.1	9.8	3.6	1.6	0.0	0.2	0.0	0.0	0.0	0.2	0.0	0.0	0.0	0.0
A	0.4	0.0	0.1	0.4	3.2	81.8	7.1	4.5	1.0	0.1	0.3	0.0	0.7	0.0	0.3	0.0	0.0	0.0
A−	0.0	0.0	0.0	0.2	1.3	5.6	75.5	9.7	4.5	1.6	0.5	0.3	0.3	0.2	0.0	0.0	0.0	0.3
BBB+	0.0	0.0	0.0	0.0	0.2	0.3	4.4	75.7	9.6	4.7	2.3	0.6	0.0	0.9	0.2	0.6	0.3	0.2
BBB	0.1	0.3	0.0	0.0	0.3	0.3	1.1	5.6	76.9	9.7	1.4	1.3	0.6	0.4	0.5	0.0	1.0	0.5
BBB−	0.2	0.0	0.0	0.0	0.0	0.5	0.2	0.8	8.3	74.2	7.5	2.4	2.4	1.0	0.5	0.3	0.8	0.8
BB+	0.2	0.0	0.0	0.0	0.2	0.7	0.0	0.5	2.3	9.7	68.1	7.6	4.2	2.3	0.2	1.6	0.7	1.6
BB	0.0	0.0	0.3	0.3	0.0	0.3	0.0	0.0	0.0	2.2	9.4	70.2	8.3	4.1	2.8	0.6	0.8	0.8
BB−	0.0	0.0	0.0	0.0	0.0	0.0	0.2	0.6	0.2	0.8	2.4	8.5	73.2	5.4	4.6	1.4	1.3	1.4
B+	0.0	0.0	0.0	0.0	0.0	0.0	0.1	0.0	0.3	0.0	1.0	2.5	6.3	72.1	8.7	4.5	2.5	2.2
B	0.0	0.0	0.0	0.0	0.0	0.0	0.2	0.5	0.0	0.5	0.2	0.3	1.9	9.1	68.4	8.8	5.3	5.0
B−	0.0	0.0	0.0	0.0	0.0	0.0	0.2	0.0	0.4	0.0	0.4	0.2	1.5	2.7	11.0	64.2	13.5	5.8
CCC	0.0	0.0	0.0	0.0	0.0	0.2	0.0	0.0	0.0	0.4	0.2	0.4	0.4	1.2	2.8	8.7	69.8	15.8

Table A.7 Large corporate – hard landing

	1c AAA	1c AA+	1c AA	1c AA–	1c A+	1c A	1c A–	1c BBB+	1c BBB	1c BBB–	1c BB+	1c BB	1c BB–	1c B+	1c B	1c B–	1c CCC	1c@ Default
AAA	93.2	1.0	5.2	0.0	0.5	0.0	0.0	0.0	0.0	0.0	0.0	0.0	0.0	0.0	0.0	0.0	0.0	0.0
AA+	2.0	77.6	6.8	13.6	0.0	0.0	0.0	0.0	0.0	0.0	0.0	0.0	0.0	0.0	0.0	0.0	0.0	0.0
AA	1.5	3.0	79.0	11.4	2.6	1.8	0.4	0.0	0.4	0.0	0.0	0.0	0.0	0.0	0.0	0.0	0.0	0.0
AA–	0.2	1.3	1.6	83.1	7.8	2.9	1.8	0.4	0.0	0.2	0.2	0.0	0.4	0.0	0.0	0.0	0.0	0.0
A+	0.0	0.2	0.5	4.0	81.9	9.7	3.4	0.3	0.0	0.0	0.0	0.0	0.0	0.0	0.0	0.0	0.0	0.0
A	0.2	0.0	0.3	2.8	4.2	76.8	10.9	2.2	1.2	0.3	0.3	0.2	0.0	0.0	0.2	0.0	0.1	0.2
A–	0.1	0.3	0.3	0.6	0.8	5.5	74.8	9.8	4.4	1.4	0.3	0.3	0.6	0.4	0.3	0.1	0.1	0.0
BBB+	0.0	0.3	0.1	0.0	0.0	1.6	4.3	76.9	10.6	3.7	0.7	0.9	0.3	0.1	0.0	0.0	0.1	0.4
BBB	0.1	0.1	0.0	0.4	0.3	0.5	2.4	5.4	75.4	10.6	2.3	1.0	0.4	0.1	0.5	0.4	0.0	0.0
BBB–	0.0	0.0	0.0	0.2	0.0	0.5	1.2	2.6	9.6	69.9	5.2	3.4	3.3	1.9	0.3	0.0	0.9	1.0
BB+	0.0	0.0	0.0	0.0	0.0	0.2	1.9	0.8	1.9	8.8	71.0	3.5	5.6	1.9	2.1	1.2	0.0	1.2
BB	0.0	0.0	0.0	0.0	0.0	0.0	0.0	0.2	0.7	2.7	7.5	67.9	9.0	2.3	5.4	1.8	0.9	1.6
BB–	0.0	0.0	0.0	0.0	0.0	0.0	0.0	0.0	0.1	1.0	2.8	3.9	70.2	3.2	8.2	4.2	1.4	5.0
B+	0.0	0.0	0.1	0.0	0.1	0.2	0.0	0.1	0.0	0.7	0.7	1.5	4.0	69.4	5.8	7.9	3.4	6.1
B	0.0	0.0	0.1	0.1	0.0	0.0	0.1	0.4	0.3	0.0	0.5	0.5	1.7	4.3	67.9	6.8	7.0	10.3
B–	0.0	0.0	0.2	0.0	0.2	0.0	0.2	0.0	0.0	0.2	0.0	0.4	0.5	2.1	2.3	62.3	12.8	18.9
CCC	0.0	0.0	0.0	0.0	0.0	0.0	0.0	0.0	0.0	0.0	0.0	0.0	0.0	0.5	0.0	2.5	67.7	29.3

Table A.8 Large corporate – soft landing

	1c AAA	1c AA+	1c AA	1c AA–	1c A+	1c A	1c A–	1c BBB+	1c BBB	1c BBB–	1c BB+	1c BB	1c BB–	1c B+	1c B	1c B–	1c CCC	1c@ Default
AAA	91.7	3.6	2.3	1.0	1.0	0.3	0.0	0.0	0.0	0.0	0.0	0.0	0.0	0.0	0.0	0.0	0.0	0.0
AA+	2.4	83.2	5.6	2.8	3.6	0.8	0.4	0.8	0.0	0.0	0.4	0.0	0.0	0.0	0.0	0.0	0.0	0.0
AA	0.5	4.6	81.7	4.9	4.1	2.0	1.7	0.0	0.0	0.0	0.0	0.0	0.2	0.2	0.0	0.0	0.0	0.0
AA–	0.1	0.7	3.6	81.5	6.1	5.5	1.2	0.4	0.1	0.4	0.0	0.1	0.0	0.0	0.0	0.0	0.0	0.0
A+	0.1	0.1	0.7	5.2	81.4	6.1	2.6	0.7	0.7	0.3	0.8	0.8	0.2	0.3	0.0	0.0	0.0	0.0
A	0.0	0.1	0.3	0.5	4.5	84.5	5.3	2.2	1.5	0.5	0.1	0.1	0.2	0.1	0.1	0.0	0.1	0.0
A–	0.0	0.0	0.1	0.0	1.5	7.9	78.5	5.9	2.5	2.4	0.4	0.3	0.1	0.2	0.1	0.2	0.0	0.0
BBB+	0.1	0.0	0.0	0.1	0.3	3.3	6.8	78.7	5.8	2.6	1.2	0.0	0.4	0.5	0.1	0.0	0.0	0.0
BBB	0.0	0.2	0.0	0.1	0.0	1.2	3.1	6.6	80.5	4.9	1.7	0.2	0.5	0.5	0.4	0.2	0.0	0.0
BBB–	0.0	0.0	0.0	0.0	0.0	0.7	0.5	3.7	9.2	75.1	6.7	1.9	0.9	0.5	0.2	0.3	0.0	0.3
BB+	0.0	0.0	0.0	0.1	0.1	0.0	0.7	0.9	5.0	9.2	70.1	6.1	3.9	1.0	1.6	1.0	0.1	0.2
BB	0.0	0.0	0.0	0.0	0.0	0.1	0.1	0.7	0.8	2.8	9.1	67.9	9.6	2.9	3.3	1.4	0.6	0.6
BB–	0.0	0.1	0.0	0.0	0.1	0.1	0.2	0.5	0.2	0.6	3.0	4.7	68.5	10.5	5.9	3.0	0.8	1.8
B+	0.0	0.0	0.0	0.1	0.1	0.0	0.2	0.0	0.2	0.0	0.5	2.5	7.1	67.9	12.3	4.2	1.9	3.1
B	0.0	0.0	0.0	0.0	0.0	0.1	0.0	0.1	0.0	0.1	0.3	0.8	2.4	7.9	65.8	10.7	6.5	5.3
B–	0.0	0.0	0.0	0.0	0.0	0.0	0.0	0.3	0.0	0.0	0.0	0.4	1.0	4.5	7.6	66.7	11.4	8.0
CCC	0.0	0.0	0.0	0.0	0.0	0.0	0.0	0.0	0.2	0.2	0.2	0.0	0.7	1.1	2.3	4.5	74.8	15.9

Corporate Transition Matrices

Table A.9 Corporate – recovery

	1c AA	1c AA–	1c A+	1c A	1c A–	1c BBB+	1c BBB	1c BBB–	1c BB+	1c BB	1c BB–	1c B+	1c B	1c B–	1c CCC	1c@ Default
AA	54.9	35.8	8.0	0.0	1.3	0.0	0.0	0.0	0.0	0.0	0.0	0.0	0.0	0.0	0.0	0.0
AA–	18.1	26.8	39.0	7.5	3.2	0.0	5.4	0.0	0.0	0.0	0.0	0.0	0.0	0.0	0.0	0.0
A+	0.0	11.3	35.8	31.0	6.6	15.3	0.0	0.0	0.0	0.0	0.0	0.0	0.0	0.0	0.0	0.0
A	2.2	6.5	14.4	21.9	31.1	16.4	4.8	0.0	2.6	0.0	0.0	0.0	0.0	0.0	0.0	0.0
A–	0.0	0.0	9.6	22.8	23.6	25.8	13.4	2.7	2.2	0.0	0.0	0.0	0.0	0.0	0.0	0.0
BBB+	0.0	0.0	0.0	3.6	21.5	28.2	33.3	11.8	1.2	0.0	0.2	0.1	0.0	0.0	0.0	0.0
BBB	0.0	0.6	0.0	1.1	3.4	16.4	28.1	30.9	12.0	6.5	0.8	0.2	0.0	0.0	0.0	0.0
BBB–	0.0	0.0	0.0	0.0	3.0	4.9	22.9	31.4	18.7	13.2	5.2	0.2	0.5	0.1	0.0	0.0
BB+	0.0	0.0	0.1	0.0	0.3	1.6	2.6	18.1	40.6	23.1	8.7	3.3	0.3	0.0	0.0	1.3
BB	0.0	0.0	0.0	0.1	0.4	0.8	2.5	7.3	34.3	37.6	12.9	2.6	1.3	0.3	0.1	0.0
BB–	0.0	0.0	0.0	0.0	0.0	0.0	1.0	0.8	5.6	44.2	33.9	7.5	4.7	0.2	0.0	2.0
B+	0.0	0.0	0.0	0.0	0.0	0.0	1.4	0.0	1.2	13.4	35.1	35.5	5.8	3.1	0.1	4.2
B	0.0	0.0	0.0	0.0	0.0	0.0	0.0	0.0	3.2	8.2	16.4	31.7	28.6	5.7	1.4	4.8
B–	0.0	0.0	0.0	0.0	0.0	0.0	0.0	0.0	0.0	4.7	4.9	24.7	34.4	13.0	2.9	15.5
CCC	0.0	0.0	0.0	0.0	0.0	0.0	0.0	0.0	0.0	0.0	5.4	9.8	23.0	30.3	15.4	16.1

Table A.10 Corporate – overheat

	1c AA	1c AA–	1c A+	1c A	1c A–	1c BBB+	1c BBB	1c BBB–	1c BB+	1c BB	1c BB–	1c B+	1c B	1c B–	1c CCC	1c@ Default
AA	54.2	36.3	2.2	7.2	0.0	0.0	0.0	0.0	0.0	0.0	0.0	0.0	0.0	0.0	0.0	0.0
AA–	11.5	37.0	25.7	13.8	4.9	7.1	0.0	0.0	0.0	0.0	0.0	0.0	0.0	0.0	0.0	0.0
A+	5.2	11.1	24.0	29.8	13.7	16.0	0.0	0.3	0.0	0.0	0.0	0.0	0.0	0.0	0.0	0.0
A	2.7	8.0	13.2	19.9	20.9	23.2	4.6	1.1	6.5	0.0	0.0	0.0	0.0	0.0	0.0	0.0
A–	0.0	0.0	8.2	12.5	19.3	29.9	22.1	3.9	2.6	0.5	0.9	0.0	0.0	0.0	0.0	0.0
BBB+	0.0	0.0	2.1	0.9	10.7	23.7	34.8	18.9	8.6	0.0	0.0	0.3	0.0	0.0	0.0	0.0
BBB	0.0	0.0	0.0	0.6	2.1	12.4	22.4	33.7	8.9	18.9	0.9	0.1	0.0	0.0	0.0	0.0
BBB–	0.0	0.0	0.0	0.5	0.6	1.6	19.5	29.8	27.4	10.1	7.8	1.1	0.3	0.1	0.0	1.2
BB+	0.0	0.0	0.1	0.0	0.0	1.0	2.9	18.4	35.3	24.3	7.6	4.4	0.1	0.1	0.3	5.5
BB	0.0	0.0	0.0	0.1	0.0	0.0	0.0	5.4	26.1	36.7	18.6	9.3	1.2	0.1	0.0	2.5
BB–	0.0	0.0	0.0	0.0	0.0	0.2	0.4	2.2	7.2	42.4	33.4	8.0	3.5	0.2	0.1	2.2
B+	0.0	0.0	0.0	0.0	0.0	0.0	0.6	0.0	9.7	11.2	25.4	35.6	10.2	3.0	0.2	4.2
B	0.0	0.0	0.0	0.0	0.0	0.0	0.0	3.5	1.4	2.1	11.8	33.6	31.7	5.7	1.5	8.6
B–	0.0	0.0	0.0	0.0	0.0	0.0	0.0	0.0	0.0	1.5	10.8	11.3	51.1	12.5	3.9	8.8
CCC	0.0	0.0	0.0	0.0	0.0	0.0	0.0	0.0	0.0	0.0	2.7	15.0	32.8	28.8	11.8	8.9

Table A.11 Corporate – hard landing

	1c AA	1c AA–	1c A+	1c A	1c A–	1c BBB+	1c BBB	1c BBB–	1c BB+	1c BB	1c BB–	1c B+	1c B	1c B–	1c CCC	1c@ Default
AA	52.7	36.7	4.6	5.3	0.6	0.0	0.0	0.0	0.0	0.0	0.0	0.0	0.0	0.0	0.0	0.0
AA–	14.1	33.4	29.0	8.7	8.6	6.2	0.0	0.1	0.0	0.0	0.0	0.0	0.0	0.0	0.0	0.0
A+	7.4	15.3	26.8	32.6	14.4	3.4	0.0	0.0	0.0	0.0	0.0	0.0	0.0	0.0	0.0	0.0
A	4.0	34.6	11.2	12.1	20.5	7.3	3.6	1.6	4.9	0.1	0.0	0.0	0.0	0.0	0.0	0.0
A–	5.5	0.0	5.2	12.1	19.0	30.0	21.3	3.3	1.5	0.4	1.5	0.0	0.0	0.0	0.0	0.0
BBB+	0.0	0.0	0.0	4.6	11.0	25.3	40.3	15.7	2.8	0.0	0.4	0.0	0.0	0.0	0.0	0.0
BBB	0.0	1.6	0.0	1.2	4.0	11.0	20.3	33.8	13.5	14.1	0.5	0.0	0.0	0.0	0.0	0.0
BBB–	0.0	0.0	0.0	0.5	3.8	4.7	20.9	26.0	17.5	13.2	9.7	2.0	0.2	0.0	0.0	1.4
BB+	0.0	0.0	0.0	0.0	1.4	2.0	2.6	18.9	41.5	12.5	11.4	4.0	0.8	0.1	0.0	4.7
BB	0.0	0.0	0.0	0.0	0.0	0.2	1.9	6.8	21.2	36.1	20.8	5.2	2.5	0.4	0.0	4.9
BB–	0.0	0.0	0.0	0.0	0.0	0.0	0.4	3.3	10.2	23.6	38.8	5.7	7.6	0.7	0.2	9.4
B+	0.0	0.0	0.0	0.0	0.0	0.0	0.0	0.0	8.1	7.9	18.3	38.7	7.6	5.9	0.3	13.3
B	0.0	0.0	0.0	0.0	0.0	0.0	0.0	0.0	5.2	3.9	11.7	17.6	35.0	4.9	2.2	19.5
B–	0.0	0.0	0.0	0.0	0.0	0.0	0.0	0.0	0.0	3.6	5.6	12.7	15.2	17.2	5.3	40.4
CCC	0.0	0.0	0.0	0.0	0.0	0.0	0.0	0.0	0.0	0.0	0.0	14.4	0.0	19.3	27.1	39.2

Table A.12 Corporate – soft landing

	1c AA	1c AA−	1c A+	1c A	1c A−	1c BBB+	1c BBB	1c BBB−	1c BB+	1c BB	1c BB−	1c B+	1c B	1c B−	1c CCC	1c@ Default
AA	61.6	17.7	8.3	6.3	3.4	0.6	1.5	0.4	0.3	0.0	0.0	0.0	0.0	0.0	0.0	0.0
AA−	26.8	26.7	18.5	13.5	4.6	4.9	3.8	0.2	0.6	0.2	0.0	0.0	0.0	0.0	0.0	0.1
A+	10.9	19.0	25.8	19.7	10.8	7.5	4.7	0.5	0.7	0.2	0.1	0.0	0.0	0.0	0.0	0.0
A	6.0	10.3	19.7	21.8	16.6	12.1	7.4	4.3	1.8	0.1	0.0	0.0	0.0	0.0	0.0	0.0
A−	2.0	4.4	10.6	18.9	21.7	19.7	13.4	6.2	2.1	0.4	0.3	0.0	0.0	0.0	0.0	0.2
BBB+	1.0	1.6	4.2	9.8	17.4	25.9	21.8	11.2	4.7	1.4	0.5	0.2	0.0	0.0	0.0	0.3
BBB	0.4	0.5	1.2	3.6	6.9	18.1	29.4	21.5	13.5	3.3	1.0	0.2	0.0	0.0	0.0	0.4
BBB−	0.0	0.2	0.4	0.7	1.9	7.4	21.9	30.7	24.7	7.8	2.9	0.6	0.2	0.1	0.0	0.5
BB+	0.0	0.0	0.1	0.2	0.5	2.0	6.8	18.8	39.3	21.0	7.7	2.0	0.6	0.1	0.1	0.9
BB	0.0	0.0	0.0	0.0	0.2	0.6	2.2	6.7	24.6	34.6	21.2	6.4	1.5	0.3	0.0	1.6
BB−	0.0	0.0	0.0	0.0	0.1	0.2	0.6	2.0	10.3	26.0	34.8	17.3	5.0	0.5	0.1	3.2
B+	0.0	0.0	0.0	0.0	0.0	0.1	0.3	0.9	4.5	11.2	28.0	32.5	14.0	2.7	0.1	5.7
B	0.0	0.0	0.0	0.0	0.0	0.0	0.0	1.0	2.5	5.5	14.5	28.8	30.1	6.9	1.8	8.9
B−	0.0	0.0	0.0	0.0	0.0	0.0	0.4	0.4	2.2	3.3	7.9	19.7	36.6	13.5	3.4	12.6
CCC	0.0	0.0	0.0	0.0	0.0	0.0	0.0	0.0	0.0	1.3	5.6	16.9	31.8	18.2	15.3	10.9

SME Corporate Transition Matrices

Table A.13 SME corporate – recovery

	1c BBB	1c BBB–	1c BB+	1c BB	1c BB–	1c B+	1c B	1c B–	1c CCC	1c@ Default
BBB	33.9	53.4	9.9	2.5	0.0	0.0	0.0	0.3	0.0	0.0
BBB–	14.0	55.3	19.2	8.1	3.1	0.1	0.3	0.0	0.0	0.0
BB+	0.3	14.4	50.4	22.9	6.8	3.6	0.4	0.0	0.0	1.2
BB	0.1	2.1	31.7	47.9	13.3	2.1	2.0	0.3	0.4	0.0
BB–	0.0	0.1	2.6	38.2	43.2	8.2	4.7	0.4	0.3	2.0
B+	0.0	0.0	0.4	7.4	32.2	46.2	6.4	3.4	0.7	3.2
B	0.0	0.0	1.1	4.7	12.0	35.4	31.4	8.9	2.2	4.3
B–	0.0	0.0	0.0	1.9	2.3	21.3	33.5	17.6	8.8	14.7
CCC	0.0	0.0	0.0	0.0	1.2	7.6	12.1	31.8	14.5	32.8

Table A.14 SME corporate – overheat

	1c BBB	1c BBB–	1c BB+	1c BB	1c BB–	1c B+	1c B	1c B–	1c CCC	1c@ Default
BBB	27.1	58.3	7.3	7.3	0.0	0.0	0.0	0.0	0.0	0.0
BBB–	11.4	50.2	26.9	5.9	4.4	0.5	0.2	0.0	0.0	0.4
BB+	0.3	14.7	44.0	24.2	5.9	4.8	0.1	0.2	0.4	5.2
BB	0.0	1.5	23.3	45.1	18.6	7.2	1.8	0.1	0.2	2.1
BB–	0.0	0.4	3.4	37.0	43.1	8.8	3.6	0.4	1.0	2.3
B+	0.0	0.0	3.1	6.3	23.9	47.5	11.4	3.4	1.1	3.3
B	0.0	0.0	0.5	1.2	8.5	36.9	34.3	8.7	2.3	7.6
B–	0.0	0.0	0.0	0.6	4.9	9.5	48.5	16.6	11.9	8.1
CCC	0.0	0.0	0.0	0.0	0.7	13.1	19.4	34.1	12.4	20.4

Table A.15 SME corporate – soft landing

	1c BBB	1c BBB–	1c BB+	1c BB	1c BB–	1c B+	1c B	1c B–	1c CCC	1c@ Default
BBB	41.5	43.5	13.0	1.5	0.0	0.0	0.0	0.5	0.0	0.0
BBB–	13.3	54.0	25.5	4.8	1.7	0.3	0.1	0.0	0.1	0.2
BB+	0.7	15.7	51.3	21.9	6.3	2.3	0.7	0.2	0.1	0.9
BB	0.1	1.9	22.8	44.0	21.9	5.1	2.3	0.3	0.2	1.4
BB–	0.0	0.3	4.7	22.3	44.1	18.7	5.0	0.9	0.7	3.3
B+	0.0	0.0	1.4	6.3	25.9	42.7	15.5	3.1	0.8	4.4
B	0.1	0.0	0.9	3.1	10.5	31.7	32.6	10.5	2.8	7.9
B–	0.0	0.3	0.3	1.3	3.7	17.1	35.9	18.5	10.7	12.0
CCC	0.0	0.0	0.0	0.0	1.4	15.2	19.3	22.1	16.6	25.5

Table A.16 SME corporate – hard landing

	1c BBB	1c BBB−	1c BB+	1c BB	1c BB−	1c B+	1c B	1c B−	1c CCC	1c@ Default
BBB	24.4	58.4	11.1	5.4	0.0	0.0	0.0	0.7	0.0	0.0
BBB−	13.9	49.8	19.5	8.8	6.3	1.0	0.2	0.0	0.0	0.6
BB+	0.3	15.3	52.6	12.7	9.1	4.4	0.9	0.2	0.0	4.5
BB	0.1	1.9	19.2	45.1	21.1	4.1	3.7	0.4	0.3	4.2
BB−	0.0	0.5	4.7	20.2	48.8	6.1	7.6	1.4	1.2	9.5
B+	0.0	0.0	2.5	4.3	16.6	50.0	8.3	6.5	1.7	10.1
B	0.0	0.0	1.9	2.2	8.6	19.8	38.7	7.7	3.4	17.6
B−	0.0	0.0	0.0	1.4	2.4	10.1	13.7	21.7	15.2	35.5
CCC	0.0	0.0	0.0	0.0	0.0	8.2	0.0	14.9	18.6	58.3

SME Retail Transition Matrices

Table A.17 SME retail – recovery

	1c BBB	1c BBB−	1c BB+	1c BB	1c BB−	1c B+	1c B	1c B−	1c CCC	1c@ Default
BBB	33.9	53.4	9.9	2.5	0.0	0.0	0.0	0.3	0.0	0.0
BBB−	14.0	55.3	19.2	8.1	3.1	0.1	0.3	0.0	0.0	0.0
BB+	0.3	14.4	50.4	22.9	6.8	3.6	0.4	0.0	0.0	1.3
BB	0.1	2.1	31.7	47.9	13.3	2.1	2.0	0.3	0.4	0.0
BB−	0.0	0.1	2.6	38.2	43.2	8.2	4.7	0.4	0.3	2.2
B+	0.0	0.0	0.4	7.4	32.1	46.1	6.4	3.4	0.7	3.6
B	0.0	0.0	1.1	4.6	12.0	35.3	31.3	8.8	2.1	4.8
B−	0.0	0.0	0.0	1.9	2.2	20.9	32.9	17.3	8.7	16.1
CCC	0.0	0.0	0.0	0.0	1.1	7.3	11.6	30.4	13.8	35.7

Table A.18 SME retail – overheat

	1c BBB	1c BBB−	1c BB+	1c BB	1c BB−	1c B+	1c B	1c B−	1c CCC	1c@ Default
BBB	27.1	58.3	7.3	7.3	0.0	0.0	0.0	0.0	0.0	0.0
BBB−	11.4	50.2	26.9	5.9	4.4	0.5	0.2	0.0	0.0	0.5
BB+	0.3	14.7	43.8	24.1	5.9	4.8	0.1	0.2	0.4	5.7
BB	0.0	1.5	23.2	45.0	18.6	7.2	1.8	0.1	0.2	2.3
BB−	0.0	0.4	3.4	37.0	43.0	8.8	3.6	0.4	1.0	2.5
B+	0.0	0.0	3.1	6.3	23.8	47.3	11.4	3.4	1.1	3.6
B	0.0	0.0	0.5	1.2	8.4	36.6	34.0	8.7	2.3	8.3
B−	0.0	0.0	0.0	0.6	4.8	9.4	48.0	16.4	11.7	9.0
CCC	0.0	0.0	0.0	0.0	0.6	12.7	18.9	33.1	12.1	22.5

Table A.19 SME retail – hard landing

	1c BBB	1c BBB–	1c BB+	1c BB	1c BB–	1c B+	1c B	1c B–	1c CCC	1c@ Default
BBB	24.4	58.4	11.1	5.4	0.0	0.0	0.0	0.7	0.0	0.0
BBB–	13.9	49.8	19.5	8.8	6.3	1.0	0.2	0.0	0.0	0.6
BB+	0.3	15.3	52.3	12.6	9.0	4.4	0.9	0.2	0.0	5.0
BB	0.1	1.9	19.1	44.9	21.0	4.0	3.7	0.4	0.3	4.6
BB–	0.0	0.5	4.6	20.0	48.3	6.1	7.5	1.3	1.2	10.4
B+	0.0	0.0	2.5	4.3	16.5	49.5	8.2	6.5	1.7	11.0
B	0.0	0.0	1.8	2.2	8.5	19.4	38.0	7.5	3.4	19.2
B–	0.0	0.0	0.0	1.3	2.3	9.7	13.2	20.8	14.6	38.0
CCC	0.0	0.0	0.0	0.0	0.0	7.6	0.0	13.8	17.2	61.4

Table A.20 SME retail – soft landing

	1c BBB	1c BBB–	1c BB+	1c BB	1c BB–	1c B+	1c B	1c B–	1c CCC	1c@ Default
BBB	41.5	43.5	13.0	1.5	0.0	0.0	0.0	0.5	0.0	0.0
BBB–	13.3	54.0	25.5	4.8	1.7	0.3	0.1	0.0	0.1	0.2
BB+	0.7	15.7	51.2	21.9	6.3	2.3	0.7	0.2	0.1	1.0
BB	0.1	1.9	22.7	44.0	21.9	5.1	2.3	0.3	0.2	1.6
BB–	0.0	0.3	4.7	22.2	44.0	18.6	5.0	0.9	0.7	3.6
B+	0.0	0.0	1.4	6.2	25.8	42.5	15.4	3.0	0.8	4.9
B	0.1	0.0	0.9	3.1	10.4	31.4	32.3	10.4	2.8	8.7
B–	0.0	0.3	0.3	1.3	3.6	16.9	35.4	18.2	10.6	13.2
CCC	0.0	0.0	0.0	0.0	1.3	14.7	18.7	21.3	16.0	28.0

Notes

Chapter 4 – Integrated Pricing Model in USA

1. This results from imperfections in the loan accounting systems of financial institutions. For example, following a merger of two institutions, the loan accounting systems may be integrated and the date of defaults may be lost in the integration.
2. A famous example of a sampling issue leading to an incorrect forecast was in 1948 when the Chicago Daily Tribune printed papers that read "Dewey Defeats Truman" the day after the election. The forecast was based on telephone surveys that created a biased sample because it turned out that at the time of the survey, telephones were relatively rare and having a telephone was systematically related to household income, which, in turn, was systematically related to supporting Dewey.
3. These variables are often ratios but not always. For example, one measure of profitability is Net Income to Total Assets, which is a ratio, and one measure of size is Inflation Adjusted Total Assets, which is not a ratio.
4. By non-parametric, we mean that the T(xi) is a continuous function of x not requiring a specification of a specific closed (or parametric) functional form. We estimate these transforms using a variety of local regression and density estimation techniques.
5. We implement operating cash flow as EBITDA plus changes in accounts payable less changes in accounts receivable less changes in inventories. This implementation requires seven inputs including three from the previous year's financial statement.
6. Excessive multicollinearity may reduce the stability of parameter estimates.
7. The corresponding accuracy ratios are 54.3% (FSO) vs. 49.5% (RiskCalc v1.0) for the 1-year horizon and 35.7% (FSO) vs. 30.7% (RiskCalc v1.0) for the 5-year horizon.
8. The log likelihood can be thought of as a measure of closeness of the predicted EDF values to the actual default rates.
9. For further definitions and technical discussion of the testing procedures in Section 4 please refer to the Technical Document.
10. As Woolridge (2000) shows, VIF is inversely related to the tolerance value (1–R2), such that a VIF of 10 corresponds to a tolerance value of 0.10. Clearly, any threshold is somewhat arbitrary and depends on the sample size. Nevertheless, if any of the R2 values are greater than 0.75 (so that VIF is greater than 4.0), we would typically suspect that multicollinearity might be a problem. If any of the R2 values are greater than 0.90 (so that VIF is greater than 10) we then conclude that multicollinearity is likely to be a serious problem.
11. The out-of-sample ARs are 53.6% and 37.7% for the 1-year and 5-year models, respectively. These out-of-sample ARs are 1.0 and 0.6 points lower than the in-sample ARs and 5.9 and 6.0 points higher than RiskCalc v1.0, for the 1- and 5-year models respectively.
12. For a discussion of the issues surrounding exploratory analysis contaminating the holdout sample (also known as data snooping), see Campbell *et al.* (1997, pp. 523–24).

13. The in-sample power gains are not directly comparable to the pure out-of-sample gains since they are based on different samples. See Stein (2002) for a discussion of issues in comparing validation results from tests on different samples.
14. Specifically, FEDFt-1,t = (CEDFt- CEDFt-1)/(1-CEDFt-1), where FEDFt-1,t is the forward EDF from years t-1 to t, and CEDFt is the cumulative EDF for year t.
15. Specifically, AEDFt = 1 - (1 -CEDFt)1/t, where AEDFt is the annualized EDF for year t.

Chapter 5 – Integrated Pricing Model in Japan

1. The success of many types of project finance firms depends largely on the outcome of a particular project. We recommend using separate models for such firms. This characteristic is explicitly recognized by the Basel Capital Accord.
2. The 5-year to 1-year mean default ratio of 3.9 is close to the previous version of RiskCalc v1.0 Japan.
3. These variables are often ratios of two (or more) financial statement items, but do not always have to be ratios. For example, one measure of profitability is Gross Profit to Total Assets, which is a ratio, and one measure of size is inflation adjusted Net Sales, which is not a ratio.
4. By non-parametric, we mean that the T(xi) is a continuous function of x not requiring a specification of a specific closed (or parametric) functional form. We estimate these transforms using a variety of local regression and density estimation techniques.
5. For further details, see Dwyer and Stein (2004), Technical Document on RiskCalc v3.1 Methodology.
6. cf. Bohn and Crosbie, 2003, and Dwyer and Korablev, 2007.
7. With the credit cycle adjustment, the model's performance improves by three percentage points of accuracy ratio at the 5-year horizon (51.6 versus 48.5), but loses almost five percentage points at the 1-year horizon compared with RiskCalc v3.2 FSO (53.1 versus 58.0).
8. Altman *et al.*, 1995.
9. Altman *et al.*, 1995.
10. As Woolridge (2000) shows VIF is inversely related to the tolerance value (1–R2), such that a VIF of 10 corresponds to a tolerance value of 0.10. Clearly, any threshold is somewhat arbitrary and depends on the sample size. Nevertheless, if any of the R2 values are greater than 0.75 (so that VIF is greater than 4.0), we would typically suspect that multicollinearity might be a problem. If any of the R2 values are greater than 0.90 (so that VIF is greater than 10) we then conclude that multicollinearity is likely to be a serious problem.
11. For a detailed discussion of these improvements, refer to the Technical Document.
12. Specifically, FEDFt-1,t = (CEDFt- CEDFt-1)/(1-CEDFt-1), where FEDFt-1,t is the forward EDF credit measure from years t-1 to t, and CEDFt is the cumulative EDF credit measure for year t.
13. Specifically, AEDFt = 1 - (1 -CEDFt)1/t, where AEDFt is the annualized EDF credit measure for year t.

Chapter 6 – Integrated Pricing Model in China

1. The success of many types of project finance firms depends largely on the outcome of a particular project. We recommend using separate models for such firms. This characteristic is explicitly recognized as part of the Basel Capital Accord.
2. Wang (2003) provides an industry-based classification of large corporate, medium size, and small firms in China. While the classification methods rely on asset size, sales, and number of employees, using asset size as a proxy, our sample covers all three firm types.
3. The east, middle, and west areas account for 60%, 23%, and 17% of the GDP in 2007, respectively. GDP data was compiled from the Statistical Yearbook of China, 2008.
4. These variables are often ratios, but not always. For example, one measure of profitability is Net Income to Total Assets, which is a ratio, and one measure of size is Inflation Adjusted Total Assets, which is not a ratio.
5. For further details, see Dwyer and Stein, 2004, "Technical Document on RiskCalc v3.1 Methodology" (Technical Document).
6. As listed in the previous section, the 13 industries are Agriculture, Automobile, Business Products, Communication, Construction, Consumer Products, High Tech, Mining, Services, Trade, Transportation, Utilities, and Unassigned.
7. See Altman *et al.*, 2007.
8. As Woolridge (2000) shows, VIF is inversely related to the tolerance value (1–R2), such that a VIF of 10 corresponds to a tolerance value of 0.10. Clearly, any threshold is somewhat arbitrary and depends on the sample size. Nevertheless, if any of the R2 values are greater than 0.75 (so that VIF is greater than 4.0), we would typically suspect that multicollinearity could be a problem. If any of the R2 values are greater than 0.90 (so that VIF is greater than 10) we conclude that multicollinearity is likely to be a serious problem.

Chapter 7 – Integrated Pricing Model in Russia

1. Guriev and Tsyvinski, 2010.
2. Aslund and Kuchins, 2009.
3. In 1998, Russia started the Program of Accounting Reform, based on international financial reporting standards (IFRS). The Ministry of Finance announced plans to adopt IFRS in Russia in July 2004. Currently, listed firms are permitted to prepare consolidated statements under IFRS; commercial banks are required to prepare annual standalone financial statements under IFRS in addition to Russian Accounting Standards (see PWC, 2010).
4. See International Monetary Fund (2010).
5. See http://www.estandardsforum.org/russia/standards/international-financial-reporting-standards. Accessed 25 June 2010.
6. The success of many types of project finance firms depends largely on the outcome of a particular project. We recommend using separate models for such firms. This characteristic is explicitly recognized as part of the Basel Capital Accord.

7. Sales Growth is defined as
8. The weights are assigned as follows: if Sales >$10M then weight = 1, if Sales = $10M then weight = 0.09.
9. Map source: http://openbudget.karelia.ru/budnord/english/fo_main.htm.
10. The Central, Northwest, South, Volga, Urals, Siberia, and the Far East accounted for 37%, 10%, 8%, 15%, 15%, 11%, and 5% of the GRP in 2007, respectively. GRP data compiled from the Federal Statistics Services – Rosstat.
11. These variables are often ratios but not always. For example, one measure of profitability is Net Income to Total Assets, which is a ratio, and one measure of size is Inflation Adjusted Total Assets, which is not a ratio.
12. By non-parametric, we mean that the $T(x_i)$ is a continuous function of x not requiring a specification of a closed (i.e., parametric) functional form. We estimate these transforms using a variety of local regression and density estimation techniques.
13. As listed in the previous section, the nine industries are Agriculture, Business Products, CommHiTech, Construction, Consumer Products, MiningTransUtility, Services, Trade, and Unassigned.
14. Example 2 of Section 6.6, Hogg and Craig (4th edn, 1978) provide the posterior distribution for the mean of a normal distribution (u) where the variance of the distribution is known; in the prior, the mean comes from a normal distribution, and a sample mean of observations drawn from this distribution is observed. The expected value of the posterior distribution of u is a weighted average of the mean of the prior and a sample mean. We use the following formulas to assign weights: weight_industry=, and weight_overall =, where N is number of firms in the industry. One can derive our weighting scheme from the Bayesian expression for the mean of the posterior by using the average of distance-to-default for all of Russia in that month as the prior for the industry distance to default, assuming that the variance of the prior is equal to one-tenth the variance of the sample. This technique allows the weight on the industry DD to increase as the number of firms with traded equity in the industry increases over time. The technique is motivated by Vasicek (1973).
15. CDS spread data acquired from Markit Partners. We use median sovereign CDS spread by date for the Russian Federation.
16. iPath S&P GSCI Crude Oil TR Index ETN (OIL).
17. We used the Z-score model presented in Altman (2000).
18. The power results on the model run in CCA mode are skewed due to a data collection issue: the majority of defaults in the data cluster around 2006–7, a period of Russian economic expansion. Consequently, results presented here are for the model in FSO mode.
19. As Woolridge (2000) shows, VIF is inversely related to the tolerance value (1–R2), such that a VIF of 10 corresponds to a tolerance value of 0.10. Clearly, any threshold is somewhat arbitrary and depends on the sample size. Nevertheless, if any of the R2 values are greater than 0.75 (so that VIF is greater than 4.0), we would typically suspect that multicollinearity could be a problem. If any of the R2 values are greater than 0.90 (so that VIF is greater than 10), we then conclude that multicollinearity is likely to be a serious problem.
20. The percentage of defaults presented in the 0 – Table 13 is based on the original, non-weighted observation count.
21. In our development sample all annual statements have December as a statement month. The last default we used is October 2009. Therefore, if we use statements

that are at least 360 days prior to default, we can only use 2007 statements to predict defaults in 2009.

Chapter 8 – Integrated Pricing Model in India

1. Includes firms with audited and unaudited financial statements. Korean accounting rules require that middle-market firms with assets greater than 7 billion won have their financial statements audited.
2. The success of many types of project finance firms depends largely on the outcome of a particular project. We recommend using separate models for such firms. This characteristic is explicitly recognized as part of the Basel Capital Accord.
3. These variables are often ratios but not always. For example, one measure of profitability is Net Income to Total Assets, a ratio; and one measure of size is Inflation Adjusted Total Assets, which is not a ratio.
4. By non-parametric, we mean that the T(xi) is a continuous function of x not requiring a specification of a closed (i.e., parametric) functional form. We estimate these transforms using a variety of local regression and density estimation techniques.
5. For further details, see Dwyer and Stein, 2004, "Technical Document on RiskCalc v3.1 Methodology" (Technical Document).
6. As Woolridge (2000) shows, VIF is inversely related to the tolerance value (1–R2), such that a VIF of 10 corresponds to a tolerance value of 0.10. Clearly, any threshold is somewhat arbitrary and depends on the sample size. Nevertheless, if any of the R2 values are greater than 0.75 (so that VIF is greater than 4.0), we would typically suspect that multicollinearity may be a problem. If any of the R2 values are greater than 0.90 (so that VIF is greater than 10) we then conclude that multicollinearity is likely to be a serious problem.
7. See FAQ529 "The RiskCalc™Emerging Markets Model Adjustment Factor".

Chapter 9 – Integrated Pricing Model in Italy

1. Continental European firms used to compute the distance-to-default factor are as follows: Austria, Belgium, Denmark, France, Germany, Greece, Italy, Luxembourg, the Netherlands, Portugal, Spain, and Switzerland.
2. In this context, a public company is a company with publicly traded equity. There are too few public firm defaults in Italy to construct a meaningful default rate at this time.
3. The log likelihood can be thought of as a measure of closeness of the predicted EDF values to the actual default rates.
4. For further definitions and technical discussion of the testing procedures in Section 4 refer to the Technical Document.
5. As Woolridge (2000) shows VIF is inversely related to the tolerance value (1–R2), such that a VIF of 10 corresponds to a tolerance value of 0.10. Clearly, any threshold is somewhat arbitrary and depends on the sample size. Nevertheless, if any of the R2 values are greater than 0.75 (so that VIF is greater than 4.0), we would typically

suspect that multicollinearity could be a problem. If any of the R2 values are greater than 0.90 (so that VIF is greater than 10) we then conclude that multicollinearity is likely to be a serious problem.

6. The out-of-sample ARs are 75.2% and 60.5% for the 1-year and 5-year models, respectively. The 1-year out-of-sample power is .3%.
7. Specifically, FEDFt-1,t = (CEDFt- CEDFt-1)/(1-CEDFt-1), where FEDFt-1,t is the forward EDF from years t-1 to t, and CEDFt is the cumulative EDF for year t.
8. Specifically, AEDFt = 1 - (1 -CEDFt)1/t, where AEDFt is the annualized EDF for year t.

References

Altman, E., 1968, "Financial Ratios, Discriminant Analysis and the Prediction of Corporate Bankruptcy", *Journal of Finance*, Vol. 23, pp. 589–609.

Altman, E., John B. Caouette and Paul Narayanan, 1998, *Managing Credit Risk: The Next Great Financial Challenge*, Wiley.

Annunziata, M., 2011, *The Economics of the Financial Crisis. Lessons and New Threats*, Palgrave Macmillan.

Banks, E., 2010, *Dark Pools. The Structure and Future of OFF-Exchange Trading and Liquidity*, Palgrave Macmillan.

Blanco, R., S. Brennan, and I. W. Marsh, 2005, "An Empirical Analysis of the Dynamic Relation Between Investment-Grade Bonds and Credit Default Swaps", *Journal of Finance*, Vol.60, pp. 2255–81.

Burgstahler, D. C. and R. Libby, 1997, "Earnings, Adaptation and Equity Value", *The Accounting Review*, Vol. 72, pp. 187–215.

Chan-Lau, J. A., 2006a, "Is Systematic Default Risk Priced in Equity Returns? A Cross-Sectional Analysis Using Credit Derivatives Prices", IMF Working Paper, no.148.

Chan-Lau, J. A., 2006b, "Fundamentals-Based Estimation of Default Probabilities: A Survey", IMF Working Paper.

Chan-Lau, J. A., and Yoon-Sook Kim, 2005, "Equity Prices, Credit Default Swaps and Bond Spreads in Emerging Markets", *ICFAI Journal of Derivatives Markets*, Vol. 2, pp. 26–48.

Coda, V., 1966, *Introduzione alle Valutazioni dei Capitali Economici di Impresa*, Giuffrè.

Chua, L., D. W. Dwyer and A. Zhang, 2009, "Moody's KMV Risk Calc V3.2 Japan", Moody's KMV.

Damodaran, A., 1996, *Investment Valuation*, Wiley.

Damdaran, A., 1997, *Corporate Finance. Theory and Practice*, Wiley.

Damodaran A., 2010, *The Dark Side of Valuation: Valuing Young, Distressed, and Complex Business*, FT Press.

Damodaran, A., 2011. *Equity Risk Premiums (ERP): Determinants, Estimation and Implications – The 2011 Edition*, Stern School of Business.

Dwyer, D. W. and A. E. Kocagil, 2004, "Moody's KMV Risk Calc V3.1 United States", Moody's KMV.

Dwyer, D. W., I. Korablev and J. Y. Zhao, 2010, "Moody's Analytics Risk Calc v3.1 Russia", Moody's Analytics.

Fama, E. F., and K. R. French, 1993, "Common Risk Factors in the Returns on Stocks and Bonds", *Journal of Financial Economics*, Vol. 33, pp. 3–56.

Fama, E. F., and K. R. French, 1996, "Multifactor Explanations of Asset Pricing Anomalies", *Journal of Finance*, Vol. 36, pp. 55–84.

Guatri, L., 1998, *La Valutazione delle Aziende*, Egea.

Guatri, L. and M. Bini, 2009, *Nuovo Trattato sulla Valutazione delle Aziende*, Egea.

Hamada, R.S., 1969, "Portfolio Analysis, Market Equilibrium and Corporate Finance", *Journal of Finance*, Vol. 24, pp. 30–31.
Hood III, F. and D. W. Dwyer, 2006, "Moody's KMV Risk Calc v3.1 Italy", Moody's KMV.
Hull, J., M. Predescu and A. White, 2004, "The Relationship between Credit Default Spreads, Bond Yields, and Credit Ratings Announcements", *Journal of Banking and Finance*, Vol. 28, pp. 2789–811.
Likert R., 1970, "Putting a Value on Human Resources", *International Management*, October,.
Longstaff, F. A., S. Mithal and E. Neiss, 2005, "Corporate Yield Spreads: Default Risk of Liquidity Risk? New Evidence from the Credit Default Swap Market", *Journal of Finance*, Vol. 60, pp. 2213–53.
Oricchio, G., 2011, *Credit Treasury. A Credit Pricing Guide in Liquid and Non-Liquid Markets*, Palgrave Macmillan.
Oricchio, G., L. Izzi and L. Vitali, 2012, *Basel III Credit Rating Systems. An Applied Guide to Quantitative and Qualitative Rating Models*, Palgrave Macmillan.
Rietz, T., A., 1988, "The Equity Risk Premium. A Solution", *Journal of Monetary Economics*, Vol. 22, pp. 117–31.
Vassalou, M., and Y. Xing, 2004, "Default Risk in Equity Returns", *Journal of Finance*, Vol. 59, pp. 831–68.
Zanda, G., 1996, *Casi e Valutazione delle Aziende*, Giappichelli
Zanda, G., 2012, *Corporate Management in a Knowledge-Based Economy*, Palgrave Macmillan.
Zanda G. and M. Lacchini, 1989, "La stima del valore del capitale umano ai fini della valutazione d'azienda", *Rivista Italiana di Ragioneria e di Economia Aziendale*, luglio-agosto.
Zanda, G., M. Lacchini and T. Onesti, 2005, *La valutazione delle Aziende*, Giappichelli.
Zanda G., E. D'Amico, E. Laghi, G. Oricchio, 1996, "Le metodologie di valutazione delle aziende: brevi richiami", in G. Zanda (ed. by), *Casi ed applicazioni di valutazione delle aziende*, Giappicheli.
Zhang, J., D. W. Dwyer and J. Y. Zhao, 2010, "Moody's Analytics Risk Calc v3.1 China, Moody's Analytics.
Zhao, J. Y., D. W. Dwyer and S. Xu Zhang, 2010, "Moody's Analytics Risk Calc v3.1 Emerging Markets", Moody's Analytics.
Zmijeski, M. E., 1984, "Methodological Issues Related to the Estimation of Financial Distress Prediction Models", *Journal of Accounting Research*, Supplement on Current Econometric Issues in Accounting Research, pp. 59–82

Index

www.ingramcontent.com/pod-product-compliance
Lightning Source LLC
Chambersburg PA
CBHW071556220925
32987CB00004B/374
* 9 7 8 0 2 3 0 2 9 1 4 4 7 *